D0914964

OP

# DRAMATIC DOCUMENTS FROM THE ELIZABETHAN PLAYHOUSES

Walter Wilson Greg

UNIVERSITY MICROFILMS, INC.
*A Subsidiary of Xerox Corporation*
*Ann Arbor*

XEROX

This "O-P Book" Is an Authorized Reprint of the
Original Edition, Produced by Microfilm-Xerography by
University Microfilms, Inc., Ann Arbor, Michigan, 1966

# DRAMATIC DOCUMENTS

FROM THE

# ELIZABETHAN PLAYHOUSES

STAGE PLOTS : ACTORS' PARTS : PROMPT BOOKS

BY

W. W. GREG

COMMENTARY

OXFORD
AT THE CLARENDON PRESS
1931

## CONTENTS

OXFORD UNIVERSITY PRESS
AMEN HOUSE, E.C. 4
LONDON EDINBURGH GLASGOW
LEIPZIG NEW YORK TORONTO
MELBOURNE CAPETOWN BOMBAY
CALCUTTA MADRAS SHANGHAI
HUMPHREY MILFORD
PUBLISHER TO THE
UNIVERSITY



PRINTED IN GREAT BRITAIN

## PLATES

## INTRODUCTION

THE papers reproduced and discussed in these volumes are actual playhouse documents used in the original productions of Elizabethan plays. They tell us something at least of the conditions of performance, and something about the nature of the texts in use, thus supplying as it were a material scheme within the limits of which both the bibliographical critic and the textual editor must work.

Generally speaking it may be said that for every piece in the repertory of an Elizabethan theatrical company there must have existed three playhouse documents or sets of documents. First and foremost there was the *Book*, or authorized prompt copy. Two early examples that have preserved their original vellum wrappers are found inscribed respectively 'The Booke of Sir Thomas Moore' and 'The Book of Iohn A kent & Iohn a Cumber', while this technical use of the word is likewise seen in the term 'book-holder', as the prompter was called in the Elizabethan theatre. Next there were the *Parts* of the several characters, written out for the actors on long paper scrolls, if we may rely on the evidence of the solitary example that has survived. This unluckily is mutilated and has lost any heading it ever had: analogy would suggest that, since the play took its title from the hero, it may have been inscribed simply 'The Part of Orlando Furioso'. It belonged to Edward Alleyn; another of his rolls may have been headed 'The Part of the Moore in the Battell of Alcazar'. Last there were the *Plots*, skeleton outlines of plays scene by scene, written on large boards for the use of actors and others in the playhouse. Of these some half dozen, belonging to the two principal companies, have come down to us from near the end of the sixteenth century. All those sufficiently preserved show generally similar headings: 'The plott of the First parte of Tamar Cam', though only known in reprint, is typical.

Of course, where several examples of these types of document are extant they differ in a measure among themselves, both in details and to some extent in general character, and we must not arbitrarily assume that all those that must have once existed conformed in any close way to the few that have survived. But it is difficult to see how the business of such a stage as that of the Elizabethan and early Stuart period could have been carried on without something of the nature of the three classes of documents enumerated above. Prompt copies there must always have been save in the most exceptional circumstances, and the custom of inscribing thereon the official licence lent them a degree of authority which has certain important bibliographical implications: it is probable that in their general features they conformed to a fairly constant pattern, though certain individual peculiarities they likewise no doubt possessed. It is respecting actors' Parts that we are least well informed and most care is needed in drawing inferences; but at the same time the fact that the main features of our Elizabethan example are in a measure supported by the few fragments that survive from earlier times suggests that the range of variation was probably not very wide. With the Plots it is somewhat different. There is some reason for suspecting that those we have belong to a closely related group, and it is consequently uncertain how far they should be taken as typical of their class. Moreover, they differ appreciably among themselves. The necessity, however, of some such guide for the actors would be pretty obvious in a repertory theatre, and there seems every probability that, whatever their particular form, documents essentially similar to those before us were usual, if not universal, in the Elizabethan playhouses.

But though it is desirable to point out the caution needed in arguing from a restricted number of extant documents, it would be a serious error not to recognize their great importance for criticism. Every item of historical evidence performs a two-fold function: positively it enlarges the basis we have to build on, and enables us to extend the structure of valid inference; negatively it is often of even greater service in limiting the field of admissible conjecture. That is why to a certain type of mind all fresh evidence is so extremely distasteful. In the present case, when we have made reasonable allowance for individual variation, the documents we are considering afford

a very considerable and very valuable body of evidence. In so far as the printed texts of the Elizabethan drama—using that term in an extended sense—ultimately hale from the playhouses—and to this conclusion recent criticism seems generally tending—it is documents such as these that lie behind the early editions, and it is in terms of these that the latter must be criticized and judged. It is hardly too much to say that the Plots and the Part reproduced in this collection, and the Books of which specimens are given, form an indispensable background to all useful thought, and a framework to which must conform all valid conjecture, concerning the textual phenomena and history of the Elizabethan drama.

I make this claim as an article of critical faith, and I do not make it lightly. It is to-day less revolutionary than it would have been a generation ago; to some it may sound trite. But I should be sorry to appear magisterial, or to put the claim higher than reason will warrant. It may be that the mere fact of a conjecture or a theory being at variance with the evidence of these documents would be no conclusive ground for its rejection, though I think that any view that provoked such a conflict would need remarkably urgent reason for presenting itself. On the other hand the fact of its being in accord with that evidence would be a very strong argument in favour of its respectful consideration. And some suggestions which have from time to time been advanced, but of which indeed criticism has rightly grown shy, a study of the documents does afford us conclusive grounds for rejecting. We can, for instance, no longer believe that the exhibition of locality boards was a general or even a usual practice of the Elizabethan stage; we know that lists of personae and careful division into acts and scenes are not characteristic features of copy derived from the playhouse, but quite the reverse; nor should we now venture to assume that stage-directions of a descriptive type necessarily imply a text taken down at a performance.

Chance and convenience have conspired to place the three sections of this work in what is really the reverse of their logical order: we start with the Plots, proceed to the Parts, and work back to the Books at the end. So far as the first two of these are concerned the extant remains are reproduced entire, and it is possible therefore to discuss them with a fair measure of completeness if not perhaps of finality. Of the prompt books, of course, only specimen pages can be reproduced. An attempt, indeed, has been made to give a list of possible prompt copies known to be still in existence and to record their main features. But neither the list nor the discussion can pretend to be exhaustive, for the field is a wide one, and it is still very imperfectly explored. That despite its importance it should not hitherto have attracted workers is a curious fact and not without significance; but it is impossible in such a work as the present to do more than draw attention to the want and point the way for further investigation. The thorough survey of this field seems to me the most urgent task at present awaiting the critical student of the early drama, and I shall consider that my work has not been wasted if by a preliminary survey I succeed in arousing the interest and lightening the labour of those who shall come after.

I have special reasons for wishing to record the amiable generosity with which the Delegates of the Clarendon Press assumed responsibility for a venture which is, I fear, hardly like to prove remunerative. To Sir Edmund Chambers's encyclopaedic works and learning I owe a debt that will be only too obvious to the reader. More personally I am indebted to him both for the Note on certain disputed points of theatrical history which I have been able to include in this volume, and even more for his unfailing kindness and patience in many conversations and much correspondence, which have resulted in narrowing very considerably the field in which we incline to different views. I think it is safe to say that the points that remain at issue between us are such as will trouble none but the closest students of a very technical subject. Nevertheless, it seemed desirable to have them clearly defined, since in a subject such as that we have been exploring one can never tell when a seemingly trivial detail will be found to have a bearing upon, or even hold the key to, some problem of more general concern.

My thanks are due to the authorities of the British Museum,

Dulwich College, and the Society of Antiquaries for leave to reproduce the documents concerned. For information on particular points I am further under obligations to Mr. R. B. Haselden of the Huntington Library, California, Mr. H. D. Hughes of the Cathedral Library, Durham, Professor W. L. Renwick of Armstrong College, Newcastle, Dr. Henry de Vocht of Louvain, Mr. R. G. Howarth, Mr. Edward Heawood, and Miss Rebecca Rhoads. I fear that in course of the decade during which this work has been slowly shaping itself I must have incurred many other debts the precise nature of which now eludes my memory. It is not from want of gratitude that they pass unacknowledged here.

When, more years ago than I care to think, I read before the Shakespeare Association the nucleus of the present work in the form of a paper on Elizabethan Theatrical Plots—and attracted a large audience under the impression that I was going to talk about the plots used by Elizabethan dramatists—the chair was taken by a very distinguished man, the late A. B. Walkley, who like the rest had been brought there on false pretences. In an impish spirit, perhaps a little akin to his own, I resolved to commemorate that occasion by placing his name in the forefront of the present volume when it reached completion. Fate was unkind, and it now appears unsponsored.

# STAGE PLOTS

## THE DOCUMENTS

THEATRICAL Plots are documents giving the skeleton outline of plays, scene by scene, for use in the theatre, a small group of which has survived from the last twelve years or so of Elizabeth's reign. In this sense the word 'Plot'[1] is a highly specialized term of the early playhouses. Essentially it is the same word that we use in speaking of the plot of a play or novel, the original meaning being ground-plan. But among playwrights it very naturally assumed the meaning of an outline sketch serving as a guide for the composition of a play, especially when this was to be written by several authors in collaboration. Thus we find Henslowe recording that Jonson was engaged on a play of which 'he showed the plotte vnto the company' and that Chapman wrote a tragedy 'of bengemens plotte', which may refer to the same.[2] This was clearly not a Plot in the technical sense. It may, however,

[1] Among writers on dramatic history it became at one time the rather misleading, if possibly convenient, custom to call these documents 'Plats'. This was merely due to the accident of the word being spelled 'platt' in the heading to the one (2 *Seven Deadly Sins*) that first found its way into print. In the four others that preserve their headings the spelling is 'plott'. According to the *N.E.D.* 'plat', which was not uncommon in the sense of plan in the sixteenth and seventeenth centuries, is a mere by-form of 'plot' arising through confusion with a distinct word 'plat', a cognate of 'plate'. The vogue of the term 'Plat' may have been helped by its resemblance to 'platform'. Collier speaks of 'plats', 'platforms', or 'plat-forms' indifferently. The word 'platform', originally meaning a ground-plan or chart, was certainly in use in the sixteenth century in the sense of a pattern or sketch: it might well have been used as an equivalent of 'plot' in its non-technical use, but there seems to be no evidence whatever that it was applied to the documents in question.

[2] The entries in question run: 'lent vnto Bengemen Iohnson the 3 of desembʒ 1597 vpon a boocke w$^{ch}$ he showed the plotte vnto the company w$^{ch}$ he promysed to dd vnto the company at cryssmas next the some of —xx$^{s}$', and 'Lent vnto Robart shawe & Iewbey the 23 of octobʒ 1598 to lend vnto m$^{r}$ Chapmane one his playe boocke & ij ectes of a tragedie of bengemens plotte the some of —iij$^{li}$'. In these cases we must suppose that the plot meant a written sketch of the play. It is possible that the drawing up of such plots, as a recognized branch of the playwright's profession, may be implied in Nashe's claim of Greene 'subscribing to me in any thing but plotting Plaies, wherein he was his crafts master' (ed. M$^{c}$Kerrow, iii. 132), and in Meres's well-known description of Munday as 'our best plotter', though it is unlikely that anything more is meant than that their plays were well constructed.

have included, though it can hardly have been confined to, a list of scenes with the characters appearing in each, such as we find illustrated in a note among Henslowe's correspondence to which I shall return later (p. 5). A list of this character would need little elaboration to convert it into a theatrical Plot of the simplest type, as seen in *The Dead Man's Fortune*, and it is easy to suppose that it was from such a beginning that the documents we are considering were evolved.[1]

So far as I am aware no contemporary allusion to these Plots has been discovered, and although the object for which they were prepared is pretty obvious from internal evidence, their exact nature has been the subject of some misapprehension, and it is only of recent years that their full significance has been recognized. The four Plots completely preserved were printed more than a hundred years ago in the famous 'Variorum' editions of Shakespeare, but the early critics made little attempt at interpretation, and Steevens's suggestion that 2 *Seven Deadly Sins* may have consisted only of dumb-show and chorus hardly indicates a very close study of the document.[2] Serious criticism began with Collier, who, in 1831, maintained that the Plots

[1] The use of 'plot' in the sense of a rough sketch continued in theatrical circles. The manuscript of *The Faithful Friends*, assigned therein to Beaumont and Fletcher (Dyce MS. 10), most likely belongs, in spite of the late character of the writing, to the second quarter of the seventeenth century. On p. 69 occurs the following:

The Plott of a Scene of mirth
to conclude this fourth Acte.

Enter Sr Pergamus the foolish knight like a Bridegroome leading Flauia his Bride, Bellario the singing Soldier, Black Snout the Smith, Snipp Snapp the Tayler and Cauleskin [*sic*] the Shomaker.
An Altar to be sett forth with the Image of Mars' Dindinus [*sic*] the Dwarfe bearing Sr Per: Launce and sheild wch are hung vp for trophees' and Sr Perg' Vowes for the loue of Flauia neuer to beare Armes agen, the like dos Bla: snout who hangs vp his Sword and takes his hammer vowing to God Vulcan neuer to Vse other Weapon, The Taylor and the Shoomaker to vowe the like to God Mercury Then Bellario [to] Sings a songe how they will fall to there old Trades, a clapp of Thunder and all run of /

finis 4 Act

After this is inserted a leaf, of smaller size and written in another hand, which contains the text for the scene in question.

[2] Steevens actually noted that 'On the outside of the cover is written, "The *Book* and Platt, &c."' but apparently failed to draw the obvious inference (Malone's *Supplement*, 1780, i. 61). Even apart from this the fact that two scenes are specified as being in 'Dumb show' suffices to prove that others were not.

were scenarios of impromptu plays imitated from the Italian *commedia dell' arte*.[1] The idea must, one would suppose, have been suggested by the fact that *The Dead Man's Fortune* contains characters (Pantaloon, &c.) evidently borrowed from the improvised comedies of Italy, but curiously enough Collier made no mention of this, and his arguments based on *The Seven Deadly Sins* hardly call for examination. It was unfortunate that no attention was paid to the fragmentary plots, since these include one of *The Battle of Alcazar*, and this well-known play of Peele's, printed in 1594, was assuredly not composed extempore.[2] The Plot was acquired with others by the British Museum in 1836 and a facsimile published in 1860, but this did not prevent Collier reproducing his account of the matter without material alteration in 1879, nor A. W. Ward endorsing it so late as 1899. His view is now generally discarded, and it is significant that Creizenach did not consider it even worth mention.

It is clear to us now that there was nothing exceptional about the plays for which Plots were required. Although we are without external information on the point we may suppose that these were prepared for the guidance of actors and others in the playhouse, to remind those concerned when and in what character they were to appear, what properties were required, and what noises were to be made behind the scenes. The necessity for some such guide would be evident in a repertory theatre, and we may feel assured that the Plot was exhibited in a place convenient for ready reference during performance. There

[1] Collier does not actually use the term 'scenario', but his description of the plays in question as 'experiments in the nature of the Italian *Commedie al improviso*', indicates what he had in mind. In point of fact there is little resemblance between the Plots and the Italian *scenari*, which always provide not only an outline of the action but a summary of the dialogue as well, though I learn from Miss K. M. Lea, who has made a special study of the subject, that they are not always as elaborate as those printed by Ferdinando Neri in his *Scenari delle maschere in Arcadia* (1913).

[2] Although *The Battle of Alcazar* is the only instance in which both the Plot and text of a play have survived, we know from the endorsement that a Book of 2 *Seven Deadly Sins* once accompanied the Plot, while a Book of *Tamar Cam* belonged to Alleyn in 1602. Moreover, Chettle and Dekker were writing a *Troilus and Cressida* at an appropriate date, and Dekker also worked on a play whose title it is hard to dissociate from the other fragment.

seems, indeed, every probability that documents similar in general character to those we possess were usual, if not universal, in Elizabethan playhouses. At the same time the extant Plots differ to some extent in detail, and we cannot of course be certain how far the few we possess are typical of the many that must have perished. Further evidence of their precise nature can only be obtained from a close analysis of the documents themselves, and it is the main purpose of the present study to perform this necessary task or at least to furnish the necessary basis for further investigation.

The surviving Plots are here collected from several sources. From Dulwich comes the Plot of 2 *Seven Deadly Sins*, where it is now classed as MS. XIX (see G. F. Warner, *Catalogue of the Manuscripts and Muniments of Dulwich College*, 1881, p. 341).

From the British Museum come five Plots, now all bound up together in a volume classed as MS. Add. 10449. These are *The Dead Man's Fortune* (fol. 1), *Frederick and Basilea* (fol. 2), *The Battle of Alcazar* (fol. 3, imperfect), 2 *Fortune's Tennis* (fol. 4, fragmentary), and *Troilus and Cressida* (fol. 5, fragmentary).

The Plot of 1 *Tamar Cam* is now only known from its inclusion in the Prolegomena to the 'Variorum' edition of Shakespeare published in 1803 (iii. 114), where it was printed by the editor, Isaac Reed, from a transcript by George Steevens.

It may be mentioned at once that the *Troilus and Cressida* fragment is written in the same hand as the Plot of *Alcazar*, and the *Fortune's Tennis* fragment in the same as that of the *Deadly Sins*; also that the latter is the hand of one of the contributors to the play of *Sir Thomas More* (B.M., MS. Harl. 7368), namely the one designated 'C' in the Malone Society's edition, who, whether himself an author or not, certainly acted as stage reviser for the whole.

For the sake of comparison I have included in the present collection, besides the seven genuine Plots above mentioned, a type-facsimile of a broadside entitled 'The Plot of the Play, called *Englands Ioy*. To be Playd at the Swan this 6. of Nouember. 1602', from the only known copy in the collection of the Society of Antiquaries (no. 98). This is not properly

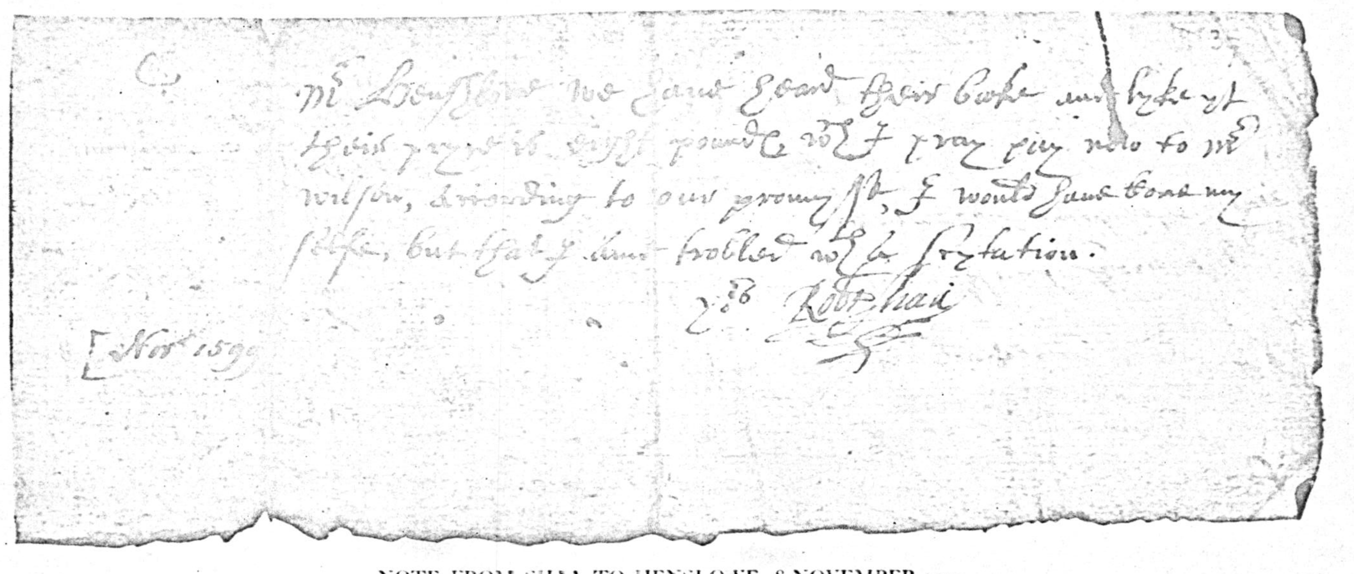

Mr Henshlowe we haue heard their booke and lyke yt
their pryce is eight pownds wch I pray paye now to Mr
wilson, according to our promysse. I would haue come my
selfe, but that I ame trobled wth a scytation.

yors Robt Shaa

[Nov 1599

NOTE FROM SHAA TO HENSLOWE, 8 NOVEMBER 1599

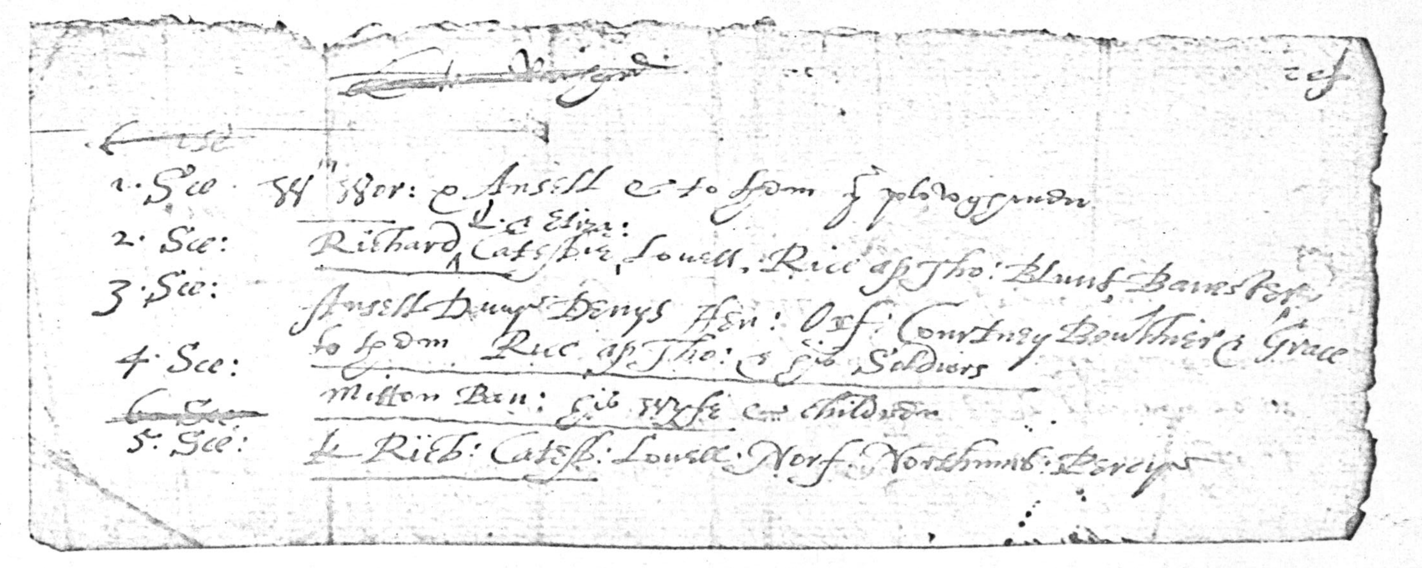

1. Sce: [illegible] & Ansell & to them [illegible]
2. Sce: Richard, Catesbie, Lovell, Ric ap Tho: Blunt, Banester.
3. Sce: Ansell Dawes? Denys Hen: Oxf: Courtney Bourchier & Grace to them Ric ap Tho: & his Soldiers
4. Sce: Mitton Ban: his Wyfe & children
5. Sce: K Rich: Catesb: Lovell: Norf: Northumb: Percy

MEMORANDUM OF SCENES FOR A PLAY ON THE BACK OF THE SAME

a theatrical Plot at all, and it is doubtful how far the word in the heading is coloured by the technical use, but since it may be in some measure modelled on the genuine documents it is of interest in suggesting a contemporary familiarity with their form. A full account of Vennar's impudent fraud may be read in Sir Edmund Chambers's *Elizabethan Stage* (iii. 500). No further notice need be taken of it here.

To complete the evidence available on the subject of Plots I also add here a facsimile and print of the scribbled fragment of a Plot or list of scenes already mentioned as occurring among Henslowe's correspondence. It is found on the back of an undated note of 8 Nov. 1599 from Robert Shaa, an actor of the Admiral's company, and appears to be in his handwriting. The script is mainly Italian with a considerable admixture of English. The note relates to a play, 2 *Henry Richmond*, apparently by R. Wilson and others, and the scenes evidently belonged to the same piece (Dulwich MS. 1, art. 26; see Warner's *Catalogue*, p. 16).

[Enter Richard]

1·*Sce* · *Wm Wor:* & *Ansell &* to them ye plowghmen

——— *Q.* & *Eliza:*

2·*Sce:* *Richard* ^ *Catesbie, Louell, Rice ap Tho: Blunt, Banester* ^ ·

———

3·*Sce:* *Ansell Dauye Denys Hen: Oxf: Courtney Bou'chier* & *Grace* to them *Rice ap Tho:* & his *Soldiors*

4·*Sce:* ———————

*Mitton Ban:* his *wyfe & children*

[6·*Sce:*] ———

5·*Sce:* *K Rich: Catesb: Louell · Norf: Northumb: Percye*[1]

———

[1] One other document perhaps deserves passing mention. In a manuscript copy of Fletcher's tragedy of *Bonduca*, written, probably about the middle of the first half of the seventeenth century, by a playhouse scribe, and now in the British Museum (MS. Add. 36758), we find the following (fol. 24a):

Actus: Quintj: Scæna: pria:

[Here should be A Scæne of the Solemnitye of]

[Pænius his ffunerall: mournd by Caracticus:]

Here should A Scæne · be betwene Iunius · & petillius: (Iunius mocking petillius for being in loue wth Bonducas Daughter that Killd her Selfe: to them · Entred Suetonius: (blameing petilius for the Death of pænius:

The history of the documents, so far as it can be traced, lends colour to the supposition that they were all at one time in the possession of Edward Alleyn and from him presumably passed into the keeping of Dulwich College. Only one, however, namely the Plot of 2 *Seven Deadly Sins*, is now to be found in the College library, and even in this case it may have been only the accident that it had at one time formed the wrapper of a manuscript play called *The Telltale* that led to its identification and recovery. The pilfering of the Dulwich records, presumably with the connivance of their custodians, began early. There is a story, which may or may not be authentic, that in the eighteenth century a large collection of printed plays from the College library was exchanged for volumes of contemporary theology: be that as it may there is no doubt that long before Collier made his mischievous forgeries in Henslowe's diary and possibly abstracted entries therefrom, the volumes had been pillaged to supply a number of autograph signatures now to be found among Malone's books in the Bodleian.[1] The diary, we know, was discovered shortly before

The next Scœne · the Solemnitye of pænius his ffunerall mournd by Caracticus:
The begining of this following Scæne betweene petillius & Iunius is wanting.
— the occasion. why these are wanting here. the booke where [it] by it was first Acted from is lost: and this hath beene transcrib'd from the fowle papers of the Authors wch were found:

This must have been written from memory, for the description of the missing scenes is incorrect, but the arrangement and the phrase 'to them' suggest that the scribe had a Plot of the play in mind.

[1] Collier, defending himself against the charge of forgery, wrote in his *Reply to Hamilton* (1860, p. 46) as follows: 'Let it be borne in mind that the documents, which Malone here and elsewhere refers to [as "now before me" and "in my possession": *An Inquiry into the Authenticity of certain Papers*, 1796, p. 215], were, in fact, the property of the Master, Warden, and Fellows of Dulwich College—that Malone had quietly taken possession of them—that they remained in his hands for several years—that he did exactly what he liked with them—that he cut off signatures of old dramatists and players to place them on the title-pages of his own books—and that he or others mutilated *Henslowe's Diary* in such a way, that some of the most valuable portions are now entirely lost. Even the books, the title-pages of which he decorated with the old autographs, had belonged to Dulwich College; for he contrived to persuade the Master, Warden, and Fellows, of that day, that Old Plays and Old Poetry did not half so well become their shelves, as the musty divinity, dull chronicles, and other volumes of the same sort, which he substituted. Hence the bulk of his collection; and he must have chuckled amazingly at his success in persuading unsuspecting people to make an exchange of works, which would sell for hundreds of pounds, for others not worth as many shillings. So of the Manuscripts: they

1790 and immediately forwarded to Malone (*Shakespeare*, 1790, vol. i, pt. ii, p. 288; Warner's *Catalogue*, p. ix). Ten years earlier the first of the Plots, *The Seven Deadly Sins*, had found its way into print in his *Supplement to the Edition of Shakespeare published in 1778* (1780, i. 60). It would seem from his rather

seem to have allowed Malone to carry away such as he pleased, to keep them as long as he pleased, and to return them as he pleased, in the state which he pleased. Some that he did not return found their way again to their old home after his death; and it is not very long since the College, most properly, bought back a bundle of papers that must have originally come out of its archives.' It is never wise to accept Collier's testimony unsupported, and Collier on his defence is not likely to have been more scrupulous than usual. The value of his evidence can be judged by his statement that from Henslowe's diary 'some of the most valuable portions are now entirely lost', since if they were entirely lost he could have no knowledge of their value. I do not doubt that if, as I suppose, Malone did cut signatures from the Dulwich documents, it was done, as Collier himself implies, with the concurrence of the owners. The story of the exchange is, so far as I can discover, wholly uncorroborated. Indeed it looks like a perversion or confused recollection of a story told by Malone himself in his *Supplement* (1780, i. 49). In this he says that there were over five hundred volumes in the Cartwright collection at Dulwich and that Garrick 'some years ago obtained a few of them, in exchange for some other books', and that they were 'added to his large collection'. This presumably is the basis of a statement by Joseph Knight in the *D.N.B.* (*s.v.* William Cartwright, actor) to the effect that 'Cartwright's collection after quitting Dulwich became the nucleus of the famous Garrick collection'. It is to some extent borne out by the manuscript of a play called *The Wizard* now in the British Museum (MS. Add. 10306) which was certainly once in Garrick's possession (being sold among his books) and which bears a modern pencil inscription to the effect that it was once in Cartwright's collection. At the same time Miss Eleanore Boswell, who has made a close study of the litigation that followed Cartwright's death, assures me that it is improbable that his library contained anything like five hundred volumes. If Malone really did obtain any of his plays from Dulwich, it is of course possible, though I think highly improbable, that they already contained signatures cut from the diary or elsewhere. As to Collier's possible depredations, it is certain that he owned the fragment from the diary now in MS. Egerton 2623 (fol. 19), and possible that he cut it out, for it was quoted by Malone in his *Inquiry* (1796, p. 245, note) as from 'Henslowe's Register'. Collier's own explanation is that he found it lying loose in a volume of old plays he had bought at an auction (*History of Dramatic Poetry*, 1831, iii. 89, note). This is, of course, possible, but I am more inclined to suspect that he found it lying in one of Malone's volumes in the Bodleian, just as a memorandum of Porter's was subsequently discovered (*English Literary Autographs*, plate XII). Another fragment evidently from the diary, containing receipts by Chapman and Dekker, is now in MS. Add. 30262 (fol. 66). Its history previous to a sale at Puttick's in 1878 is not known, but as it very likely comes from the same leaf as the Porter fragment one may suspect that its adventures have been similar. I should add that there is a suspicion that a volume of manuscript plays bought by the British Museum at the Charlemont sale in 1865 (now MS. Egerton 1994) may have been obtained by Malone from Dulwich and lent to Lord Charlemont, remaining in his hands on Malone's death.

loosely-worded account, that what Malone had before him was not the original, which is stated to have been 'met with in the library of Dulwich college', but a transcript made by Steevens.[1] The actual document may have come into his hands later; but he did not reprint it, as one might have expected, in the 'Historical Account of the English Stage' prefixed to his edition of Shakespeare in 1790. Meanwhile, however, Steevens had been collecting materials for an edition, and these included not only *The Deadly Sins* with his own and Malone's observations on it, but the Plots of *The Dead Man's Fortune*, *Frederick and Basilea*, and 1 *Tamar Cam* as well. It is probable that he also knew of *The Battle of Alcazar*, 2 *Fortune's Tennis*, and *Troilus and Cressida*, but in view of their defective condition thought them unworthy of notice. Steevens died in 1800, and the materials were used by Reed in 1803 in what is known as the 'First Variorum' edition of Shakespeare. After giving (iii. 404) the matter previously published by Malone, Steevens's account proceeds (iii. 414) to the additional Plots and states: 'The originals are in my possession. There is reason to suppose that these curiosities once belonged to the collection of Alleyn, the founder of Dulwich College'. The 'First Variorum' was reprinted in 1813, and another large edition of Shakespeare, generally, though perhaps inaccurately, called the 'Third Variorum', appeared in 1821 under the editorship of James Boswell the younger, to whom Malone, on his death in 1812, had entrusted the completion of his Shakespearian labours, and in whose hands his collections remained till 1821, the year before Boswell's own death. In both of these editions (1813 and 1821) the Plots were duly reprinted. It will be noticed that Steevens, though he possessed the three additional Plots, never claimed

[1] Malone wrote (i. 58): 'I shall subjoin a transcript of a very curious paper now in my possession, entitled, *The Platt of the Secound Parte of the Seven Deadlie Sinns*'. And to the print of the Plot he appended some remarks of Steevens, who wrote (i. 61): 'This singular curiosity was met with in the library of Dulwich college . . . The *Platt* (for so it is called) is fairly written out on pasteboard in a large hand . . . and has been converted into a cover for an anonymous manuscript play entitled *The Tell-tale*. From this cover I made the preceding transcript'. It would seem that the strict interpretation of Malone's words is 'I shall subjoin a transcript [sc. a print] of a very curious paper [i.e. Steevens's transcript] now in my possession'.

to have had that of *The Deadly Sins*. This is borne out by the catalogue of the sale of his library at King's auction room on Tuesday, 13 May 1800, and the ten following days, wherein the only relevant entry is lot 1216, namely:

> The Plot of the Plays of *Frederick* and *Basilea*, and of the *Deade Man's Fortune*, the original papers which hung up by the Side Scenes in the Playhouses for the Use of the Prompter and the Actors, *earlier than the Time of* Shakspeare.

The lot was bought by Malone for the sum of £11, which shows that the interest of these 'curiosities' was appreciated. It is possible that Steevens had handed over *The Deadly Sins* (together with *The Telltale*) to Malone at an earlier date; if not, and more probably, Malone may have obtained it from Dulwich subsequently. In any case we know that they came into the possession of Boswell, for when his library in turn was put up to auction at Sotheby's on Tuesday, 24 May 1825, and the nine following days, the last day's sale included the following lots:

3136 The Plotte of the Second Parte of the Seven Deadlie Sinnes.
3137 The Plotte of the Deade Man's Fortune.
3138 The Plotte of Frederick and Basilea.
3139 The Plott of the Battell of Alcazar. This fragment . . . is unfortunately in a terrible state of decay. To it is added a fragment of another Plott.[1]
3140 The Tell Tale, a Comedy, MS. The curious Plotte of the Seven Deadly Sinnes formed the cover of this comedy when it was discovered at Dulwich.[2]

Lots 3136 and 3140 were claimed as the property of Dulwich College and surrendered to the Governors before the sale.[3]

[1] The other Plot was no doubt *2 Fortune's Tennis*. That of *Troilus and Cressida*, which has lost its heading and is in the same hand as *The Battle of Alcazar*, was presumably mistaken for part of that Plot.

[2] It is sometimes incorrectly stated that the Plot formed, or was pasted into, the binding of the comedy. It can never have been more than a loose wrapper or folder.

[3] I do not regard this as any evidence that the other Plots had not also come from Dulwich, though it is difficult to get beyond Steevens's conjecture. There was no proof of their provenance on which the Governors could have acted. Indeed I suspect that it was primarily *The Telltale* that was traced and that the Plot of *The Seven Deadly Sins* was surrendered because it was known to have accompanied it.

The rest were bought by Thorpe, the bookseller; 3137 for 18*s*., 3138 for 13*s*., and 3139 for 8*s*., a sad falling off from the price paid by Malone. Presumably Thorpe sold them to Richard Heber, for in Part XI (manuscripts) of his sale at Evans's on Wednesday, 10 Feb. 1836, and the nine following days, the last day's sale included lot 1640, described as:

> Theatrical. The Plotte of the 'Deade Mans Fortune.' The Plotte of Frederick and Basilea. And two more very imperfect.

This time Thorpe obtained them for 15*s*. and seems to have sold them to another bookseller, Rodd, from whom the British Museum purchased them in April following. The fragments probably still formed a loose bundle, and were first sorted out, mounted, and bound at the Museum, though I have not found any actual record of the fact. The work was skilfully and intelligently done and is generally successful, though the loose fragments of *Alcazar* were misplaced. Of the Plot of 1 *Tamar Cam*, transcribed by Steevens, nothing further seems to have been heard.

The Plot of 2 *Seven Deadly Sins* was again printed, ostensibly from the original, in Collier's *History of Dramatic Poetry and Annals of the Stage*, 1831 (iii. 394), and in the later edition of 1879 (iii. 198). Collier complained that the reprint of 1821 contained 'many errors and variations of greater or less importance', but his own text is by no means accurate and indeed reproduces not a few of the mistakes of his predecessors. In 1860 Halliwell reproduced *The Battle of Alcazar*, *Frederick and Basilea*, and *The Dead Man's Fortune* in full-size lithographic facsimile for private circulation as *The Theatre Plats of Three Old English Dramas*. Of *The Seven Deadly Sins* a reduced facsimile, also lithograph, was given by William Young in his *History of Dulwich College*, 1889 (ii. 5), while a collotype, likewise reduced, of *Frederick and Basilea* illustrates an article by Mr. J. W. Lawrence in *A Book of Homage to Shakespeare*, 1916 (p. 208). All seven plots, so far as they are preserved, were printed in my collection of *Henslowe Papers* in 1907 (Appx. II, p. 127), together with notes, but I was not at the time able to devote to their study the attention necessary to an adequate

[illegible] Plot of a Second Dead Man [illegible] [illegible] [illegible], presumably [illegible] [illegible], in Collier's *History of Dramatic Poetry and Annals of the Stage*, [illegible] [illegible] [illegible] [illegible] Malone's edition, [illegible] (iii. [illegible]). Malone complained that the text [illegible] contained many errors and [illegible] [illegible] [illegible] [illegible] [illegible] [illegible] [illegible] [illegible] [illegible] [illegible] and added [illegible] [illegible] and a few [illegible] [illegible] [illegible] [illegible] [illegible] [illegible] [illegible] [illegible] [illegible] [illegible] [illegible] [illegible] [illegible] [illegible] [illegible] [illegible] [illegible] [illegible] [illegible] [illegible] [illegible] [illegible] [illegible] [illegible] [illegible] [illegible] [illegible] [illegible] for [illegible] [illegible] [illegible] [illegible] [illegible] [illegible] [illegible] [illegible] [illegible] [illegible] [illegible] [illegible] [illegible] [illegible] [illegible] [illegible] [illegible] [illegible] [illegible] [illegible] [illegible] [illegible] [illegible] [illegible] [illegible] [illegible] [illegible] [illegible] [illegible] [illegible] [illegible] [illegible] [illegible] [illegible] [illegible] [illegible] [illegible] [illegible] [illegible] [illegible] [illegible] [illegible] [illegible] [illegible] [illegible] [illegible] [illegible] [illegible] [illegible] [illegible] [illegible] was not at the time [illegible] [illegible] [illegible] [illegible] adequate

elucidation, and unfortunately neither the texts nor the notes are very satisfactory. I hope in the present work to have redeemed the errors of past years. Lastly, in 1923 I gave in my essay on *Two Elizabethan Stage Abridgements* (pp. 21, 26 ff.) both a reduced collotype facsimile of the Plot of *Alcazar* and a reprint with attempted reconstruction of the defective portions. This is, I believe, substantially accurate, though further study has suggested a few modifications. It was accompanied by an elaborate commentary and comparison with the text of the play as printed in 1594, a subject which lies beyond the scope of the present work, and I may therefore be allowed to refer the curious to what I then wrote.

It might be supposed that it would be sufficient on the present occasion to accompany the facsimiles and transcripts with some general description of the character of the various examples and to leave details of occasion and origin to the debate of historians of the stage. But the documents in question are so important for the study of the companies to which they relate, and conversely the fortunes of the companies throw so much light on the documents, that it is difficult to avoid some historical digression, and the discussion having so far been scattered through larger treatises and periodical publications, I have thought it best to enter into the matter at some length and give a detailed account of my own interpretation of the evidence. For convenience I may here summarize the results of later discussion in a table giving the main facts about the different Plots.

| No. | p. | Title | Source | Company | Theatre | Date |
|---|---|---|---|---|---|---|
| I | 94 | Dead Man's Fortune | B.M., MS. Add. 10449. f. 1 | Admiral's (?) | Theatre (?) | *c.* 1590 |
| II | 105 | 2 Seven Deadly Sins | Dulwich MS. XIX | Strange's (?) | Curtain (?) | *c.* 1590 |
| III | 123 | Frederick & Basilea | B.M., MS. Add. 10449, f. 2 | Admiral's | Rose | *c.* 3 June 1597 |
| IV | 130 | 2 Fortune's Tennis (?) | B.M., MS. Add. 10449, f. 4 | Admiral's | Rose | *c.* 1597–8 |
| V | 138 | Troilus & Cressida (?) | B.M., MS. Add. 10449, f. 5 | Admiral's | Rose | *c.* May 1599 |
| VI | 144 | Battle of Alcazar | B.M., MS. Add. 10449, f. 3 | Admiral's | Rose | *c.* 1598–9 (?) |
| VII | 160 | 1 Tamar Cam | 1803 Variorum, iii. 414 | Admiral's | Fortune | *c.* 2 Oct. 1602 |

The seven extant Plots fall into two clearly-marked groups. Two, *The Dead Man's Fortune* and *The Seven Deadly Sins*, belong to about 1590, and are connected either with Lord Strange's or the Lord Admiral's company, or with some amalgamation of the two. The other five were all prepared for the later Admiral's men and range in date from 1597 to 1602. Between the groups lies the plague of 1592–4 which so powerfully affected the organization of the London stage. If it is only in the light of the history of the companies concerned that the Plots can be fully understood, it is also true that for the theatrical history itself the Plots are among the leading documents. The interpretation of the evidence therefore is a rather complicated task, and not only is the subject one upon which it would be foolish to dogmatize, but it is one upon which somewhat different views have been, and indeed still are, held by those who have devoted most attention to it. I shall here give my own account of the theatrical history of the critical period from 1589 to 1594, and incidentally explain the evidence upon which I rely, but detailed reference to and criticism of the authorities is for the most part now unnecessary in view of the admirable treatment of the question by Sir Edmund Chambers, and it is only to points on which I have the misfortune to disagree with him that I need devote any minute discussion. I have endeavoured to be as uncontroversial as circumstances permit, and to a large extent the narrative here set forth represents an agreed view of events which are rather matter of plausible speculation than ascertained fact, and readers will have the benefit of studying Sir Edmund's own statement of the points on which our views diverge in the note he has kindly contributed to this chapter.[1]

[1] The treatment of the evidence in my edition of *Henslowe's Diary* and in the *Henslowe Papers*, in the latter of which the whole of the Plots were for the first time printed, has I think formed the basis of most recent work on the subject, but much of it is now out of date and should not be relied on. The comprehensive and masterly discussion in Sir E. K. Chambers's *Elizabethan Stage* (1923) is likely to remain classical, but the scale of his work made it impossible to deal with minute points as fully as one would have liked. My own diver-

The seven extant Plots fall into two clearly marked groups. Two, *The Dead Man's Fortune* and *The Seven Deadly Sins*, belong to about 1590, and are connected either with Lord Strange's or the Lord Admiral's company, or with some amalgamation of the two. The other five were all prepared for the later Admiral's men and range in date from 1597 to 1602. [illegible] the groups [illegible] the [illegible] power [illegible] of the [illegible] stage. It is only in the light of the history of the companies concerned that the Plots can be fully understood. It is also true that for the theatrical history itself the Plots are among the leading documents. The interpretation of the evidence here is a matter of complexity [illegible] not [illegible] the one upon which it would be [illegible] of dogmatic, but it is one upon which somewhat different views have been, and indeed still are, held by those who have [illegible]. I shall here [illegible] the critical [illegible] the evidence [illegible] criticism of the [illegible] view of the [illegible] [illegible] to [illegible] discussion. [illegible] circumstances [illegible] set forth [illegible] will [illegible] statements [illegible] kindly [illegible]

[illegible]

We know that in Nov. 1589 Strange's and the Admiral's men formed separate companies, for in that winter season they were acting at different inns in the City, the former at the Cross Keys, the latter elsewhere, when they were suppressed by the Lord Mayor. The following winter, on 27 Dec. 1590 and 16 Feb. 1591, performances were given at Court by a company which one official document calls Strange's and another the Admiral's. About the same time, in Nov. 1590 and May 1591, a company described as the Admiral's was playing at the Theatre and quarelled with the owner, James Burbage. From Feb. to June 1592 (and possibly earlier), and again from Dec. to Feb. following, a company described as Strange's, but which appears to have included Edward Alleyn, the leader of the Admiral's, was acting at Henslowe's playhouse, the Rose, on Bankside. Between 1591 and 1594 the provincial records yield frequent mention of the two companies, sometimes separately, sometimes together, sometimes even in association with other bodies. On 6 May 1593, by which time the plague had made further acting in London clearly impossible, the Privy Council granted a travelling licence to a company described as the servants of Lord Strange, the six members of which are specified by name, the first being Edward Alleyn, who is particularly designated as servant of the Lord High Admiral.[1] On 25 Sept. 1593 Lord Strange succeeded to the earldom and his company became known as Derby's men. On 16 Apr. 1594 he died. On 16 May a company under the patronage of his widow performed at Winchester.[2] The company under his successor

gences from his views were set forth in an article on 'The Evidence of Theatrical Plots for the History of the Elizabethan Stage' which appeared in *The Review of English Studies* for July 1925 (i. 257–74). Many of the points at issue have also been discussed in appendixes to *Two Elizabethan Stage Abridgements* (1923, pp. 17 ff., 85 ff.).

[1] The six members of the company were Edward Alleyn (Admiral's), William Kempe, Thomas Pope, John Hemings, Augustine Phillips, and George Bryan. These officially constituted the company, but it presumably included hired men and boys as well.

[2] Also 'my L. Morleys players and the Earle of Darbyes' performed at Southampton in 1594 at a date between 15 and 19 May inclusive, that is, not more than three days after the performance at Winchester. This was presumably therefore the same company. The entry has been previously misdated 1593, *c.* 18 May; I owe the correction to Sir E. K. Chambers.



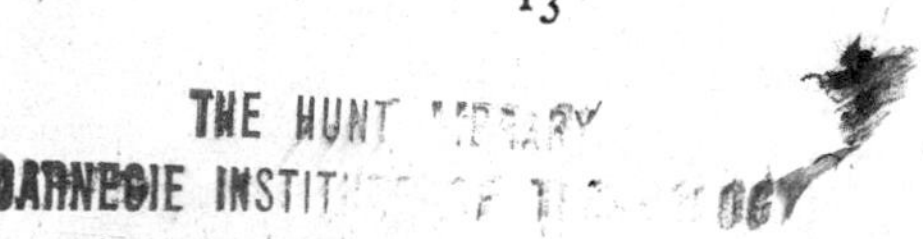

William sixth Earl of Derby, can be traced first on 15 Sept. (at Norwich), and it remained essentially a provincial troop (though it gave performances at Court in 1600 and 1601). Meanwhile on 14 May (that is, two days before the Winchester performance) a company calling itself the Lord Admiral's men, and presumably led by Alleyn, began playing in London as lessees of Henslowe. They were followed early in June (Henslowe says the 3rd, but it was more likely the 5th) by another company, styled the Lord Chamberlain's men, which probably included the other five members of Strange's 1593 licence. For ten days the two performed either jointly or alternately at Newington Butts, after which the Admiral's men returned to the Rose, while the Chamberlain's moved (whether directly or not) to the Theatre, and the companies started on their separate and prosperous careers, eventually becoming the famous Prince's and King's men of the following reign.

From this bare summary of facts that are not in dispute it would appear that, even before the plague temporarily put an end to acting in and about London, there had occurred some sort of fusion, amalgamation, or at least co-operation between the Admiral's and Strange's servants, that this possibly became closer as time went on and endured throughout 1593, while in the spring of 1594, on the other hand, a fission of the joint body gave rise to the later Admiral's, Chamberlain's, and possibly Derby's men. But whether this fission represented a segregation of original elements, and indeed the exact nature of the union in 1592 and 1593, still more in 1591 or earlier, are questions upon which, though speculation may not be unprofitable, it must be admitted that we are very imperfectly informed.[1]

[1] The problems that the investigator has to face should be kept clearly in mind, and those connected with the fusion are more important than those connected with the fission. What was the precise nature of the amalgamation and at what date did it begin? That, whatever it may have been, it was operative in May 1593, may be taken as proved by the licence: that it was so in 1592, during the tenancy of the Rose, is at least highly probable, for Strange's men produced *A Knack to Know a Knave* on 10 June 1592, and when this play was printed in 1594 was said to have been 'sundrie tymes played by Ed. Allen and his Company': that this tenancy dated in fact from the spring or summer of 1591, though unproved, is quite possible. The only indication that anything of the kind obtained in 1590 is afforded by the Court payments, which may imply no more than

A great deal depends of course upon the personnel of the various organizations, but while the Plots afford us a considerable body of evidence on the point, it does not become available until we are in a position to assign these to their proper companies. Apart from the Plots our knowledge of the composition of the early Strange's and Admiral's men, down to 1590–1, is sadly defective, though it would be a mistake to suppose it altogether absent, or too uncertain to afford a basis for argument. It is in respect to Strange's that we are worst off. It is doubtful whether John Symons was ever a member;[1] in any case he cannot be traced with them after 1588, and was certainly with the Queen's men in 1589. Their payee in 1590–1 was George Ottewell or Attewell, but as it was for the joint performances at Court that he was paid, it is not absolutely certain to which company he belonged. Five years later he too was with the Queen's men. With regard to the Admiral's we are rather better informed. A company of the name is traceable in 1585–7, sometimes in alliance with the then Lord Chamberlain's (a company of course quite distinct from that which started in 1594). They disappear till Christmas 1588–9. The evidence for their personnel is not altogether clear, but it is

sporadic co-operation. The real problem then is whether the fusion followed on the City restraint of Nov. 1589 or on the Theatre quarrel of May 1591. It would seem to have been the Admiral's company that had been getting into difficulties, and Strange's that was the predominant partner in the amalgamation. This inclines me to lay stress on the Theatre quarrel, which the evidence serves to connect specifically with the Admiral's men, rather than the City restraint, in which it was Strange's who got into trouble.

As regards the nature of the amalgamation, all that the evidence of the 1593 licence or the Henslowe documents for 1592 warrant our assuming is that Edward Alleyn, retaining his position as servant of the Lord Admiral, allied himself with Strange's company. The Admiral's men had lost several of their number in the course of 1589–91, and it must be matter of speculation whether any followed Alleyn in his association with Strange's, supposing that to have begun in 1591. It is known that at least two were with him at the Theatre in the winter of 1590–1.

Unfortunately the names that we find applied to the companies in contemporary records are not very helpful. If there was an effective amalgamation of the two, they very likely possessed and used on their travels warrants from both lords, and the titles would be used indiscriminately. Even if it was only Alleyn who associated himself with Strange's, his reputation as leader of the Admiral's might possibly lead to the popular use of that title for the company. This makes the interpretation of the provincial records in particular rather uncertain.

[1] Sir E. K. Chambers has altered his view on this point.

tolerably certain that Edward Alleyn was already their leader and that his brother John Alleyn, James Tunstall or Donstone, Richard Jones, Robert Browne, and perhaps Edward Browne, were likewise members.[1] Of these Edward Alleyn, Edward Browne, Tunstall, and Jones were members of the later Admiral's company; John Alleyn disappears, Robert Browne went abroad, as did Jones for a time. It may be added that two minor members of the 1593 company (known not from the licence but from Alleyn's correspondence) namely Thomas Downton and Alleyn's boy John Pyk (or more familiarly Pig), were also members of the later Admiral's men.[2] We have here a list of some eight actors whose presence would be possible with the Admiral's men at the time when they were entering into relation with Strange's.[3]

Let us now turn to the two earliest of the extant Plots, those of *The Dead Man's Fortune* and *The Seven Deadly Sins*. The probability that they were both at one time (as one still is) among Alleyn's papers suggests that they originally belonged to one of the companies with which he was associated, and since this was clearly not the later Admiral's, we are driven back upon the earlier Admiral's, the joint company, or through this Strange's. The occurrence of the name of Richard Burbage in each Plot would most naturally connect them with the

[1] Tunstall, Jones, and the two Brownes had been fellows of Edward Alleyn in Worcester's company in 1583–4. On 3 Jan. 1589 Edward Alleyn bought of Richard Jones the latter's share in certain theatrical stock held jointly with himself, his brother John, and Robert Browne; while between then and 1591 the Alleyns made further purchases of stage apparel, to some of which Tunstall was witness. This points to their all being connected with the same company, namely the Admiral's of which both Alleyns are known to have been members.

[2] The correspondence also mentions Richard Cowley, who was later a member of the Chamberlain's company.

[3] The evidence must certainly not be pressed as regards the personnel of the company in, say, 1590. It looks as though Jones had been bought out early in 1589. Robert Browne was in Leyden by Oct. 1590, and it is possible that Edward Brown was with him (Henslowe first mentions him in 1599). Pig was still apparently quite a small boy in 1593. I assume that the 'Mr Doutone' of Alleyn's correspondence is Downton (whom Henslowe often calls 'Dowton'). It is suggested that he might be Edward Dutton, also afterwards an Admiral's man, but he is not heard of till some years later than Downton. Of course there is no proof that Downton was with the company before 1593 or that he was not a member of Strange's. The only three who can be assigned with some certainty to the Admiral's men in 1590 are the two Alleyn's and Tunstall.

Theatre, which his father James Burbage owned, and where in 1590–1 a company called the Admiral's was performing. This also serves to limit the date, since it is unlikely that, when owing to the quarrel with James Burbage in May 1591 the Admiral's men presumably left the Theatre, young Richard would have continued acting with them or with the joint company which we apparently find located (under Strange's name) at the Rose a year later.[1] The backward date is less determined, but there is no evidence to connect either company with the Shoreditch houses before 1590, and indeed what little evidence there is seems against the supposition.

The natural inference then is that the two Plots were drawn up between Nov. 1589 and May 1591—say roughly in the course of 1590—for the Admiral's men (or possibly a joint company) then acting at the Theatre. This is, indeed, the view taken by Sir Edmund Chambers. But before the inference is accepted as correct we must see whether it is adequately borne out by the internal evidence.

Let us first consider the cast of *The Seven Deadly Sins*, which is exceptionally complete. We know the name, or at least the initials or nickname, of the actor for every speaking part[2] except two, these being important roles that could not be doubled. The first point that strikes one about the list is the absence of the name of Edward Alleyn.[3] This would not by itself have any significance, since he might of course have taken one of the two unallotted parts. It becomes more noteworthy when we observe that none of the actors enumerated above as possible members of the old Admiral's company appears to have taken part in the performance for which the Plot was drawn up.[4] Perhaps, in view of the uncertainty of the

[1] On the possibility, or rather impossibility, of the Plot belonging to 1592, see pp. 110–2.

[2] The seven Sins were evidently mutes, and Mercury only appears in a dumb-show.

[3] He was certainly not the boy Ned who played Rhodope in 'Sloth', any more than the boy Will who played Itys in 'Lechery' was Shakespeare.

[4] The suggestion that Thomas Goodale who appears in it was an Admiral's man is without foundation. A document of 18 May 1593 connects him with John Alleyn and Robert Lee, the former certainly, the latter possibly, an Admiral's man in 1590; but the evidence, if significant at all, points to their

company's personnel, it would be unreasonable to rely very much upon this evidence. What does, however, lend it significance is the fact that, whereas the documents relating to the quarrel between the Burbages and the Admiral's men at the Theatre preserve the names of only two members of the company (apart from young Richard, who of course sided with his family) namely John Alleyn and James Tunstall, these are both otherwise known as Admiral's men but neither is found in the Plot.[1] These considerations seem to me to point to the conclusion that the play was acted neither by the Admiral's men nor by the joint company, and therefore not at the Theatre, and consequently I hesitate to accept the obvious inference upon which Sir Edmund relies.

How then are the two lines of argument to be reconciled? I do not think that there need be any serious difficulty if we assume that Richard Burbage was attached rather to his father's interest than to the company that happened to occupy his house. For there was at this date a working agreement whereby the Curtain was treated as an easer ('Esore') to the neighbouring Theatre, the profits being 'pooled under an arrangement between Henry Lanman and the Burbadges' (*Elizabethan Stage*, ii. 402), so that it would be a matter of indifference to James at which his promising son performed: and if the companies occupying the two houses were also, like the Admiral's and Strange's, in mutual relation, they may well have found it convenient to share his activities as occasion served. Thus I do not think that the appearance of Richard Burbage in a play about 1590 can be taken as evidence that it was necessarily

association in the joint company of 6 May 1593, not in the Admiral's of two or three years before. By 1593 John Alleyn had probably given up playing. Sir Edmund recognizes this.

[1] John Alleyn and Tunstall *might* of course be the two unnamed actors, but that would leave Edward Alleyn unaccounted for, and we should have to suppose that he *happened* not to be cast for that particular play. This is logically possible, but such coincidences strain probability. I may add that the two 'chorus' parts of Henry VI and Lydgate, for which no actors are named, though perhaps prominent are clearly not 'star' parts, and it seems to me highly improbable that either of them was taken by Edward Alleyn. It would be a malicious stroke of fortune if one of the unnamed actors was William Shakespeare, but the possibility should not be forgotten, and the part of Henry VI could be fitted to him better than to Alleyn.

performed at the Theatre, but only that it was performed at one or other of the Shoreditch houses.

My conclusion is therefore that *The Seven Deadly Sins* was probably acted about 1590 by Strange's men alone at the Curtain. That no other company can be in question is sufficiently proved by three of the principal actors in the Plot being named in the Privy Council licence of 1593, while the Curtain is the only alternative to the Theatre consistent with the appearance of Richard Burbage. This leaves us free to assign *The Dead Man's Fortune* to the Admiral's men at the Theatre. The two Plots are very different in character, the latter being much less elaborate, and if approximately contemporary are unlikely to have been prepared for the same company. This view is borne out by the evidence, such as it is, of the cast, since of the three minor actors named along with Burbage not one appears in the very full list of *The Seven Deadly Sins*. They are Robert Lee, Darlowe, and a boy (?) called Sam. Darlowe does not otherwise appear in theatrical records, but a Richard Darloe, player, was living from 1595 to 1602 in the parish of St. Botolph, Aldgate, where Robert Lee and Thomas Goodale also resided. Lee may not improbably have been a member of the joint company in May 1593 when he is found associating with Goodale who had acted in *The Seven Deadly Sins*. Ten years afterwards he was with Queen Anne's men, having in the interval (on 22 Feb. 1598) sold an old play to the later Admiral's company, though he does not seem to have been a member of it. Of Sam nothing definite is known: he may quite likely have been Samuel Rowley, the later Admiral's man, or less probably Samuel Gilburne, the Chamberlain's man, who is described as a 'late apprentice' in 1605.

The view of these Plots that I have outlined above is of course nothing more than a working hypothesis; it is certainly not susceptible of proof on the evidence at our disposal. I claim for it merely that it covers the facts with the least straining of probability. Sir Edmund Chambers's view that both Plots were probably prepared for use at the Theatre by a company that at least included actors drawn from the Admiral's—though it accounts naturally for the presence of Burbage and the possession of the Plots by Alleyn at a later date—seems to me to rely too much upon negative coincidence in the matter of personnel. Sir Edmund is entitled to argue, on the other hand, that my assumptions that Burbage divided his services between the companies, and that a play with which Alleyn was not originally concerned nevertheless came later into his hands, do in fact run counter to probability. 'Both these things would be a little exceptional', he mildly protests. To which I reply, as regards Burbage, that the circumstances were themselves admittedly exceptional, both in respect of the companies and the houses. And as regards the play it must be borne in mind that at least in 1593 the union of the companies and their management must have been virtually complete and their stock of plays common; while in the following year some sort of share out must have taken place. That Alleyn obtained plays that were new during the period of collaboration we know from the case of *Tamar Cam*. I see nothing whatever unlikely in supposing that he may equally have obtained some old plays of Strange's dating from before that period, if he saw in them greater possibilities that his colleagues recognized. Why should Sir Edmund assume a strict segregation of repertory when, as we shall see in a moment, he is reluctant to believe in a segregation of personnel?

I must revert for a moment to the cast of *The Seven Deadly Sins*, since it is of some importance for the later history of the company. The Plot specifies just twenty actors. Of these, three are dignified by the title 'Mr.', namely Bryan, Phillips, and Pope, and eight others are given their full Christian and surnames: these eleven are all otherwise known and no question arises as to their identity. The nine others are less fully distinguished and their identity with actors elsewhere recorded is necessarily conjectural. For two prominent parts, which cannot have been doubled with any others, the names of the performers are not given.

The prefix 'Mr.' undoubtedly distinguishes the leading members of the company—the sharers, it is natural to assume, though this is a point to which I shall have to return later. But it is impossible to believe that in the company which acted *The*

*Seven Deadly Sins* the sharers or leaders were only three in number, or that only three of them were called upon to take part in a performance which made considerable demands on their resources. It is therefore reasonable to assume that the two unnamed actors of prominent parts were also of this rank, and this would raise the number to five. But the licence granted to Strange's men in 1593 names exactly five leading actors (apart from Alleyn) and again it is natural to suppose that these were sharers. The three named leaders of the Plot all duly appear in the licence, namely Thomas Pope, Augustine Phillips, and George Bryan. The other two licensees are William Kempe and John Hemings. Alleyn being specified as servant to the Lord Admiral, we are bound to assume that all the rest were servants of Lord Strange, and we might therefore expect to find Kempe and Hemings in the Plot two or three years earlier. Thus the natural inference would be that it was they who filled the two unassigned roles. There are, however, certain considerations which make this improbable. Will Kempe was not merely a comic actor but a recognized 'clown': it is almost inconceivable that he should have taken the part either of Henry VI or of Lydgate while another was chosen to act 'Will Foole'. As regards Hemings we cannot speak with the same certainty. But he was with the Queen's company earlier, is said to have been 'long time servant' to her Majesty, appears to have married on 10 Mar. 1588 the widow of William Knell of that company, and though he is not in their subsidy list (perhaps incomplete) of 30 June 1588, there is certainly no evidence that he was with Strange's. It is best to admit that we do not know who the unnamed actors were.[1]

This being so we must content ourselves with regarding only eleven actors of the Plot as fully identified. One of these, Thomas Goodale, may possibly have been a member of the joint company in 1593 and has achieved some notoriety as the

[1] In *Henslowe's Diary* (ii. 374) I assigned Lydgate to Hemings and Henry VI to Shakespeare, and though it was a mere guess I am by no means convinced that it was wrong. Kempe was presumably with the company when it performed *A Knack to Know a Knave* ('With Kemps applauded Merrimentes') at the Rose on 10 June 1592, and most likely joined when the move was made, probably in 1591. It may also have been then that John Alleyn ceased playing.

one actor named in the Book of *Sir Thomas More*, but his later career is not known. One, Robert Pallant, is not heard of again till 1602, when he was with the later Worcester's men: since Kempe, Duke, and Beeston are found in the same company, it is just possible that he was like them a member of the Chamberlain's in the interval.[1] One, John Holland, is not otherwise recorded, and the appearance of his name as that of a rebel in 2 *Henry VI* (1623, IV. ii. 1) is as likely to be confirmation of his membership of Strange's company *c.* 1590 as evidence that he was with the Chamberlain's in 1594 or later.[2] The other eight, namely George Bryan, Augustine Phillips, Thomas Pope, Richard Cowley, John Duke, William Sly, John Sincler, and Richard Burbage, were all subsequently members of the Chamberlain's company, probably from its inception in 1594, though Burbage is unlikely to have maintained his association throughout. Besides the three leaders, Richard Cowley can be traced through the joint company of 1593, thanks to Alleyn's correspondence. This being so, it is clear that, if any attempt is made to identify the nine less fully specified performers, it is among the Chamberlain's men (or of course their successors the King's men) that they are most likely to be found at a later date. Nor is it likely to be a coincidence that we have in the Plot the rather unusual Christian names Sander and Kit, while Alexander Cooke and Christopher Beeston appear in the records of the Chamberlain-King's company; while it is not seriously disputed that the 'Ro. Go.' of the Plot is the Robert Gough of the later organization. The musician Vincent, considering the name is uncommon, may well have changed his calling and be the Thomas Vincent who is said to have been prompter at the Globe apparently before 1603. And if we

[1] The argument is not of much weight, though I think it worth considering. Kempe, Duke, and Beeston all appear to have left the Chamberlain's men in 1598 or 1599, but it is not known whether they left together; perhaps not, since Kempe alone acquired a share in the Globe and is recognized in the Folio list. Duke and Beeston are not known to have gone abroad as Kempe is believed to have done. Nor is it known when or how they joined Worcester's men. Duke, Beeston, and Pallant, but not Kempe, remained with this company when it became Queen Anne's.

[2] His name has recently been discovered in a manuscript play, *John of Bordeaux*, but at present the history of that piece is not known.

further suggest, slight as the connexions may be, that Harry was none other than Henry Condell, and Nick perhaps Nicholas Tooley, who claimed Burbage as his 'master', the speculation seems at least innocent if no more can be claimed for it. It is less likely that Will was the William Tawyer, Hemings's man, who appeared with a trumpet in *A Midsummer-Night's Dream*. For T. Belt and Ned no plausible identifications have I believe been proposed.

Before passing to the consideration of the later Plots, which all belong to the Admiral's company subsequent to the plague years, I will here recapitulate briefly, in the light of the foregoing discussion, what I conceive to have been the course of events from 1590 to 1594. The occasional co-operation of the Admiral's and Strange's men, of which we have evidence—and which I believe to be all for which we have evidence—in the former year, led, after the Admiral's had left the Theatre in May 1591, to some more formal association. The Admiral's company was indeed at this time to some extent disrupted: Robert Browne and possibly Jones had left them some time before, and both may have been already abroad; others now probably travelled in the country, while Alleyn and a skeleton formation joined up with Strange's. It was almost certainly this composite organization that occupied the Rose in 1592 or possibly earlier, and some hint of its nature may be gleaned from the licence of 1593, which seems to indicate that Alleyn was accorded a position and voice in the management as representing the Admiral's contribution to the joint concern.[1] So matters continued till Derby's death on 16 Apr. 1594. Immediately afterwards Alleyn, together with the old Admiral's contingent such as it was and possibly a few personal adherents of later date, separated himself from the joint body and sought his fortune in London. The remainder continued for a few weeks under the protection of the widowed Countess, and then transferred their services in a body to Lord Hunsdon, and, following their quondam fellows to London, established them-

[1] That Alleyn was indeed the leader of the troop may be inferred from the fact that his name stands first in the licence taken in conjunction with the title-page of *A Knack to Know a Knave* (1594) on which the body that performed the play is described as 'Ed. Allen and his Company'.

selves as the Chamberlain's men. The later Derby's men were a wholly distinct company, though a few minor members of the former troop may perhaps have joined them. This assumed segregation of earlier elements is of course a deduction from, and cannot be cited in corroboration of, my views respecting the earlier companies,[1] but it is permissible to observe that none of the actors traceable as possible members of the old Admiral's men were ever associated with the Chamberlain's company, though several are found in the later Admiral's; while none of the actors in *The Seven Deadly Sins* are later traceable with the Admiral's, and that assuming the piece to have been Strange's there can be no doubt of the substantial identity of personnel between that company and the Chamberlain's.[2]

The five remaining Plots all belonged manifestly to the later Admiral's men, and it will suffice if we trace the career of that company to the end of Elizabeth's reign. They opened at the Rose on 15, or more likely 17, June 1594, and for two years and a half their history was uneventful. Then some time in the winter of 1596–7, not improbably on 12 Feb., two of their principal members, Richard Jones and Thomas Downton, broke away, and joining with several others, servants of the Earl of Pembroke, entered into contract to play at the Swan from 21 Feb. 1597. The venture ended in disaster, and the scandal attending their performance of *The Isle of Dogs* involved not only their own disruption but a general inhibition of theatrical activity from the end of July to the end of October

[1] The segregation, which is indeed a matter of very slight importance, is of course denied by Sir Edmund Chambers since he denies the validity of my earlier inference.

[2] There is one link between *The Seven Deadly Sins* and the later Admiral's men, namely the writer of the Plot, who also prepared that of *Fortune's Tennis* for the later company. Between writing the two Plots, presumably, he edited the Book of *Sir Thomas More*. Whether he was ever with the Chamberlain's is not known; equally unknown are the circumstances in which he joined the Admiral's. It is, however, worth observing that his one Plot for the later company was written soon after its amalgamation with Pembroke's, while the only Plot written for it before that amalgamation is in a different hand. To follow out the possible implications of this it would be necessary to discuss at length the very involved problem of Pembroke's company, for which this is no suitable occasion. Suffice it to say that it seems possible that some actors who were with Strange's men in 1592 did find their way into the later Admiral's company in 1597, but that they did so in a manner that does not affect the segregation of 1594.

1597. The prodigals returned to the Admiral's fold bringing most if not all of their late comrades with them, and Henslowe proceeded to secure himself against a repetition of the escapade by a series of contracts with the leading members of the troop. For a while the re-formed company was known as the Lord Admiral's and Lord Pembroke's men, but the second title was dropped by the end of the year. This reorganization may have had considerable influence on the Admiral's men's affairs, for it would seem that Alleyn now loosened his connexion with them, while on the other hand his father-in-law assumed, I fancy, a more active share in the management or at least in the financing of the company. It is clear, however, that their prosperity was not seriously interrupted, and in 1600 Alleyn returned to the stage and built his new playhouse, the Fortune, whither the company removed apparently towards the end of the year. On the death of Elizabeth, and her successor's restriction of theatrical patronage to the royal family, the company passed into the service of Henry, Prince of Wales, and its subsequent fortunes do not concern us here.

With respect to the personnel of the company we are pretty well informed from other sources, and this enables us to determine with some accuracy the relation of the various Plots. The earliest is that of *Frederick and Basilea*, a play first performed on 3 June 1597, and the absence of Richard Jones and Thomas Downton, who were with Pembroke's men at the time, confirms the assumption that it was prepared for the original performance. In it the names of Edward Alleyn and Edward Juby are regularly distinguished by the honorific 'Mr.'. This also occurs irregularly with those of James Dunstan or Dunstone, Thomas Towne, and Martin [Slaughter], an inconsistency which is unexplained, for all three were presumably sharers. The other actors were Richard Alleyn, Thomas Hunt, Charles [Massey], Samuel [Rowley], Robert Ledbeter, and Edward Dutton, besides a 'super' known as Black Dick, Alleyn's boy Pig, Dutton's boy Dick, and two other boys called Griffin and Will. The only actor whom there is reason to suppose was a sharer at this date but whose name does not appear in the Plot is John Singer.

In the reconstruction of Oct. 1597 Slaughter or Slater, Dunstan or Dunstone, and possibly Edward Alleyn, retired, while Jones and Downton returned bringing with them Robert Shaa or Shaw, William Birde *alias* Borne, Gabriel Spenser, and two men of the name of Jeffes, Humphrey and Anthony. The next Plot appears to be that of *Fortune's Tennis*, which is a mere fragment written by the same hand as that of *The Seven Deadly Sins*. John Singer appears, duly distinguished as 'Mr.', Sam and Charles reappear, likewise a Dick (? Dutton's boy). We also find three minor actors, George [Somerset], Robert Tailor, and William Cartwright, of whom there is no trace in *Frederick and Basilea*, but who figure in later Plots, and were therefore probably brought in as hired men at the time of the reconstruction. We can also trace a Somerton who is most likely the same as Somerset, a Pavy who apparently lived to be a sharer in Prince Henry's company, and an unspecified Thomas, presumably Hunt. The extensive decay of the Plot has deprived us of any further information.

We may next take the other small fragment, which apparently formed part of the Plot of *Troilus and Cressida*, a play on which Chettle and Dekker were engaged in Apr. 1599. It is natural to suppose that the Plot was prepared soon after, perhaps in May. The evidence of cast it preserves is very meagre. But Richard Jones appears, duly distinguished as 'Mr.', and Thomas Hunt now has the same title. Jones also has a boy (who, we happen to know, was called James), and Alleyn's boy Pig reappears. A minor part was taken by one Stephen, who may possibly be Stephen Maget a tireman mentioned by Henslowe in 1596.

This fragment is in the same hand as the important though imperfect Plot of *The Battle of Alcazar*, of which the exact date is a good deal disputed, and the two should be considered in relation. In *Alcazar* no less than ten actors have the honorific 'Mr.'. That Edward Alleyn, Thomas Downton, Edward Juby, Thomas Towne, Robert Shaa, and Richard Jones are so distinguished goes without saying: they were all sharers in Oct. 1597 and (with a reservation in the case of Alleyn) continued as such till Jones and Shaa retired in 1602. Death had removed

Spenser in 1598; Singer and Birde are likewise absent, though one or other presumably took the part of Sebastian, for which no actor is assigned. This accounts for all the sharers of 1597. But we likewise find the 'Mr.' bestowed, not only on Thomas Hunt (as in *Troilus and Cressida*), but on Richard Alleyn, Sam [Rowley], and Charles [Massey]. Sam and Charles are known to have been sharers before the end of 1598, but Hunt and Alleyn involve difficulties to which I shall have to return. The other adult actors are the two Jeffes (who are not styled 'Mr.', though they probably held one share between them), Cartwright, Tailor, and Somerset (already known from *Fortune's Tennis*), one William Kendal, who had been hired by Henslowe on 8 Dec. 1597, and Thomas Drom, who is not otherwise known and may possibly have been a boy. There are also no less than eight boys, of whom three filled important roles. The actor of Calipolis is not named but was possibly the Will of *Frederick and Basilea*. His two chief supporters were Dick Juby, who was probably Dutton's boy Dick of that Plot, and a James, who was probably the James Bristow whom Henslowe 'bought' on 18 Dec. 1597. There remain Thomas Parsons, who is known to have been Downton's boy in 1599; Alleyn's boy, presumably once again our friend Pig; Dab, who may possibly be the 'Dobe' mentioned in a list of the company's wardrobe in 1597/8; also Towne's boy and a Harry, neither of whom is otherwise known.

The last Plot, that of 1 *Tamar Cam*, is supposed to have been prepared for a revival of that piece in the autumn of 1602, of which we perhaps find an indication elsewhere. The eight actors distinguished as 'Mr.' are Edward Alleyn, Downton ('Denygten'), Birde ('Bourne'), Towne, Singer, Edward Juby, Sam, and Charles. Jones and Shaa do not appear, having retired from the company in the preceding February; Richard Alleyn and Hunt have also disappeared, and the former had died in Nov. 1601. The Jeffes are there without the honorific. Cartwright, George [Somerset], and Parsons reappear, but not Kendal (whose term of service was up at the end of 1599), Tailor, or Drom; William Parr and Thomas Marbeck are newcomers. What seem to be the two female parts are unassigned:

perhaps James Bristow and Will were still available; Dick Juby seems now to be taking men's parts. Two minor boys are called 'Jack Grigerie & Mr. Denygtens little boy [Will]'. There are also probably nine others who appear as 'supers' in a final march past, including a James, who may be Jones's boy of *Troilus and Cressida*, a Ned Browne, who if he be the Edward Browne of Alleyn's early days has come sadly down in the world, and one who is merely described as the red faced fellow.

It will be seen that the casts of the Plots fit in comfortably with what we know from other sources of the personnel of the Admiral's men. It will also be noticed that as a rule the actors honoured with the designation 'Mr.' coincide with those who are otherwise known to have been sharers in the company, though here occasional difficulties arise. It is indeed in the interpretation of this prefix that the problem of the later Plots centres, for upon it depends the possibility of more precise dating.

There are three possible views as to the meaning of the 'Mr.' in these Plots. (i) The first is that no particular significance attaches to the designation, which is added as a mere mark of respect towards a leading member of the troop.[1] This seems to me in itself unlikely and unsupported by evidence. (ii) The second is that it indicates a sharer.[2] This agrees so well with the evidence in almost all cases that we should hesitate to abandon it even in the face of occasional difficulties. (iii) The third, according to a very ingenious conjecture of Sir Edmund Chambers, is that 'It may indicate appointment as a household servant of the company's "lord", a status which, as the history of the King's and Queen Anne's men seems to show, was independent of the contractual relations between the

[1] Sir E. K. Chambers seems to have been influenced by this view when he wrote in *The Elizabethan Stage* of R. Alleyn and T. Hunt that their 'long service had apparently earned them the dignity of the "Mr."' (ii. 175). Their long service, however, is an assumption which Sir Edmund no longer advances. Also I suppose I took this view when, in editing Henslowe's diary, I wrote (ii. 103) that 'the plots cannot be relied on to distinguish between the sharers and the hired men'. Further examination of the evidence has convinced me that I was wrong, and that Fleay, despite his incidental blunders, was right.

[2] Sir Edmund admits that this is 'in accordance with the ordinary usage of the Dulwich documents' (ii. 125).

members of a trading association of players using the lord's warrant' (*Two Elizabethan Stage Abridgements*, p.93, n.1). I am perfectly prepared to accept this interpretation as technically correct, but I regard it as practically equivalent to the former.[1] Such licensed servants would officially constitute the company; it is their names that would appear in the warrant, the other members of the troop only coming under its protection in virtue of being the hired servants of the licensees. But in general the body of licensees and the body of sharers no doubt would be the same, and I think it would be risky to assume that they diverged in cases where we have no definite evidence on the point.[2] Moreover, the distinction does not really help to solve the problem set us in the Plots, since there is independent evidence that one at least of the men distinguished as 'Mr.' but absent from the regular lists of sharers, was nevertheless treated as such in the company's affairs. Let us therefore examine rather more carefully the cases in which the use of the honorific appears to be anomalous.

And at the start attention may be directed to the care and consistency generally shown in its use. I have already mentioned the exceptions in the Plot of *Frederick and Basilea*. There Towne's name occurs five times but only once has the 'Mr.', that of Martin [Slaughter] occurs four times with the prefix and four times without, Dunstan's six times in all and only once without. All were apparently sharers at the time.

[1] It may also be suggested that whatever technical distinction there may have been the real social distinction in the company, which we should expect to find reflected in the playhouse documents, must have been between the financial sharers and those they hired at a weekly wage, that is to say as usual between masters and men.

[2] With this, as a general proposition, I understand that Sir Edmund would agree. I imagine that theatrical servants would not normally be appointed individually, their position would be the result of the 'lord' appending his name to the warrant authorizing them to act. And the body applying for such a warrant would naturally be those having contractual relations as a trading association of players. If subsequently other men became sharers they would not necessarily become technically servants of the 'lord', and it seems unlikely that other 'servants' would join the company as non-sharers. If therefore we find men acquiring the dignity of 'Mr.' during the career of a company, it seems more probable that they do so by becoming sharers than by becoming recognized 'servants'. It is true that in the royal companies the procedure was different, individual actors being formally appointed as grooms of the chamber.

The irregularity then can only be due to carelessness on the part of the scribe. No other errors of the sort occur, and if we accept the proposed date of 1597–8 for *Fortune's Tennis*, the Plots are mutually consistent, no actor having once acquired the distinction being ever deprived of it again.

Further, the close general correspondence between the use of the honorific 'Mr.' and the position of sharer is obvious. This may be seen at a glance by comparing the actor-lists of the Plots (in the accompanying volume of facsimiles) with the usual lists of recognized sharers in the Admiral's company, such as will be found in Sir Edmund Chambers's *Elizabethan Stage* or my edition of Henslowe's diary. But when this comparison is made certain discrepancies will also be observed. They are as follows. The two Jeffes, who appear among the sharers, are never given the honorific prefix in the Plots; while, on the other hand, Richard Alleyn and Thomas Hunt, who are distinguished as 'Mr.' in certain Plots, are absent from the lists of sharers.

It will be necessary, in order to get a clearer view of the problem before us, to consider in greater detail than has been hitherto thought necessary the evidence available respecting the sharers in the company. This, excluding as we must for the moment the Plots themselves, is derived from three main sources. (i) To begin with, we have in Henslowe's diary certain lists of the principal actors, composed in several instances of signatures appended in confirmation of the accounts: these actors are admittedly sharers. (ii) Next, there is a series of agreements between Henslowe and various members of the company, some of which specify a weekly wage, in the absence of which it is natural to assume that they apply to sharers. (iii) Lastly, Henslowe's accounts frequently mention individual actors as authorizing payment on behalf of the company, and since it would be the sharers as a body who would be responsible for the debt so incurred, we may assume that only a sharer would be authorized to contract it. None of these sources of information, any more than the Plots, is altogether satisfactory—since the lists are in some instances admittedly incomplete, the interpretation of the contracts is not beyond possible question, and the evidence under the third head is no

more than fragmentary—still I believe that between them they are capable of solving our problem with a reasonable approach to certainty.

(i) Henslowe's lists of the company are five in number. (1) The first is not of great importance, being a mere string of names entered for no apparent purpose presumably in the winter of 1594–5. (2) The next is contained in the heading to the accounts of 'my lord admeralles players' that began immediately after the reconstruction: it is dated 11 Oct. 1597, though I do not think that it was actually entered till the end of the year.[1] (3) A few months later there was a reckoning, and the sharers appended their signatures in acknowledgement of the company's debt sometime between 8 and 13 Mar. 1598. (4) Another reckoning was made on 10 July 1600 preparatory to the move to the Fortune, and the sharers again appended their autograph signatures. (5) The last acknowledged reckoning was made between 7 and 23 Feb. 1602 on the retirement of Jones and Shaa: the signatures in this instance are not autograph but were written by Shaa. The names in these five lists run as follows:[2]

| fol. 3 | Pemb. | fol. 43$^v$ | fol. 44$^v$ | fol. 70 | fol. 104 |
|---|---|---|---|---|---|
| 1594–5 (?) | Feb 1597. | 11 Oct. 1597 | 8–13 Mar. 1598 | 10 July 1600 | 7–23 Feb. 1602 |
| E. A[lleyn] | | | | | |
| J. Syngr | | Synger | J. Singer | J. Singger | Jhon Singer |
| R. Jonnes | • | Jonnes | Richard Jones | Richard Jones | |
| T. Towne | | Towne | Thomas Towne | Thomas Towne | Thomas Towne |
| Mr. Slater | | | | | |
| Jube | | Jube | | Edward Jubye | Edward Juby |
| T. Dowten | • | Dowten | Thomas Downton | Thomas Downton | Thomas Downton |
| Donstone | | | | | |
| | • | Borne | William Birde | W. Birde | William Byrd |
| | • | Gabrell [Spenser] | Gabriell Spenser | | |
| | • | Shaw | Robt. Shaa | Robt. Shaa | |
| | (•) | ij Geffes { | Humfry Jeffes | Humfry Jeffes | Humphrey Jeffs |
| | | | | Anthony Jeffes | Anthony Jeffs |
| | | | (Charles Massye) | Charles Massye | Charles Massy |
| | | | (Samuell Rowlye) | Samuell Rowley | Samuel Rowley |

[1] *Diary*, fol. 43$^v$. The first four items, of 21 Oct. to 1 Dec. 1597, duplicate rough entries on fol. 37, and the next seven items, of 1 to 28 Dec., duplicate entries on fol. 37$^v$. The following item is dated 5 Jan. 1597/8. It is interesting to observe that in the original rough entries of 23 Oct. and 5 Nov. Henslowe styles the company 'my lorde admeralls men & my lord penbrockes', but that by 8 Dec. he had settled down to 'my lord admeralles men' again.

[2] The order of the names as here given is only original in the case of the first list. In the third and fourth the order cannot be definitely determined. I have

The name most conspicuous by its absence is that of Edward Alleyn. He had in fact 'leafte [p]laynge' before the end of 1597 and apparently retired for a time from active participation in the affairs of the company, and since, as I have already remarked, the heading to the October accounts was probably not written till the end of the year, it is natural that his name does not appear in it. But he certainly resumed his share in the organization when the company moved to the Fortune towards the end of 1600, and the absence of his name from the last list is best explained on the supposition that the intimacy of his relations with Henslowe made formal acknowledgement unnecessary. Otherwise it is only the third list which is obviously incomplete. The absence of Juby can only, so far as I see, be explained as an oversight, and this may very likely account for the absence of Anthony Jeffes as well, though we shall find that in his case another explanation is possible. In the same list the names of Massey and Rowley may conceivably have been added later (see p. 34).

(ii) We must next consider the contracts, of which there are twelve in all:[1]

(1) 27 July 1597. Thomas Hearne. Hired to serve as a player for two years at 5*s*. a week the first year and 6*s*. 8*d*. the second.

(2) 3 Aug. 1597. John Helle, the clown. Bound in £40 to continue playing at the Rose till Shrovetide 1598 (as security for a loan of 10*s*.).

(3) 6 Aug. 1597. Richard Jones. Bound in 100 marks to continue playing with the Admiral's men at the Rose or in the country for three years from Michaelmas 1597.

(4) 6 Aug. 1597. Robert Shaa. Jones bound himself in 100 marks that Shaa (who was in prison at the time) would observe a circular undertaking.

(5) 10 Aug. 1597. William Borne (Birde). Bound in 100 marks to come and play with the Admiral's men at the Rose for three years from the end of the restraint.

(6) 6 Oct. 1597. Thomas Downton. Bound in £40 to play at the Rose till Shrovetide 1600.

indicated by a star in the second column those actors who joined in the reformation of Pembroke's company in Feb. 1597.

[1] They are all preserved in the *Diary*, fols. 230$^{v}$–233, except (7), which once formed part of fol. 231 but has been cut out and is now in MS. Egerton 2623, fol. 19.

(7) 8 Dec. 1597. William Kendall. Hired as a covenant servant to play at the Rose for two years at 10*s.* a week in London and 5*s.* a week in the country.

(8) 18 Dec. 1597. James Brystow, Henslowe's boy. Bought of William Augustine, player, for £8.

(9) 25 Mar. 1598. Richard Alleyn. Bound in £40 as a hired servant for two years.

(10) 25 Mar. 1598. Thomas Heywood ('hawoode'). Hired and bound in £40 as a covenant servant to play at the Rose for two years.

(11, 12) 16 Nov. 1598. Charles Massey and Samuel Rowley. Hired and bound in £40 apiece as covenant servants to play at the Rose till Shrovetide 1600.

There are a good many points to be considered in respect of these agreements. No. 8 for the purchase of James Bristow of course stands apart and need not trouble us further. Nos. 3–6 relate to known sharers and are clearly designed to bind them to the company and to Henslowe's house. Nos. 1 and 7, in which wages are specified, relate no less clearly to hired men.[1] Nos. 9–12 are all agreements to serve, and at first sight might be also supposed to relate to hired men. But it must be observed that the names of Massey and Rowley occur in the sharer lists, and moreover a covenant with a hired man which failed to specify a wage would be futile. It is true that Helle, the clown, was presumably such, and that in his agreement (no. 2) no wage is mentioned. But this bond is not quite on a par with the rest; it is security for a loan and for a short term only, and I interpret it to mean that Helle gave Henslowe an undertaking not to break his already existing contract with the company before he had had time to repay the debt. I fancy therefore that the hiring of Alleyn, Heywood, Massey, and Rowley as 'servants' may have been of the nature of a legal fiction, and it is significant that whereas in nos. 1 and 7 we merely have hiring for a wage, in 9–12 the point is a bond, just as it is in nos. 3–6. I conclude therefore that these eight agreements (3–6 and 9–12) all relate to sharers.[2]

[1] With these may be compared a contract of 25 Jan. 1599 [/1600?] whereby Thomas Downton hired an unnamed covenant servant to play for two years from Shrove Tuesday at 8*s.* a week and half wages if they were idle for more than a fortnight (*Diary*, fol. 20$^{v}$).

[2] It is just conceivable that R. Alleyn, Heywood, Massey, and Rowley, who,

If this is admitted we may draw a further inference that is not without importance. Jones, Shaa, Birde, and Downton were joining the Admiral's from Pembroke's company: Jones and Downton as sheep returning to the fold, Shaa and Birde as new-comers. Their contracts are all before the beginning of the accounts in October, and three out of the four are specified to begin when acting was expected to recommence in the autumn. It was then that the actors in question would become in effect sharers. The other four contracts are later, two on 25 Mar. and two on 16 Nov. 1598, and on the analogy of the others we should expect them to mark the inception of sharership. We are here met with a slight difficulty, for Massey and Rowley, whose contract is dated 16 Nov. 1598, signed the reckoning of the previous March. It is however to be remarked that their signatures appear together rather apart from the rest, and the graphic evidence is consistent with, and perhaps rather suggests, the supposition that they were added at a later date.[1] It is significant in this connexion that, though Rowley was one of the most frequent representatives of the company in authorizing payment on behalf of his fellows, his name occurring forty-two times in all, he acted in that capacity for the first time on 12 Dec. 1598.

The contracts then appear to afford us the names of eight sharers. In six out of the eight cases their testimony is confirmed by Henslowe's lists. In the other two there is an ap-

if sharers, had all acquired that position since the reorganization of Oct. 1597, may have been hired as 'servants' just because they were not technically servants of the Lord Admiral. But I rather hesitate to suggest this since the contracts were made with Henslowe and not with the company.

It is a pleasure to add that correspondence with Sir Edmund Chambers has resulted in a substantial measure of agreement respecting the interpretation of these documents. He writes: 'I think your theory that wageless contracts are for sharers is very likely sound; sharers being bound to each other by a "composition" and to Henslowe by a contract of service'. And he adds: 'The theory helps to clear up a phrase which has always puzzled me in the Burbadge lawsuit. John Alleyn says in his deposition of 6 Feb. 1592 that he "did as a servaunt wishe the said James Burbage to have a conscience in the matter".' Burbage of course stood to the company occupying his house much in the same position as Henslowe, so it may not have been the latter who invented these covenants.

[1] By analogy we should expect to find the names of Alleyn and Heywood added, but with Henslowe's methods it would be mainly a matter of chance whether new sharers were called upon to acknowledge the company's debt.

parent contradiction. Thomas Heywood is not otherwise heard of in connexion with the Admiral's men whether as sharer or hired man, though he was writing for them in 1596, 1598–9, and 1602–3.[1] Richard Alleyn was certainly an actor in the Admiral's company at this time, but his name does not appear in any of Henslowe's lists. Both contracts however are dated 25 Mar. 1598, which is after the reckoning of 3–13 Mar. and the two years for which they ran would be up at Lady Day 1600, so that Heywood and Alleyn may have left before the reckoning of 10 July that year. We naturally look for confirmation of this conjecture, and in the case of Alleyn we find it in the authorizations of payments on behalf of the company. His name appears twice, first (jointly with Birde's) on 17 Jan. 1599, within a year of his contract, and again (alone) on 6 May 1600, which is some weeks after its expiration, but still a couple of months before the next reckoning.[2] In view of this I cannot doubt that the interpretation of the contracts suggested above is correct, and that Richard Alleyn and Thomas Heywood were sharers in the Admiral's company from Lady Day 1598 till the spring of 1600.[3]

[1] Sir Edmund remarks that 'Heywood may not have acted much, holding his share in return for his services as a playwright, as Shakespeare may have done in his later years. He seems, however, still to have been paid for plays while a sharer.' He may, of course, have had an agreement to supply one or two pieces a year and have been paid for extra work.

[2] Richard Alleyn also accompanied Thomas Towne to Court on 7 Apr. 1599. This of course does not prove that he was a sharer though it looks as though he was a person of some consequence in the company.

[3] Sir Edmund, when he denied this in *The Elizabethan Stage*, was forced to argue that in the contracts, being only Henslowe's memoranda and not formal documents, the mention of wages had in some cases been inadvertently omitted. Such an assumption seemed a little arbitrary, and moreover it failed in the case of Massey and Rowley. As already mentioned Sir Edmund has since modified his view.

It is possible that objection might be taken to the theory that Richard Alleyn and Heywood (and also as we shall see later Hunt) were for two years sharers in the Admiral's company, on the ground that sharers on retirement are believed to have been paid £50 by the company for their interest in the concern, and that Henslowe's diary records no payment of the sort in favour of these men. Such an allowance was certainly made to Jones and Shaa *jointly* when they left in 1602, and there is other evidence of the custom. To which it may be replied that if it was paid in the case of R. Alleyn and Heywood (and Hunt), the company may have found the money without having such recourse to Henslowe as they had in that of Jones and Shaa. It is noticeable that Henslowe kept this

(iii) With respect to the evidence of sharership derived from the authorization of payment, little more need be said. We have found it of use both as regards Samuel Rowley and Richard Alleyn, and its significance is not disputed. Out of the fourteen actors whom I suppose to have been sharers in 1598, eight appear as appointing payment before the move to the Fortune in 1600. They are Shaa, Downton, Rowley, Juby, Birde, Jones, Towne, and Richard Alleyn; the first three acting frequently, the rest occasionally. The only hint of a non-sharer authorizing payment is afforded by certain entries in which the name 'w$^{m}$' Juby appears. No such person as William Juby is otherwise known, and there is good reason to suppose that in each case 'w$^{m}$' is no more than a slip of the pen for 'm$^{r}$', the actor intended being the sharer Edward Juby (*q.v.* in Actor Lists).[1]

We must now see how the information we have acquired can be applied to the problem of the Plots. The observed anomalies in the use of the honorific 'Mr.' are as follows. Richard Alleyn, who was not formerly regarded as a sharer, appears without it in *Frederick and Basilea* but with it in *The Battle of Alcazar* (he did not act in *Tamar Cam*). Thomas Hunt, of whom there is no hint among the sharers, also appears without the 'Mr.' in *Frederick and Basilea* (and probably in *Fortune's Tennis*) but with it in *Troilus and Cressida* and *The Battle of Alcazar* (he

advance distinct from the ordinary debt of the company, and further that when, on Edward Alleyn's temporary retirement in 1597, they presumably made him a like payment of £50, they discharged most of it privately before 10 July 1600, when they borrowed from Henslowe a balance of £11 needed to complete the payment.

[1] One other source of evidence as to sharers is to be found in the payees for performances given by the company at Court during the Christmas festivities. For the sake of completeness I append a list of the payees for the Admiral's men, 1594–1603, taken from *The Elizabethan Stage* (Appx. B), iv. 165–7.

1594–5: Edwarde Allen, Richarde Jones & John Synger (15 Mar. 1595).
1595–6: Edwarde Allen and Martyn Slater (13 Dec. 1596).
1596–7: no performance.
1597–8: Roberte Shawe and Thomas Downton (3 Dec. 1598).
1598–9: Robert Shawe and Thomas Downton (2 Oct. 1599).
1599–1600: Robert Shawe (18 Feb. 1600).
1600–1: Edwarde Allen (31 Mar. 1601).
1601–2: Edward Allen (28 Feb. 1602).
1602–3: Edwarde Allen (22 Apr. 1603).

too is absent from *Tamar Cam*). In the case of the Jeffes the position is reversed: they were clearly sharers, but while they appear both in *The Battle of Alcazar* and in *Tamar Cam*, in neither are they accorded the prefix.

Now as regards Richard Alleyn the discrepancy is not between the Plots and the diary, but between the different categories of evidence supplied by the diary itself, and we have already seen that even if the Plots were absent we should yet have to infer that he was at one time a sharer. This conclusion is confirmed by the Plots. But his case and that of Thomas Hunt really stand or fall together. The evidence of the Plots is essentially the same in each, and neither actor appears in Henslowe's lists. But the other evidence from the diary has proved that the Plots are to be trusted and indicated how the contradiction is to be overcome. It has been shown that Alleyn became a sharer at some date after 8 Mar. (probably on 25 Mar.) 1598 and ceased to be one before 10 July 1600, and the same explanation is open in the case of Hunt. It is true that with respect to Hunt we lack the confirmation we have in respect to Alleyn, but this is not an objection of any weight. Henslowe may either not have made any contract with Hunt, or he may have omitted to record it in his diary, or the record of it may have been lost (as Kendall's very nearly was): whether or not he authorized a payment during his sharership would be merely a matter of chance. I conclude, therefore, that Hunt was a sharer and that his career with the company was essentially the same as Alleyn's.[1]

[1] It is a curious coincidence that, on the evidence of the contracts (see p. 33), Thomas Heywood was a sharer in the company for two years from 25 Mar. 1598, though there is no other trace of him in connexion with them (except as a writer), while on the evidence of the Plots, Thomas Hunt was a sharer some time between Mar. 1598 and July 1600, though he is not traceable in the diary (unless he was the Thomas Honte mentioned, possibly as a member of the company in Oct. 1596). By all the rules of the game they ought to be the same person, and I long toyed with the idea that Hunt was Heywood's stage name—much as Borne seems to have been Birde's. But there was always a difficulty in reconciling the subsequent careers of the two, and now that Professor Sisson has discovered Heywood's signature among the Chancery depositions and I have had an opportunity of comparing it with Hunt's in the Dulwich documents, this fanciful speculation must be abandoned. There remains a possibility that in Henslowe's contract the name 'hawoode' is a mere slip for Hunt, but this seems rather less likely in view of the circumstance that, whereas the witnesses

There remain the Jeffes—sharers without the prefix—and I think that in their case the clue is to be found in an account of Jan.–Mar. 1598 dealing with some obscure transaction of Henslowe's relative to 'humfreye Ieaffes hallffe share'. From this I infer that the two Jeffes held only a single share between them, and that though this necessitated their acknowledging the reckonings, it was not held to entitle them to the honorific in the Plots.[1] This conjecture finds some slight confirmation in the fact that the documents relating to Pembroke's company, whence they presumably joined the Admiral's, do not name them and hesitate between seven and eight as the number of its members.[2] It might also account for Henslowe being content with the signature of one only to the reckoning of Mar. 1598.

My conclusion, therefore, is that the distinctive 'Mr.' of the Plots does indicate a sharer, either explicitly or because all recognized servants of the lord were sharers. In a few exceptional cases a sharer appears without the honorific, but no non-sharer is ever graced with it. From this it follows that the Plots of *Troilus and Cressida* and *The Battle of Alcazar*, in both of which the 'Mr.' is prefixed to the name of Thomas Hunt, must have been drawn up between Mar. 1598 and July 1600. Further, if our reasoning is correct, *The Batile of Alcazar*, in which Massey and Rowley are distinguished by the prefix,

to the other contracts are mostly actors, those to Heywood's include his fellow dramatist Antony Munday.

[1] It is of course possible that they held a share but were not technically servants of the Lord Admiral—if that is the correct interpretation of the prefix 'Mr.'. Professor T. W. Baldwin, in an article entitled 'Posting Henslowe's Accounts' (*Journal of English and Germanic Philology*, 1927, xxvi. 42 ff.), offers a different explanation (p. 60), namely, that by Jeffes's half share is meant his portion of the half share of certain receipts due to the company, and this is to some extent borne out by the actual amounts recorded. The possibility had occurred to me, but I doubt whether it should be entertained. The agreement of the sum is not very close, and Jeffes's half share seems to me an unnecessarily misleading way of referring to his 'eighth share of the quarter gallery' takings. Mr. Baldwin finds a similar correspondence in 'Bengemenes Johnsones Share' on 28 July 1597, but there seems no possibility of Jonson having been a member of the Admiral's company at that date.

[2] Five members are named: Shaa, Jones, Spencer, Birde, and Downton. The Jeffes (counted as one or two) would make six or seven. The seventh or eighth was almost certainly Ben Jonson, who was imprisoned as both actor and part author of *The Isle of Dogs*. He did not join the Admiral's men as a player, but began writing for them about this time (Dec. 1597).

must be after 16 Nov. 1598. There is every reason to believe that *Troilus and Cressida* belongs to the spring of 1599, and it certainly need not surprise us to find that *The Battle of Alcazar*, which is written by the same hand and in the same style, is approximately contemporary.

But this dating of *The Battle of Alcazar* raises a difficulty, for Edward Alleyn, whose name figures in the Plot, was, it is contended, in retirement from the autumn of 1597 to that of 1600.[1] That he did withdraw from the stage about this time is not questioned: it is implied in the Court payments; according to Henslowe he had 'leafte [p]laynge' by 29 Dec. 1597; the company paid him £50, which looks like the bonus of a sharer on retiring; on 11 Nov. 1600 they made a new 'composicion' with him preparatory to opening at the Fortune; and, perhaps most significant of all, the warrant for the erection of that theatre issued on 8 Apr. 1600 mentions the pleasure taken by the Queen in Alleyn's acting 'wheareof, of late he hath made discontynuance'. But I see no reason to assume that his retirement was necessarily absolute or of a nature to preclude his occasional appearance on the boards. I conjecture therefore that he consented to grace in this manner the revival of Peele's play, an old Admiral's piece, in which he had probably filled the leading role some ten years before, and in which we may suppose popular interest to have been revived by the recent death of the author. I may also point out that in casting the

[1] Sir Edmund was formerly so impressed with the difficulty that he rejected the evidence respecting sharers we have been considering. I would gladly, if I could, avoid the assumption of Alleyn's exceptional reappearance, but I cannot see how to do so. Even apart from the problem of the 'Mr.', the Plot can hardly be put after his return, for one of the boy actors in it was married and had a child probably within eighteen months of that event. With this Sir Edmund 'now on the whole' agrees. And before Alleyn's retirement there is really no time. Reference to the list of Henslowe's contracts shows that the presence of Kendall places it after 8 Dec. and that of James presumably after 18 Dec. 1597. But Henslowe tells us that Alleyn had retired *before* 29 Dec., and there is nothing in the account, in the heading to which he gives us this information (*Diary*, fol. 43), to lead us to suppose that his retirement was quite recent. It is much more likely to have taken place in October. At the outside there would have only been a little over a week for the casting, rehearsing, and production of the play. In a choice between improbabilities a desire for what I regard as the lesser would still lead me to postulate Alleyn's exceptional reappearance, even were I not driven to that conclusion by what seems to me the cogent evidence of sharership.

play one of the leading actors of the troop, either Singer or Birde, was held in reserve and would be available to take Alleyn's place when he again withdrew. But I think that Alleyn is more likely to have made such an occasional reappearance in the winter than in the summer, which we know he sometimes spent in the country, and in the earlier than the later part of his retirement, when the Fortune warrant suggests that he had been using his 'discontynuance' as a lever in Court circles. It is therefore to the winter of 1598–9, shortly before the composition of *Troilus and Cressida*, that I conjecturally assign the Plot of *The Battle of Alcazar*.[1]

## Note by Sir E. K. Chambers

Dr. Greg has been good enough to give me an opportunity of commenting upon two points which have been in controversy, public and private, between us.

The first is as to the nature of the relations between Alleyn, the 'Admiral's' men, and 'Strange's' men from 1589 to 1594. As to this I have attempted elsewhere to restate the conclusions

[1] Edward Alleyn is of course distinguished as 'Mr.' in the Plot, though the evidence suggests that he had surrendered his share in the company. I have little doubt that he would in any case have retained the title by courtesy, but if it belonged technically to a servant of the company's lord, there is no reason to suppose that he had not a right to it.

It has been argued, and I have argued myself, that traces of *Alcazar* may be found in an inventory of theatrical goods belonging to the Admiral's men and dated 10 Mar. 1598. The true date of this inventory is 1597/8 not 1598/9, and it is earlier than the Plot. If therefore it does contain any properties for Peele's play, these must have been used for an earlier revival. But I now very much doubt whether there is any connexion. The crucial entry in the inventory runs: 'Item, The Mores lymes, and Hercolles lymes, and Will. Sommers sewtte'. It is clear from the mention of Sommers that there is no necessary connexion between the other two, though it is a curious coincidence if their association here is accidental, seeing that the Moor and Hercules are both characters in *Alcazar*. But there are weighty considerations against the identification. For one thing, it is rather the body than the limbs of the Moor that the text demands. Hercules is not even killed in the extant version, and though he very likely was in the original, there is no reason to suppose that he was hacked to pieces. Next, the item in question appears, not in the list of 'properties', but in that of 'sewtes'. Lastly we find that the Revels Office had 'legges ffeete Armes and hands' of moors that were nothing but black velvet tights (A. Feuillerat, *Revels of Elizabeth*, 1908, p. 24). Such 'lymes' might be used in many plays besides *The Battle of Alcazar*. Also the two parts of a play of *Hercules* appear among the 'bookes' in the same inventory.

of my *Elizabethan Stage* in the light of Dr. Greg's criticisms.[1] I still think it probable that, at any rate from the winter of 1590, the association was a close one, and amounted, for London if not for provincial work, to an amalgamation. If I am right, the plots of *The Seven Deadly Sins* and *The Dead Man's Fortune*, datable by the presence in them of Richard Burbage as earlier than the breach with his father in May 1591, may represent performances either by Strange's or by the Admiral's or by the amalgamated company, and therefore do not tell us which members of that company, as we find it in 1593, had originally been Strange's and which Admiral's men. Dr. Greg, on the other hand, not convinced that the amalgamation, if it was one, preceded the breach with James Burbage, inclines to look at the plots from a different angle, and to regard the cast of *The Seven Deadly Sins* as definitely a cast for Strange's and that of *The Dead Man's Fortune* as definitely a cast for the Admiral's. I do not think that there is any adequate material for a confident decision between the two hypotheses. Dr. Greg and I now have our *data* in common, and what remains between us is little more than a difference of speculative feeling on an issue as to which we agree that the *data* are insufficient to allow of more than speculation.

The second point is as to the date of the *Battle of Alcazar* plot. Here Rowley, Massey, Hunt, and Richard Alleyn all have the designation 'm$^{r}$'. I now agree with Dr. Greg that, whatever the precise technical sense of 'm$^{r}$', it is probable that an actor so designated in a plot was a 'sharer' at the date of that plot. I also agree that the contract of 16 November 1598 with Rowley and Massey was probably a contract for service as sharers. I am not so clear that it marks the beginning of their sharerships, in view of their signatures to the debt acknowledgement of March 1598, since we cannot be sure that those signatures were added at a later date. However this may be, Hunt and Richard Alleyn signed neither the acknowledgement of March 1598 nor that of July 1600, and as there is no obvious reason for regarding the signatures as incomplete, I suppose

[1] See *William Shakespeare, a study of facts and problems* (Oxford, 1930), chap. ii, particularly pp. 48–52.

we must infer that these men were only sharers for short periods between the two dates, and that the *Alcazar* plot also fell between them. I am therefore reluctantly driven to admit that Dr. Greg's theory of a temporary return by Edward Alleyn holds the field.

8 *December* 1930.

## ACTOR LISTS

In the summary notes that follow I have endeavoured to collect the main relevant facts concerning the actors who figure in the Plots and their relation to the companies concerned. I have not however attempted to compile complete biographies, nor to give detailed references to authorities. The latter are as a rule easily ascertained from Sir Edmund Chambers's *Elizabethan Stage* and my own editions of *Henslowe's Diary* and the *Henslowe Papers*. The ground was also partly covered in my *Two Elizabethan Stage Abridgements* (appendixes to Chapters II and IV, together with the notes on the Cast and Personae in IV). I have occasionally drawn on Dr. T. W. Baldwin's *Organization and Personnel of the Shakespearean Company* (Princeton, 1927), on an article by Miss E. M. Denkinger, 'Actors' Names in the Registers of St. Botolph Aldgate', in the *Publications* of the Modern Language Association of America (1926, xli. 91–109), and on information kindly supplied by Mr. G. E. Bentley, whose gleanings from the parish records of St. Saviour, Southwark, were printed under the heading of 'Shakespeare's Fellows' in *The Times Literary Supplement*, 15 Nov. 1928, while those from St. Giles, Cripplegate, appeared in the *Publications* already mentioned in Sept. 1929 (xliv. 789–826). I have had the advantage of checking the proofs of my notes with the material carefully collected by Dr. E. Nungezer in his *Dictionary of Actors before 1642* (1929).

### *The Earlier Plots—I & II*

The chief lists of the Chamberlain's and King's men referred to in these notes are as follows: 'The Names of the Principall Actors in all these Playes' given in the Shakespeare Folio of 1623, 'The principall Comædians' or 'Tragædians' in several of Jonson's plays given in his Works in 1616 (*Every Man in his Humour*, 1598, *Every Man out of his Humour*, 1599, *Sejanus*, 1603, *Volpone*, 1605, *The Alchemist*, 1610, *Catiline*, 1611), the list in the patent of 19 May 1603, and the identical list in the livery warrant of 15 Mar. 1604. There were later patents of

27 Mar. 1619 and 24 June 1625, and warrants of 19 May 1619, 7 Apr. 1621, 27 Mar. 1625, and 6 May 1629. The two Plots here referred to by numbers are:

I—The Dead Man's Fortune.
II—2 Seven Deadly Sins.

BEESTON, CHRISTOPHER. *See* KIT.

BELT, T. In II 'T Belt' played a Servant in the Induction, and Panthea, who has a single entrance in Lechery. He is an otherwise unknown boy.

BRYAN, GEORGE. II 'mr Brian' 'mr Bry'. He played Damasus, a lord or counsellor, in Envy, and Warwick in the Conclusion. He is first heard of abroad in 1586–7, and is in the licence for Strange's men in 1593. As a Chamberlain's man he first appears as payee on 21 Dec. 1596 for plays of the previous winter at Court, but is not traceable with them later, and probably left before 1598 to become an ordinary Groom of the Chamber, a post he is known to have held in 1603 and later. He is in the Shakespeare Folio list, but in none of Jonson's.

BURBAGE, RICHARD. I 'Burbage': II 'R Burbadg'. It is a conjecture that the former was Richard, but he is the only one of the family known to have acted. His part in I is rendered uncertain by the confused text. It was probably not the Messenger, as usually supposed, but may have been Urganda. In II he played Gorboduc and Tereus, leading parts, but does not seem to have been a sharer. He cannot have been much over, and was probably not much under, twenty when in 1590–1 he took a prominent part in a brawl at the Theatre, in which a company called the Admiral's was concerned, and which perhaps led to the migration of that body and Strange's to the Rose in 1591 or 1592. Richard presumably stayed with his father James at the Theatre, but what if any company acted there we do not know. He must presumably have found some occupation during the next few years, but the suggestion that he led Pembroke's men appears to me without foundation: he is not named in the 1593 licence. He was, however, probably an original member of the Chamberlain's company in the spring of 1594, for on 15 Mar. 1595 he, Shakespeare, and Kempe were payees for the Court performances of the preceding Christmas. He was, of course, the leading member of the company, with which he remained after it became the King's till his death on 13 Mar. 1619.

CONDELL, HENRY. *See* HARRY.

COOKE, ALEXANDER. *See* SAUNDER.

COWLEY, RICHARD. II 'R Cowly' 'R Cow'. He played several small male parts, including the Lieutenant of the Tower in the Induction and

Giraldus in Sloth. He is not in the licence of May 1593, but we know from Alleyn's correspondence that he joined the company at Bristol at the end of July bringing letters from London. The stage-directions in *Much Ado* (IV. ii: Q 1600 and F 1623) show that he played Verges, perhaps about 1598, and he is in the Shakespeare Folio list. Otherwise he is not recorded with the Chamberlain's men till 1601, when he was payee on 31 Mar., though he was probably with them from 1594. He was still with the King's company in 1605, but had no share in either playhouse. His will, of 13 Jan. 1618, was witnessed by Hemings and Cuthbert Burbage, and he was buried in St. Leonard's, Shoreditch, on 12 Mar. 1619.

DARLOWE. I 'Darlowe' 'Dar'. His name is given three times as playing an Attendant. A Richard Darloe, player, baptized and buried three children in St. Botolph's, Aldgate, between 1595 and 1602.

DUKE, JOHN. II 'John duke' 'J(o) Duke' 'J Duk'. He played several small male parts including one in Sloth called Will Fool. He was later with the Chamberlain's men and may have joined them in 1594, though he is first recorded as acting in *Every Man in his Humour* in 1598: he is also in the Shakespeare Folio list. But he was in relation with Henslowe as early as 1600, and was a member of Worcester's company by 18 Aug. 1602, after their amalgamation with Oxford's; he appears in their draft patent as Queen Anne's men in 1604, and again in that of 15 Apr. 1609. He is not heard of later, and since he is also only traceable in the registers of St. Leonard's from 1604 to Jan. 1609, he may have died soon after. The occurrence of his name in an exemplification of the patent dated 7 Jan. 1612, and in later notes of the same, is hardly evidence that he was still alive.

GOODALE, THOMAS. II 'Th(o) Goodale' 'T Good'. He played several small male parts, including Lucius, a lord or counsellor, in Envy, and Phronesius in Sloth. There was a Thomas among the children of John Goodale of Stratford upon Avon (1562–6), and a Thomas Goodale was one of Lord Berkeley's players committed to the Counter in July 1581 in consequence of a brawl with Inns of Court men. The name also appears in a marginal stage-direction in the Book of *Sir Thomas More* (sc. viii, fol. 14) 'Mess[enger] T Goodal'. Lastly, a Thomas Goodale, mercer, along with John Allein, innholder, and Robert Lee, gent., signed a bond for the payment of £19 to John Allen, gent., on 18 May 1593. It is reasonable to suppose that this Lee was the actor of the name in I, and certain that John Allein, innholder, was Edward Alleyn's elder brother, and the document suggests their association about the date of the Strange-Admiral's licence (6 May 1593—though John Alleyn may have already ceased acting) but throws no light on their earlier connexions. Goodale appears as a player in the St. Botolph registers in 1594 and 1599.

GOUGHE, Robert. There is little doubt that in II the 'R Go' who played Aspasia in Sloth and the 'Ro' who played Philomele in Lechery are the same and identical with Robert Goughe, though it is true that either inference depends to some extent on the other. He was of course a boy. Later he was a King's man and appears in the list of 1619 and in the Shakespeare Folio. Presumably he had been with the Chamberlain's men, possibly from 1594, for he was a legatee under Pope's will, 22 July 1603, and a witness in 1605 to that of Phillips, whose sister he married on 13 Feb. 1603. He is traceable in St. Saviour's from 1604 to his burial on 19 Feb. 1624. The Book of *The Second Maiden's Tragedy* (fol. 48ᵃ, l. 1724) shows that he played a part, probably that of Memphonius, in 1611, and the Book of *Sir John Barnavelt* (fol. 9ᵃ, l. 839) that he was still with the company in 1619, though he clearly did not play Leidenberg as has been suggested.

HARRY. In II 'Harry' or 'Hary' played Ferrex in Envy, besides a Lord in Lechery, and was therefore an actor of some importance. He may have been Henry Condell, who is first named in the cast of *Every Man in his Humour* in 1598. He was then, of course, a Chamberlain's man, but how long he had been with the company there is nothing to show. He is in the Shakespeare Folio list, and with Hemings edited that volume in 1623. He had then given up acting, though his name still appears in the patent of 1625. The same year he was living at his country house at Fulham, where he made his will on 13 Dec. 1627 and was buried on the 29th.

*HENRY VI.* No actors are assigned in II for the parts of 'Henry the sixt' and 'Lidgate', and speculation is perhaps unprofitable. Neither part is likely to have been of a kind to attract Edward Alleyn (supposing him to have been in the cast, which I doubt). The part of Henry might have suited Shakespeare (but there is again no evidence that he was acting with the company). The suggestion that the parts were filled by Kempe and Hemings (see p. 21) cannot be entertained as regards the former and is unsupported as regards the latter.

HOLLAND, John. The 'J Holland' or 'J Holl' who is down for several small male parts in II is presumably the John Holland who acted a rebel according to the stage-directions of 2 *Henry VI*, IV. ii. 1 (F 1623). But it is doubtful what significance his appearance in that play has for his career, since the manuscript may possibly have belonged in turn to Strange's, Pembroke's, and the Chamberlain's men. The name John Holland is also found in marginal annotations to a manuscript play to which the title of *John of Bordeaux* has been given.

KIT. In II 'Kitt' (once 'Kit') played several small male parts. He may have been Christopher Beeston, who is described as the 'servant' of Phillips in the latter's will. He was with the Chamberlain's men in 1598 according to the cast of *Every Man in his Humour*. In 1602 he is found, like Duke, with Worcester's men, and remained with them under Queen Anne's patronage till 1619, after which he took a leading part in several theatrical ventures and owned the Cockpit. He is traceable till 1637 and was evidently dead two years later.

LEE, ROBERT. In I 'Robart lee' appeared twice as an attendant and once perhaps as a messenger. A Robarte Lee, gent., was associated with Thomas Goodale (q.v.) and John Alleyn about the date of the Strange-Admiral's licence of 1593, and may conceivably have taken part in that amalgamation. He sold an old play, *The Miller*, to the later Admiral's men in 1598, but does not seem to have belonged to that company. He is not known to have been with the Chamberlain's or Worcester's (cf. Duke, Kit, Pallant) but was with Queen Anne's from 1604 to 1619. After the Queen's death he became leader of the company, which was then known as the Red Bull players or the Children of the Revels, till it broke in 1623.

*LYDGATE*. No actor is assigned in II either for 'Lidgate' or for 'Henry the sixt' (q.v.).

NED. A boy in II who played Rhodope in Sloth but cannot be identified. He was certainly not Edward Alleyn who was twenty-four in 1590, the earliest likely date for the Plot.

NICK. A boy in II who played Pompeia in Sloth besides a lady in Envy. He may possibly have been Nicholas Tooley, who is in the King's men's patent in 1619 though not in the lists of 1603–4. Phillips's will of 3 May 1605 makes him his 'fellow', so he was probably a sharer by that date and no new comer. His own will of 3 June 1623 (he was buried two days later) makes Richard Burbage his 'master', so he had probably at one time been the latter's 'boy' or 'man'. In 1590 Burbage was hardly old enough for this, and II shows him still a hired man. Presumably therefore the relation must have existed after 1594 when Burbage was leading the Chamberlain's men. Tooley may then have been a boy in Strange's company and have stayed on with the Chamberlain's (with Burbage as his 'master') as a hired man before becoming a sharer. A 'Nicke' appears as a messenger in *The Taming of the Shrew* (III. i. 82, F 1623) and as a rebel in Pembroke's men's *Contention* (sc. xiii, Q 1594 = 2 *Henry IV*, IV. ii. 1), but in the former case it is not certain that the name is an actor's, and in the latter improbable. The Nick of the Plot can hardly have been the boy of that name who is heard of with the Admiral's men in 1601 and 1603.

PALLANT, Robert. II 'R(o) Pallant' 'R Pall' 'R Pa' 'R P'. He played several small male parts including Nicanor in Sloth and Julio in Lechery. He is next heard of with Worcester's men in 1602 and remained with Queen Anne's nominally till 1619, though he was apparently with Lady Elizabeth's in 1614 and Prince Charles's in 1616. There must, however, have been a younger actor of the name, for he cannot have played Cariola in *The Duchess of Malfi* with the King's men as recorded in 1619. This was, no doubt, the 'Robert Pallant, son of Robert, a player', baptized at St. Saviour's on 28 Sept. 1605. The elder Robert was probably the 'man' of the name buried on 4 Sept. 1619. His association both earlier and later with Duke (q.v.) and perhaps Beeston, suggests the possibility of his having been with the Chamberlain's men in 1594–8 (but see p. 22 note).

PHILLIPS, Augustine. As 'mr Phillipps' in II he played Sardanapalus in Sloth. He is in the licence of 1593, and was with the Chamberlain's men, probably from 1594, though he is not recorded very early. He appears however in all the regular lists from 1598 to 1604 and in the Shakespeare Folio. An Awgustyne Phillips was buried in St. Saviour's in 1592, and the player is traceable there from 1593 (in Bullhead Alley) to 1604 (in Horseshoe Alley). He was living at Mortlake on 4 May 1605 when he made a will that was proved on the 13th.

POPE, Thomas. As 'mr Pope' in II he played Arbactus in Sloth. He is first heard of abroad in 1586–7, is in the licence of 1593, and was probably with the Chamberlain's men from 1594 on. In any case he was their payee on 27 Nov. 1597 for Court performances of the previous Christmas, played in both Jonson's *Humour* plays, 1598–9, and is in the Shakespeare Folio list. In 1598 there was litigation between him and William Birde of the Admiral's, and Rowlands couples him with John Singer of that company as acting clowns' parts. He was a sharer in the Globe in 1599, but retired before the company became the King's servants. His will was made on 22 July 1603 and proved on 13 Feb. following.

SAM. I 'b samme' 'sam'. He played attendants, Validor's man, and apparently Euphrodore, parts which in no way force us to interpret the 'b' as 'boy', though this is perhaps the most likely explanation. Speculation as to his identity is rather idle, though the name is not common. Indeed there seem to be only three possible Samuels recorded. A Samuel Crosse is in the Shakespeare Folio list, though not known in the Chamberlain-King's company. He may have been the Crosse mentioned by Heywood as before his time: in that case he belonged to the earliest days of Shakespeare's career, and was certainly not a boy or a

subordinate actor in or about 1590.[1] Samuel Gilburne, also in the Shakespeare Folio list, is at least known to have belonged to the Chamberlain-King's company, since Phillips, in his will made in 1605, calls him his 'late apprentice'. This expression, however, suggests that the apprenticeship was fairly recent, and if Gilburne was say twenty in 1605 he can hardly have been acting as early as 1590. Lastly there is Samuel Rowley, the 'Sam' of the later Plots, who can first be traced with the Admiral's men in the summer of 1597 and became a sharer the following year. He must have had an earlier career on the stage, and might still have been just called a boy in 1590. It is true that he has been credited with being already a playwright in the early nineties, which would make us doubt his extreme youth, but his authorship is hardly proved, and moreover 'b' may not stand for 'boy'. He is on the whole the most likely of the three.

SAUNDER. He was one of the leading boys in II, playing Queen Videna in Envy, and Progne, wife of Tereus, in Lechery. Possibly he was Alexander Cooke. In his will Cooke speaks of Hemings as his 'master', so he had probably once been the latter's 'boy' or 'man' in the Chamberlain's company. Phillips calls him his 'fellow' in his will in 1605, so he was probably a sharer by that date though he is not in the lists of 1603–4. He is in the Jonson lists of 1603 to 1611, and in the Shakespeare Folio. He appears to have been already married in Oct. 1603 and had a son baptized two years later. He lived in St. Saviour's from 1604 and was buried there on 25 Feb. 1614, when his share of the company's stock was worth £50. He had a brother John, who may possibly have been the author of *Greene's Tu Quoque*, 1614. In *The Taming of a Shrew* acted by Pembroke's men 'Sa(u)nder(s)' is the name given to the character called Grumio in *The Shrew*, and 'San.' is the prefix given to a Player in the Induction (sc. i, Q 1594: where *The Shrew* in F 1623 has 'Sincklo'). It need not be an actor's name. Nor need it indeed be a Christian name: a William Sanders is among 'musitions and other necessary attendantes' of the King's company mentioned in a 'protection' of 1624.

SINCLER, JOHN. II 'John Sincler' 'J sincler' 'J Sinc'. He played several small male parts, appearing once as a musician. Otherwise he is chiefly known from the accidental preservation of his name in stage-directions. Thus he played a Beadle in 2 *Henry IV* (v. iv, Q 1600), a Player in the Induction to *The Taming of the Shrew* (F 1623), and a

[1] *Eliz. Stage*, ii. 313. Recently Sir E. K. Chambers has conjectured that he was an otherwise unrecorded actor whom he supposes to have formally become a member of the King's company in 1604 and to have died almost at once. I do not know the ground of this conjecture, but if it is correct he may of course have been the boy Sam fourteen years before.

Keeper in 3 *Henry VI* (III. i, F 1623). For the significance of the last (possibly the last two) cf. Holland. In the first he is represented as of a lean and cadaverous appearance, and this has suggested that he may have played the Apothecary in *Romeo and Juliet* (see A. Gow in *Anglia*, 1925, N.F. xxxvii, 289). He also appears, among other actors of the King's company, in the 'Induction' to *The Malcontent* (1604).

SLY, WILLIAM. In II 'w sly' played Porrex in Sloth and a Lord in Lechery, an actor evidently of some importance. In the autumn of 1594 he bought a jewel of Henslowe, and in Mar. 1598 the Admiral's men possessed a suit which had once been his ('Perowes sewt which W^m^ Sley were'). This may have been a relic of a joint wardrobe of 1592–3, for there is no reason to suppose that he was ever with the later Admiral's men. He was with the Chamberlain's men, perhaps from 1594, certainly from 1598; may be traceable in Southwark as early as 1588 and as late as 1596, had an illegitimate son in St. Giles's, Cripplegate, in 1606, and was buried in St. Leonard's, Shoreditch, 16 Aug. 1608. He is in the Jonson lists from 1598 to 1605, and in the Shakespeare Folio, also in the official lists of 1603–4, but he only acquired an interest in the playhouses at the very end of his life.

TOOLEY, NICHOLAS. *See* NICK.

TIRE-MAN. In I a 'tyre man' was called on, together with Darlowe, to play 'atendantes & others'. Cf. Stephen in the later Plots.

VINCENT. He appears in II as one of '3 musitions' in a single scene of Sloth. The others are Cowley and Sincler, but Vincent does not seem to have been a regular actor. He may, of course, have been a professional musician. According to John Taylor a Thomas Vincent was 'book-keeper or prompter' at the Globe, apparently between 1599 and 1603 (see Baldwin, p. 124). But if it is Thomas who is in question here he can hardly have already held that post, since the prompter was the one man who could not be called on as a 'super'. There was another Thomas Vincent, fellow of Trinity College, Cambridge, whose Latin *Paria* was acted in 1628 and printed in 1648.

WILL. In II a boy 'will' played Itys in Lechery. As he took no other part we may perhaps conclude that he was a very small boy. One of the rebels in Pembroke's *Contention* (sc. xiii, Q 1594 = 2 *Henry VI*, IV. ii. 92) is called Will, but there is no reason to suppose that this is an actor's name. There was a William Tawyer or Toyer, Hemings's 'man', who was one of the 'Musitions and other necessary attendantes' with the King's men in 1624, and who died in 1625, and 'Tawyer with a Trumpet before them' is a stage-direction in *A Midsummer Night's Dream* (v. i. 128, F 1623; not in Qq), but this is too remote to be of any significance.

## *The Later Plots—III-VII*

These all belonged to the later Admiral's company, 1594–1603. The five sharer lists given by Henslowe, from 1594–5 to 1602, are printed at p. 31, the list of his contracts with individual actors at pp. 32–3. The company became servants of Prince Henry in the winter of 1603–4: there is a livery warrant for the coronation procession of 15 Mar. 1604, but no patent till that of 30 Apr. 1606. The difficult question of the boy actors is further discussed in a note on pp. 66–9. The Plots are here referred to by numbers and abbreviated titles as follows:

III—Frederick and Basilea—*Frederick.*
IV—2 Fortune's Tennis—*Tennis.*
V—Troilus and Cressida—*Troilus.*
VI—The Battle of Alcazar—*Alcazar.*
VII—1 Tamar Cam—*Tamar.*

ALLEN, Richard. *See* ALLEYN, R.

ALLEYN, Edward. III 'Mr Allen(n)': VI 'mr Ed: Allen': VII 'Mr. Allen'. As the leader of the company he naturally took important roles: Sebastian in *Frederick*, the Moor in *Alcazar*, the title-role in *Tamar*. There is no trace of him in the fragments; he was probably in retirement at the time and only returned for a special revival of *Alcazar*. He withdrew from the company probably in Oct. 1597, certainly before the end of the year, and remained away about three years, only rejoining when it moved to the Fortune late in 1600 (see pp. 39–40). He finally retired probably in 1604 (his name is in the livery warrant but not the patent, and he was payee on 19 Feb. but not on 17 Apr.), but it is doubtful whether he acted after Elizabeth's death.

ALLEYN'S BOY. VI 'mr Allen's boy'. He may have been Pig (q.v.).

ALLEYN, Richard. III 'Richard Alleine' 'R Allen(n)': VI 'mr Rich: Allen'. The first perhaps justifies the spelling adopted, but he is not known to have been related to Edward. He spoke the Prologue and Epilogue in *Frederick* and acted as Presenter in *Alcazar*: further he filled the male title-role in the former and a minor part in the latter. Presumably an actor of good presence rather than histrionic gifts. He is first mentioned by Henslowe, probably in 1594, when he was possibly with the Queen's men. He was borrowing small sums of Henslowe in 1597–8, and on 25 Mar. 1598 bound himself to him for two years, and witnessed a similar bond on Heywood's part. He accompanied Towne to Court on some business connected with the company on Easter Eve

1599, and authorized payments on 17 Jan. 1599 and 6 May 1600. He is not, however, in any of Henslowe's lists, and if he was ever a sharer it must have been between the reckonings of Mar. 1598 and July 1600, within which dates his contract falls (see p. 37). He lived in St. Saviour's, Southwark, but his residence cannot be certainly traced, for the name is a common one. However, he had daughters baptized there in 1599 and 1601, and 'Richard Allen, a man' was buried there on 18 Nov. 1601 (this extract of Collier's is confirmed). It is apparently not correct that 'man' means player, but that the entry refers to him is made probable by advances of Henslowe to a 'm^rs alleyn widow' in Sept. 1602.

ATTENDANTS. In *Frederick* 'attendaunts' are called upon to impersonate certain 'lords' (sc. viii); presumably also a 'Guard' (sc. xi) and possibly 'Soliors' (Soldiers, sc. v).

BARNE or BORNE, WILL. VII 'little will Barne'. *See* WILL.

BIRDE *alias* BORNE, WILLIAM. VII 'Mr. Burne' 'Mr. Bourne' 'Mr. Boorne'. He always signed himself Birde, but was generally called Borne: these can hardly be variants of the same name, and moreover Henslowe twice connects them with the word 'alles' (alias). He had sons baptized in the name of Borne at St. Saviour's in 1600 and 1602. He doubled the parts of Colmogra and Artabisus in *Tamar*, and probably appeared in *Alcazar* as Sebastian (q.v.). He is first heard of with Pembroke's men in Feb. 1597, and after they broke in July he bound himself to Henslowe on 10 Aug. for three years from the end of the restraint; he was thenceforward one of the leading members of the Admiral's company and its successors, and is traceable till 1622. He also wrote for the stage, collaborating with Samuel Rowley in 1601–2 on additions to *Faustus* and a play called *Judas*. He is credited with having played female parts, but 'bornes womones gowne', on which the suggestion rests, was almost certainly worn by Will Barne (*see* Will).

BLACK DICK. *See* DICK.

BORNE alias BIRDE, WILLIAM. *See* BIRDE, W.

BRISTOW, JAMES. *See* JAMES.

BROWNE, NED. He represented a Crim in the procession in *Tamar*. An Edward Browne appears with Edward Alleyn in the licence for Worcester's men in 1583; an Edward Browne, player, had a son baptized at St. Saviour's on 1 Oct. 1596; and one of the name was pretty certainly with the Admiral's men in 1599 or 1600, when he joined Henslowe and Massey in witnessing an agreement whereby Downton engaged an unnamed actor as his covenant servant. The two latter are probably the one in the Plot, but if this was the former Worcester's man he had come down in the world. He may, of course, after retirement,

have busied himself with odd jobs about the theatre, but he is distinguished from another 'old' Browne.

BROWNE, 'Old'. He was a Cannibal in the procession in *Tamar*.

*CALIPOLIS*. For the chief female part in *Alcazar* no actor is assigned. It may have been played by Will Barne (*see* Will).

CARTWRIGHT, WILLIAM. IV 'w· Cartwright': VI 'w· Cartwright': VII 'W. Cart.', once only 'W. Cartwright'. The parts he took were many but small. He is not heard of before the reconstruction of Oct. 1597, but by 21 Apr. 1598 was associated with Jones in borrowing money of Henslowe. He remained with the company and later came to the fore; he does not seem to have been a sharer till it became the Palsgrave's in 1613, but was a lessee of the Fortune in 1618, and appears to have been intimate with Alleyn. He was living in Upper Whitecross Street near the Fortune in 1623, and was still with the Palsgrave's men the following year. He probably joined the King's Revels in 1629, and was with them at Norwich in 1635; in 1634 and 1636 he was at the Fortune, presumably with the same company. He appears to have married and buried quite a number of wives in St. Giles's between 1621 and 1651, but probably more than one man is concerned. It is not certain whether he was the father of the Restoration actor of the same name, who, however, had also been a member of the King's Revels, and whose books and pictures passed to Dulwich College.

CHARLES. *See* MASSEY, C.

DAB. A minor boy appearing in *Alcazar* only, in which he played a young brother of the Moor, afterwards a ghost, and the young son of Rubin Arches. We may perhaps trace him in 'Dobes cotte of cloth of sylver' in the Admiral's men's inventory of 10 Mar. 1597/8.

DICK. III 'Dick' 'E Dutton his boye': IV 'dick (J?)': VI 'Dick Jubie': VII 'Dick Jubie'. In *Frederick* the actor of the female title-role is usually given as Dick, but once when Philippo and Basilea enter together the actors are recorded as 'E Dutton [&] his boye'. Dick was therefore Edward Dutton's 'boy'; he is distinguished from a minor adult actor Black Dick in the same Plot. In *Tennis* the graphic evidence makes it likely that the Dick who played a Child was Dick Juby. In *Alcazar* Dick Juby is named as playing Abdula Rais (Abdil Rayes), who is the wife of Abdelmelec, and a youthful courtier, Christophero de Tavora. In *Tamar* Dick Juby is again named for the chorus and a number of small male parts: he was apparently no longer a boy. Moreover, by 1602 he seems to have been married and had a son Richard baptized at St. Saviour's on 1 May. There is every likelihood that it was the same actor who appeared in all four Plots. He is not otherwise known, and his relation to Edward Juby is uncertain.

DICK, 'Black'. He is thus distinguished from Edward Dutton's boy Dick in *Frederick*, in which he played several small male parts.

DONSTONE, JAMES. *See* DUNSTAN, J.

DOWNTON, THOMAS. VI 'm^r Doughton': VII 'Mr. Denygten' twice. 'Denygten' must be a misreading of 'Doughton' written in English secretary script. Henslowe often calls him 'Dowton', but the autograph form does not vary. He played Abdelmelec in *Alcazar*, and Mango Cham in *Tamar*, besides appearing in the procession as a Tartar. Both are rather important if short parts. A Thomas Dowtonne, 'misysyan', had a son baptized at St. Saviour's on 27 Dec. 1592, and a 'm^r doutone' seems to have been travelling with Alleyn in 1593. I think the latter must be Downton, not Dutton (see p. 16, n. 3). As Thomas Dowton he had three sons (one base-born) baptized at St. Saviour's in 1597, 1600, and 1601. Later he lived in St. Giles's, Cripplegate, where the records show him as Thomas Doughton, Doughten, or Downton from 1606 to 1625. He buried a wife 'Annes' (Agnes) in 1613, married Anne Roye in 1614, buried her in 1617, married Jane, widow of a vintner, in Feb. 1618, and made a will appointing her executrix on 25 July 1625. He was with the Admiral's men in 1594–5, but is not heard of again till Feb. 1597, when he had left them for Pembroke's. He returned, however, in the summer, and on 6 Oct. bound himself to Henslowe till Shrovetide 1600. Except for this adventure he was probably a sharer in the Admiral's company and its successors from 1594 till about 1618. On 31 Oct. the latter year he witnessed the lease of the Fortune, but as he was not himself a lessee we may presume that he had retired and become a vintner himself.

DOWNTON'S BOY. *See* PARSONS, T., *and* WILL.

DROM, THO. He is twice mentioned in *Alcazar* as playing Nemesis in a dumb-show, and was therefore perhaps a boy, but is not otherwise known.

DUNSTAN, JAMES. III 'M^r Dunstan(n)' (six times, the last without the prefix). He played a Governor and a Friar in *Frederick*. His name appears in a bewildering variety of forms. The Plot supports 'Dunstan', Guilpin's *Skialetheia* has 'Dunston', Henslowe alternates between 'Donston', 'Donstone', and 'Donstall'. As James 'Tunstall' he appears in the licence for Worcester's men in 1583, the Norwich records preserve the same form the same year, and as 'Tvnstall' or 'Tonstall' he witnessed several deeds for Alleyn between 1585 and 1591. Since the signatures are presumably autograph they perhaps give the authoritative form. He was probably with Alleyn as a member of the earlier Admiral's company before its association with Strange's, and was clearly a sharer in the later Admiral's company in 1594–5 and 1596, but he is last heard of on

3 Aug. 1597, when he witnessed Henslowe's agreement with John Helle the clown, and he did not join in the reconstruction of the following October.

DUTTON, EDWARD. III 'E(d) Dutton' 'Dutton(n)'. He played Philippo in *Frederick*, not an onerous part. He was borrowing money in Mar. 159[?6/]7 and in July 1597 of Henslowe (who spells his name 'Dutten') but as he is not otherwise recorded with the company he probably left it at the reconstruction in October. Daughters of an Edward Dutton, player, were baptized at St. Saviour's on 16 Jan. 1600, 2 Oct. 1600, and 16 Apr. 1602; but there is surely something wrong here, unless the first ceremony had been postponed.

DUTTON'S BOY. *See* DICK.

GATHERERS. In *Frederick* 'Gatherers' are called upon to impersonate a 'Guard' twice in sc. ix, 'confederates' in sc. x, and 'Soliors' (Soldiers) in sc. xviii; also probably one of the Guards in sc. xi. Gatherers were the playhouse attendants who collected the money either at the door or in the galleries. From various references it would seem that their number was sometimes considerable, that they were not always honest, and that women were sometimes employed (*Henslowe Papers*, pp. 89, 85, 63).

GEORGE. *See* SOMERSET, G.

GIBBS. He appeared as a 'Geat' in the procession in *Tamar*.

GIDEON. 'Gedion' appeared as the same.

GILES'S BOY. 'Gils his boy' appeared as a Pigmy in the same.

GREGORY, JACK. VII 'Jack grigerie' 'Jack Grigorie'. A boy who played one of Tarmia's sons and the nymph Heron in *Tamar*, besides appearing as an Amazon in the procession.

GRIFFIN. A boy 'Griffen' played Athanasia in *Frederick*, a small part involving only a single appearance.

HARRY. He played a young brother of the Moor (later a ghost) in *Alcazar*. He is, of course, distinct from the Harry of *The Seven Deadly Sins*.

HUNT, THOMAS. III 'Th(o). Hunt': IV 'Tho . . .': V 'mr Hunt': VI 'mr Hunt'. He played several small male parts in *Frederick* and *Alcazar*, and probably a similar one in *Troilus*. In *Tennis* only the christian name is preserved, and this also belonged to Towne, Downton, Drom, and Marbeck. But the first two should have had the 'Mr.' at the date most likely for the Plot, while the last two are not known to have yet been with the company. We may therefore reasonably though not confidently assume that Hunt was intended. His part is not preserved. He was, no doubt, the Thomas Honte to whom the company paid 6*s.* 8*d.* (perhaps a week's wages) in Oct. 1596. Nothing further is heard of him, apart from the Plots, till 29 Aug. 1611, when his name appears among the signatures of duplicate bonds to Henslowe from what was evidently the newly formed Lady Elizabeth's company, while on 15 Apr. 1621 he dined with Alleyn apparently as one of the Palsgrave's men.

JAMES. V 'mr Jones his boy': VI, VII 'Jeames'. In *Troilus* Jones's boy played Cressida's maid and a Beggar; in *Alcazar* a James played Ruben (a female part) and Sebastian's Page; in *Tamar* a James appeared in the procession as an Hermaphrodite. There were at least two boys called James connected with the company at this period. (i) There was James Bristow, 'my boye' whom Henslowe 'bowght' for £8 on 18 Dec. 1598 of 'william agusten player', and for whose wages at the rate of 3*s*. a week the company owed Henslowe £6 9*s*. to 15 Feb. 1601, Anthony Jeffes being in some way personally responsible for the debt. ['Wm. Augustine player' had a daughter baptized at St. Botolph's, Aldgate, on 19 Nov. 1595.] (ii) Richard Jones had a boy James, as we learn from a memorandum wherein Henslowe records that on 17 Nov. 1599 he lent 'mr Jonnes player' 40*s*. 'wch is boye Jemes feched'. The distribution of the parts in the Plots is discussed in the note on boy actors (pp. 67–8).

JEFFES, ANTHONY. VI 'Antho(ny) Jeffes': VII 'A. Jeffs'. He played young Mahomet, the Moor's son, in *Alcazar*, but in *Tamar* only appeared as the satyr Linus, walked on as an olive-coloured Moor, and possibly carried a drum. He appears with the Admiral's men after the amalgamation with Pembroke's in Oct. 1597, and is in Henslowe's lists (except that of Mar. 1598) down to 1602. He in some way represented the company in dealing with Henslowe over the wages of the latter's boy, James Bristow. He remained with the company when it became Queen Anne's, but retired before 1613 apparently, receiving £70 on the occasion. It is natural, though not necessary, to suppose that he was the brother of Humphrey (q.v. for further details). He is presumably the Anthony, son of Richard Jeffes, baptized at St. Saviour's on 14 Dec. 1578, and possibly married Faith Jones there on 19 Feb. 1601. If so he moved soon after to St. Giles's, Cripplegate, where children of Anthony Jeffes, player, are recorded between 11 June 1602 and 1 May 1609. He seems to have become a brewer, and as such is mentioned from 1610 to 1621. Thus he was still alive on 22 Oct. 1620, when a 'mr Jeffe' dined with Alleyn.

JEFFES, HUMPHREY. VI 'H Jeffes': VII 'H. Jeffs'. He played much more important parts than Anthony, namely Muly Mahomet Xeque, besides a Devil and perhaps a Captain, in *Alcazar*, and Otanes, who is on in fourteen scenes, in *Tamar*. He is usually supposed to be the

'Humfrey' who appears as a Keeper in the stage-directions of 3 *Henry VI* (F 1623, III. i. 1), and on the whole this seems probable, though whether it implies membership of Strange's, Pembroke's, or the Chamberlain's company is uncertain. There is also a serving-man who is addressed as 'Humphery' in *Look about You* (sig. G 1), a play printed in 1600 as 'lately played' by the Admiral's men. The two Jeffes appear to have joined the Admiral's company at the time of the amalgamation with Pembroke's in Oct. 1597, but are not among the five named out of seven or eight who belonged to that company in the preceding February. They were sharers evidently from 1597 till 1602 (though only Humphrey acknowledged the first reckoning in Mar. 1598) and were later servants of Queen Anne. But neither has the prefix 'Mr.' in the Plots. An account begun by Henslowe on 14 Jan. 1598 mentions 'humfreye Jeffes hallffe sheare' and suggests that the two may have held one share between them, a supposition that might account for several facts just mentioned. Each is found authorizing payment on behalf of the company on a single occasion in 1602. After Anthony had retired and the company had become the Palsgrave's Humphrey was one of its leading members, and was in trouble over its irregularities in 1615 and 1616. He had a daughter baptized at St. Saviour's on 25 Jan. 1600, and was the 'supposed' father of another three months earlier. He was himself buried at St. Giles's on 21 Aug. 1618.

JONES, Jack. His name appears in a deleted passage in *Tamar*. The passage was evidently somehow a mistake, and it would be risky to infer that he actually played Palmeda (as seems to be implied) since he is not mentioned elsewhere. The registers of St. Botolph's, Aldgate, mention 'John Jones a Player in Houndsditch' in 1615, probably also in 1609–10, possibly as marrying a Joan Jones on 7 Feb. 1607.

JONES, Richard. V, VI 'm^r^ Jones'. In *Troilus* he took the part of Priam, in *Alcazar* those of Luis de Silva, a Spanish Ambassador, and at least one other, possibly only an Attendant. He cannot have been the Black Dick of *Frederick*, since he was not with the company when that play was acted. He was with Alleyn in Worcester's company in 1583, and presumably in the old Admiral's. On 3 Jan. 1589, however, he sold his share of the common stock—apparel, play books, instruments, and other commodities—to Alleyn for £37 10*s*., and must be assumed to have parted from his fellows. In Feb. 1592 he accompanied Robert Browne overseas. [To this occasion has usually been referred a letter to Alleyn on which the latter lent him £3. There are, however, difficulties which induced Chambers (ii. 287) to assign it rather to *c*. 1615. Baldwin (p. 325, note 24) argues inconclusively in favour of the earlier date. The point is doubtful and not very important.] In the autumn of 1594 his relations with Henslowe point to his being with the later Admiral's men in London, and he is in the list of 1594–5. He was one of the seceders who joined Pembroke's company in Feb. 1597 (hence his non-appearance in *Frederick*) but on its failure in July he returned and on 6 Aug. bound himself to Henslowe for three years, becoming at the same time surety for a similar undertaking by Shaa. The two completed their contract, and followed the company to the Fortune, but retired together in Feb. 1602 (before the reckoning that month) when they received £50 between them from the company. On 4 Jan. 1610 Jones was one of the patentees of the Children of the Queen's Revels. He was abroad again a few years later, for he wrote to Alleyn on business either before Henslowe's death on 6 Jan. 1616 or at least before he had heard of it, and he was still away on 1 Apr. 1620, when his wife wrote to Alleyn from Danzig, and in 1622–4 when he was a musician at the Court of Pomerania. A Richard Jones is traceable in Southwark from 1588 to 1607 and on 14 Feb. 1602 married Anne Jube, perhaps a relation of Edward and Richard Juby. But in 1620 Jones's wife was called Harris.

JONES'S BOY. *See* JAMES.

JUBY, EDWARD. III 'M^r Jubie' 'M^r Juby': VI 'm^r Jubie': VII 'Mr. Jubie'. He played the King in *Frederick*, Calcepius and Avero in *Alcazar*, but only the satyr Pitho in *Tamar* besides walking on as an olive-coloured Moor in the procession. He was evidently a sharer from 1594–5 to 1602; the absence of his name in the 1598 list must be accidental. He remained with the company when it became the Prince's, and seems to have been its leader or manager about 1613, when it was probably already the Palsgrave's, and was one of the lessees of the Fortune in 1618. He and his wife dined with Alleyn on 13 Sept. that year, but he was probably buried on 20 Nov. His widow Francis was one of the lessees in 1622. He seems to have resided in Southwark from 1598 till his death, and was a tenant of Henslowe in 1602–3: he had children baptized at St. Saviour's in 1599, 1600, 1603, 1606, 1610, 1612, and 1614. His relationship to Dick Juby is not known. It should be mentioned that a 'w^m' Juby appears seven times in Henslowe's accounts as authorizing payment on behalf of the Admiral's men between 20 Jan. 1599 and 21 Oct. 1602. Also on two occasions, 1 Mar. 1598 and 8 Sept. 1602, 'w^m' has been crossed out and 'edward(e)' substituted. This William Juby is not otherwise known—Edward's son William was not born till 1606—and that a man of whom we have no independent record should have occupied a position of trust in the company is most unlikely. It may seem a violent hypothesis, but I believe that all nine cases were blunders, though only two were corrected. Henslowe's tendency to call Edward 'm^r' Juby, together with the frequent appearance of 'w^m' Birde

as authorizer, seems to have led to a confusion between the two contractions. It is significant that the same error is found elsewhere, for Henslowe's 'w^m stonard', a servant of the Master of the Revels, signs himself 'Tho: Stonnard'.

JUBY, RICHARD. *See* DICK.

KENDALL, WILLIAM. VI 'w · Kendall'. He played Abdelmunen, afterwards a ghost, Hercules, a Janizary, and perhaps other characters in *Alcazar*. On 8 Dec. 1597 Henslowe hired him as a covenant servant for two years, to play at his house (or rather with the company) at the rate of 10*s*. a week in London and 5*s*. in the country. He was accused, in some verses printed in 1615, of having shirked a challenge on the Fortune stage (*Eliz. Stage*, ii. 191), and would therefore seem to have been with the company after 1600, but unless he left within two years we should expect to find him in *Tamar*. He had a son baptized at St. Saviour's on 5 Jan. 1615, but whether it was he who married Bettris Seele there on 1 Aug. 1619 and was living in Maid Lane the following year is uncertain.

LEDBETER, ROBERT. III 'le(a)dbeter' 'Rob: le(a)db'. In *Frederick* he played Pedro and a Lord, perhaps one character. He is not otherwise recorded with the company and must have left soon afterwards, for he is traceable abroad in 1599, 1601, and 1606.

MAGET, STEVEN. *See* STEPHEN.

MARBECK, THOMAS. He took several small male parts in *Tamar*. A Thomas Marbeck, musician, had a son baptized at St. Saviour's on 26 June 1603. A Richard Marbecke may have been a tenant of Henslowe in 1602–3.

MARTIN. *See* SLAUGHTER, M.

MASSEY, CHARLES. III 'Charles': 'IV 'Cha . . .': VI 'm^r Charles': VII 'Mr. Charles'. He played Thamar in *Frederick*, apparently an Attendant in *Tennis*, Zareo, the Duke of Barcellis, and a Spanish Ambassador in *Alcazar*, and Artaxes in *Tamar*. They seem to be roles of some importance. He is not traceable earlier than *Frederick*, but his appearance there shows that he was with the company before its amalgamation with Pembroke's. His name is not in the sharer list of Oct. 1597: it appears, however, coupled with Rowley's, in that of Mar. 1598, though it is possible that both were added later (see p. 34). His contract, entered into jointly with Rowley, is dated 16 Nov. 1598, and ran to Shrovetide 1600. He is in all subsequent lists, was a lessee of the Fortune in 1618 and 1622, and probably remained with the company till his death which took place before 6 Dec. 1635. He seems traceable as 'Masey', 'Marcy', or 'Mercy' in St. Giles's, Cripplegate, from 1610 to 1625, in which year he was buried on 3 Aug. He also wrote for the stage apparently, producing *Malcolm King of Scots* and *The Siege of Dunkirk* for the company in 1602 and 1603.

MUTES. In *Troilus* some playhouse attendants were called in as 'mutes' to personate beggars.

*PALMEDA.* For the chief female parts in *Tamar*, Palmeda and Tarmia, no actors are assigned (but see J. Jones). Palmeda is on in the last scene and the actor therefore cannot have taken part in the procession. He may have been Henslowe's boy, James Bristow (see note on boy actors, p. 67).

PARR, WILLIAM. VII 'W. Parr'. He played several small parts in *Tamar*. There is no reason to suppose that he was the boy Will of *Frederick* (see p. 67). 'A cloth of silver for par^r' is among the 'Gownes' in an undated inventory in Alleyn's hand; but the 'Gownes' were not all 'wemens gowns', and the inventory need not be as early as that of 10 Mar. 1597/8. Parr was with the Prince's men in 1610, and was one of the Palsgrave's men in trouble over an irregular licence in 1616; he became a lessee of the Fortune in 1618, and is apparently traceable as late as 1620.

PARSONS, THOMAS. VI '(Tom?) Parsons': VII '(Tho.) Parsons'. He played a Fury in the dumb-shows of *Alcazar*, and in *Tamar* several small parts, apparently including a Nurse, and walked in the procession as an Hermaphrodite. Henslowe mentions 'Thomas dowtones biger boye' on 19 Dec. 1597, 'Thomas dowton boye Thomas parsones' on 16 Apr. 1599, and 'Thomas dowton . . . his boye' on 5 June 1600. Since Parsons appears to have been still a boy in 1602, he is perhaps unlikely to have been the 'biger boye' of 1597, but it would account for one of the Wills in *Tamar* being described as 'Mr. Denygtens little boy' irrespective of his actual size.

PAVY. A 'Pauy' probably acted Mauritius in *Tennis*. This seems to have been in 1597–8, and as there is no reason to suppose that this was a boy's part, he cannot have been Jonson's Salathiel, the Chapel child who died aged thirteen in 1603. It is curious that we should find no other trace of him in the Plots or later lists, for he can hardly be any but the 'Wylliam Pavye one of y^e princes players dwelling by the Mynoryes', whose burial on 8 Sept. 1608 is recorded in the register of St. Botolph's, Aldgate, and who was clearly a sharer in the company, since Massey, writing *c.* 1613, mentions that 'm^res pavie' had been paid the customary £50 on her husband's death. William may, of course, have been Salathiel's father.

PIG. III 'Pigg': V 'pigg': VI 'm^r Allens boy'. In *Frederick* he played

Andreo, presumably a youth, and though the part may not have been a large one it involved five entries. In *Troilus* we only know that he played a Beggar. In *Alcazar* Alleyn's and Towne's boys played two Moorish Pages, and parallelism may account for his not being given his name. He is always called Pig, but there is an undated letter signed 'Iohn pyk' and a power of attorney to Alleyn in 1594 witnessed by Edward Griffin, scrivener, and 'Iohn pik'. The signatures are ill written, but the hand may be the same. One would hardly expect a child to witness a legal instrument, but I do not know whether two witnesses were required, and Pig's may have been added as a joke. He and James [Bristow?] were informal witnesses to a loan on 27 Mar. '1598' (?1599). The letter, the body of which is in Alleyn's hand, was written to Mrs. Alleyn while the company was travelling, perhaps in 1593, though this is uncertain. It clearly is, or purports to be, the composition of a young child, and it refers to Alleyn as 'my mayster'. No doubt then Pig was Alleyn's 'boy', and one gathers that he had lived in the Henslowe-Alleyn household. Still it is not altogether certain that Pig was the boy in *Alcazar*. Two entries in Henslowe's diary have been taken to imply that he played the title-role in *Alice Pierce* in the winter of 1597–8, which would make him a much more important actor than we gather from the Plots; but this is probably a mistake, the passage should apparently be read: 'laid owt mor the same tyme [i.e. 8 Dec. 1597] for makynge [allce perces bodeyes] & a payer of yeare [i.e. hair] sleavfe for the bodeyes of pyges gowne.' The inventory of 10 Mar. 1597/8 records 'j payer of bodeyes for Alles Pearce' without mention of Pig, though it elsewhere duly records 'j red sewt of cloth for pyge'. See further in the note on boy actors (p. 67).

*PROCTOR*. Apparently a 'proctor' is a character in *Troilus*, though Chambers once thought it was an actor's name. As explained in the notes on the Plot, the part was almost certainly played by Thomas Hunt.

RED FACED FELLOW. One of the 'supers' called in to personate a 'Nagar' (? negar, nigger) in the procession of *Tamar* is described as 'the red fast fellow'.

RESTER. He appeared as a Cannibal in the same.

ROWLEY, SAMUEL. III, IV 'Sam': VI 'mr Sam': VII 'Mr. Sam'. He played Heraclius in *Frederick*, apparently an Attendant in *Tennis*, several small parts in *Alcazar*, the most important being Pisano, and the spirit Ascalon in *Tamar*. His career is closely parallel to that of Massey (q.v.). He is first mentioned by Henslowe on 3 Aug. 1597 when he witnessed an agreement with Helle, the clown. His name is in the sharer list of Mar. 1598, but may have been added later. His contract is dated 16 Nov. 1598 and ran till Shrovetide 1600, and he authorized payment for the first of many times on 12 Dec. 1598. Several notes written by him to Henslowe in 1601 on the affairs of the company are extant. He became the servant of Prince Henry and the Palsgrave as the company acquired these patrons, but never took any share in the Fortune lease. He also wrote for the stage, collaborating with Birde in *Judas*, 1601, and in additions to *Faustus*, 1602, and producing his *Joshua* alone the latter year. His extant play on Henry VIII was acted by the company after it became the Prince's and printed in 1605. He seems to have been still writing, though perhaps not acting, in 1623–4, when Herbert licensed three plays by him for the Palsgrave's men. (A Samuel Rowley, Merchant-tailor, was buried in St. Giles's, 'at Christes Church', on 23 Nov. 1620.) Whether he is the 'S. R.' whose *Noble Soldier* was printed in 1631 is uncertain. A case, not I think conclusive, has been made out for his authorship of, or at least participation in, several plays of the early nineties, notably *The Taming of a Shrew*, 1594, and *The Famous Victories of Henry V*, 1598. If he happens to be the boy (?) Sam of *The Dead Man's Fortune* he is the only actor who appears both in the earlier and the later Plots.

ROWLEY, THOMAS. He appeared as a 'Nagar' (? negar, nigger) in the procession of *Tamar*, but is otherwise unknown.

SAM. *See* ROWLEY, S.

*SEBASTIAN*. The part of Sebastian, King of Portugal, in *Alcazar*, is an important if not a very large one, but no actor is assigned for it. It would double very conveniently with that of Abdelmelec, which was played by Downton, and this may well have been the intention when the play was written. But it cannot have been necessary in the performance for which the Plot was prepared, for there are two sharers unemployed, namely John Singer and William Birde. Probably one was held in reserve to replace Alleyn if and when he withdrew. This would perhaps be the senior actor Singer: so that Birde most likely played Sebastian.

SHAA, ROBERT. VI 'm$^{r}$ Shaa'. Shaa is the only autograph spelling, and it is worth noting that an otherwise unknown John Shaa, a witness in Henslowe's diary, spells his name the same way. No doubt the name is the same as Shaw, and this, or Shawe, is the almost consistent non-autograph spelling: Chettle, however, writes Shaa, and Henslowe, the first time he wrote it, Shaee. It is a little curious, therefore, to find the name spelled Shaa certainly twice, probably three times, in the Plot. The hand of the Plot can be compared with that of Shaa's note reproduced at p. 5. I do not think they can be the same.

Shaa played the Irish Bishop and the Governor of Tangier, also probably Celebin, in *Alcazar*. He is closely associated with Jones, and is first mentioned by Henslowe when Jones entered into an agreement on

his behalf on 6 Aug. 1597 to play at Henslowe's house for two years. He was with Pembroke's men the previous February, was arrested after the performance of *The Isle of Dogs* in July, and was not released from the Marshalsea till 8 Oct. Three days later he appears in the list of Admiral's sharers, and he reappears in those of 1598 and 1600; but just before the next, entered between 7 and 23 Feb. 1602, he and Jones retired, receiving £50 jointly from the company. He had been one of the most active in authorizing payments, and became surety for the payment to Henslowe of James Bristow's wages when Anthony Jeffes and the company fell in arrears. Later he is found selling apparel to Worcester's men and an old play to the Admiral's, but is not traceable after Mar. 1603 at latest. On 10 Apr., however, a Robert Shawe, player, had a son baptized at St. Saviour's, and Robert Shawe, 'a man', was buried there on 12 Sept. following.

SHAW, ROBERT. *See* SHAA, R.

SINGER, JOHN. IV 'mr singer': VII 'Mr. Singer'. In *Tennis* he seems to have played a character whose name began with the letters 'Co'. In *Tamar* he played Assinico, probably a clown, who comes on drunk, and was probably the missing Bactrian of the procession. This agrees with Rowlands who couples him with Pope, and Dekker who couples him with Tarlton and Kempe, as a clown. We need not suppose, however, that he only took comic parts, for Pope played Arbactus in Sloth, whom there is no reason to suppose comic, and left Will Fool to Duke. The absence of his name in *Frederick* is therefore a little surprising, seeing that Dunstan had to take two parts. In *Alcazar* he was probably held in reserve to replace Edward Alleyn in the Moor's part, though he possibly played Sebastian (q.v.). He may have been the John Singer who owed money at Canterbury in 1571; he was probably with the Queen's men in 1583 and 1588, and concerned in a homicide. His name is in all Henslowe's lists, usually at the head. On 13 Jan. 1603 the company paid him £5 'for his playe called Syngers vallentarey': this Chambers takes to mean 'valedictory', but it might with better authority be interpreted as 'choice' or 'improvisation'.[1] He appears no more with the company and became an ordinary Groom of the Chamber the same

[1] According to the *N.E.D.* 'valedictory' as a substantive is nineteenth century only, while even the adjective is not recorded before the middle of the seventeenth. There is no authority for 'vallentarey' as a spelling of 'voluntary', but that would not trouble Henslowe. The sense of free will or device seems to occur only in phrases, but the musical sense of a composition added to a set piece at the will of the performer was well established in the sixteenth century. It is true that the extension of this meaning to an impromtu or optional writing is not recorded till the end of the seventeenth. I should imagine the 'playe' to have been some unusually elaborate jig. Such pieces were supposed to be largely extempore, but were in fact often carefully prepared.

year. He lived in 'Awstens Rents' in St. Saviour's, and had children baptized there in 1597, 1599, 1600, 1601, and 1603.

SLATER, MARTIN. *See* SLAUGHTER, M.

SLAUGHTER, MARTIN. III 'Martyn(n)' 'Mr Martyn', each four times. The spelling of his name varies from Slater to Slawghter, and I am not quite clear that Slaughter or Slawter and Slater or Sclater are the same name. (In *The True Tragedy of Richard III*, 1594, one of the murderers is called Sluter—perhaps a misprint for Slater—or Slawter, and the pronunciation is guaranteed by a pun on 'slaughter'.) He may have been the Martin Slawter, 'a servant', buried at St. Saviour's on 4 Aug. 1625. He appears, as 'mr slater', in the first of Henslowe's lists, and was clearly the Martin (with inconsistent prefix) who played Theodore in *Frederick*; but some six weeks later, on 18 July 1597, Henslowe recorded that 'martin slather went for the company', and since he is not in the October list we may conclude that he at least went 'from' it. There was evidently a quarrel, and legal proceedings were at any rate threatened between him and Birde, Downton, and Spencer the following spring, possibly over the ownership of five old play Books which he eventually sold to the company for £8 on 16 May and 18 July 1598. He was still borrowing money of Henslowe in 1604, and was then married. Meanwhile he had been acting in Scotland in 1599, presumably with Laurence Fletcher, and was payee on 20 Apr. 1603 for a Court performance given by Lord Hertford's men on Twelfth-night. Later he was with Queen Anne's company in 1606, was a manager of the King's Revels in 1608, when he is described as an ironmonger, and of the Children of her Majesty's Royal Chamber of Bristol in 1618–9, with the status of servant to the Queen, though no longer of her London company.

SOMERSET, GEORGE. IV 'Geo . . .' (? 'Somerton'): VI 'George', once 'Georg Somersett': VII 'George'. In *Tennis* he probably played a Serving-man, and is almost certainly identical with Somerton (q.v.). In *Alcazar* he took several small male parts, the most important being County Vinioso, and the same in *Tamar*. In the latter he seems at one point (l. 78) to be cast for a child, but this is probably a misunderstanding. There is no reason to suppose that he was a boy, though his frequent association with Parsons and Dick Juby suggests that he was still quite young. He has left singularly little trace outside the Plots. Among the Dulwich papers is, or was, a note, written probably soon after Oct. 1601, of 2*d*. spent 'for a Staple for Georg Sommersetts Dore', while on 3 Sept. 1624 a son of John Wilson was buried at St. Giles's from the house of George Sommerset, musician.

SOMERTON. In *Tennis* occurs the name 'somerton' (preceded by a

deletion). This can hardly be a character name, but if it is an actor's his part cannot be identified and he is otherwise unknown. However, the Plot also mentions a Geo[rge] who can hardly be other than George Somerset, and I find it impossible to believe that there were two actors of such similar and unusual names as Somerset and Somerton acting in the same play. Since, moreover, *Alcazar* gives George his surname on a single occasion only, *Tennis* may have done the like, and done it more reasonably on his first appearance. I conclude therefore that 'somerton' is a variant of, or possibly an error for, Somerset (q.v.). It can hardly be relevant that Somerton is in fact in Somerset.

STEPHEN. His name appears as playing a Beggar in *Troilus*. Since he was clearly a 'super' he may have been the tire-man Steven Maget mentioned by Henslowe several times in 1596.

TAILOR, Robert. IV 'R Tail.r': VI 'Ro(bin) Tailor'. In *Tennis* he was entered for a Serving-man, but struck out again, presumably because, like his fellow Cartwright, he was required in the following scene, perhaps as a Wine-presser. In *Alcazar* he took several small parts, including Jonas, certainly a man's, and a Fury, not necessarily a boy's. A Robert Tailor was the author of a play, *The Hog hath Lost his Pearl* (1614), which caused some scandal at the time, wrote commendatory verses to a work of John Taylor's the same year, and published settings to *Sacred Hymns* the next.

*TARMIA*. One of the principal female characters in *Tamar*, for whom however no actor is assigned. Since she was not on in the last scene, her impersonator no doubt appeared in the procession, and I conjecture him to have been Will Barne (see Will).

THOMAS. A 'Tho . . .' appeared in *Tennis* whom I conjecture to have been Thomas Hunt (q.v.).

TOWNE, Thomas. III 'Tho: Towne' four times, 'Mr Towne' once: VI 'mr Towne': VII 'Mr. Towne'. In *Frederick* he played Myronhamec, in *Alcazar* Stukeley, in *Tamar* the Shah of Persia, besides an Oracle and in the procession a Tartar. They were leading parts. His name is in all Henslowe's sharer lists and he repeatedly authorized payment. He appears to have remained with the Prince's men till his death in 1612: he was buried in St. Saviour's on 9 Aug., and his widow, Agnes or Ann, received £50 from the company. By his will of 4 July he left money to his fellows Borne, Downton, Juby, Rowley, Massey, and H. Jeffes, for a carouse. His name occurs in a stage-direction, 'Enter Towne like a sweeper', in 1 *Honest Whore* (sig. I 3), a play written by Dekker and Middleton for the Prince's men in 1604 and printed the same year.

TOWNE'S BOY. In *Alcazar* 'mr Townes boy' is coupled with 'mr Allens boy' as playing a Moorish Page, evidently mute.

TUNSTALL, JAMES. *See* DUNSTAN, J.

WILL. III 'Will': VII (*a*) 'Mr. Denygtens little boy' 'the other little boy' 'little Will', (*b*) 'little will Barne'. There are at least two, possibly three, Wills here. (i) There is the Will who played Leonora, the second lady in *Frederick*. (ii) In *Tamar* Jack Gregory is always accompanied by a boy severally described as Downton's little boy (perhaps to distinguish him from his bigger boy Parsons, q.v.), the other little boy, or little Will, as personating Tarmia's sons, Nymphs, and in the procession Amazons. (iii) In the same procession 'little will Barne' walked as a pigmy. The question is whether either of the Wills in *Tamar* can be identified with the one in *Frederick*. There is an interval of over five years, so that the actor of Leonora may well have grown up. It is clear that Downton's Will was quite a small boy and cannot possibly be the one in question. At first sight Will Barne, the pigmy, hardly looks more promising. But there is a curious piece of evidence which proves, I think, that he was actually taking female parts as early as 1597. On 1 Dec. that year Henslowe recorded the purchase of 'tensell for bornes womones gowne'. This has been taken to refer to William Borne *alias* Birde, and to prove that this grown man, a sharer in the company, played female parts. (It has been assumed, further, that Birde was the Will of *Frederick*, but we now know that he was with Pembroke's men at the date that piece was acted.) This I find impossible to believe. Moreover, the name Birde or Borne occurs nearly seventy times in Henslowe's diary, but (if we exclude the bare list that heads the accounts of Oct. 1597) never without the christian name except in the present instance. I infer, therefore, that the reference here is not to the sharer but to the boy Will Barne. This makes it probable that it was Will Barne who appeared in *Frederick*, and that he was one of the principal boys of the company during the whole period covered by the Plots. I conjecture that in *Tamar* he also played the part of Tarmia. See further in the note on boy actors (pp. 67–8).

## *Note on the Boy Actors*

The boy actors, of whom about a dozen seem traceable in the later Plots, present a rather complicated problem, owing mainly to four causes: that they were commonly called by their christian names only, that in some instances there was more than one boy of the same name, that they are sometimes distinguished not by their own names but by those of their masters, and that the boys filling several of the most important female roles are unspecified in the Plots. In face of these difficulties it is not possible to arrive at a complete or certain solution of

the problem, but I think that certain probabilities may be established, and that speculation will at least be harmless.

For about half the number, and these the less important, we have what information is necessary, and they need not detain us: it will suffice to refer to the actor list for Griffin, Parsons, Dab, Harry, and Gregory. Towne's boy and Giles's boy may possibly be the same as others named elsewhere, though there is nothing to point to an identification. But with respect to the rest, including all the more important, some more or less serious question arises in each case.

Pig does not give much trouble except for the doubt whether he is identified with Alleyn's boy. From the Plots themselves one would not necessarily gather that Pig was a boy at all, but we know from other sources that he was certainly a child about 1593 and was still acting women's parts in 1597. He is the only boy known to have been associated with Alleyn. At the same time the part of a Moorish Page assigned to Alleyn's boy in *Alcazar* seems to be a smaller one than that played by Pig in *Frederick*, namely Andreo, who though perhaps not important, at least appeared in five scenes. In *Troilus* he is only known to have played a beggar, and this part apparently could not be doubled with any of the four female parts preserved, but there must have been others, e.g. Hecuba, and he may have taken one of these. If he did, and was not Alleyn's boy in *Alcazar*, he may have been a leading boy and taken some of the unassigned parts. Still there is little basis for the supposition, and I prefer in the interests of economy to suppose that Pig and Alleyn's boy were the same.

Nor need Dick Juby worry us seriously. He played Abdula Rais (Abdil Rayes) wife of Abdelmelec, in *Alcazar*, and was therefore a boy. In *Tamar* he took several small male parts besides acting as Chorus, and had apparently grown up. Indeed by this time he was married and had a son. In *Tennis* a Dick played the part of a child, and graphic evidence rather suggests that the name Juby followed. Of course, he may have played, and probably did play, some other part as well. In *Frederick* we find a Dick, who took the important role of Basilea, distinguished from a Black Dick who took small male parts. The former is once described as Edward Dutton's boy. There is every reason to suppose that we have to do with Dick Juby throughout. If so, he was clearly one of the principal boy actors.

There remain the tangles of the Jameses and Wills, and the two are intertwined. Take the former first. We know that in 1599 Richard Jones had a boy James, and it was therefore he who played a waiting-maid and a beggar in *Troilus*. They are very minor parts and cannot have been doubled with others preserved (though as before there is the possibility of Hecuba). Henslowe, however, also had a boy James Bristow, and we find a James acting an important female part in *Alcazar*, namely Rubin Arches, and doubling it with Sebastian's Page. Now this James of *Alcazar* must have taken one of the leading roles in *Troilus*, with its heavy call for female parts, and it is natural to suppose that the other James was called Jones's boy to distinguish him from Henslowe's James. The latter then would be the more important, and the one named in *Alcazar*. To the James who appeared as an Hermaphrodite in the procession of *Tamar* we shall return in a moment.

A Will meets us first in *Frederick*, taking the second female part, Leonora. It is not easy to trace this boy later, for no other Will is named before the two in *Tamar* some five years later. If he grew up he may have been Will Cartwright or Will Parr, or even Will Kendall. But the last named was apparently a new comer six months after *Frederick*, while all three usually took very minor parts. No doubt a boy at adolescence may belie his earlier promise; still one hardly expects to find a leading lady doing hack work on the stage. One of the Wills in *Tamar* is described as Downton's 'little boy', 'the other little boy', and 'little Will', and appeared as one of Tarmia's sons, a nymph Thia, and an Amazon in the procession, his identity throughout being guaranteed by his constant companion Jack Gregory. These are apparently small parts for a small boy and cannot have been taken by the Leonora of five years before. The other Will named in *Tamar* is 'little Will Barne', of whom we are only told that he was a Pigmy in the procession. For this he cannot have been very big, but he was presumably bigger than plain 'little Will', and most likely the insistence on his size was mainly an attempt to distinguish 'little will Barne' or Borne from big Will Borne or Birde. For there can, I think, be no doubt that it was for Barne and not for Birde that Henslowe purchased 'bornes womones gowne' on 1 Dec. 1597. But this was within six months of *Frederick*, and makes it very probable that Barne was the Will who acted Leonora.

But if this conjecture is right and Will Barne was a leading lady, it is impossible to suppose that he only appeared as a Pigmy in *Tamar*. Now in this Plot the two leading female parts, Palmeda and Tarmia, are unassigned. The former remained on in the last scene and the actor cannot have taken part in the procession. But Tarmia's last appearance is in v. i, and in view of the severe demands made by the procession it is certain that her impersonator reappeared in it. It would follow that Barne played Tarmia, and I have very little doubt that this inference is correct. The only alternatives are Giles's boy (Barne's fellow Pigmy) and James (the Hermaphrodite). Of the former we know nothing. But it will be remembered that there are two Jameses. The Hermaphrodite

may reasonably be supposed to have been Jones's quondam boy (Jones had lately retired) who took the two small parts in *Troilus*, and this would leave Henslowe's boy, James Bristow (the Rubin Arches of *Alcazar*), free to play Palmeda.

Having settled this at least to my own satisfaction, I invite attention to other lacunae in our information. Who fed and grew fat as fair Calipolis in *Alcazar*? The only possible boy part that will double with it is the Fury played by Parsons. But neither Abdula Rais nor Ruben is doubled, so that it is unlikely that the more important lady was: moreover there is no hint that Parsons was capable of filling a leading part. We are forced back on some one outside the named cast, and assuming Pig to be Alleyn's boy, I naturally choose Will Barne for the part.

In *Troilus* we observe that none of the female parts whose names are preserved, Cassandra, Cressida, Helen, Polyxena, will double with the beggars, consequently none of these can have been played by Pig or Jones's James. Presumably Hecuba appeared, and if so she may have been played by Pig. Dick Juby, apparently the oldest of the boys, might be cast for the tragic Cassandra. Will Barne, whom I have a fancy for regarding as the principal boy, might be given the title-role of Cressida. Polyxena, seemingly a small role and a young one, would naturally fall to Griffin, who took the diminutive part of Athanasia in *Frederick*. This leaves James Bristow for Helen.

Of *Tennis* we know too little for guessing to be much fun. If Dick Juby acted a child, Bella (or whatever her name was) would fall to Barne or Bristow: Pig, Griffin, and Jones's boy would be available for the Ladies.

But, except in the case of *Tamar*, the foregoing speculation rests on a remarkably slender foundation, and serious criticism will no doubt treat it with the contempt it deserves.

## GENERAL CHARACTERISTICS

Materially the Plots seem to have been all constructed on a uniform plan. It is true that only two out of the seven are perfectly preserved, namely *The Dead Man's Fortune* and *Frederick and Basilea*, but these fortunately belong to different groups and dates, and since there is nothing in others to suggest structural divergence, we may suppose that none existed. The Plot, then, consisted of a thin pulp board, with an extreme measurement of seventeen inches high and thirteen wide, on either side of which was pasted a sheet of stout paper. The sheets were divided, by lines ruled in ink, into two main columns, between which was left a narrow margin, and towards the top of this was cut a small oblong hole by which the Plot might be suspended on a peg in the wall.

The variations in size are not great. The board of *The Dead Man's Fortune* measures $16\frac{7}{8} \times 12\frac{1}{2}$ inches, the sheets about $\frac{1}{4}$ inch less each way: the board of *Frederick and Basilea* $16\frac{1}{4} \times 12\frac{1}{4}$, the sheets again about $\frac{1}{4}$ inch less. The front sheet of *The Seven Deadly Sins* probably measured $16\frac{1}{8} \times 12\frac{1}{8}$, certainly not less, the front sheet of *The Battle of Alcazar* not less than $16\frac{7}{8} \times 11\frac{7}{8}$; that of *Troilus and Cressida* was not less then $12\frac{1}{8}$ in width. In each case a whole untrimmed sheet was used (such varied appreciably in size) and the board cut to suit it. The sizes suggest that the sheets used were rather large samples of the smaller of the two most common makes, corresponding to what we should call 'foolscap'.

Other formal details vary to some extent in the different Plots. Except *The Dead Man's Fortune* (and, of course, *Troilus and Cressida*, which has presumably lost it) every Plot has an elaborately written gothic heading extending across above both columns. In *The Dead Man's Fortune* the title is written at the head of the first column in the same script as the rest of the Plot. In *The Seven Deadly Sins*, and in *Fortune's Tennis* by the same scribe, the heading is enclosed in a somewhat elaborate frame, but there is no other rule across the top. In *Frederick and Basilea* there are rules both above and below the heading, in *The Battle of Alcazar* there is a rule below only,

and possibly this was also so in *Tamar Cam.* If in *Tamar Cam* the direction for the first Chorus was written across immediately below the heading as represented in the print, it was, so far as we know, a unique feature.

Let us next take the two main columns. In *The Seven Deadly Sins* these are not bounded by any rules on the outer edges, and the same may have been the arrangement in the fragmentary *Fortune's Tennis* by the same scribe. In all the other Plots both columns are bounded by rules. They do not vary very greatly in width, but tend to grow narrower, the three earlier measuring over, and the three later under, five inches. The narrowest is the left column of *Troilus and Cressida* with 4¼ inches, the widest ruled the left (used) column of *Frederick and Basilea* with nearly 5½, while the unruled left margin of *The Seven Deadly Sins* runs at its widest to 5¾. The two columns sometimes differ slightly, but not by more than a quarter of an inch in the ruled examples. Generally no line is drawn across the foot of the columns, except in *The Battle of Alcazar* in which the second column is so bounded because it ends a scene. The print of *Tamar Cam* may be inaccurate in this respect.

The central margin is in two cases narrower than in the others: in *The Dead Man's Fortune* it measures three-quarters of an inch, in *Frederick and Basilea* only one-half. In all the others it appears to be approximately one inch, subject to the reservation that in *Fortune's Tennis* it is mutilated (not less than ¾ inch) and that in *Tamar Cam* we have only the print to go by.

In *The Seven Deadly Sins* the columns are not bounded by rules and consequently no side margins exist. In *Fortune's Tennis* we cannot tell what the arrangement was, but may assume that it followed the other Plot by the same scribe. In *Frederick and Basilea* the columns are bounded by rules, but these come near the edge of the paper leaving no appreciable margins available. In all other cases there is a left margin of ¾ to 1 inch in width and a right margin usually slightly narrower. In *The Dead Man's Fortune* the margin was not itself bounded by rules: in *Tamar Cam*, if we can believe the print, only the left margin was so bounded: in *The Battle of Alcazar* and

*Troilus and Cressida* both margins. *Troilus and Cressida* is peculiar in the thickness of the rules used.

Where margins existed they were used for notes. In *The Dead Man's Fortune* both the left and central margins are used, but only for notes written after the completion of the Plot and partly in a different hand. In *The Battle of Alcazar* and *Troilus and Cressida* both the left and central margins are freely used for properties and noises. In *Tamar Cam* the left margin is so used, but the central one contains nothing but the numbers of the procession: this, however, may be an accidental omission in the print. In no instance are there notes in the right margin.

In *Frederick and Basilea*, with its abnormally narrow central margin, the peg hole measures little over $\frac{1}{2} \times \frac{1}{4}$ inch. In all other cases, so far as we can tell, the variation from an average of $\frac{3}{4} \times \frac{1}{2}$ was slight. In *The Dead Man's Fortune* the hole is barely more than $1\frac{1}{2}$ inches from the top of the board[1]: in all other cases for which we possess evidence the distance seems to be between 4 and 5 inches.

In *Frederick and Basilea* the Plot occupies the first column only. In *The Battle of Alcazar* and *Troilus and Cressida* it overflowed the second column and was presumably completed on the back sheet. In *The Dead Man's Fortune*, *The Seven Deadly Sins*, and *Tamar Cam* it ends somewhere in the lower half of the second column. In *Fortune's Tennis* we only know that it ran into a second column.

The Plot of *The Dead Man's Fortune* is in a large English or secretary script, Italian being only used sporadically here and there for a character name, and also for the additions by a second hand. All the other Plots are written in Italian script, with trifling exceptions. In *The Battle of Alcazar* there is a solitary marginal direction in English, apparently in the same hand but possibly added later. As to *Tamar Cam* we have of course no direct evidence: the presumption is that it was written in an Italian hand, but there is evidence that one actor's name at least was in English.

We may now pass from the material and formal arrangement

[1] This is probably due to the writing in the central margin. The hole would naturally be cut after the Plot was complete.

of the Plots to their more essential character. In its most fundamental aspect a Plot consists of the record of the successive entrances of the characters of a play, with some record expressed or implied, and varying much in completeness, of the corresponding exits. This is the essential, but almost all examples exhibit in very varying degrees two other features: namely, some record of properties and other requirements of the stage, and some record of the actors assigned for the individual parts. It is evident therefore that for the preparation of the fundamental Plot what would be required, and all that would be required, would be the Book or prompt copy of the play, but that there was usually available and in use a second document, namely a Cast showing the distribution of the characters among the available actors.[1] To the question of the detailed relation of the Plot to the Book, and to the question of the use made of the Cast, we shall return later.

The basic principle of the record of entrances and exits is bound up with the problem, not free from difficulty, of the division into scenes. Every Plot is divided up into sections by rules drawn across the column, and with very few, though not insignificant, exceptions every section begins with the word 'Enter', a word that is not normally used in any other position. It is clear, however, that it is not only at the beginning of sections that entrances occur: internal entrances are frequent, but these are indicated by the words 'to them (him, her)', the word 'enter' being in these cases understood.[2] In some in-

[1] I imagine that for every play produced there must have been a Cast drawn up, and that even after the information it contained had been embodied in the Plot it would still be of sufficient convenience for reference to ensure its preservation along with the other documents relating to the play. No example, however, is known to survive, and we are left to speculate as to the origin of the Casts printed in a few late quartos. Of course several academic plays have Casts written in the Books themselves.

[2] This formula is peculiar to the Plots and is not derived from the corresponding Books. It is, as Sir Edmund Chambers points out to me, distinctly rare whether in manuscript or printed plays. Combining our notes the record is as follows. In manuscript, it is found in *John a Kent* (l. 368): 'Enter Pembrook, . . . Amery, to them this crew marching . . .' (also l. 582); in *Richard II* (*Thomas of Woodstock*) (l. 2875): 'To Them Enter lancaster, yorke & Surry: & beats them all away Manet the King', cf. also (l. 2887): 'Enter Baggot Busshy & Scroope to the King'; in Heywood's *Captives* it is used eight or ten times by the stage reviser (fols. $58^b$, $62^a$, $63^b$, $68^b$, $70^a$, $70^b$, $71^a$, $71^b$; see Specimens, no. 7)

stances every section ends normally with the word 'exeunt' or 'exit', in others this appears to be assumed; and again, internal exits for individual characters are in some cases specified, but more frequently only implied, either in the action itself or in the form of the description. After allowing for some uncertainty in procedure and for occasional ambiguities or errors in some of the Plots, it is quite evident that the sections correspond to scenes divided in the usual Elizabethan manner, that is as a general rule whenever all the characters go off, and consequently that the word 'Enter' is to be interpreted to mean: Enter on a clear stage.

The exceptions to the usual procedure are not without interest, and it will be well to particularize briefly the evidence of the individual Plots. In general it may be said that the scene-division is perfectly regular so far as the preservation of the Plots allows us to judge, and in this respect that of *The Battle of Alcazar* is particularly important, since the existence of a printed version of the play enables us to check the dispositions of the Plot and verify our conclusion that they are perfectly normal. The only clear departure from the rule occurs in *The Dead Man's Fortune*, in which the end of the last act is improperly broken up into a number of separate sections. There is here quite certainly an error or at least uncertainty of treat-

but never by Heywood himself; Heywood, however, does once use a similar phrase in *The Escapes of Jupiter* (fol. 93[a]): 'Enter Amphitrio in a rage . . . To whome at another doore Enter Gamimed'; it also occurs in the scribe's Plot-like note of the missing scenes in the manuscript of Fletcher's *Bonduca* (fol. 23[a]): 'Here should A Scæne · be betwene Iunius · & petillius: . . . to them · Enterd Suetonius'. In print, the phrase is found twice in *The True Tragedy of Richard III*, namely in the heading of sc. i (l. 1): 'Enter Truth and Poetrie. To them the Ghoast of George Duke of Clarence', and again in that of sc. ii (l. 75): 'Enter Edward the fourth, Lord Hastings, Lord Marcus, and Elizabeth. To them Richard'; and repeatedly in the quarto of *Nero* (1624), e.g. in Act III: 'A Romane to them'; in the Shakespeare folio it occurs once, namely in the heading of 1 *Henry VI*, III. iv: 'Enter the King, . . . Exeter: To them, with his Souldiors, Talbot', while a somewhat similar formula is found in 2 *Henry VI* in the headings of III. i: 'Enter King, Queene, . . . and Warwicke, to the Parliament', and III. iii: 'Enter the King, Salisbury, and Warwicke, to the Cardinal in bed'. The formula is also freely used by Jonson in the 1616 folio of his works, but then of course his method of scene division, and consequently the significance of his directions, differs from that of the popular stage. The same system of division is found in the manuscript *Timon*, and in this the phrase again occurs twice (fols. 3[a], 8[a].)

ment, though its extent must remain a matter of conjecture. It is curious that the scribe of *Frederick and Basilea* showed a tendency to the same error at the same point, though he was careful to correct what he had written.

The practice of beginning every scene with 'Enter' is one of the best established throughout, and so, with certain exceptions, is that of confining the word to that position. In *The Dead Man's Fortune* the scribe's error at the end has of course involved abnormality in this respect, but it is to be observed that formally the rule is rigidly followed, every division (whether correct or not) beginning with the word 'Enter'. Such relaxation of the rule as occurs is not insignificant. In the lengthy description of V. ii (probably dumb-show) we get the expression '& ther Enters' showing the original stage-direction usurping upon the succincter terminology of the Plot. In II. ii 'and Enter' indicates a re-entrance. Further, in III. iv we have an internal 'enter' following upon a peculiar sign (=) not found outside this Plot. Taking the description as a whole there can be little doubt that the characters already on the stage were concealed, and that it might consequently be misleading to make the later comers enter 'to them': these enter upon a stage ostensibly though not technically clear. Lastly, the second scribe, who added in the central margin the description of V. i, was evidently unconcerned for the convention, for he uses 'Enter' three times in the course of what is presumably a single scene.

In *The Seven Deadly Sins* it is interesting to notice that, while every scene of the three Sin plays begins with the word 'Enter', none of the divisions belonging to the framework (I, II, IX, XVII, XXIII, XXIV) do so. There is, of course, an obvious reason for this since Henry is discovered asleep at the beginning and remains on the stage throughout, so that he at least can never 'Enter'. It is true that in II a Keeper is said to 'Enter' where the words 'to him' would have sufficed, but this is a trifling irregularity, while the really anomalous direction in the same division 'Exit then enter again' no doubt serves a specific purpose, namely to indicate that certain characters leave the main stage and reappear in the balcony.

In *Frederick and Basilea* the abnormal 'To them Enter' in sc. xviii is merely due to the scribe having originally and erroneously begun a new scene at this point, while the quite unusual 'To the queen Theodore' of sc. xvii is no doubt an attempt to indicate a discovery. In the fragment of *Fortune's Tennis* there is apparently one internal 'Enter', but it probably marks an appearance of the Chorus and should properly have been separated from the rest of the scene.

So far the irregularities observed have rather confirmed than weakened the general rule. The three remaining Plots, very likely all the work of one scribe, are even stricter. In *The Battle of Alcazar* there is no departure whatever from the rule: in *Tamar Cam* the only exception concerns the procession at the end, each pair in which is said to 'Enter'. *Troilus and Cressida* has one internal '& Enter', but it is significant that this is connected with the attempt to indicate internal exits which is peculiar to the three later Plots.

It can hardly, I think, be denied that this rigid observance of a purely arbitrary rule in all the extant Plots is rather remarkable.

We now come to consider the exits. Since the line drawn across the column indicates the close of a scene according to the Elizabethan method of division, it is of course, when correctly placed, equivalent to the direction 'Exit' or 'Exeunt (omnes)'. Strictly therefore there was no need for such an indication at the end of a scene, nor are any found in what are generally the simplest Plots, *The Dead Man's Fortune* and *Frederick and Basilea*. In *The Seven Deadly Sins* it occurs twice, first at the end of I where 'and so Exeunt' marks the departure of the seven Sins while Henry remains asleep on the stage, and in XXIV where 'and so Exitts' marks the final departure of Lydgate after speaking the epilogue. For the practice in *Fortune's Tennis* the surviving evidence is scanty, but so far as we can judge final exits were not marked.

The remaining group, on the other hand, make a general practice of marking them. *The Battle of Alcazar*, so far as it is preserved, is perfectly consistent in this respect. In *Troilus and Cressida* seven scenes out of ten for which evidence remains

have a direction (one 'exit', five 'exeunt', one even 'exeunt omnes') while three are without it (one consists of a single character entrance only, one has an equivalent direction—'beat Hector in'—and in one the line was already full). In *Tamar Cam*, out of nineteen scenes, fourteen have a direction (four 'Exit', ten 'Exeunt') while five have not. These five include the final scene (not preserved in either *Troilus and Cressida* or *The Battle of Alcazar*) and one in the last line of which there was no room: in the other three no reason can be assigned for the omission.

In this case we see the emergence of an apparently useless convention, but the appearance of final exits in these Plots is evidently connected with an attempt to mark internal exits that is first made in the same three. In the first three Plots, though internal exits are frequently implied by the context, they are very seldom marked. There is one instance in *The Dead Man's Fortune*, II. ii, necessitated by the fact that a character goes off and at once re-enters disguised. In *The Seven Deadly Sins* we find (in II) the direction 'Exit then enter againe' already discussed as implying the passage of characters from the main to the upper stage, but elsewhere it is only in descriptions of dumb-shows that characters are said to 'exit' (l. 24) or 'Vanish' (l. 84). In *Frederick and Basilea* no exits whatever are marked. In *Fortune's Tennis* no evidence remains.

Of course the object of the Plot was to get the actors on to the stage at the right point. Once started they could be trusted to get off again or the prompter would see that they did. Thus a direction for an exit would only get into the Plot either accidentally, when the scribe was copying stage-directions more closely than usual, as he was apt to do in the case of dumb-shows, or else in cases where some unusual business had to be provided for and the omission of the 'exit' would have left the description obscure.

Unmarked internal exits can often be inferred in one of two ways. When a character enters a second time in the course of a single scene, it is obvious that he must have previously gone off. Or when, following the entry of several characters, we find the direction 'to him' or 'to her' it is evident that all but one of them has departed. In the latter case there is apt of course to be ambiguity as to which character or characters have left the stage, unless the gender of the pronoun affords an indication. Sometimes, as in *The Seven Deadly Sins*, II, we can assign the exits with some confidence, but at others, as in *Frederick and Basilea*, sc. xii, and even in sc. xviii, real doubt remains.

It is not clear what it was that suggested to the scribe of the last three Plots the desirability of marking internal exits. He may have felt the awkwardness of recording the entrance of a character who, so far as appeared from the Plot, was already on the stage. Or the change may have been introduced less consciously as the result of closer attention to the directions of the Book. Internal exits are freely marked in *Troilus and Cressida*, section E being particularly noticeable in this respect, but it is difficult to say how far the practice was consistent. The scribe has made no attempt at doing so in the rather difficult section K, and it is uncertain whether or not the 'exit' at the end of A implies that Cassandra remains alone on the stage after the others have gone off. In *The Battle of Alcazar* there are frequent internal exits marked, particularly in II. iii: there do not appear to be any irregularities in this respect. The same is generally true of *Tamar Cam*, but there are in this case a few doubtful points. Exits are certainly required in IV. i and V. iii, and it is uncertain whether their absence is due to the scribe or the transcriber (see notes to ll. 86 and 105). Other anomalies are probably only apparent (see notes to ll. 26–8, 33–4, 53).

Consequential upon this practice of marking internal exits is the use of the term 'manet'. It is of course not essential when the characters going off are specified, and is not always used. Thus in *Troilus and Cressida* (E) the scribe wrote 'manet Pandarus to him Deiphobus, exit Deiphobus to him [sc. Pandarus] Helen & Paris' and in *Tamar Cam* (I. iv) 'Exit Colmogra To them [sc. the rest] Colmogra & Mango'. The second instance is quite unobjectionable, but in the first a certain awkwardness is observable, and it is natural that in section A of *Troilus and Cressida* for example the scribe should have preferred to write (if we may so restore the passage) 'exeunt

Vlisses, Diomed, Hector & Deiphobus, manet the rest & Herraulds, to them Menelaus' &c. The term 'manet' also has the further convenience that it enables the scribe, if he wishes, to leave unnamed the characters who go off. Thus in *Troilus and Cressida* (E) he writes 'exeunt manet Pandarus', and there are a number of similar instances of this succincter use. Occasionally 'manet the rest' is used redundantly before another exit as in *Tamar Cam* (l. 9).

It is worth noting that although the scribe of these Plots uses both 'Exit' and 'Exeunt', and generally uses them correctly, he never employs the plural 'manent'. Thus we find not only 'manet the rest' repeatedly, but even 'manet Stukeley & Duke of Auero' in *The Battle of Alcazar*, III. i. I fancy that 'manent' will also be found to be distinctly rare both in prompt books and in quartos printed from playhouse manuscripts.[1]

We now pass from the division of scenes and related topics to the question of act division. In general it may be said that the Plots ignore act division, but this broad statement is subject to some qualification. In no case is there any numbering of acts [2]: but then neither is there any numbering of the scenes that the Plots are generally so careful to mark. That several of the plays of which Plots survive were regularly divided into five acts is obvious from the entrances of a chorus. This is most evident in *Tamar Cam*, hardly less so, in spite of mutilation, in *The Battle of Alcazar*. Further, it is clear that in *The Seven Deadly Sins* the three Sin plays were divided so as to furnish a total of five acts apart from the historical framework. Even in the fragmentary *Fortune's Tennis* there is at least a hint (at l. 26) of the appearance of a chorus which may have indicated a similar division. But in all these cases, although the structural division may be evident and find reflection in the Plot, there is no insistence on the division, nor any formal recognition such as might suggest that any theatrical importance was attached to the feature. It is perhaps significant that the scribe instead of emphasizing has rather obscured the

[1] The only instance of 'manent' I have noticed in a manuscript play occurs in *The Poor Man's Comfort*, fol. 280[a].

[2] Unless we regard the numbering of the dumb-shows in *The Battle of Alcazar* as an equivalent.

structural divisions in *The Seven Deadly Sins*. The Plot of *Frederick and Basilea* shows no act-division whatever, neither does that of *Troilus and Cressida*, and though the latter is of course fragmentary, enough survives to make inference at least plausible. The one outstanding exception is *The Dead Man's Fortune*, which is formally divided into five sections with direction for music in the intervals. But—and this is the really significant thing about it—this division is not original, but was introduced by a second hand that subsequently revised or at least corrected the Plot.

Thus, if we take the Plots as first written we find no recognition whatever on the part of the scribes of any division into acts, however obvious a feature this may be in the structure of the play as designed by the author. But I think we may go further than this, and say that it is unlikely that any formal division appeared in the prompt books upon which the Plots were based. It seems on general grounds unlikely that such a feature, if present in the Books, should so consistently have been omitted in the Plots, and in this connexion the original absence of division in *The Dead Man's Fortune* seems particularly significant. It is moreover supported by further evidence, for the most natural explanation of the omission of v. i in that Plot seems inconsistent with any very clear division of acts in the Book; while an apparently similar error is found at the beginning of the fourth act of *Tamar Cam*. I conclude therefore that in general act division was not formally recorded either in the prompt books or in the Plots of the companies from which specimens of the latter have reached us.

But it would be rash from this to draw the further conclusion that no such division was recognized in the actual performance. In *The Seven Deadly Sins*, *The Battle of Alcazar*, *Tamar Cam*, and perhaps *Fortune's Tennis*, the structure of the play itself necessitated this division, which would have been evident in performance whether or not any actual intervals were allowed. In *The Dead Man's Fortune* we know that there were intervals, and that they were filled with music. Thus, out of seven plays, possibly five were fully divided in performance. Touching *Troilus and Cressida* we are in a position unfavourable to

speculation. Lastly we have *Frederick and Basilea*, in the Plot of which there is not the slightest trace of division; yet when we examine it closely we find the necessities of costume changes apparently demanding an interval between scenes iii and iv. Thus I am forced to conclude that in performance the division into five acts was common if not universal in the companies in question, and may have obtained even in those pieces in the Books and Plots of which no trace of any such division can be found. I do not attempt to explain this peculiarity, but I doubt whether we can safely argue from the state of extant texts to contemporary stage practice in this respect. I shall have to return to the subject when we come to discuss the extant play Books, but I should like to remind readers at this point that the Books that survive are for the most part considerably later than the latest of the Plots.

The other class of matter which the Plots derived from the Books is the enumeration of properties required and of incidental stage noises and the like. The only Plot entirely devoid of such information is *Frederick and Basilea*, in which the nearest approach to a property mentioned is 'the walls' in sc. xi, which of course means no more than the balcony or upper stage. In *The Dead Man's Fortune* we find a fairly full record of properties, all mentioned in the text and not in the margins. The latter, however, contain directions for 'Musique' between the acts: otherwise the only indication of noises are the 'satires plaing on ther Instruments' in IV. ii and 'the musicke plaies' in V. ii. In *The Seven Deadly Sins* no use is made of the margins and the properties mentioned in the text are comparatively few. As regards noises we find 'A Larum' twice, 'A senitt' once, and what may be implied by the presence of a drum. There was at any rate some mention of properties in the text of *Fortune's Tennis*, but the fragmentary condition of this Plot conceals its general practice. On the other hand, *Troilus and Cressida* in spite of mutilation is seen to be very explicit as regards stage noises, which, however, are recorded in the margins and not in the text. In this and other Plots the term 'Excursions' presumably indicates stage fighting and not a specific noise: on the other hand, I take 'a retreat' to mean a particular blast on the trumpet. There seems to be only one actual property mentioned in the extant portion, and that in the text. *The Battle of Alcazar* follows the preceding exactly in the matter of noises, but it is also very explicit as regards properties both in text and margins, one marginal direction being added in a different script, though probably by the same hand. Lastly, in *Tamar Cam* we again find the same practice as regards noises (the absence of any in the middle margin being I suspect due to the transcriber), and this Plot resembles *Troilus and Cressida* in its comparative reticence as regards properties. It should be added that, although the last three Plots are very likely all by the same hand, the profusion of stage noises is the natural result of the martial character of many of their scenes.

We now pass to the material that the Plots in general drew from a Cast rather than the Book, namely information regarding the actors that filled the different parts. Here our two earliest Plots present some very interesting features. In the case of *The Dead Man's Fortune* the scribe appears to have been without a Cast to work from: he made no attempt generally to record actors. In two scenes he assigned a few minor parts; in a third he most likely entered the name of an actor by mistake for the character he impersonated. In this same scene and in one other he subsequently added the actors for minor parts. But all told he only mentions five performers in connexion with twelve appearances of characters, not all of which can be certainly identified. None of the chief characters have actors assigned. Since sporadic notes of the actors taking incidental parts are a common feature in prompt books it is natural to assume that such was the source of the irregular records of this Plot. If the mention of Burbage is correctly taken to be a mistake for the name of a character, the error would not be without parallel in the other Plots, and it may have arisen from the scribe's own knowledge of the casting: at the same time it is not impossible that the actor's name may have found its way into the Book in place of a character name, especially if the appearance of the character was due to revision or there were other confusion in the manuscript such as seems here reflected in the Plot. In any case all the information that the Plot affords

us is that Richard Darlowe, Robert Lee, and a boy (?) named Sam were the three supernumerary actors generally available in the company for odd parts, that on occasion it was possible to call in the help of the tire-man—just as that of another (or possibly the same) tire-man may have been used in *Troilus and Cressida*—and that Richard Burbage, an actor of a very different standing, played some uncertain part in the play.

In contrast with this the record of actors in *The Seven Deadly Sins* is very full. The latter was a play in which from its nature the doubling of parts was unusually heavy, and it was therefore desirable that a clear scheme of distribution should be readily accessible. We can imagine that, even if such had not been customary in the company before, the experiment might have been made in the case of the present piece; and there is even some hint that this may indeed have been so, since for the two characters who remain present throughout, and for whom therefore doubling was out of the question, no actors are assigned.[1] These two are the only main characters left unprovided, but it is noteworthy that for eight mute personae the actor is again not specified. Unless this means that these eight were not members of the regular cast (which seems improbable) I am at a loss to account for the omission.

In all five remaining Plots, so far as we can judge, it seems to have been the intention of the scribe to mention the actor for every part in the play, whether major or minor, and that where he failed to do this it was due to mere oversight.

Except, therefore, in *The Dead Man's Fortune* we have a practically complete record of the actors in each play. There are, nevertheless, certain minor differences in the methods of record employed. Errors and irregularities apart the chief differences are as follows: the name of the actor may be mentioned every time a character appears, or only on the occasion of his first appearance; and where several characters enter together the name of the actor of each may be given immediately after that of the character, or the names of the characters may be massed in a consecutive list followed by another massed list of the names of the actors in the order of their parts. Our know-

[1] See, however, p. 117, note.

ledge of the actual use to which the Plots were put is insufficient to allow us to decide the comparative merits of the different methods. All we can say is that the development seems to have been from constant repetition of actors' names to mention on first entrance only; while as regards massing, an attempt to abandon the practice and link the names individually seems to have been made only to be abandoned. It is easier to appraise the relative convenience of the methods from our own point of view and to see the type of error into which they respectively led. Constant repetition of actors' names seems to us a clumsy and redundant practice, and it actually led in some cases to a habit of so abbreviating the names as to give rise on occasions to actual ambiguity. On the other hand, when the intention was to mention an actor's name only on his first appearance, there was a danger of its not being mentioned at all, and it is no doubt to the development of this practice that our ignorance of several of the performers in the later Plots is due. Massing is the obvious and easy method for a plotter to adopt: he copies down from the Book the list of characters entering and then supplies their actors' names from the cast. It, too, seems a very clumsy method to us, and is very irritating to the critic who is trying to check the accuracy of the plotter. Moreover, it does lead in practice to considerable laxity in the order of the actors' names: especially when characters habitually enter in pairs, the scribe seems quite indifferent whether the order of the actors agrees with that of the characters. As a rule, of course, the ambiguity can be resolved, but there remain occasional cases of real uncertainty. At the same time it is possible that as the Plots were actually used at performance, massing may have been the more convenient method: in any case its drawbacks seem to have been insufficient to cause a change of practice.[1]

In *The Seven Deadly Sins* repetition is usual but not consistent, and massing is the general rule. The nature of the play

[1] To make sure that everything was in readiness for a given entrance the prompter or stage manager might find it sufficient to check the list of characters or the list of actors: either would show whether the proper number were present. In this case massing would be the more convenient. On the other hand, in a play in which there was much doubling and in which the casting of minor parts

made repetition less cumbersome and perhaps more desirable than usual, but it led to severe abbreviation. Massing led to frequent irregularity of order. In *Frederick and Basilea* repetition is the rule, though there is little abbreviation: the names are massed. In *Fortune's Tennis* repetition is clearly not the rule, but the names were certainly sometimes massed. In *Troilus and Cressida* repetition must have been definitely abandoned, but the fragment affords no evidence on the subject of massing. Nor in *The Battle of Alcazar* is there any repetition except occasionally in the case of minor characters and in those like Ghosts and Furies that occur in groups. As a result some actors have remained unspecified. An attempt was made at the beginning to avoid massing but it seems not to have been altogether successful. Since repetition had been abandoned the question of massing was only important in the earlier scenes. Lastly, in *Tamar Cam* the absence of repetition has led to some omissions. Massing is the rule again, but there is an endeavour at least to separate different groups. In this Plot too a novel but feeble attempt is made to number the actors impersonating group characters.

The ability of the scribes who prepared the Plots varied to some extent, and though the plotter who prepared *The Seven Deadly Sins* and *Fortune's Tennis*, and even more the one apparently responsible for the last three Plots, attained a high degree of technical competence, none avoided error and confusion altogether. Their individual lapses are discussed in the descriptions of the several Plots, but do not appear to be of any general significance. The most common are ambiguities affecting the minor characters, which appear to be due to a failure adequately to digest the sometimes vague directions of the Books.

One of the most important functions of the plotter, or perhaps rather of the person who determined the details of casting, was to bring the requirements of the Book into harmony with the capacity of the company at the time. It is

might vary, it might be desirable to check the actors against the characters, and massing would then prove inconvenient. The evidence of the Plots suggests that the latter alternative was not generally important. But groups who have to enter by different doors are kept distinct.

common for an author to make extravagant demands in the way of 'supers', and it was the business of the stage manager to make use of the resources of the company in the most adequate and effective way. But since, no doubt, the resources varied from time to time it was convenient to make the adjustment not in the Book itself but in the more ephemeral Plot. Even in this the adjustments were not always exact and the actors specified are at times inadequate to afford the demand for attendants, guards, and the like retained in it. The relation of Plot to Book in this respect may of course be best studied in *The Battle of Alcazar* (see p. 157, note on l. 10; also *Two Elizabethan Stage Abridgements*, pp. 58, 59, 109, 118).

In the case of necessary characters the adjustments were of course made principally by doubling the parts. Of this there cannot have been very much in *The Dead Man's Fortune*, but the lack of record of the actors leaves us quite in the dark. Doubling was certainly and of obvious necessity resorted to in *The Seven Deadly Sins*, but its application to mute characters has been left curiously vague. It is slight in *Frederick and Basilea*, which is an interesting example of the apparent adaptation of a new play to the temporary circumstances of the company performing it (see p. 126). In *The Battle of Alcazar* a majority of the actors had to take more than one part, while, on the other hand, in *Tamar Cam* doubling is not heavy apart from the final procession.

In all the Plots except *The Dead Man's Fortune* certain actors are distinguished by the prefix 'Mr.'. The exact significance of this honorific is in doubt, but that in practice it designates a sharer in the company may be accepted. In *The Seven Deadly Sins* only three actors are so distinguished, but it is likely that the two whose names are not recorded also had a right to it. *Frederick and Basilea* is the only Plot in which the designation is not used with perfect consistency.

That in every case the Plot must have been prepared from the Book is more or less self-evident, and the relation of the two, particularly the influence of the latter on the construction and wording of the former, is an important and interesting study. Writers on the drama have sometimes made the quite

unwarranted assumption that a prompt Book must have been purely and severely theatrical in form and disposition. An examination of the extant examples shows that this in an error. While individual examples, as we shall see in a later section, differ considerably in their technical character, they all preserve stage-directions and other features of a literary type very imperfectly assimilated to the requirements or the point of view of stage representation. They are documents that have come from the hands of authors who, while often experienced dramatists, appear to have thought or at least expressed themselves rather in literary or ideal terms than in those of the material conditions of the playhouse, and even when they have been extensively worked over by a stage reviser the assimilation to a technically theatrical type and language has been but imperfectly effected. So much is evident from the surviving Books themselves. But it could be inferred with hardly less certainty from a study of the Plots. For these are purely technical documents produced in the playhouses, and yet they constantly preserved features and phrases of a literary rather than theatrical character.

The Plots differ a good deal in the degree to which the influence of the Book appears in them. Traces are perhaps least evident in *Frederick and Basilea*, a particularly bare and simple Plot, and in *Tamar Cam*, in which technical development has succeeded in eliminating almost all extraneous features. On the surface there is in these nothing beyond an occasional phrase—a redundant '&c' or an explanatory 'his daughter' that can have no theatrical significance—to point to dependence on the Book, but there is good reason to suspect that even here certain ambiguities and anomalies are due to imperfect assimilation or understanding of directions in the same source. It is no doubt a conjecture that an error in *Tamar Cam* was due to carelessness in turning the leaves of the Book, but the same explanation fits a similar error in *The Dead Man's Fortune*, a Plot in which the influence of the Book is more manifest. This is likewise apparent in *The Seven Deadly Sins* and *The Battle of Alcazar*, and it can also fairly be traced in the two fragments.

The most notable survivals in the Plots of the technique of

the Book are the descriptive directions for certain scenes, particularly those in or involving dumb-show. As a very rough generalization one may say that the stage-directions in prompt Books were on the whole meagre beyond notices of entrance and exit, the dialogue being sufficient as a rule to indicate the necessary action. But where dialogue failed descriptive directions of some elaboration were inserted. It was natural therefore that the plotter, working his way through the directions of the Book, should embody much of these descriptions, especially as they frequently involved a fairly elaborate series of entries and exits. And the wording of the Plots suggests that in some cases such descriptive directions were transcribed almost without alteration. They are conspicuous in *The Dead Man's Fortune* and *The Seven Deadly Sins*; less so in *The Battle of Alcazar*: they are absent from *Frederick and Basilea* and *Tamar Cam*, nor are any preserved in the two fragments. Presence or absence seems to depend less upon the character of the plotting than upon the presence or absence of dumb-show, though it is true that the wording of the directions in *The Battle of Alcazar* has been pretty thoroughly digested, and that we might have expected some indication of the nature of the finale of *Tamar Cam*.

A few individual points are of interest. I have previously suggested that the sporadic records of actors in *The Dead Man's Fortune* are derived from the Book rather than from a proper cast, and it is tempting to suppose that the curious difficulty over Mr. Hunt and the Proctor in *Troilus and Cressida* had its origin in additions clumsily worked into the Book after the formal cast had been drawn up. The possibility that vague directions in the Book may be the source of certain ambiguities in the Plots has been already mentioned in discussing the actors, and so has the particular value of *The Battle of Alcazar* for the relation of Book to Plot. One of the most interesting points of all is the persistence here and there even in these highly technical Plots of purely literary phrases that must go back for their origin to the author himself. Even the severely theatrical *Frederick and Basilea* has in one place 'vpon the walls' instead of the technical 'above'. Similarly in *Troilus and*

*Cressida* 'they on the walls descend', and there is mention of Achilles' 'Tent'. 'A tent' is also 'plast on the stage' in *The Seven Deadly Sins*, but in spite of the explicitness of the direction it is uncertain whether anything more than the alcove is intended. Later in the same Plot Sardanapalus enters 'w[th] as many Iewels robes and Gold as he can cary', and a curious mixture of phraseology appears where Ferrex enters 'one way' and Porrex 'At a nother dore'. Even in *The Battle of Alcazar*, in which the language is for the most part strictly technical, the scribe stumbled on the phrase 'Carrie him out' which from the theatrical point of view should of course be 'in'.

It will probably have been noticed that a development of technical form is in some degree observable in the Plots, nor does this seem to rest entirely upon the fact that I have placed the rather elementary *Dead Man's Fortune* at the beginning of the series, and that the elaborate *Tamar Cam* definitely stands at the end. The period covered from one to the other is probably no more than twelve or thirteen years; in all only seven Plots are preserved, several imperfectly. These facts must be borne in mind, for the surviving documents can be but a small proportion of those that once existed and we have little to show whether they are typical or not. The evidence at our disposal is far too scanty to justify any far-reaching generalization as to the history and evolution of the Plot from a technical point of view. Nevertheless, when we subject them to the analysis here attempted there do seem to emerge certain definite lines of development and certain links with external history, and, always subject to the reservations just made, I propose to indicate in outline what it appears to me that development is and what the guiding circumstances may have been.

I previously mentioned the rather remarkable fact that all the seven extant Plots follow the same rather arbitrary convention as to the technical use of the term 'Enter'. That it was a convention and possibly a recent one is suggested by the fact that it was not recognized by the scribe who made the additions to *The Dead Man's Fortune*. That this Plot stands, in its elementary and I think one may fairly say comparatively primitive character, apart from the rest, is obvious on the face of it. Its English script and the absence of any ornamental heading distinguish it on the material side, just as its merely incidental mention of actors does on the theatrical. Noteworthy too is its uncertainty respecting scene division, and its marking of act division with intervening music, though the latter is not an original feature. The whole suggests, if only faintly, that the technique was still in an experimental stage—no later plotter would have begun a section with the words 'Enter to them'—and it is possible that we here see the Plot in the act of emerging from something even more primitive. If it belonged to the same company as *The Seven Deadly Sins*, it is difficult to believe that it is not appreciably the elder: if the two are of approximately the same date—as seems on the whole most likely—then it is difficult to believe that they can have been drawn up for the same company. For in *The Seven Deadly Sins* the Plot has in all essentials reached maturity. In particular we find as in all later examples (if sufficiently preserved) a practically complete list of actors. And yet here again there is a suggestion of experiment. For a record of the actors was particularly desirable in a play such as this, whose composite structure rendered doubling necessary and frequent, and the significance of the fact that for the two characters who could not be doubled no actors are specified cannot be dismissed. It would be illegitimate to argue that a systematic record of actors had never before been attempted; but on the other hand, if the attempt was indeed made here for the first time the motive would at least be apparent. Similarly with the distinctive gothic heading which now first makes its appearance. There is no evidence that the scribe of *The Seven Deadly Sins* invented it: at the same time it is legitimate to observe that he placed very similar headings on the Books of *Sir Thomas More* and *John a Kent*, and that such headings were not, to the best of our knowledge, a common feature of prompt Books. Both these early Plots then have some suggestion of experiment about them, and their differences suggest no very intimate relation between them. Without wishing to press the evidence I may at least suggest that if *The Seven Deadly Sins* belonged to

Strange's men, it is not unreasonable to suppose that *The Dead Man's Fortune* may have been prepared for the Admiral's.

On passing to the later group, all belonging to the later Admiral's company, it is curious to observe the same contrast in a manner repeating itself. The earliest of these, the only one dating from before the reconstruction of Oct. 1597, is *Frederick and Basilea*, and this again is in some ways a rather bare and meagre Plot. It is the only one tolerably preserved that has no record of properties or noises required, and it is the only one with a full record of actors that is inconsistent in its use of 'Mr.'. It is also written in a smaller hand than the rest and is the only Plot confined to one column. Like *The Dead Man's Fortune* it gives the impression of standing in technical character somewhat apart from its fellows. It has even some peculiar features in common with that Plot. Thus there is the curious tendency to improper scene division at the end, while on the formal side the two agree in the narrowness of the central margin and in the fact that while the columns are bounded by rules there are no further rules forming outside margins. On the other hand, *Frederick and Basilea* of course separates itself from *The Dead Man's Fortune* and follows *The Seven Deadly Sins* in recording the cast fully, and even agrees with the latter in repeating and massing the actors' names. The next Plot is *Fortune's Tennis*, which was drawn up by the same scribe who wrote *The Seven Deadly Sins* some seven years before. Its fragmentary character has deprived us of much possibly valuable information, but it is natural to assume, where there is no evidence to the contrary, that the scribe persisted in his earlier methods. One important innovation, however, he did make: he abandoned the practice of repeating actors' names. This of course made the practice of massing (which he retained) of much less importance since it confined opportunity for it mainly to the opening scenes. It may be added that in the four Plots just considered practically no exits, whether internal or final, are marked, that properties are fairly frequently mentioned in the text in all except *Frederick and Basilea*, and that in no case is any use made of the margins except in *The Dead Man's Fortune* and then only by an afterthought.

The last three Plots form a close group by themselves. *Troilus and Cressida* and *The Battle of Alcazar* are written in the same hand, and if *Tamar Cam* is not, as is probable, the work of the same scribe, it is that of a very close imitator. Moreover the scribe of these Plots was clearly a disciple of the scribe of *The Seven Deadly Sins*: he takes over intact his technical procedure, as we may suppose it stood in *Fortune's Tennis*, and contents himself with slightly developing it. He regularly uses ruled margins in which he records noises, and in *The Battle of Alcazar* properties as well. He consistently abandons repetition, as did the scribe of *Fortune's Tennis*, and experiments with the avoidance of massing, coming in *Tamar Cam* to a compromise on the matter. He introduces the practice of marking final exits (and actually does so consistently in one case, so far as we know) presumably as part of an attempt to mark exits generally (including internal), though of this we can only say that his practice was not always consistent. In connexion with this attempt he introduces a new term, 'manet'. Whether his practice differed at all between his two earlier Plots the fragmentary condition of *Troilus and Cressida* prevents our observing. No differences are apparent, and if I am right in supposing the two written within a few months of one another, perhaps none existed. In *Tamar Cam*, three years later, the scribe seems to be again experimenting if we can trust the extant print and our inferences from it. The position of the direction for the first chorus is unique: there is an attempt in the case of the procession, and very imperfectly elsewhere, to add numbers to the enumeration of a group of actors, and finally there may have been an attempt to distinguish between the names of characters and those of actors by the use of Italian and English script respectively.

To sum up: it is possible, in spite of their scanty number and imperfect preservation, that the Plots that have come down enable us to watch to some extent at least the genesis and development of the type. We have in *The Dead Man's Fortune* an early and rather rudimentary example, prepared by a scribe that has not yet acquired either the amenities or technical adaptation that the conditions suggest. He worked, I con-

jecture, for the earlier Admiral's company. Meanwhile with Strange's men experiments were being made by another scribe, to whose technical ingenuity and appreciation of theatrical requirements we largely owe the development of the stage Plot as it appears at the end of Elizabeth's reign. It must be borne in mind that this scribe was also the stage editor of the play of *Sir Thomas More*. These two are our early Plots dating probably from about 1590 or 1591. The remaining five were prepared for the later Admiral's company between 1597 and 1602 inclusive. Of these the earliest, *Frederick and Basilea*, is to some extent a regression. While adopting the principle of a full record of actors, it certainly adds nothing by way of technical development to *The Seven Deadly Sins*, and even reverts in certain details of form and arrangement to the type of *The Dead Man's Fortune*. Of course the close association which seems to have existed from about 1590 to 1594 between the Admiral's and Strange's companies would lead us to expect that at least the more important innovations of theatrical routine of either company would become familiar to the other, but if there was in fact, and apart from Alleyn's leadership, any continuity between the older and later Admiral's men it would be easy to understand some minor features of their Plots persisting. Then the scribe of *The Seven Deadly Sins* reappears on the scene with *Fortune's Tennis*. The date of this is probably the winter of 1597–8, that of *Frederick and Basilea* June 1597, and the contrast between them suggests the possibility that the scribe joined the Admiral's men on their amalgamation with Pembroke's in the autumn of that year. He produced no more Plots that we know of, but he found a pupil and successor who not only adopted his technical procedure but developed it further on the same lines, and was still experimenting with the form at the close of Elizabeth's reign.

Such is the story that the Plots suggest to me concerning their development, but I know how slender is the evidence on which it rests, and if any denying spirit objects that it is fanciful I shall not demur.

*Preservation.*—This is one of the two Plots perfectly preserved. It retains its original board, which is covered with paper on both sides; and on the back is an abortive beginning of the Plot. The peg hole goes right through, but it has been closed with paper in modern times. The Plot has at some time been folded in two, as have those of *The Seven Deadly Sins* and *Frederick and Basilea*, perhaps with a view to forming a protection for the Book.

*Identification.*—Nothing whatever is known of this play apart from the Plot. The rather primitive character of the latter as compared with that of *The Seven Deadly Sins*, which itself belongs to 1591 at latest, suggests that it was prepared either at an earlier date or for a different company. The appearance of Burbage's name serves, at the period in question, to connect it with the Theatre, or at least with one of the Shoreditch houses. I have elsewhere (p. 19) given my reasons for assigning it to the Admiral's men at the Theatre about 1590.

*The Action or Fable.*—A peculiarity of the play is the double plot: a main plot supplied by a romantic tragi-comedy with supernatural machinery, and a sub-plot modelled on the Italian impromptu farce. As the Plot stands these seem to be entirely disconnected, but we shall see that this appearance is probably deceptive. The characters of the sub-plot are clearly traditional, and it is worth notice that while in some instances 'Panteloun' is treated as a proper name (ll. 14, 21, 31, 44) in others it has the article prefixed (ll. 9, 33, 62, 65) showing that it was recognized as a stock designation. But there is no reason to suppose that the sub-plot, let alone the play as a whole, was performed extempore (see, however, the note on p. 98).

The sub-plot need not further detain us, but the discussion of various obscurities in the interpretation of the Plot will be greatly facilitated if we can form some idea of the story furnishing the main fable, and the following is an attempt to recon-

struct an outline from the necessarily rather meagre data. While the relation of the characters is in general pretty clear, the details of the action and the motives suggested are of course conjectural, and it is perhaps unlikely that they have been always correctly imagined. Certain anomalies of the Plot have been interpreted in accordance with the analysis to be attempted later on: the reconstruction of IV. i is particularly problematic.[1]

Laertes and Eschines, befriended by the magician Urganda, are suitors to Alleyane and Statyra, whom, however, their fathers, Tesephon and Allgerius, destine for the wicked rivals Carynus and Prelior. Laertes first makes the acquaintance of the fathers (I. iii), while on Urganda's advice Eschines takes a disguise as Bellveile (II. ii). The rival pairs of suitors appear before the ladies and their fathers to prefer their suits, and when the ladies refuse to bow to their parents' wishes by renouncing their chosen lovers they are committed to prison (II. iv). Here they overhear a plot by the wicked suitors (III. i), and with the help of the Jailor are able to summon their lovers (III. ii), thus defeating their fathers' plan of marrying them off under the influence of a drug administered in their meat (III. iii). While, however, Tesephon and Allgerius are congratulating themselves on the success of their plot, news is brought by a messenger that their daughters have died, and Urganda (Burbage) then accuses them of poisoning the meat, and has them arrested by an officer named Euphrodore (IV. i). Next Urganda visits Carynus and Prelior and by means of a magic mirror (IV. ii) drives them mad (IV. iii). The last act opens with a scene (added later to the Plot) in which Urganda restores the ladies to their true lovers (V. i). There follows a spectacular entry, in which, before King Egereon, the condemned fathers are brought out to execution. Carynus and Prelior follow, but the catastrophe is interrupted by another magic show, in which three antic fairies dismiss the executioner and free the victims (V. ii), whereupon Urganda enters with the united couples (V. iii) and the play ends in mutual reconciliation.

[1] I owe the basis of the reconstruction to Sir Edmund Chambers.

*Characteristics.—The Dead Man's Fortune* is the most primitive of the Plots and differs from the rest in several particulars. The following points especially deserve notice: (i) the inconspicuous heading, (ii) the secretary script, (iii) the general absence of actors' names, (iv) the uncertainty of the arrangement, particularly as regards scene division, and (v) the use of a sign of uncertain significance (=) not found elsewhere. It is the only extant Plot written in an English hand, though even in this Italian script is used for the word '*finis*', for an occasional name, and also for the additions in another hand (cf., however, the remarks on the lost original of *Tamar Cam*, p. 162).

The most important difference from later custom is in the record of the actors. The scribe evidently had no intention of recording the names of the players who filled the various parts as a general rule. All he did was to mention the actors who played a few minor and purely incidental characters, actors who had either to be borrowed from other parts or called in specially for the occasion, and even so some of the names were only added as an afterthought (ll. 17, 34, and probably 36). These notes for supernumerary characters are exactly such as we often find jotted down in the margins of prompt Books, and it is reasonable to suppose that that is in fact the source from which they are here derived. The Plot affords us, for instance, rather more information respecting the actors than does the Book of *Edmond Ironside*, and somewhat less than that of *Barnavelt*. With the regular casting of the piece the scribe is not concerned: we should not from his silence conclude that there was no doubling, though this cannot have been extensive among the principal parts. (The mention of Burbage in l. 35 is probably exceptional and due to an error, as suggested in the notes.)

The play was divided into five acts, the divisions being marked by rows of crosses superimposed on or placed above a line drawn across the column. That these indicate actual intervals in the performance is shown by the directions for music in the margins. They seem, however, to be additions to the Plot as originally written, for it is likely (as explained in the note to ll. 48–9) that the crosses were added at the same time

as the directions, and these are written in another hand, which also inserted, at the beginning of Act v, a scene probably omitted by the original scribe. This result is of some importance since it suggests that, although the actual performance was divided into acts, there may have been no indication of this in the Book.

The Plot is also ostensibly divided into scenes by rules drawn across the column, but there is some uncertainty as to what these divisions represent. It cannot have been the scribe's intention to begin a fresh scene whenever there was a change in the characters on the stage, since internal entries occur in many of the divisions, while an internal exit is noted in II. ii, and others implied in II. iii, III. iv, and IV. iv. It is natural to conclude, therefore, that the scribe of this plot agreed with others in recognizing scene division on the Elizabethan plan, and that he intended to mark a new scene only when the stage was empty, even though final exits are not recorded. But in that case the rule above V. iii is clearly wrong, since the words 'Enter to them' in l. 60 imply that some characters are already present. There is, moreover, reason to suspect that this is not an isolated slip. It has already been remarked that as the Plot stands the main intrigue and the under-plot are throughout distinct, without any point of contact, which though perhaps not unparalleled is at least unusual. Again, 'the cheste or truncke' that Panteloun produces at the end (all by himself!) must surely contain 'the deade mans fortune', and it would be rather surprising if the play took its title from an incident belonging to the sub-plot alone. Lastly, the sequence of disconnected scenes (V. iv–vii) with which the play ends suggests a curious departure from the usual Elizabethan technique, and this becomes all the more suspicious when we observe similar sequences in the sub-plot elsewhere, namely three scenes at the end of Act IV, and two at the end of Act III. There are other suspicious details discussed in the notes (ll. 62, 63), and we are bound, I think, to conclude that the scribe's divisions are unreliable, that in the last act scenes ii–vii are really continuous, and that both plots are involved in the catastrophe.

The scribe began in the first instance to write the Plot on

what is now the back or reverse of the board, but after completing six lines he discovered that he had overlooked the second scene[1]: he made no attempt to alter or even delete what he had written, but turned the board over and began again. The probability is that he made another mistake at the beginning of Act v, where a scene has been inserted by another hand, for in view of his earlier mistake it seems more likely that the scribe accidentally omitted the scene than that it was later added to the play. The most likely explanation of this error, of which he evidentally remained in ignorance, is that at the conclusion of Act iv at the bottom of a page he accidentally turned over two leaves of the Book at once, and finding the next page begin with an important entry assumed that he was at the beginning of Act v (cf. *Tamar Cam*, ll. 74–5). If this conjecture is correct it confirms our previous inference that the act divisions were not marked in the Book, or at least that there were no act or scene headings. The omission was subsequently rectified by the same hand that added the directions for music between the acts.

We find a fairly extensive record of properties, all mentioned in the text and not the margin: 'ruffes', whatever they may be (ii. v), Peascod's 'apparell' (ii. vi), meat (iii. iii), spectacles (iii. iv), a looking-glass and musical instruments (iv. ii), a 'flasket of clothes' (suggestive of Falstaff's buck-basket) twice (iv. vi), a block, sword, and halbards (v. ii), and finally 'the cheste or truncke' (v. vii).

The influence of the Book is seen in several ways. If I am right in suggesting that it was the source of the mention of occasional actors, the example is apparently unique. More certain and more obvious is the lengthy description of v. ii. Here we may suppose the action to have been largely dumb-show: such business was necessarily described rather fully in the Book and we shall see that the descriptions always tended

[1] The scene he overlooked was the first scene of that sub-plot which shows such marked affinity with the extempore drama of Italy. If any one chose to argue that he overlooked it because it was not in the Book, and that it was not in the Book because the sub-plot was an improvised addition to the play to be rendered by the actors impromptu, I do not think it would be very easy to refute the suggestion, though I see no reason to entertain it.

to be copied faithfully into the Plot. Such a phrase as 'then after that the musicke plaies & ther Enters' is particularly noticeable for its descriptive quality, which is quite at variance with the usual terse formality of even this comparatively primitive Plot: equally significant are such details as 'dancynge on after a nother' and 'as they entred so they departe'. This is the language of the descriptive directions for such shows found in prompt Books: as in *The Second Maiden's Tragedy*, 'On a sodayne in a kinde of Noyse like a Wynde, the dores clattering, the Toombstone flies open . . . His Lady as went owt, standing iust before hym all in white' (ll. 1926 ff.) and 'They bringe the Body in a Chaire drest vp in black veluet . . . He standes silent awhile letting the Musique play' (ll. 2225 ff.); or in *Hamlet* (Q 2), 'anon come in an other man, takes off his crowne, . . . wooes the Queene with gifts, shee seemes harsh awhile, but in the end accepts loue' (III. ii). The 'prysoun' in which the Ladies speak in III. i is clearly from the Book, and on the stage would probably be represented by the balcony; and I suspect that the phrase 'whiles he speakes validore passeth ore the stage' in l. 21 must come from the same source. The vague 'others' in l. 35 points in the same direction, and no doubt the trouble over 'the laydes' (ll. 26, 28) and 'ther laides' (l. 61), and over Peascod's father (l. 4) and Panteloun's man (l. 14), as well as the slighter difficulties respecting Asspida (ll. 14–5) and Rose (l. 20), have arisen through the scribe reproducing phrases which may have been perfectly clear in the Book but became ambiguous apart from the context. At the same time it should be observed that phrases of the sort are not always clear even in the Book, and that it is part of the business of a good plotter to interpret them in a specific manner.

*The Casting.*—As originally written, and apart from the mention of Burbage in l. 35, the only actors named in the Plot were 'Darlowe: lee: b samme' for attendants in I. iii, and '· b · samme' for Validore's man in III. iv. Later the scribe again assigned 'Dar lee sam' as attendants in II. iv and also turned his attention to IV. i. Here he had already entered Burbage's name, but this (as I have argued in the notes) was almost certainly a mistake for the name of a character. The scene further required 'atendantes & others', 'a messenger', and 'Euphrodore', at least six in all in addition to the regular characters. There were only four actors available, even after pressing the tire-man into service. The scribe allotted the messenger and Euphrodore to 'Robart lee & b samme' and left 'Dar & tyre man' to do the best they could for 'atendantes & others'. Such reduction of the demands of the Book is common.

'Burbage' is no doubt Richard Burbage, who was about twenty in 1590, and it is very unfortunate that we cannot determine with certainty which character he played. Even if we were to suppose that he and not Lee was the messenger (which is extremely unlikely) we should still have to assume that this was not his only appearance but that he played at least one more important part as well. Richard Darlowe and Robert Lee were both minor actors: the little that is known about them will be found recorded elsewhere, but throws little light on the Plot. Sam may be Samuel Rowley (or less probably Samuel Gilburne): the '· b ·' is usually interpreted to mean 'boy', which is plausible but not necessarily correct (but cf. p. 49).

The ambiguities of the casting, none of which apart from 'Burbage' are very serious, are fully discussed in the notes. I have assumed that Peascod is Panteloun's 'man' and that his 'father' is a different character.

In drawing up the tabular analysis (in the volume of facsimiles) I have merely displayed the characters as they appear in the different scenes. I have made no attempt to make use of the scant data as to actors, which are indeed mostly confusing, nor have I tried to indicate the possibilities of doubling. There is, in any case, little scope for this among the regular characters. It is excluded in the case of Urganda, Laertes, Eschines, Tesephon, Allgerius, Allcyane, Statyra, Carynus, Prelior, Panteloun, Peascod, Asspida, Validor, Rose. This gives fourteen main actors besides Darlowe, Lee, and Sam. These seventeen with the tire-man suffice. Eschines and Bellveile are identical: Peascod's father, if not Panteloun, will double with him (or with Carinus or Prelior): Panteloun's man, if not Peascod, will double with him: the Jailor will double

with Urganda (or Rose): the Satyrs of IV. ii with characters of the sub-plot. In V. ii the five main characters of the sub-plot together with the tire-man will supply the Executioner, three Fairies, and two Officers (who all go off at l. 59), while Darlowe, Lee, and Sam will furnish King Egereon and two Lords, who presumably stay on to the end of the play. The Prologue of course could be spoken by any of the actors other than those who take the parts of Urganda, Laertes, and Eschines, or even by one of these if the usual black cloak was worn (cf. *Frederick and Basilea*, l. 2).

## *Notes*

4. Since Peascod is subsequently attached to Panteloun it would seem natural, at first sight, to suppose that it is the latter who is here referred to as 'his father'. But it is noticeable that the first time Panteloun has any one attached to him his satellite is merely called 'his man' (l. 14). This 'man' is mentioned nowhere else, and unless he is identical with some other character we might expect an actor to be specified for the part (as in the case of Validore's 'man', l. 32). I therefore conclude, though not with complete confidence, that Peascod is not Panteloun's son but his 'man', and that he here takes leave of his father before seeking his fortune in service.

6. It has been usual to assume that here and in ll. 32, 36 'b samme' stands for 'boy Sam'. This may be correct, but unless Euphrodore, whom Sam possibly impersonates in IV. i, is a female character (which there seems no reason to suppose) the inference lacks cogency. We have a 'Black Dick' in *Frederick and Basilea*: one can imagine 'b samme' standing for 'Black Sam' or for various other sobriquets. The question has some relevance to the identification of the actor.

13. There seems no doubt that 'for Bell veile' means disguised as Bellveile. The usual term in the later Plots is 'like', e.g. *Fortune's Tennis*, l. 22, and *Tamar Cam*, l. 52; but 'for' is Shakespearian, and occurs in *As you Like it*, II. iv. 1: 'Enter Rosaline for Ganimed, Celia for Aliena'. Bellveile appears to be throughout no more than a disguise for Eschines, for the latter is absent after II. ii for seven scenes of the main plot, during which it is Bellveile who is Laertes's companion, and when he reappears in V. i, we find the significant warning 'Enter wt out disguise'.

14. 'his man' is presumably Peascod; cf. l. 4.

14–5. It seems safe to suppose that 'his wife asspida' is a case of apposition and that only one character is involved, since Asspida frequently reappears and there is no other mention of Panteloun's wife.

15. The phrase 'to hir' implies that Panteloun and Peascod have gone off.

19–20. The phrase 'cutting of ruffes' is obscure. Neither the cutting out nor the cutting up of ruffes, in the sense of collars, seems a reasonable occupation. It has been suggested to me that cutting might mean pleating with a crimping iron, but the proper term for this was 'setting'. It is perhaps worth noting that some early glossaries give 'ruff' for the wick of a taper: so that the words might possibly here mean 'snuffing the candles'.

20. No doubt 'the maide' here and at l. 24 is identical with Rose, who attends on Asspida in IV. iv, vi and V. vi.

25. The mark (=) used here, and again at ll. 31, 36, is found in no other Plot, and its meaning is not quite clear. It seems, however, to be used as a dash to mark a break of some kind in the description. Here the two sets of characters on the stage apparently keep apart; the ladies, presumably in the balcony, perhaps overhearing the conversation of their suitors without revealing themselves. In III. iv it also appears to mark concealment: since Asspida does not enter 'to' the others they are presumably hidden, and they subsequently reappear seemingly in farcical disguise. Lastly in IV. i it seems merely to mark off the addition of the actors' names.

25–6. There is some uncertainty, here and at l. 28, as to who 'the laydes' (i.e. ladies) may be, but they are presumably the same as in V. iii. There, at first sight, one might suppose that there were three of them, one each for Urganda, Laertes, and Eschines. On the other hand, Allcyane and Statyra seem to be the only characters available, and if the proposed reconstruction of the story is correct it explains the apparent anomaly.

31. 'pateloun', a scribal slip for 'panteloun'.

32. The phrase 'to hir' again implies that Panteloun and Peascod have gone off or at least retired (cf. l. 25, note).

34–6. The interpretation of this scene presents difficulties which have some bearing on the history of the Plot. Of the actors' names 'Burbage' is part of the original writing (like the names in I. iii and III. iv), while 'Dar & tyre man' certainly, and 'Robart lee & b samme' probably, are additions. At the beginning of the scene the Plot demands 'atendantes & others', but for these the company can only provide two actors. It seems indifferent whether we make them both 'aten-

dantes', or Darlow an 'atendant' and the tire-man an 'other' (as I have done in the tabular analysis)—we do not know sufficient of the story to tell whether the 'others' are significant. At first sight it looks as though Burbage took the part of 'a messenger', and this has hitherto been generally assumed. But, if that is so, it must be observed (1) that the actor's name precedes instead of following the part he plays, which is anomalous; (2) that Richard Burbage (who must be meant) was by 1590 an actor of very different calibre from any of the others mentioned in this Plot, which is suspicious; and (3) that, in spite of the shortage already noticed, two actors would be assigned for the part of Euphrodore, which is certainly incorrect. I have very little doubt that the explanation of the confusion is that 'Robart lee & b samme' were added as the actors of the messenger and Euphrodore, and that in the original writing Burbage's name was accidentally inserted instead of that of the character he played (for a similar error see *The Battle of Alcazar*, l. 111). What part Burbage filled is a matter of conjecture, but if our reconstruction of the story is approximately correct it is at least probable that Urganda, who seems to play the part of guardian angel in the catastrophe, appeared in this scene which must have witnessed the arrest of the principal villains. I therefore conjecture that in place of 'to them Burbage a messenger' the scribe should have written either 'to them Urganda and messenger' or perhaps 'to them Urganda to them a messenger'.

42. Once more the phrase 'to hir' implies an exit for Peascod.

48–9. It will be noticed that in this instance the row of crosses that indicates a fresh act is placed above the rule separating the scenes instead of on it as in the earlier instances. The object appears to be to make it clear that the additional scene, the index for which descends from the rule, belongs to Act V and not to Act IV. It follows that these crosses are not the work of the original scribe but were added by the second hand.

52–9 (central margin). This is evidently an additional scene which has been supplied in the Plot by another hand. The writer does not follow the same convention as the main scribe, as is shown by the repetition of 'Enter'. The last repetition is apparently an afterthought and refers to Eschines, who, since II. ii, has been disguised as Bellveile. There is no reason to suppose that the addition includes more than a single scene, or that it is not distinct from what follows. More doubtful is the question whether the scene is a later addition to the play, or had been accidentally omitted by the original compiler of the Plot. The union of the lovers under the auspices of Urganda, previous to their public appearance in V. iii, would not be a necessity of the action and might therefore be a later embroidery: at the same time it would offer a situation which a romantic playwright would be unlikely to forgo, and it seems on the whole more probable that we have to do with an accidental omission by the scribe.

50. 'wth his' was first written 'wthis' by mistake.

56. The 'a' in 'waye' not being very clear, the scribe repeated it above.

60. The phrase 'Enter to them' shows that this cannot properly be a new scene, and that the scribe was wrong in drawing a rule above it.

62. There seems no reason why the scribe should have written 'then' if he originally meant 'the'. Considering that the technical phraseology of this Plot is less crystallized than that of others, it looks as though he were about to use some such phrase as that in l. 23, and that it really implied 'Enter to them'. If so the action is again continuous, and the rule an error.

63. The deletion in this line is another indication that the scene division was uncertain hereabouts.

OUTSIDE OF THE PLOT, AS MOUNTED
*(much reduced)*

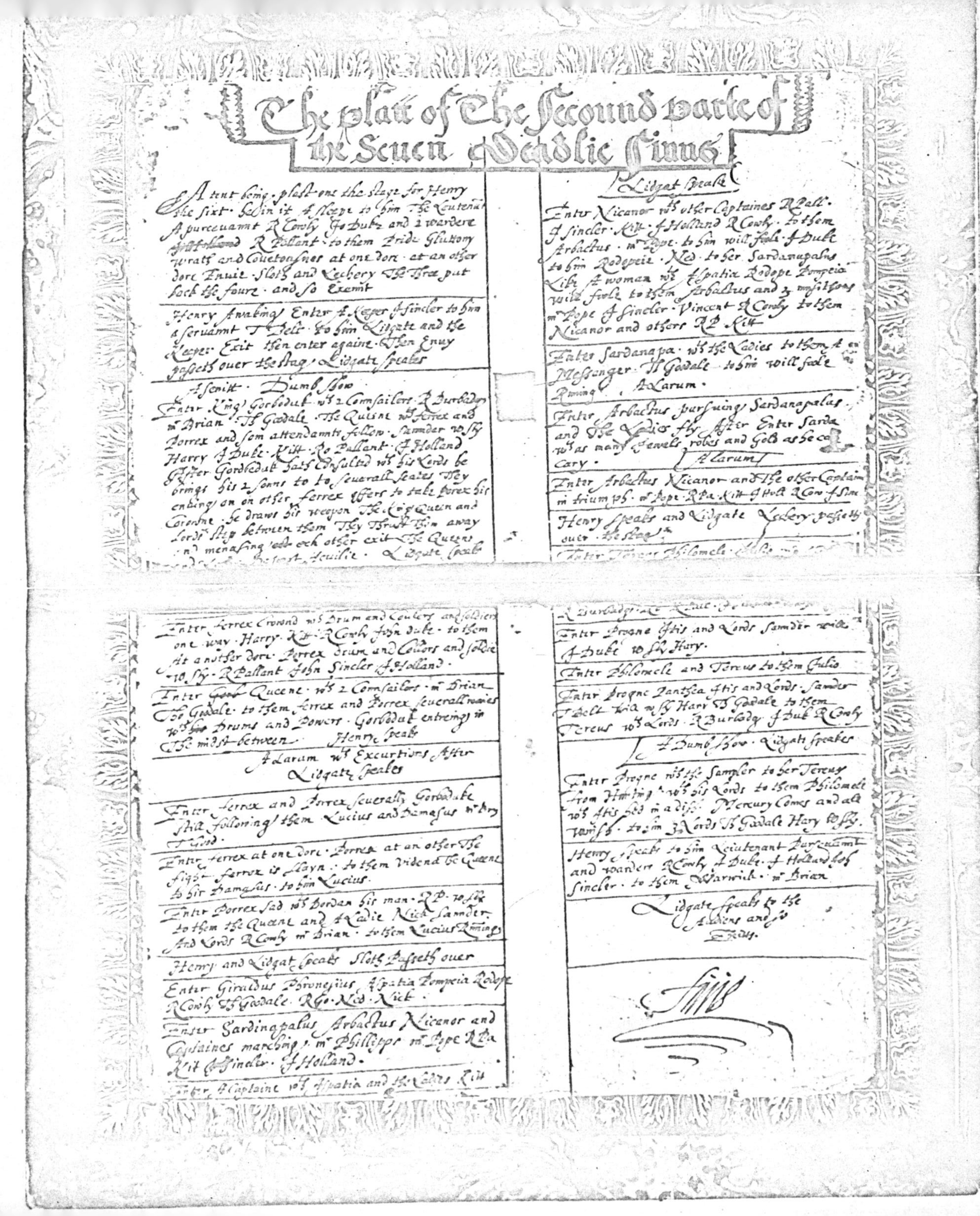

The platt of The secound parte of the Seuen Deadlie sinns

A tent being plast one the stage for Henry the sixt. he in it A sleepe to him The Leutenant A purceuaunt R Cowly Jo Duke and 1 wardere ~~Jo Holland~~ R Pallant. to them Pride. Gluttony wrath and Couetousnes at one dore. at an other dore Enuie. Sloth and Lechery The Three put back the foure. and so Exeunt

Henry Awaking Enter A Keeper J Sincler to him a seruaunt T Belt. to him Lidgate and the Keeper. Exit then enter againe. Then Envy passeth ouer the stag. Lidgate speakes

A senitt. Dumb show.
Enter King Gorboduk wth 2 Counsailers. R Burbadg mr Brian. Th Goodale. The Queene wth Ferrex and Porrex and som attendaunts follow. Saunder w Harry. J Duke. Kitt. Ro Pallant. J Holland. After Gordbeduk hath Consulted wth his Lords he brings his 2 sonns to to seuerall seates they enving on on other Ferrex offers to take Porrex his Corowne he draws his weapon The King Queen and Lords step between them They Thrust Them away and menasing ech other exit The Queene and Lords Depart Heauilie. Lidgate speaks

Enter Ferrex Crownd wth Drum and Coulers and soldiers one way. Harry. Kitt. R Cowly John duke. to them At a nother dore. Porrex drum and Collors and soldie w Sly. R Pallant John Sincler J Holland.

Enter Queene. wth 2 Counsailers. mr Brian Th Goodale. to them Ferrex and Porrex seuerall waies wth Drums and Powers. Gorboduk entreing in The midst between. Henry speaks

Alarum wth Excursions After Lidgate speakes

Enter Ferrex and Porrex seuerally Gorboduk still following them Lucius and Damasus mr Bry T Good.

Enter Ferrex at one dore. Porrex at an other The fight. Ferrex is slayn. to them Videna the Queene to hir Damasus. to him Lucius.

Enter Porrex sad wth Dordan his man. R P. w Sly. to them the Queene and A Ladie Nick Saunder. And Lords R Cowly mr Brian. to them Lucius Running

Henry and Lidgat speaks Sloth Passeth ouer

Enter Giraldus Phronesius Aspatia Pompeia Rodope R Cowly Th Goodale. R Go. Ned. Nick.

Enter Sardinapalus Arbactus Nicanor and Captaines marching. mr Phillipps mr Pope R Pa Kit J Sincler. J Holland.

Enter A Captaine wth Aspatia and the Ladies Kitt

Lidgat speake

Enter Nicanor wth other Captaines R Pall. J Sincler. Kitt. J Holland R Cowly. to them Arbactus. mr Pope. to him will foole J Duke to him Rodopeie. Ned. to her Sardanapalus Like A woman wth Aspatia Rodope Pompeia Will foole to them Arbactus and 3 musitions mr Pope J Sincler. Vincent R Cowly to them Nicanor and others R P. Kitt

Enter Sardanapa. wth the Ladies to them A Messenger. Th Goodale to him will foole Running. A Larum.

Enter Arbactus pursuing Sardanapalus and the Ladies fly. After Enter Sarda wth as many Jewels robes and Gold as he ca cary.
Alarum

Enter Arbactus Nicanor and The other Captains in triumph. mr Pope R Pa. Kitt J Holl R Cow J Sinc

Henry speaks and Lidgate Lechery passeth ouer the stag

Enter Tereus Philomele [illegible]

R Burbadg [illegible]

Enter Progne Itis and Lords Saunder Will. A Duke w Harry.

Enter Philomele and Tereus to them Julio

Enter Progne Panthea Itis and Lords. Saunder T Belt Will wth Harry Th Goodale to them Tereus wth Lords. R Burbadg J Duk R Cowly

A Dumb show. Lidgate speakes

Enter Progne wth the Sampler to her Tereus from Hunting wth his Lords to them Philomele wth Itis hed in a dish. Mercury Comes and all vanish. to him 3 Lords Th Goodale Hary w Sly.

Henry speaks to him Leiutenant Pursuevant and warders R Cowly J Duke. J Holland Iohn Sincler. to them Warwick. mr Brian

Lidgate speaks to the Audiens and so Exits.

PLOT OF 2 SEVEN DEADLY SINS, AS MOUNTED

*(much reduced)*

*Preservation.*—The earliest description of this document we possess is that given by Steevens, who writes (flourishes apart): 'This singular curiosity was met with in the library of Dulwich college . . . The *Platt* (for so it is called) is fairly written out on pasteboard in a large hand . . . It has an oblong hole in its centre, sufficient to admit a wooden peg; and has been converted into a cover for an anonymous manuscript play entitled *The Tell-tale*. From this cover I made the preceding transcript...On the outside of the cover is written, "The *Book* and Platt, &c."' (see p. 8, note).

I see no reason to doubt this account, and conclude that when Steevens saw the document at Dulwich, at some unspecified date before 1780, the sheet of paper on which the Plot was written was still mounted on its original thin board (such as survives in *The Dead Man's Fortune* and *Frederick and Basilea*), that this was backed by another sheet of paper on which was written the inscription he records, that the whole was folded across the middle, and that within the case so formed were laid, or perhaps lightly sewn, the sheets of *The Telltale*. There can be no question of any more substantial binding being involved, since in that case the Plot must have suffered far more than it has. It is also evident from the note on the back that the Plot was originally accompanied, not by the seventeenth-century *Telltale*, but by the Book of *The Seven Deadly Sins* itself.

It is, however, a mistake to suppose—as I am afraid I, and perhaps others, have done—that the sort of elaborate 'folder' to the inside of which the Plot is now attached is the cover of *The Telltale* described by Steevens, or that the stout boards of which it consists formed that of the original document. This is evident from the facts, that the boards are some four inches too large for the Plot (or for the sheets of *The Telltale* or any other known theatrical Book), that the peg-hole goes through the paper only and not the board, and that the edges of the Plot show extensive worm-holes that leave the boards unaffected. Clearly the document has been remounted by some one who realized that it had no connexion with *The Telltale*, presumably after Steevens wrote his description. It is significant that the Plot and the play formed separate items in the Boswell sale.

Whoever was responsible for the remounting took some care to preserve the character of the document. Not only was the inscription on the back replaced, but its chance use as a 'folder' was rather misleadingly imitated. The mounter took a large stout board, round the edge on one side of which he pasted (or found pasted) a strip of curious engraved pattern forming a sort of frame. This board he cut in two, and pasted the two halves of the Plot, stripped from its original card, one on each half of the same. He then jointed the two halves together with a strip of thin red morocco, so as to resemble the cover of a book, lining this back with a narrow strip of thicker brown leather. On the red he lettered in gold the title:

THE PLATT OF THE SECOUND PARTE OF THE SEUEN DEADLIE SINNS

Next on the outside of one of the halves he pasted a label, apparently cut from the back sheet of the original document, and bearing the inscription:

*The Booke and Platt of the ſecond*
*part of The ·7 deadly ſinns*

This is written in the same Italian hand as the Plot itself but larger.[1] Lastly he covered the outside of the boards with marbled paper, turning this over the edges and cutting a hole in it to show the label. It is possible that having done this he replaced in the 'folder' the sheets of *The Telltale*. These have in recent times been bound as a separate volume; but with them, as fol. 1, is a leaf of different paper which clearly does not belong. I conjecture that it formed one half of the original back sheet of the Plot, for it is much discoloured. It too bears an inscription, again in the same hand:

*The Booke and platt of the*
*ſecond part of the 7 deadly ſinns*

[1] The label now also bears the number '3136', and again, deleted and in a different hand, '1135'. The former is that of the 'lot' in the Boswell sale. The latter I am unable to interpret. It may be a preliminary number affixed in the course of cataloguing. It does not refer either to the Steevens or Heber sale.

INSCRIPTION ON THE ORIGINAL BACK SHEET OF THE PLOT

In order to make this account of the document as clear as possible reduced facsimiles have been provided showing the outer and inner sides of the folder exactly as they now appear, and also a facsimile of the inscription from the first leaf of *The Telltale*.

*Identification.*—That there was a 'play the seven deadly sins' written by the famous comic actor Richard Tarlton is known from contemporary allusions. Gabriel Harvey, in his *Four Letters* of 1592 (ed. Grosart, i. 194), describes Nashe's forthcoming *Pierce Peniless* ironically as follows:

> A strange title, an od wit, and a mad hooreson, I warrant him: doubtles it wil proue some dainty deuise, queintly contriued, by way of humble Supplication To the high, and mighty Prince of Darkenesse: not Dunsically botched-vp, but right-formally cōueied, according to the stile, and tenour of Tarletons president, his famous play of the seauen Deadly sinnes: which most-dea[d]ly, but most liuely playe, I might haue seene in London: and was verie gently inuited thereunto at Oxford, by *Tarleton* himselfe, of whome I merrily demaunding, which of the seauen, was his owne deadlie sinne, he bluntly aunswered after this manner: By God, the sinne of other Gentlemen, Lechery.

To this attack Thomas Nashe replied the same year in his *Strange News of the Intercepting of certain Letters* (ed. McKerrow, i. 304) in which he addresses Harvey thus:

> Hang thee, hang thee, thou common coosener of curteous readers, thou grosse shifter for shitten tapsterly iests, haue I *imitated* Tarltons *play of the seauen deadly sinnes in my plot* of *Pierce Penilesse?* ... [and again, pp. 318–9] Wherein haue I borrowed from *Greene* or *Tarlton, that I should thanke them for all I haue?* Is my stile like *Greenes*, or my ieasts like *Tarltons?* ... This I will proudly boast ... that the vaine which I haue ... is of my owne begetting, and cals no man father in England but my selfe, neyther *Euphues*, nor *Tarlton*, nor *Greene*. Not *Tarlton* nor *Greene* but haue beene contented to let my simple iudgement ouerrule them in some matters of wit.

The account of the subsequent fortunes of this play that has hitherto been accepted is in fact a very ingenious theory designed by Fleay to embrace and interpret several disconnected but possibly interrelated items of evidence. Tarlton was of course a leading member of the Queen's company when these men were at the height of their fortunes, and there can be little doubt that it was they who originally performed his *Seven Deadly Sins*. Now in the accounts of the Revels Office for 1584–5 there are two entries respecting this company which run as follows (ed. Feuillerat, *Revels of Elizabeth*, p. 365):

An Inuention called ffiue playes in one presented and enacted before her maiestie on Twelfe daie at nighte in the hall at Grenewiche by her highnes servauntes wheron was ymployed a greate cloth and a battlement of canvas and canvas for a well and a mounte .xv ells of sarcenet .ix yardes of sullen cloth of gold purple.

An Inuention of three playes in one prepared to haue ben shewed before her highnes on Shroue sondaye at night and to haue ben enacted by her maiesties servauntes at Somerset place. But the Quene came not abroad that night. yet was ymployed on the same one howse & a battlement.

Next, among the plays recorded by Henslowe as performed by Strange's men at his theatre, the Rose on Bankside, and under date of 6 Mar. 1592, is a piece called 'iiij playes in one'. It was not a new play, the takings were moderate, and the performance was not repeated. But the Rose had probably been in use as a theatre before Henslowe's extant accounts begin on 19 Feb. 1592, and although we lack any definite evidence it is quite possible that Strange's men were acting there the previous year, and may then also have performed the play described as *Four Plays in One*. Lastly, we have the Plot of the piece called the Second Part of *The Seven Deadly Sins*, many of the actors in which must certainly have been with the company that Henslowe calls 'my lord stranges mene' in 1592, and which consists of three Sin plays set in an historical framework, thus perhaps deserving the title of *Four Plays in One*.

The suggestion is that Tarlton's play was written in two parts, that Part I, consisting of the historical induction and four Sin plays, was acted under the name of *Five Plays in One*, while Part II, consisting of the remaining three Sin plays, was acted as *Three Plays in One*; further, that after Tarlton's death and the collapse of the Queen's company the play was acquired by Strange's men, and that these tacked the historical induction onto the Second Part, making it *Four Plays in One*; and lastly,

that it was for the performance of 6 Mar. 1592 that the extant Plot was prepared.

Fleay advanced several successive and slightly variant versions of this theory, but it was most fully expounded in 1890 in his *History of the Stage*, where he writes as follows (p. 83: cf. p. 67, also *Shakespeare*, pp. 23, 264, 296, and *Biographical Chronicle*, ii. 259):

> The composition of this company [Strange's] is so interesting, as being Shakespeare's company, that I give here in greater fulness than it would otherwise deserve an account of the plot of Tarleton's Seven Deadly Sins (second part), preserved at Dulwich and acted by them (as is evident from the names of the actors, which contain none of the Queen's players, and nearly all of Lord Strange's known to us) while they were under Alleyn, *i.e.*, before 1594. As the only play in the Lord Strange's list in Henslow which can be identified with this one is that of the Four Plays in One, which name suits it admirably (there are three sin plays and an induction in the plot), and as this identification so perfectly agrees with the names of the plays acted at Court under Tarleton himself by the Queen's men in 1585, viz., Five Plays in One for the first part (four sin plays and induction), and Three Plays in One (the three other sin plays), I venture to assume 1592, March 6, as the exact date for this performance. I cannot, in any case, be far wrong. In my 'Life of Shakespeare' I said about 1594. It must have been after Tarleton's death in 1588, and before Alleyn left the company in 1594, as the plot belonged to him.

This account of the matter I accepted *in toto* in my edition of Henslowe's diary (1904–8, ii. 153), and Sir Edmund Chambers still regarded it as generally 'plausible' in his *Elizabethan Stage* (1923, iii. 497). It is still possible that it represents in the main an accurate interpretation of the facts, but a closer examination has knocked away one of the principle supports of the theory, and it will be necessary to scrutinize this very carefully to ascertain how much remains sound.

In spite of the different companies involved there seems no sufficient ground to question that the Plot does belong to the actual play ascribed by Harvey and Nashe to Tarlton, for other pieces (e.g. *Friar Bacon* and perhaps *Orlando Furioso*) are known to have passed from the Queen's men to Strange's. If this be granted it follows that Tarlton's play was in two parts, and further that it possessed an historical framework that would necessitate a fairly elaborate induction. The piece, therefore, contained eight distinct items, and it becomes quite reasonable to suppose that the two parts were known respectively as *Five Plays in One* and *Three Plays in One*. The only objection is that the natural division of eight items would be into two pieces of 'Four Plays' each. But this anomaly is adequately explained by an examination of the extant Plot of Part II. In this we have three Sin plays, but two of these are clearly divided into two sections each, evidently with the object of providing a five-act play. Thus we actually find the Second Part consisting of a five-act piece containing 'Three Plays in One'. This leaves four Sin plays and an induction to furnish as the First Part a 'Five Plays in One' again in five acts or sections. The fact that the extant Plot explains so neatly the apparent anomaly of the division goes some way at least towards proving that the two pieces acted, or prepared for acting, at Court in 1585 were indeed the two parts of *The Seven Deadly Sins*. At the same time the plausibility of the identification has no doubt rested in part upon the further identification of the *Four Plays in One* of 1592 with the piece for which the Plot was prepared, and this is just the point at which a closer analysis has made a breach in the theory propounded by Fleay.

The first attack was delivered by Sir Edmund Chambers and its objective was the date of the Plot. It is admitted that the fact that the Plot came into the hands of Edward Alleyn proves that it must have been in existence by the spring of 1594. But from 1592 (perhaps 1591) on, Strange's men (for whom alone it can at that date have been prepared) were acting, when in London, exclusively at Henslowe's house, the Rose on Bankside. Now it is almost inconceivable that Richard Burbage, whose name occurs in the Plot, should have been acting during these years at any other house than that of his father, the Theatre in Shoreditch (or possibly at the Curtain, which was being used as an 'easer' under a pooling agreement), especially as the winter of 1590–1 had seen a violent quarrel between James Burbage and the Admiral's men, then occupying the Theatre, and that the Admiral's leader, Alleyn, was now leading

Strange's, even if there was not (as there may have been) some more extensive fusion of the two companies. The only period before 1594, therefore, at which Richard Burbage can legitimately be supposed to have been acting in company with the men whose names appear in the Plot is before the quarrel of 1590–1, when they were performing, either in conjunction with the Admiral's at the Theatre, or (as I think more probable) at the associated and neighbouring Curtain. Sir Edmund's own words are as follows (*Elizabethan Stage*, ii. 307):

> It is a little . . . difficult to suppose that at a date when the Queen's men were still active [sc. *c.* 1590] the Admiral's or Strange's had already acquired Tarlton's *Seven Deadly Sins*, in the 'plot' of which 'R. Burbadg' is cast for the important characters of Gorboduc and Tereus. But perhaps it is even less probable that, after the breach of the Admiral's with his father in 1591, he took part in the performance of the same play by the amalgamated Admiral's and Strange's men at the Rose in 1592.

Elsewhere he puts the argument somewhat differently (ii. 125) by saying that the Queen's men

> are not very likely to have parted with it before Tarlton's death in 1588 brought the first shock to their fortunes, but clearly it may have come into the possession of Strange's or the Admiral's or the combined company before ever they reached the Rose. And surely the appearance of Richard Burbadge suggests that the 'plott' was brought from the Theatre, and represents a performance there. He is very unlikely to have joined at the Rose the company which had just been driven there by a quarrel with his father.

This, I think, disposes of the suggestion that the extant Plot was prepared for the performance of *Four Plays in One* on 6 Mar. 1592 recorded by Henslowe. It is, indeed, on the face of it unlikely, for that single unsuccessful performance of an old play rather suggests the casual trial of a stock piece than the sort of formal revival for which a fresh Plot would be prepared. But the possibility of course remains that *Four Plays in One* was the play for which the Plot was prepared, not on the occasion of the performance of 1592, but when it first came into the hands of the company, say in 1590.

It is when we come to examine the Plot in detail that this assumption begins to look rather thin. The suggestion is that we have in the Plot, with its three Sin plays, the original Second

Part of Tarlton's piece together with the historical induction borrowed from Part I, making in all 'Four Plays in One'. Now in the first place this would have made a rather long play, for as we have seen the three Sin plays are so arranged as to provide five acts, and the induction must *ex hypothesi* have been of the dimensions of an act itself. There may, of course, have been reasons of popularity for the selection of the particular Sin plays chosen, but on general grounds we should have expected such a selection as would have provided five acts including the induction. Be this as it may, it will be well to look closer at the actual evidence supplied by the Plot. It is at once obvious that the historical framework was not confined to the induction, but that it formed a setting to the whole performance. The final scene and epilogue (XXIII, XXIV) therefore are the original close of the Second Part, while the interludes (IX, XVII) likewise belong. It is, then, to the first two scenes (I, II) that we must look for the induction borrowed from Part I. Some sort of introduction to the Second Part, comparable at least to the interludes between the Sin plays, there must of course always have been. But the second scene is just such an introduction, with Envy passing over the stage, and must have always belonged to Part II. Moreover, in the first scene the seven Deadly Sins appear in two parties and 'The Three put back the foure'—obviously because they have had their innings in Part I. This scene, then, likewise belongs to the Second Part and not the First. Also, if the induction could be treated as a 'play' by itself, we should expect to find it in structure comparable to one of the shorter Sin plays, say four to six scenes, and to find it reflecting the evils of Henry's reign as a pointed introduction to the Sins, and likewise the tragedy of Henry's earlier life. Instead the Plot opens with Henry already in the Tower. Surely, then, it is evident that we have in the Plot nothing but what it purports to be, namely the Second Part of *The Seven Deadly Sins*, that is presumably the original *Three Plays in One*. It would hardly have occurred to any one to question this had it not been for the red herring of the *Four Plays in One* that Fleay drew across the trail.

It remains, of course, abstractly possible that the *Four Plays*

*in One* as performed in 1592 represented some shuffling of the old 'Five Plays' and 'Three Plays', but all confirmatory evidence of the suggestion has vanished.[1]

The upshot of our inquiry is, then, that we have in the Plot nothing but the Second Part of *The Seven Deadly Sins* as originally designed by Tarlton, performed by another company between his death in Sept. 1588 and the spring of 1591 at one of the houses controlled by James Burbage. I have given elsewhere (p. 19) my reasons for ascribing it to Strange's men at the Curtain probably in 1590.

*Structure of the Play.*—The piece consists of three plays or episodes illustrating the sins of Envy, Sloth, and Lechery, in the stories respectively of Ferrex and Porrex, Sardanapalus, and Tereus, set in an historical framework dealing with an episode of the reign of Henry VI. This framework comprises the two introductory scenes (divisions I and II as marked in the transcript), the conclusion and epilogue (XXIII and XXIV), and the two interludes that separate the Sin plays (IX and XVII). The first Sin play begins and the last ends with a dumb-show to which Lydgate (a framework character) acts as expositor (ll. 25, 80). But it will be observed that Henry and Lydgate also break into the middle of the first Sin play (ll. 33–5) and Lydgate into the middle of the second (l. 52). This serves to divide the first and second Sin plays into two acts each, while the third is undivided; so that the three Sin plays together constitute five acts. A glance at the tabular analysis will, I hope, make this structure plain. Evidently Henry and Lydgate remain present as spectators throughout, commenting at appropriate points on the action of the Sin plays.

The framework deserves rather closer attention. The mention of a 'wardere' (l. 5) and 'Keeper' (l. 10)[2] shows that

[1] The identification of 2 *Seven Deadly Sins* with Henslowe's *Four Plays in One* was attacked by Mr. R. Crompton Rhodes in *The Times Literary Supplement* on 23 Oct. 1919, and defended by me. The arguments he advanced do not appear to me to carry weight, but I now believe that his conclusion was correct.

[2] This Keeper has, of course, nothing to do with the Keepers in Shakespeare's 3 *Henry VI* (III. i. 1).

Henry is already in captivity when the play opens, and 'The Leutenãt' is clearly the Lieutenant of the Tower, where the scene is therefore laid. The appearance of Warwick at the end (l. 87) proves that it is Henry's first captivity, from which he was released by the King-Maker's espousal of his cause in Oct. 1470. Actually, it would seem, it was not Warwick himself but his brother Archbishop Neville who, with Bishop Waynflete of Winchester, went to the Tower to effect his liberation on 5 Oct., but Hollinshed follows Hall in representing it as Warwick's own act, as dramatic effect demands, and is naturally followed both by Tarlton and Shakespeare (3 *Henry VI*, IV. vi). Lydgate's participation is eminently unhistorical, for he had been dead some twenty years, but as the narrator of the 'Falls of Princes' is not inappropriate.[1]

But if in the first scene Henry is already in the Tower, what is the meaning of the 'tent' that is 'plast one the stage' for him? I conjecture that Henry, who is asleep throughout the scene, is represented as dreaming that he is still encamped on the field of battle, and sees in dream the contention of the seven Sins. If so the setting probably reflects that at the beginning of the First Part, representing Henry actually so encamped and meditating the evils of the time, previous to his capture. It is possible that the occasion represented was the battle of Northampton, when he first fell into Warwick's hands, the subsequent events between 1460 and 1465 being ignored, or possibly that of Hexham on 15 May 1464, the year before his capture in Ribblesdale.

*Characteristics.*—It is natural to suppose that this Plot was produced subsequently to *The Dead Man's Fortune* or in different circumstances, since in it we find for the first time a developed technique that later examples did not materially modify. We have here the ornamented heading, the elegant Italian script, the ample record of actors, and the grasp of method, that became distinguishing features of these docu-

[1] Of the stories included in the play, however, only that of Sardanapalus is told by Lydgate, and there is no particular reason to suppose that his slight account was used by Tarlton.

ments. We also find the prefix 'Mr.' given, and given consistently, to three of the principal actors.

The structure of the play renders the divisions of the Plot rather complicated, but except in one minor matter the scribe has dealt quite competently with the problem. He has not attempted any formal division into acts, and we may suppose that none was marked in the Book, clearly as it reveals itself in the structure of the piece. On the other hand, the division into scenes is, so far as we are able to judge, perfectly normal and regular, though in the absence of final exits (except at ll. 9, 90) it is perhaps not possible to be certain (internal exits are marked at ll. 12, 24, 84, and implied at ll. 11, 41, 58, 60, 65). The interludes (IX and XVII) are also correctly marked off. The point at which the scribe bungled was in his treatment of the choruses that separate the acts of the first two Sin plays. In the case of the second (l. 52) he merely marked off the words 'Lydgat speake' like a stage-direction (as he did at ll. 67 and 80) without separating it from the ensuing scene (XIII). The earlier case (ll. 33–5) was rather more complicated, since the chorus was mixed up with a stage-direction, 'A Larum w^th^ Excurtions', belonging to the play. This direction, together with 'After Lydgate speakes', he marked off as if it were a separate scene (after the manner of the interludes), but he nevertheless placed 'Henry speakes' as part of the preceding scene (V). In arranging the tabular analysis I have treated the whole of this chorus as part of V (regarding the rule between lines 33 and 34 as an error), and the later chorus of course as part of XIII.

In general it was evidently the scribe's intention to record the actors who filled the various parts. This was of course particularly important in such a piece as the present, which comprised several distinct plays and in which consequently there was much doubling. That this was, indeed, the ruling consideration is suggested by the fact that for Henry and Lydgate, the two characters present throughout and therefore incapable of doubling, no actors are specified. But it is curious that neither are any actors assigned for what were presumably mute parts, the seven Sins and Mercury in the last dumb-show (XXII). Whether this implies that these parts were not taken by regular members of the cast but by special performers is not certain (cf. under *Casting*). Within the limits of each play the scribe does not necessarily mention the actor every time a character enters, though he tends to do so at any rate for the minor parts. A result of this frequent repetition is that the names of actors are often abbreviated even to the point of obscurity (see e.g. ll. 69, 73), a feature that is peculiar to the present Plot. Another result is that where characters enter in pairs the scribe is indifferent whether he gives the actors' names in the correct order or not. The point was to get the actors onto the stage at the proper point, they were in no danger of interchanging parts: it is only for us that the scribe's carelessness is occasionally embarrassing. Only once can any definite error be detected, namely in XIII where it would seem that a name has been entered in error (apparently 'Rodope' in l. 57). As a rule the characters are what may be called 'massed': that is, the scribe does not assign each actor to his part individually, but gives first a list of all the characters entering together and follows this up by a list of the corresponding actors in the order (more or less) of their parts. This practice may be seen in X, XVI, XIX; on the other hand, some attempt at discriminating different groups is observable in ll. 5–6, 15–8.

The properties mentioned are not very numerous, and are confined to the text, no use being made of the margins. They comprise a tent (apparently, I), seats and a crown (III), drums and colours (IV, V), jewels, robes, and gold (XV), a sampler and a head in a dish (XXII). Stage noises are similarly indicated: 'A senitt' (III), 'A larum w$^{th}$ Excurtions' (V), 'A Larum' (XIV), 'A larum' (XV). Although '3 musitions' appear in XIII, there is no direction for music.

The influence of the wording of the Book is very evident in the descriptive style of the two dumb-shows (III and XXII), particularly in such phrases as 'The Queene and Lords Depart Heuilie' and 'Mercury Comes and all Vanish', which must be direct transcripts. The first scene too must have been largely and may have been entirely dumb-show, and here too the style is descriptive: 'A tent being plast one the stage for Henry the sixt · he in it A sleepe . . . The Three put back the foure · and

so Exeunt' (the significance of the tent is discussed in the notes and under *Structure*). There are expressions of telltale vagueness, such as 'som attendaunts follow' (l. 17) and 'others' (ll. 60 and 72?). Significant, too, is the direction 'w^th^ as many Iewels robes and Gold as he can cary' (ll. 66–7) which has a distinctly literary flavour, and the phrase 'still following them' (l. 37) which can have no theatrical significance. Minor traces of the Book remain throughout and rather increase towards the end: particularly noticeable is 'one way . . . At a nother dore' (ll. 27–8), also 'Ruñing' (l. 44), 'marching' (l. 49), 'Runing' (l. 63), 'pursuing' (l. 64), 'in triumph' (l. 69).

*Casting*.—No actors are specified for the parts of Henry and Lydgate, presumably because no question of doubling can arise. Neither are we told who play the seven Sins, apparently mutes, or Mercury in the last dumb-show. This might mean that the parts were taken by supernumeraries not in the regular cast: at the same time it is difficult to believe that eight special performers were called in when the roles could easily have been filled by doubling. The natural thing to do would have been to use the six boys and two of the minor men of the company, and there is some evidence (discussed in the notes, l. 5) that this was what was in fact done. I have made no attempt to assign the parts in the table, but the following distribution would present no difficulty: Pride, Saunder; Glutony, Holland, Wrath, Nick; Covetousness, Gough; Envy, Will; Sloth, Kit; Lechery, Ned; Mercury, Belt.[1]

Over the characters for whom actors are specified no very serious difficulty arises, and minor points are discussed in the notes. Uncertainty over the extent of the error in XIII throws some doubt on the impersonators of Rhodope and Pompeia (see note on l. 56), and the loose use of the term 'the Ladies'

[1] Sir Edmund Chambers has made the very ingenious suggestion that the reason why no actors are specified for Henry, Lydgate, and the Sins is that these characters had, of course, already appeared in Part I, and had therefore been already duly assigned. But this does not account for Mercury, nor does it seem to me likely that a scribe so given to repetition within the Plot would have refrained from assigning actors because to do so involved repetition from another Plot.

introduces a slight ambiguity in l. 61. The other instances of inversion and looseness (e.g. 'others') are easily dealt with.

Three actors have the prefix 'Mr.', which, whatever its technical significance, certainly designates an important member of the company. It is, therefore, worth observing that of the three only one, Bryan, appears near the beginning, Phillips and Pope being reserved for the third act. It may have been desirable to have some authoritative person free to keep an eye on the gatherers at the beginning of a performance. Henry and Lydgate are, of course, important parts, and had the actors for them been named they would very likely have had the honorific 'Mr.'. They remain present throughout, but in the table I have only marked their presence in those sections in which they have speaking parts.

## *Notes*

1. 'Platt'. This is the only Plot that spells the word in this way, but it may have appeared so in the mutilated heading to 2 *Fortune's Tennis* which was written by the same scribe. The spelling 'Plot' is correct, the form 'Plat' being due to confusion (see p. 1, n. 1).

3. 'A tent being plast one the stage'. This is a very curious description, since, as appears almost certainly from l. 12, the stage was provided with a balcony and would therefore have an alcove beneath which would naturally be used to represent the tent. It may possibly be a relic copied from the original Book prepared for performance upon a stage of a more primitive type.

5. 'i wardere', altered from '2 warders'. No doubt the Book demanded Warders and the scribe originally allotted two. The alteration was evidently made because it was found that for some reason Holland was not available. He may have been required to act one of the Sins (see under *Casting*).

8–9. 'The Three put back the foure', obviously because the latter had already performed their turns in the First Part.

9. 'Exeunt'. Of course Henry remains on the stage asleep in the tent, so that the stage is not strictly clear between the two scenes. But since Henry is in fact present throughout the play the scribe neglects him as regards scene division even in this introductory section.

10. 'to him'. This is anomalous if, as seems likely, both Henry and the Keeper are on the stage. It may mean that the Servant enters and speaks apart to the Keeper.

11. 'to him', i.e. to Henry. This may be strictly accurate, for the Servant probably went off at once, and so did the Keeper, since he re-enters at l. 12.

12. 'Exit then enter againe'. No character being specified the 'Exit' probably applies to all three, Henry, Lydgate, and the Keeper; the 'enter' perhaps only to Henry and Lydgate. The phrase is an unusual one, and must have some special significance here; for, except in the dumb-shows (ll. 24, 84), internal exits are never marked elsewhere, though often implied (ll. 11, 41, 58, 60, 65). There can be little doubt that at this point Henry and Lydgate leave the main stage and ascend to the balcony, whence they watch as chorus the action of the Sin plays, descending presumably once more in the last scene (XXIII). Notice that each of the Sins in turn is directed to pass over the 'stag' before the play intended to illustrate its effects, while no doubt Lydgate utters appropriate sentiments above.

15. '2 Counsailers'. The identity of the actors makes it almost certain that these (who reappear in V) are the Lucius and Damasus of VI (in spite of the unseemliness of a counsellor running, l. 44) and that Damasus is included among the 'Lords' in VIII. I have assumed this in the table.

16. 'The Queene'. Her name is correctly given as Videna in l. 40.

16–8. 'ferrex and Porrex . . . w sly Harry'. It is clear from IV, where they enter separately, that the actors' names are here given in the wrong order. Sly played Porrex.

17. 'som attendaunts'. The indefinite 'som' is presumably copied from the Book; four are provided.

19. 'After'. 'A' altered presumably from 'G' (or possibly 'C').
'Gordbeduk', *sic*, elsewhere correctly called 'Gorboduk' (ll. 15, &c.).
'his Lords', i.e. the two Counsellors of l. 15 (cf. l. 44).

20. 'to to', probably for 'to two'.

21. 'on on', probably for 'one an'.

25. There is little doubt of the reading 'Lords' though the paper is damaged. Below this line two rules are drawn; one is original and is now partly lost, the other is modern, having been drawn to replace the earlier one after the Plot had been divided and mounted on its present boards.

26. 'Drum and Coulers and soldiers', cf. l. 28. In each case three actors are allowed. Since in both *Alcazar* (ll. 79, 103) and *Tamar Cam* (l. 103) Drum and Colours seem to be properties, no actors being assigned, I have assumed the meaning here to be 'soldiers bearing Drom and Coulers', and have so treated it in the table. At the same time it is

possible that 'Drom and Coulers' indicates a character (supposing one could carry both which is perhaps unlikely) and that two 'soldiers' accompany him: we are not at liberty to make 'Drom' and 'Coulers' separate characters.

27. 'one way'. This is presumably a relic of the Book: we get the strict theatrical term 'At a nother dore' in the next line.

28. 'soldie[rs]'. The scribe is somewhat given to abbreviations, especially when cramped for room.

32. 'Drums and Powers', of course their soldiers as in IV.

33. Of course 'Henry speaks' between the acts like Lydgate; there should be no rule.

34. 'Excurtions' presumably means stage fighting, or perhaps the noise of fighting behind the scenes. It is possible therefore to interpret this line as meaning 'Alarum followed by Excursions'. But it seems more natural to take 'After' with what follows, in the sense of 'after which' (cf. l. 65).

37–8. 'Lucius and Damasus m^r Bry[an] T Good[ale]'. Again the order of the names has been inverted. From l. 44 it is clear that Bryan cannot have played Lucius, since he was already on the stage when that character entered. These names do not occur in Sackville and Norton's play.

39–40. 'The fight'. On the whole it seems most likely that 'The' is a slip for 'They'.

40. 'Videna'. Since no actor is assigned this must be the name of the Queen (who has already appeared) as it is in Sackville and Norton. Geoffrey of Monmouth gives the name as Widen and so does Grafton. The *Brut* calls her Ydoyne: she is not named in the brief summary in Holinshed (which besides Geoffrey cites the *Polychronicon* and Matthew of Westminster). Unless some more immediate source than Geoffrey should be found for Sackville and Norton, we must suppose that their work was known to Tarlton (cf. l. 42).

41. 'to hir' implies that Porrex has gone off; 'to him' shows that the Queen has.

42. 'Dordan' appears in Sackville and Norton as 'a counsellor assigned by the king to his eldest sonne, Ferrex'.

'R P' is, of course, Pallant; but the actors are inverted, Sly acted Porrex (see note on ll. 16–8).

43. 'Nick saunder'. Another inversion, Saunder played the Queen (see ll. 16–7).

44. The 'Lord' whom Bryan played was presumably Damasus (see l. 15); what follows proves that he did not play Lucius (cf. ll. 37–8).

possible that Thom and Gorboe's indulgence [illegible] character (supposing one [illegible] born which is perhaps unlikely) and [illegible] [illegible] necessary that we are not as likely to make Thom and [illegible] separate characters.

[illegible] This is presumably [illegible] of the Book, we see the [illegible] [illegible] [illegible] [illegible] [illegible] lines.

[illegible] The scribe is somewhat given to abbreviations, [illegible] [illegible]

[illegible] [illegible] [illegible] [illegible]

[illegible] [illegible] [illegible] [illegible] [illegible] like Lydgate; there [illegible]

[illegible] (presumably [illegible] or perhaps the noise [illegible] the scene). [illegible] interpret this [illegible] Murus followed [illegible] but it seems more [illegible] [illegible] which [illegible]

[illegible] Damasco [illegible] [illegible] the order of the names has been [illegible] it is clear that [illegible] played Lucius [illegible] of the [illegible] when that character enters. These [illegible] do not occur in Sackville and Norton's play.

[illegible] On the whole it seems most likely that 'The' is a [illegible] for 'Thee'.

[illegible] [illegible] be the name of the [illegible] Sackville and Norton, [illegible] [illegible] and so does Grafton [illegible] the [illegible] summary [illegible] (which [illegible] Geoffrey [illegible] and [illegible] Unless some more [illegible] source than [illegible] found [illegible] Sackville and Norton, we must suppose [illegible]

[illegible] shows that the [illegible]

[illegible] Sackville and Norton [illegible] counsellor assigned [illegible] Remus [illegible]

[illegible] Tallbott [illegible] By [illegible]

[illegible] [illegible] Queen [illegible]

[illegible] played was presumably Damascus [illegible] [illegible] that he did not play Lucius [illegible]

46. 'Giraldus' is not a possible classic name and shows that the author was relying on his imagination for the minor characters, or drawing on some modern source (cf. l. 76); in fact all five are inventions.

47. 'R Go'. Presumably the same actor who is subsequently referred to as 'Ro' (l. 73) and to be identified with Robert Gough.

'Ned · Nick'. In view of l. 56 I have assumed that these names are inverted and that Ned played Rhodope. But the evident corruption in XIII prevents the conclusion being certain.

48. 'Sardinapalus Arbactus'. These alone of the character names in Sloth belong to history (or legend), and the form 'Arbactus' for 'Arbaces' shows that the ultimate source is Justin. Lydgate has the form 'Arbachus' (ed. Bergen, E.E.T.S., 1924, Pynson, 1494, 1527; 'Arbacus', Tottell, 1554) but it had become 'Arbactus' in Wayland's edition, *c.* 1555.

48–9. 'Arbactus . . . m^r Pope'. Pope had a reputation as a clown, but Arbactus cannot possibly have been even a comic character, and it is noteworthy that Will Fool, the clown, is played by Duke.

'Nicanor', played by 'R Pa[llant]', is one of the captains, as appears from l. 53.

51. 'the Ladies'. Since no actors are assigned these must be Pompeia and Rhodope as in l. 46 (cf. l. 61).

'Kitt', added as an afterthought to show which captain is intended.

55. 'will foole · I Duke', presumably a jester. Observe that the name of the character is not taken from that of the actor: but of course this is not the original cast. Duke is not otherwise known as a clown, and the minor parts he plays elsewhere are not comic.

56. 'Rodopeie · Ned'. This seems to settle the actors for Rhodope and Pompeia (see l. 47). At the same time the spelling suggests a possible confusion between the two. In any case there is an error of some sort, since, whichever lady is intended, she is subsequently made to enter to herself. I conjecture that one of the names in l. 57 has been inserted by mistake. The phrase 'to her' shows that Will Fool has gone off, but he re-enters immediately.

58. '3 musitions', altered from '2 musithons'. Two of these are doubled with captains earlier in the scene. This is unusual, but cf. *Alcazar*, I. ii. The doubling is possible because all the characters except Arbactus go off at l. 55, as is shown by the phrase 'to him'. Hence too the re-entry of Nicanor (l. 60). Arbactus also goes off at the end of l. 55 (see 'to him' in l. 56) and re-enters at l. 58.

59. Since 'Vincent' does not elsewhere appear, one would suppose that he was a regular musician. If he was Thomas Vincent he was sub-

sequently the prompter at the Globe, but it would be risky to suppose that he held that position earlier, since the prompter is the one person who could not appear as a 'super'.

60. 'others' seems to be a relic of the vague stage-directions of the Book. No doubt the 'other Captaines' of l. 53 are meant. But 'R P[allant]' played Nicanor, so only Kitt is left for the 'others'. However, Holland (cf. l. 56) is available, and his name may have been accidentally omitted.

61. 'the Ladies' who enter with 'sardanapa[lus]' here, and again at l. 65, perhaps include Aspasia as well as Rhodope and Pompeia (see l. 51).

64–5. The phrasing here is certainly curious, and the exact meaning is doubtful though the sense is clear. We might alter 'pursuing' to 'in pursuit' or 'fly' to 'flying', or we might omit the 'and'. In the latter case it would be possible to take 'fly · After' together, but it seems more likely that 'After' means 'after which' (cf. l. 34, and *The Dead Man's Fortune*, l. 52). 'Sarda[napalus]' re-enters evidently on a clear stage.

72–3. The ends of these lines are damaged. The fourth actor was evidently 'I sincler' and most likely another name followed; undecipherable traces remain, possibly of 'Kit'. This would support the reading 'others' at the end of the previous line (cf. l. 60), though what 'others' we cannot tell, presumably attendants. The actor 'Ro' is probably the 'R Go' of l. 47.

'Iulio' (cf. l. 76) is of course an addition to the legend (like the 'Panthea' of l. 77) and suggests an Italian source.

80. The object of representing the catastrophe in dumb-show may have been to save time since the whole story had to be compressed into one act. It appears to end with a theophany. Lydgate evidently acts as chorus.

81. 'Tereus'. The end of the word has been altered: there were originally three minims after the second 'e', the last of which has been converted into an 's'.

82. 'his Lords', i.e. the two who accompany Tereus in the previous scene (l. 79); the others (those of l. 77) enter at l. 84.

85. 'to him', i.e. enter to Henry.

87. 'Warwick'. The 'W' has been altered, probably from 'A'.

## III—*FREDERICK AND BASILEA*

*Preservation.*—The Plot is perfect so far as the writing is concerned: a piece is torn out of the blank second column of the front sheet. The original board survives, and so does the blank back sheet. The peg-hole visible in front, and now filled up, went right through, but there is apparently a second hole in the back sheet only, suggesting that this may have once been used for another plot. It is, however, quite blank so far as can be ascertained. The whole has at some time been folded in two, but the resultant damage is very slight.

*Identification.*—*Frederick and Basilea* was performed as a new play by the Admiral's men at the Rose on 3 June 1597. The Plot must be earlier than 18 July following, since it includes the name of Martin Slaughter who left the company on that date, and it may therefore be safely assumed to have been prepared for the original performance. Only four performances in all are recorded, the last on 4 July. Acting ceased at the end of the month, and subsequent records are incomplete, but there is no hint of a revival.

*Characteristics.*—This is a short and comparatively simple Plot: it is the only one confined to a single column, but then the writing is smaller than in any other example. There is no division into acts (see, however, the note on l. 10) and so far as we can tell the division into scenes is perfectly regular (but see the note on l. 51). No exits whatever are marked, though a number of internal exits are implied (ll. 21, 30, 38, 50, 56).

The record of actors is very full, in spite of the fact that there is comparatively little doubling. It was apparently the scribe's intention to name the actor every time a character appeared. He has not been quite consistent, but his failures have the appearance of oversights (ll. 6, 14, 18, 35, 49) and it is significant that in one instance (ll. 36–7) where he failed to mention the actors when the characters first appeared he took advantage of a re-entrance to record them. This frequent repetition has resulted in much carelessness as to order; there are many cases of inversion, as in *The Seven Deadly Sins*, though little abbreviation (see note on l. 18). The inconvenient practice of massed entries (whereby the names of all the characters who enter together are given in a string, and followed in a string by all the names of the corresponding actors) is adopted here as in *The Seven Deadly Sins*, and the only points at which the scribe has departed from it (see note on l. 30) seem to be oversights. It renders more difficult the checking of the record and probably tended to inversions and omissions. Although internal exits are often to be detected they sometimes remain ambiguous (see notes on ll. 38, 50; and cf. *The Seven Deadly Sins*, l. 11). The scribe makes use of the honorific 'Mr.', but rather inconsistently.

There are certainly a few errors of carelessness. The actor for Heraclius should have been recorded at l. 6, especially as it is his first appearance, and the more serious omission to specify 'supers' at ll. 14, 34, and 35 leads to some uncertainty. Other ambiguities occur at l. 49 where the Queen is almost certainly Basilea, and at l. 5 where the Moor is very probably Thamar; possibly at l. 11 where a Lord may be Pedro, though I rather doubt it. The most definite error appears to be the omission of a character, the King, at l. 33. Some interest attaches to the scribe's uncertainty with regard to the arrangement of sc. xviii, beginning an erroneous rule before l. 50 and deleting one after it. This tendency to split up the last scene improperly is exactly what we have already observed in *The Dead Man's Fortune*.

No properties are mentioned, neither are there any directions for stage noises.

There is a total absence of descriptive directions, nor is the influence of the Book otherwise prominent. The most obvious instance is 'the walls' of l. 36, which is interesting as showing how persistent a literary direction may be. The '&c'' of l. 34 possibly points in the same direction, namely to a stage-manager's note. No doubt the 'Moore' of sc. ii comes straight from the Book, and so probably does the anomalous description of sc. xvii. Here the meaning presumably is that the Queen is 'discovered' and that Theodore enters to her as the scene

begins. There can, I think, be no doubt that the Queen is Basilea, and that this is therefore not merely a personal name but indicates the position of the character, as presumably the wife of the King (cf. the name Basilius given to the King of Arcadia in Sidney's romance and hence in some of the plays founded on it).

*Casting.*—The doubling in this Plot is slight. Apart from the provision of 'supers', which concerns only Hunt, Black Dick, the attendants, and gatherers (and raises some difficulties), and assuming that the Moor of sc. ii is Thamar and the Queen of sc. xvii Basilea, the only instances of doubling are that Dunstan plays the Governor in scs. ii–v and the Friar in scs. xiii–xviii, and that Ledbeter, who usually plays Pedro, appears in sc. iv as a Lord attending on Myronhamec, a character which it is difficult to identify with his usual part.

The only serious confusion is that respecting the use of attendants and gatherers as 'supers'. The data are these. In sc. v Myronhamec enters with Soldiers and no actors are assigned. In sc. viii the Lords are played by theatrical attendants. In sc. ix the gatherers provide two Guards, or else a Guard twice over, and in sc. x the Confederates. The changes of costume here involved raise no difficulty. In sc. xi 'Hunt &c'' constitute one Guard, and the actors for a second are not specified. Finally, the gatherers provide the Soldiers for sc. xviii. From this it follows, I think, that the gatherers and attendants are really distinct, for there would be no time for the Confederates of sc. x to change for the first Guard of sc. xi, though there would be for the second. I assume, therefore, that the '&c'' stands for the attendants and that the gatherers only appear later. Lastly we have the Soldiers of sc. v to provide for. This would perhaps be rather early in the performance for the gatherers to be at liberty. We do not know the occupation of the other attendants, but somebody must have been available, and we may therefore suppose that they were called on. This explains my assignment of the parts in the table.

The list of characters is a short one, so short that apart from 'supers' it can be supplied by fourteen actors almost without doubling, and even so one boy only appears in a single scene. Yet for 'supers' both attendants and gatherers had to be called in. The regular cast available consisted of only sixteen members, of whom five have the honorific 'Mr.' and four (probably) were boys. This is interesting, for at the date at which the play was produced the numbers of the Admiral's men were temporarily depleted. In the case of old plays the difficulty must have been met by more doubling, but when procuring a new piece the company seems to have taken care to choose one adapted to its restricted resources.

The five actors who are given the prefix 'Mr.' are Edward Alleyn, Juby, Dunstan, Martin [Slaughter], and Towne. But the scribe was careless and only the first two have it consistently. Dunstan has it five times out of six, Martin four times out of eight, Towne only once out of five. In the circumstances it is rather strange not to find Singer in the cast: he was, of course, a 'clown', but that does not necessarily mean that he only acted comic parts (cf. Pope in *The Seven Deadly Sins*, ll. 48–9).

## *Notes*

2. Richard Alleyn, who speaks the prologue, immediately reappears as Frederick. This suggests that the prologue may have been spoken in that character, though of course the traditional dress of black cloak and bay wreath could be very quickly removed.

3. 'Frederick Kinge: Mr Iubie R Allenn'. The order of the names is clearly inverted. It contradicts l. 9, and the latter is shown to be correct by a number of passages where the characters enter severally (ll. 15–6, 20, and particularly ll. 40, 45), proving that Alleyn played Frederick.

4. 'Basilea seruant Black Dick, Dick'. Another inversion: numerous later passages (e.g. ll. 15–6, and cf. l. 26) show that Dick was the boy who played Basilea, and Black Dick the minor actor who took a variety of small parts.

5. It seems likely from the name and the identity of the actors that the character here called 'Moore' is the one who subsequently appears as 'Thamar' (scs. iv, &c.). I have assumed this in the table.

6. 'Heraclius Seruants . Tho: hunt black Dick'. There is an actor short here, and it is evident from later scenes (particularly l. 14) that Heraclius was played by Sam and not by Hunt. The former's name

must have been accidentally omitted. Hunt and Black Dick were the servants.

7–8. 'Leonora, Sebastian, . . . Mr Allen, will'. Another clear inversion, since of course a boy is needed for the female part. Moreover, subsequent scenes prove that Edward Alleyn played Sebastian (ll. 23–4, 34–5) and Will Leonora (l. 19).

'Pedro, Philippo . . . Ed Dutton, ledbeter'. Again an inversion. It is contradicted by ll. 17–8, while ll. 21 and 23–4 prove that Dutton played Philippo, and Ledbeter Pedro.

10. 'Tho. Hunt' here plays a 'Guarde': at the beginning of the next scene he appears as a 'lord', and apparently has no time to change. If the Plot is correct we must suppose that he was somehow got off the stage before the end of sc. iii, unless indeed there was here an act interval of which the Plot takes no cognizance.

11. The second 'lord' is played by 'ledbeter' who elsewhere took the part of Pedro only. It is possible that the lord is Pedro, but it hardly seems likely, since Pedro appears to be attached to Sebastian rather than Myronhamec.

'Myron-hamec' is so written here and at ll. 23, 28, and without the hyphen at l. 47, but 'Myranhamec' at ll. 14, 35, 54. 'Miran' is a Persian or Tartar name, while 'hamec' may be an error for 'hamet', i.e. 'Ahmed'.

14. 'Myranhamec Soliors'. 'Soliors', i.e. 'soljors', soldiers; a peculiar spelling, unrecorded in the *N.E.D.* and distinctive of this Plot, where it reappears at ll. 47, 54. Steevens's transcript in the 'Variorum' Shakespeare has the reading 'Goliors', i.e. jailors, and I followed this in my *Henslowe Papers*, but it is certainly wrong.

The scribe has omitted to assign any actors. Myronhamec was played by Towne (l. 11). In sc. xvi the Soldiers are played by Black Dick and Hunt, but it is doubtful whether the former would be available here and almost certain that the latter would not. Probably the theatrical attendants were called in (as at l. 24).

18. 'Thamar'. The name of his actor, Charles, has been accidentally omitted at the end of the line.

'leadb:', i.e. Ledbeter; his name alone is occasionally abbreviated, cf. ll. 32 and ('ledb:') 37.

21. 'To her' evidently because Frederick and Philippo have gone off: the former re-enters immediately.

24. 'Attendaunts', i.e. theatrical attendants called in to play the 'lords', not Attendants on Myronhamec.

26. 'Philipo Basilea E Dutton his boye'. The initial 'E' was inserted

after the rest had been written. Since we know that Dutton played Philippo (see ll. 7–8) and Dick Basilea (see l. 4) it follows from the present passage that Dick was Dutton's 'boye'.

30. 'guard gatherers'. Both here and in l. 26 above the Guard forms an exception to the scribe's usual habit of massing characters. It is probable that the 'Guard' of l. 26 left the stage before the 'guard' of l. 30 entered, since it is unlikely that there were sufficient 'gatherers' available to furnish two sets of supers, although there is reason to suppose that they were sometimes rather numerous (see *Henslowe Papers*, p. 89).

31. 'ffrederick Basilea' ('l' altered from 'e'). No actors' names are given.

32. 'Rob:' must stand for Ledbeter's christian name, since he played Pedro, but it appears nowhere else.

'Gatherers'. 'G' altered from 'S'.

33. 'ffrederick . . . M^r Iuby R Allen'. Either Juby's name appears here by error, or more likely the 'King' whom he played has been accidentally omitted.

33–4. 'Guard... Th: Hunt &c'' is a very loose expression to which there is no parallel elsewhere. If, as seems likely, it comes from the Book, it must be derived not from the original direction but from an additional note by the stage-manager, such as may have been the source of the actors' names in *The Dead Man's Fortune*. In that case it probably refers back to l. 27. Here, however, the gatherers can hardly be available, and I assume that the theatrical attendants were called on. The gatherers would then be needed and available for the later 'Guard' of l. 35.

35. 'Myranhamec Guard'. Towne's name, as acting the former, has been omitted, as at l. 14; in both cases accidentally, since no provision has been made for his attendants either. Here the 'Guard' must have been played by the gatherers, who now have had time to change from the 'confederates' of sc. x.

36–7. 'Pedro Basilea vpon the walls . come doune Pedro Basilea'. The 'walls' are of course a relic of the Book. The characters enter on the balcony and then descend to the main stage.

38. 'To hym' implies that either Theodore or Andreo has gone off, but which it is impossible to say. The failure to mark exits renders the scribe's method ambiguous in such a case.

39. 'Heraclius' ('c' altered from 'l'). The actors' names in this line are inverted, Sam played Heraclius.

49. 'To the queen Theodore'. The phrasing is anomalous (cf., however,

*Troilus and Cressida*, l. 34). There can be little doubt that 'the queen' is Basilea, even though Dick's name is omitted.

50. 'To hym' is again ambiguous, implying that either Heraclius or Thamar has gone off. Probably it was Thamar, who re-enters at l. 54.

51. Once more the actors' names are inverted; Martin played Theodore and Dunstan the Friar in scs. xiii–xv.

A rule was begun in error before this line, and one drawn in error after it had been deleted. The words 'To them' were probably added after the deletion had been made.

53. 'R Allen Dick'. These actors' names are again inverted (cf. ll. 3, 4).

'Black Dick' played the 'Messenger', who must go off again, since Black Dick reappears as a 'Solior' later in the scene.

57. 'Epilog$^{s}$'. The sign which I have printed '$^{s}$' must be intended for '$^{9}$', i.e. 'us', but it is very similar to the 's' of 'Heraclius' in l. 14, and this name is written much as it is in l. 12.

*Preservation.*—What remains is a mere fragment, or rather a collection of fragments, belonging (for the most part at least) to the upper portion of the front sheet of the Plot. They have been mounted upon a modern board by a restorer who certainly did his work with intelligence and care, but it is unfortunately not known whether for the arrangement of the several detached portions he had anything beyond internal evidence to guide him.

The position of the two main fragments is approximately fixed by the heading, a part of which appear on each. The central margin, to judge by analogy, can hardly have been less than ¾ inch wide, and thus, if we allow for some word to follow 'mute' in l. 6, the most it would be possible to reduce the space between the fragments by would be some ½ inch. Since the Plot was written by the same scribe as *The Seven Deadly Sins* we may assume that the spelling of the heading was the same, and in order to read 'The Platt of the Second Part' we should need a reduction of barely ¼ inch. The position of these fragments as repaired would therefore appear to be substantially correct.

The right edge of the big fragment from the head of the second column has been mutilated in a manner more suggestive of a deliberate cut than of accidental wear or decay. Exactly how much is missing it is impossible to tell. In the scribe's other Plot (in which the columns are not bounded by rules) the length of the lines of writing is 5 to 5½ inches, in the Plots by other hands the columns vary from about 4¼ (in *Troilus and Cressida*) to about 5½ (in *Frederick and Basilea*). In the present instance exactly 4 inches remain. The probability seems therefore to be in favour of a loss of not less than an inch. We can check this to some extent by internal evidence. From the end of l. 24 all but the first letter of 'dore' is wholly lost; from l. 29 all after, and partly including, the 'r' of 'Mauritius'; from l. 27 a whole name apparently; from l. 26 the last three letters of 'Enter' and a name as well (probably 'Chorus'). We may suppose, then, that the damage is equivalent to ten letters at least, and in the script used ten letters average just about an inch.

The maximum possible loss, on the other hand, would be about fifteen letters. These limits are rather important for any attempt at determining the cast.

The position of the third and smaller fragment (it probably is one fragment and not two) is much less determinate. Assuming that the Plot was confined to the front sheet, and that it was not bounded by rules, the fragment must belong to the right-hand edge of the first column, but whether to the upper or lower portion we cannot tell. The repairer may have had some clue now lost, though this does not seem very likely. He has made the central column an inch wide, which is approximately the width in *The Seven Deadly Sins*, and is probably correct.

Both top and bottom edges of the largest fragment suggest cutting or at least tearing, and it can hardly have come down low enough to have reached the middle fold.

*Identification.*—In spite of the fragmentary condition of this Plot sufficient evidence survives in the way of actors' names to make it certain that it belonged to the later Admiral's men. The presence of Singer shows that the date can hardly be after 1602, and that of Tailor that it is probably earlier than *Tamar Cam*. The absence of the prefix 'Mr.' before the names of Sam and Charles points to a date before *The Battle of Alcazar*, and, if my interpretation of the honorific is correct (see pp. 28–36), before 16 Nov. (perhaps before 13 Mar.) 1598. On the other hand, the presence of George and Cartwright, who appear in the later Plots but not in *Frederick and Basilea*, place it after the summer of 1597. We can hardly be wrong if we assign it to the twelve months following the reconstruction of the Admiral's company on their amalgamation with Pembroke's in 1597, and for convenience the winter of 1597–8 may be conjectured.

The mutilation of the heading makes the title of the Plot uncertain, but there is one title mentioned by Henslowe in the last section of his accounts with the Admiral's company (1597–1603) that fits in so well with the traces that remain, namely 'Fortun . . . is', that I cannot bring myself to regard the resemblance as accidental. This title he gives in the form 'the fortewn tenes', which probably stands either for *The Fortune of Tennis* or *Fortune's Tennis*. It is true that Henslowe's entry belongs to September 1600 (some two or three years after the Plot must have been drawn up) and that there is no indication of the play being in two parts. These are serious objections, but after some vacillation I have come back to my original opinion that there must be a connexion between the two.

Henslowe's record of 6 Sept. 1600 was in respect of 20*s*. lent to the company 'to paye vnto Thomas deckers for his boocke called the fortewn tenes'. Now Henslowe's wording is often careless, but as a rule when he mentions a book he means the Book of an old play, and it is quite clear that he would not have got a new play from Dekker for 20*s*. He was, therefore, probably either buying an old play from Dekker, or paying him for work done on the Book. But the usual price for an old play was 40*s*., so we are left with the latter alternative. My suggestion is that Dekker's work consisted of cutting down the two parts of the original play into a single piece, a task he may well have performed for a small fee. There is a further peculiarity of Henslowe's entry that may be significant in this connexion: if, as would appear from the Plot, the title of the piece was *Fortune's Tennis*, why does he prefix the article? Now, when a few months earlier Dekker recast the old two-part play of *Fortunatus*, Henslowe called it 'the whollе history of fortewnatus'. And if in the present instance the manuscript was inscribed 'The Booke of the Whole of Fortunes Tennis', as it may well have been, this would help to account for the peculiarity of Henslowe's entry.

But if *Fortune's Tennis* was an old two-part play when Dekker took it in hand in 1600, there ought to be some trace of its earlier history. There is no record of its being performed before July 1597, nor any record of its being purchased after October the same year. It can hardly therefore have been originally an Admiral's play. The natural inference is that it was one of the pieces that the moribund Pembroke's company contributed to the stock on amalgamation. If so it ought undoubtedly to appear among 'such bookes as belong to the Stocke' in the

inventory of 1598. There is no trace of it, at least under its proper title, but the list is known to be incomplete (*Henslowe Papers*, p. 122; *Elizabethan Stage*, iii. 374). It may, of course, only have been recovered after the inventory had been drawn up.

[There is one line of speculation in connexion with this Plot which ought perhaps to be put on record, though I should certainly hesitate to endorse it. There are, namely, certain curious points of resemblance between 2 *Fortune's Tennis* and *The Trial of Chivalry*, a play printed in 1605 as 'lately acted by the right Honourable the Earle of Darby his seruants'. There is not the slightest presumption in favour of any connexion between the repertories of Derby's and the Admiral's men, but it is singular that the printed piece includes a Duke of Orleans, a Lewis King of France, and a Bella[mira] who does appear disguised as a pilgrim. Were we to concede that this pointed to some relation between the pieces, it might further be observed that one of the chief characters in *The Trial of Chivalry* is the Duke of Bourbon, and 'burbon' (in Henslowe's spelling) is the title of an old play which the Admiral's men appear to have acquired from Pembroke's in 1597. There is some suggestion that Thomas Heywood may have had a hand in *The Trial of Chivalry*, and Derby's *Edward IV* has been very generally supposed to be his. Sir Edmund Chambers thinks it likely that some of Heywood's early work was transferred to Worcester's men when he was with them in 1602–3, and the same may have happened when Heywood joined the Admiral's men in Mar. 1598, soon after their amalgamation with Pembroke's. At the same time it should be observed that no connexion whatever is known between Pembroke's company and either Heywood on the one hand or Derby's men on the other. Already far too much fanciful history has been based on supposed agreements of this sort not to warn critics against similar imaginative indulgence. It is rather as a warning than an invitation that I record these details here.

Certain other speculations respecting the present Plot must, I think, be definitely abandoned. Elaborating an earlier guess of my own, Sir Edmund Chambers suggested (*Elizabethan Stage*, iii. 448) that 2 *Fortune's Tennis* might be identical with the *Set at Tennis*, for which Munday was paid £3 in Dec. 1602, 'probably . . . a short play . . . intended to piece out to the length of a normal performance the original *Fortune's Tennis* written by Dekker as a "curtain-raiser" for the Fortune on its opening in 1600'. He added 'This is highly conjectural', and now agrees that it is definitely ruled out by the dates.]

*Characteristics.*—This fragment is in the same hand as *The Seven Deadly Sins*, and so far as its condition allows us to judge the methods followed by the scribe appear to be generally the same as in the earlier Plot. The ruled divisions (which, since they are not consecutive, I have indicated by letters instead of numbers) seem to represent scenes divided in the usual manner. There is no trace of any formal division into acts, although there is a hint of structural division in the play itself (see note on l. 26). There seems to be a fairly full record of actors, especially of those for minor characters, as in division F, but the scribe evidently did not feel bound to name the actor every time a character appeared. Thus in E none is named for Orleans, though the three other characters appear to have had actors assigned: some divisions seem, like L, to have contained no mention of actors at all. The only obvious abnormality is the rather unusual arrangement of K, the interpretation of which is necessarily conjectural.

The only property of which mention remains is the 'Table' in N. Small indications of the influence of the Book are fairly frequent, as in *The Seven Deadly Sins*, but some depend upon more or less conjectural restorations. There appear to be allusions to somebody entering 'bare headed' and to 'ladies following mute' (A), to Orleans 'musing' (E), and Mauritius 'bleeding' (G), also to somebody dressed 'like a Pilgrim' where the simple 'disguised' would meet the requirements of the Plot (H).

Such points of casting as arise—and the evidence is necessarily very uncertain—are discussed in the notes. No problems of general importance are involved, and the scanty remains afford no trace of doubling.

## *Notes*

3. At the beginning of the remaining portion of the line the letter 'r' is practically certain, and the very top of a tall letter, not immediately preceding, is visible. There is little doubt that the word was 'bare'. The suggestion in *Henslowe Papers*, 'five', should be rejected.

'Tho'. In *Frederick and Basilea* Thomas Towne once has the prefix 'Mr.' while Thomas Hunt is without it. In *The Battle of Alcazar* both have the prefix. But no inference as to date is possible since the latter has also a Thomas Drum without prefix. If, however, the date is taken as given, then the probability is that 'Tho' is Hunt,

since Towne should have the prefix and Drum is not known to have yet joined.

4. 'somerton' can hardly be a character-name. No such actor is known, but it may be a slip for or variant of Somerset, in which case he is the same as George. It is, of course, unusual for an actor to be given two names in the same Plot, but it is significant that George once has his surname in *The Battle of Alcazar.*

5. The mark at the beginning of the line can hardly be anything but a closing parenthesis, in spite of the fact the sign appears nowhere else in the Plots. The trace that precedes I cannot identify.

'dick'. The last letter looks like a 't', but the difference between 't' and 'k' is slight (cf. l. 22) and the tear may have removed the distinguishing loop. What follows has the appearance of a small round letter followed by the tail of a long one, but the two traces may quite well be the remains of a '*J*' (cf. *The Seven Deadly Sins*, particularly ll. 5 and 75). I conjecture that the word was 'Iuby', which would likewise account for the tail of a second long letter a little farther on.

If, as seems possible (one cannot be certain), 'dick' played 'A Childe' here, he is probably the same as the Dick, Dutton's boy, in *Frederick and Basilea.* There is no proof that he was Dick Juby, but it seems not unlikely.

6. 'mute'. The letters printed 'mu' are an undifferentiated series of five minims, which, however, resembles the beginning of the word 'musing' in l. 15.

7. 'to'. The 'o' is not closed, but this happens after 't' (cf. l. 15, and notably *The Seven Deadly Sins*, l. 44). The context, of course, requires 'to'.

'A s', possibly 'A seruant'.

8. Although the paper is a good deal decayed there is no doubt that this line forms part of the same fragment as the preceding, and its position is therefore fixed. Before the 'o', the top of which is pretty clear, are traces of two letters apparently, the first a tall one. It is, however, just possible that they might together form part of a 'C', in which case the name may be the same as that at the end of l. 15. After the 'm' there appears to be a blank before the actual edge of the fragment, but the surface of the paper is evidently worn away.

9–14. It is just possible that there are two fragments here, ll. 9–11 together with the trace (of 'l', 'f', or long 's') at the beginning of l. 12 belonging to one, and the rest of l. 12 together with ll. 13–4 to the other. It is more likely, however, that it is all one.

13. What is printed as 'n' might equally well be the last two minims of 'm'.

15. 'Co'. The following trace looks like three minims: 'm' seems the most probable interpretation (cf. l. 8) but 'ro' is not impossible.

16. There would probably be ample room for one other name after 'Pauy', and we may therefore assume that Singer played 'Co...', Pavy Mauritius, and the third actor Boniface. In that case no actor is assigned for Orleans, no doubt because he had appeared earlier.

17–8. Cartwright had to appear in the following scene, hence presumably the deletion of his name here. Similarly Tailor may have been needed to play one of the wine-pressers. After 'Geo[rge]' in l. 17 there would be room for one other name, but probably not for two. If, therefore, George acted Boniface, then, on the removal of Tailor and Cartwright, either these should have been replaced by other actors (of which there is no trace) or 'seruingmen' should have been altered to the singular (which it was not). I infer that the actor for Boniface (probably given in l. 16) was not repeated here, and that George and another (possibly Kendall) played the serving-men, originally four now reduced to two. Boniface, moreover, has the appearance of being a somewhat more important character than those generally played by George.

19. After the '*E*', the top of which is fairly clear, the next trace (some way farther on) is of a tall letter, most probably an '*Ɛ*', while the '*i*' has been inferred from the dot (though this may of course be accidental). A name is, of course, required, and the tall letter is therefore probably a capital. The traces suggest 'Edwin', which would fill the space conveniently.

22. The termination 'lla' presumably implies 'bella', and suggests such names as Isabella and Annabella. It might, however, be an abbreviation for such a name as Bellamira.

23. 'he'. There is not much doubt that the first letter is 'h' though it is damaged. The next is probably a badly-formed 'e' (of the 'ε' type) though it looks more like a 'c'. The word was presumably 'the'.

24. The son of some male character enters at one door; he may be the child of l. 5.

25. The only trace left in this line is probably that of a final 'e'.

26. There seems no doubt that the second remaining letter is a badly-formed 'p' (cf. l. 19). 'Champaine' is the name that suggests itself, and the trace before 'm' is not impossible for 'a' (it could hardly be 'o') while it would seem that a tall letter preceded it. If one were to

17. [illegible]

[illegible]

read 'Campaine' it might be possible to connect it with the 'Com' (?) of ll. 8 and 15, but the identification would be very risky.

'En' can hardly stand for anything but 'Enter', especially as it is marked off by a stroke from what precedes. Such a use would be quite anomalous, and there is no room for any extensive direction. A very tempting explanation is that the words were 'Enter Chorus' and that they marked the end of an act.

27. 'ies' is presumably the end of 'ladies' (cf. l. 6). At the end of the line is a trace of a long letter that suggests '*ſ*' or '*f*' but might equally be the remains of '*M*'.

28. This line ends with a trace similar to that in the line above.

30–1. It looks as though the first of these lines had been interlined, but in that case an unusually wide space had been left above the second. Moreover both look as though they were written in a slightly different ink from the rest. It is possible that the scribe failed to complete the plot at a sitting and continued in a more cramped style.

The lower portions of the letters of the last line have been cut or torn away, but the readings outside the brackets are not in doubt. Probably it is the '[attendan]tts' played by Sam and Charles who bring in the table. For the phraseology cf. *The Battle of Alcazar*, ll. 91–2.

## V—*TROILUS AND CRESSIDA*

*Preservation.*—Of this Plot a single large fragment is all that remains, roughly the lower half of the front, or first, sheet, for like *The Battle of Alcazar* by the same scribe it was apparently continued on the back. The decay which has played havoc with the upper edge may have been started by a centre fold, which very likely broke the board in two since nothing remains of the upper half. The fragment has now been mounted on a modern card. [It is possible, though by no means certain, that the right-hand bottom corner, including the words 'to them,' is really a detached fragment. But even if this is so there can be no reasonable doubt that it has been correctly placed by the restorer. No other fragments of the Plot are preserved; cf. *The Battle of Alcazar*, textual notes, ll. 115–8.]

*Identification.*—The few actors' names preserved suffice to connect this Plot with the later Admiral's company but not to date it very closely. The mention of Jones places it before the end of Feb. 1602, and the 'Mr.' allowed to Hunt after *Frederick and Basilea*: if my interpretation of the honorific prefix is correct the limits must be March 1598 and July 1600 (see p. 37). The scenes preserved obviously belong to a play on the Trojan war, but do not come from any extant piece. However, in the spring of 1599 the Admiral's men produced a series of plays dealing with this cycle of legend. In Feb. Chettle was writing a piece called *Troy's Revenge*, which may be conjectured to have followed the wanderings of Ulysses; in April he and Dekker were at work on a *Troilus and Cressida*; in May the same authors produced an *Agamemnon* which was probably identical with *Orestes' Furies* and therefore concerned the death of the hero. Thus there is every reason to suppose that the fragmentary Plot belongs to Chettle and Dekker's *Troilus and Cressida*, and no reason to doubt that it was prepared for the original performance. Henslowe's accounts between 17 Apr. and 26 May, which presumably included the final payment for *Troilus and Cressida*, are lost: the exact date of com-

pletion is consequently not known, but the piece can hardly have been on the stage before May 1599, which may therefore be taken as the probable date of the Plot.

*Characteristics.*—This fragment was written by the same scribe as the possibly slightly earlier *Battle of Alcazar*, with which it has most features in common. Its only striking individual peculiarity is the very thick rules that bound the columns. Like its companion it ran on to a second sheet. There is no indication whatever of any division into acts, either in the Plot or the play itself, and sufficient remains to make it very improbable that any formal division existed. The scenes (which again I have marked with letters) appear to be quite regularly divided, and the method followed is clearer than before, since here for the first time we meet with a practically complete record of exits both final and internal. The latter results in some technical innovations, the use of 'manet' (l. 21) or less probably 'manent' (l. 7?) and the use of 'Enter' in the interior of a scene.

We may assume it to have been the intention of the scribe, so far at least as the main characters are concerned, to specify the actor on the first appearance but not subsequently. This at least was his practice in *The Battle of Alcazar*, and it accounts for the paucity of names in the present fragment. The only principal part for which we find an actor given is Priam, and this only when his appearance was recorded in a later correction. Actors are assigned for Cressida's 'waighting maid' in E and for the beggars who accompany her in L. If my conjectures are right, Hunt appeared as a Proctor in D and L.

The scribe fell into an error in the original construction of the Plot and also in his attempt at correction. As he wrote them the descriptions of E and I were identical. In fact E was wrong, for Priam should have appeared instead of Antenor. But the scribe inadvertently made the alteration in I. He then had to make it over again in E, and restore Antenor in I. It was in making this correction that for some reason he recorded the actor along with the character. In ll. 17 and 41–2 I have little doubt that the scribe was handicapped by obscure additions in the Book.

The Plot is very explicit as regards stage noises, and makes use of the left and central margins to record them. We get '3 · seuerall Tacketts' in A, 'Alarũ' in B, D, H, I, K, N, 'excursions' in B and C, 'a retreat' in D (?) and N. There are, however, no properties beyond 'a light' borne by the maid in the text of E. There is Achilles' 'Tent' in K, but this would of course be the curtained recess (to which we find allusion in *The Battle of Alcazar*, l. 27) just as the 'walls' in D and N mean the balcony. Both are clearly survivals from the Book, the influence of which may also be traced in a few descriptive phrases such as 'pursued' (l. 14), 'w$^{th}$ patroclus on his back' (ll. 37–8), i.e. bearing the dead body, and 'they on the wall descend [to them]' (l. 50). The direction enter 'Achillis in his Tent' is of course strictly theatrical, though it is familiar from various printed texts, and if the description at the opening of the scene is slightly anomalous it is not without parallel. On the whole the work of this scribe marks a high degree of technical development.

## *Notes*

1. Notice the fragment of a rule above 'at', which fixes this as the first line of a scene. The last letter of the word 'Enter' is also perhaps traceable. In spite of the mutilation the outline of the action is tolerably clear: 'Enter at one dore . . . (?) . . . Vlisses Aiax . . . at another dore Herraulds . . . Priam, Hector, Deiphobus . . . exeunt (Vlisses,) Diomed, (Hector) & Deiphobus, manet the rest & Herraulds, to them Menelaus Vlisses & Diomede, to them Hector Deiphobus, to them Cassandra ex(eun)t'. It is clear that Ulysses and Hector are among those who go off at l. 6 since they subsequently re-enter.
2. The traces that remain are perplexing. The first letters discernable are almost certainly 'reo' and it is not clear whether anything preceded them. There follows a badly damaged letter, and lastly a fairly clear 'e'. I am unable to offer any suggestion.
3. What remains after the 'A' looks like the trace of an 'x', so that the name was almost certainly 'Aiax'.
6. The deleted word was possibly 'to'.
7. 'the rest'. If this were part of an entry it would be a very loose phrase, though it might not be without parallel in some Books. But coming as it does between 'exeunt' in l. 6 and 'to them' in l. 8, it is almost certain that the missing word in l. 7 was 'manet' (cf. 21), and after

this 'the rest' would be quite regular. It is, however, a little strange to find the Heralds specified after it. It may be remarked that though both 'Exit' and 'Exeunt' are common, and often correctly used, and though 'manet' is not uncommon, the plural form 'manent' is almost unknown, and appears nowhere in the Plots.

9. 'Patroclus' would be too long for the space at the beginning of this line, so that the only possible alternatives are 'Achillis' and 'Vlisses'. General probability and discernible traces alike favour the latter.

10. 'exit'. The 'i' is blotted, and it looks as though an 'n' or possibly 'en' had been written over it, with a view to altering the word to 'exeunt', which is presumably required.

11. 'Alarũ'. The 'u' is quite clear, but the mark of abbreviation is lost.

12. The interlineation is in the same hand as the text, but a finer pen seems to have been used.

'exeunt'. There are only three minims for 'un'.

13. The space seems insufficient for any name but 'Aiax'. The description was apparently thought too simple to need an 'exit'.

17. The traces in the margin are very slight. It looks, however, as though 'tr' or 'etr' had stood near the middle, and possibly a 't' later, which suggests 'a retreat' as in l. 48.

'm$^{r}$ Hunt' has clearly been entered in place of a character-name, though hardly by inadvertence for that of a main character, since the scribe appears to have recognized the abnormality and to have left a blank for the character-name before adding 'exeunt'. The actor's name, therefore, but not that of the character was given in the Book, and we may conclude that the passage was a later addition. I am convinced that the confusion here is connected with that at ll. 41–2 (q.v.) and believe Hunt to have played a Proctor in both passages.

21. 'waightng', sic, there are only two minims between 't' and 'g' and no dot.

27. '& Enter' is, of course, unusual; but after an exit the usual phrase 'to them' would be awkward and perhaps even ambiguous.

28. Presumably the first word was 'Enter' and the line began a scene.

29. If the second letter is correctly read as 'e' the name must have been 'Deiphobus'.

31. 'menalay' (cf. ll. 35, 49) is a common Elizabethan variant of 'Menalaus' (l. 8).

32. Apparently the final direction was taken as equivalent to an exit.

32–3. The interlineations are again in the same hand as the text. The name 'Antenor' is added above for reinstatement in l. 33, the alteration having been made in error.

33. 'exeunt'. Again there are only three minims for 'un'.

34. 'Tent'. Only the very bottom of the letters remain, but such traces as there are fully support the reading which is suggested by the context. If we were to read merely 'Enter Diomede to Achillis' the description would be anomalous though not unparalleled (cf. *Frederick and Basilea*, l. 49), but it would necessitate an exit before the re-entry of l. 36. Why, however, should the locality be specified at this point? Diomed might be supposed to call and some one answer from 'within', but that would hardly justify the use of 'to them' instead of 'to him' immediately after. I think that the tent must be open and Achilles 'discovered'; the description being equivalent to 'Enter Diomede to Achillis in his Tent'. Then the tent must close again before the entry of Ulysses, such action not being held to require an exit.

39. Cressida has appeared before (l. 19 and no doubt previously) and it is not this scribe's custom to repeat actors' names. Pig, therefore, played the first beggar.

40. 'Stephen' may conceivably have been Steven Maget the tire-man at the Rose.

By 'mutes' must be meant the gatherers or other playhouse attendants (cf. *The Seven Deadly Sins* and *Frederick and Basilea*) who were available to play 'mute' parts on occasion. The plural shows that there were at least five beggars in all.

41. 'proctor'. Chambers no longer takes this as the name of an actor (as in *The Elizabethan Stage*, ii. 335). It must stand for a character, perhaps a steward, or possibly, from its occurrence in this scene, it may be used in its technical sense of factor of a spital-house (see note on l. 50). Being a minor character, one would expect to find an actor specified, and indeed the scribe has left a space for the addition. It is therefore the exact reverse of the case in l. 17, where we found Hunt named and a blank left for the character, and we may again suspect an addition in the Book. It is noticeable, moreover, that in both instances the character is attached to Deiphobus. I feel little doubt that in both cases Hunt appeared as the Proctor.

43. 'Hellena' is elsewhere called 'Hel(l)en' (ll. 23, 48), but the longer form would perhaps fit better in l. 26. There is no trace of Helenus in this play, though he appears in Shakespeare's.

44. The required 'exit' seems to have been omitted for want of space.

49. The last word is presumably 'Hearraulds'. It is curious that the fragment should both begin and end with a parley.

50. 'to them'. This would naturally imply that the scene continued with a further entry. At the same time it is not impossible that the words

may belong to the unusual direction that precedes, though they would not be strictly necessary. One would like to know whether this was the end of a scene. If it is we should expect 'exeunt' and a rule. The former, however, is not always present, and the previous scene in particular seems to have been deprived of it for lack of space: the rule may have been omitted at the end of a column though the analogy of *The Battle of Alcazar* is strongly against it. But even if this scene is complete it is most unlikely to have ended the play. This, after the death of Patroclus, must have included that of Hector, and a play on the Cressida story could not have left her, as this appears to do, among the Trojans.[1] Moreover, every fully preserved Plot ends with the word 'Finis'. The present one must therefore have run over on to a second sheet.

[1] It might be suggested that L, showing Cressida among the beggars, contains the end of her story, her retribution. To Shakespeare 'Cressida was a beggar' (*Twelfth Night*, III. i. 62) and a 'lazar kite' (*Henry V*, II. i. 80). It seems to have been Henryson who, in his *Testament of Cresseid*, first told of her miserable end, condemned to go

begging fra hous to hous,
With Cop and Clapper lyke ane Lazarous

a conception adopted by Heywood, who in *The Iron Age* depicts her as little else but a strumpet and in the end 'branded thus with leprosie' (2, III. i). Still the other difficulties remain, and I think it more likely that in this scene the heroine is shown playing the lady bountiful to the beggars who are later to be her follows in misfortune. The last scene preserved (N) suggests a truce that might prelude the banquet depicted by Heywood as the occasion of Cressida's defection (1 *Iron Age*, III. i).

*Preservation.*—This Plot survives in a sadly mutilated state, though it is less fragmentary than *Fortune's Tennis* or *Troilus and Cressida*. The extant remains, which have been mounted on a modern card, consist of the greater part of the first sheet (for the Plot ran over on to a second) together with some half dozen detached fragments, the position of which can only be determined by internal evidence. As mounted by the repairer not one of them is quite in its proper place. Several of them can be definitely placed, but there remain three which it is difficult to fit in. One of these is so small as to be negligible: the other two appear to have formed part of the second (or back) sheet.

In order to make the reconstruction of this Plot as clear as possible the Transcript is given in two forms. The first (VI^A^) represents the original exactly as it stands in its present mutilated and repaired condition, the second (VI^B^) is an attempt at restoring it as first written, the detached fragments being rearranged (so far as their position can be determined) and the lacunae conjecturally supplied. This restoration is based partly upon a minute palaeographical examination and partly upon a study of the extant version of the play, and follows with little variation that already given in my study of *Alcazar and Orlando*. The palaeographical side is here dealt with in the Textual Notes, but it has been impossible to enter into the very intricate problem of the printed text, and students who are curious on the subject must be referred to my earlier work.

It may be well to explain here that the Textual Notes are written with reference to the exact Transcript (VI^A^), while all references in the Critical Notes and elsewhere are to the reconstructed Transcript (VI^B^). As usual pointed brackets indicate mutilations, but for the sake of clearness they have been confined in the present instance to the main sheet of the Plot (to those portions, that is, whose position is fixed and unalterable), while in the case of the detached fragments (whose position is matter of inference or conjecture) the usual pointed

brackets have been replaced by curly ones (braces). I hope that this device will enable students to see at a glance the material conditions governing the reconstruction of any passage. In the unrestored Transcript ($VI^{A}$) all letters printed within brackets, whether pointed or curly, are such as may be considered reasonably certain though they cannot be confidently identified apart from the context. Mere traces are indicated by dots, two dots representing approximately the space of one letter. In the restored Transcript ($VI^{B}$) the portions outside the brackets are identical with the other Transcript, while those within are in the main purely conjectural.

*Identification.*—This Plot, in spite of its mutilated condition, really affords the key to the whole series, since it is the only one for which there is extant a text of the play enabling us to examine its construction in some detail. This is contained in a quarto dated 1594 with the title 'The Battell of Alcazar, fought in Barbarie, betweene Sebastian king of Portugall, and Abdelmelec king of Marocco. With the death of Captaine Stukeley. As it was sundrie times plaid by the Lord high Admirall his seruants.' The text is evidently that of an abridged version of the play, but it is sufficiently near the original, in the first four acts at least, to be valuable for comparison.

No mention of *The Battle of Alcazar* is found in the detailed records of the performances of the Admiral's company which extend from the spring of 1594 to the summer of 1597, and we must therefore suppose that the allusion on the title of the quarto is to the earlier Admiral's men before the reorganization of the former year. But for some years previously the company, so far as it existed if at all as an independent organization, was absent from London and is unlikely to have acquired any new plays, so that we may suppose the original performance to have been in 1591 at latest: there is some reason to suppose that the piece may have been written as early as the winter of 1588–9. It is true that attempts have been made to identify the play with one or another of those that appear in the records under other titles, but they have not been very successful. Nor would the position be materially altered if we were to suppose that the allusion in the quarto was not strictly to the Admiral's men at all, but to Strange's (or some joint organization) when this was under the leadership of the Admiral's servant Edward Alleyn. In any case, none of the plays that it has been sought to identify with *The Battle of Alcazar* were new pieces, and the conjectures therefore do not affect the date of the original production.

The probability is, then, that *The Battle of Alcazar*, a play ascribed on plausible grounds to George Peele, was first acted by the earlier Admiral's company early in 1589. The Plot, on the other hand, was certainly prepared for the later Admiral's company between 1594 and 1603, when they were acting first at the Rose and later at the Fortune. The precise date of this revival is the subject of some controversy. The cast places it clearly after the reconstruction of Oct. 1597, the presence of Kendal after 8 Dec., that of James probably after 18 Dec.: the presence of Jones and Shaa before Feb. 1602, that of Richard Alleyn before his death in Dec. 1601. Moreover, Dick Juby played the female part of Abdula Rais, and was therefore presumably a boy: but by 1602 he was married and had a son baptized on 1 May that year. Narrower limits depend on the interpretation of the prefix 'Mr.': my own view is that it probably belongs to the three months Dec. 1598 to Feb. 1599 (see pp. 38–9). This would place it between *Fortune's Tennis* and *Troilus and Cressida*, but since the date is not free from doubt I have consulted convenience in placing the two fragments together and discussing *The Battle of Alcazar* after instead of before *Troilus and Cressida*.

The relation of the Plot to the quarto text raises many difficult and intricate problems, which I have discussed at length in my essay on *Two Elizabethan Stage Abridgements: Alcazar and Orlando* (Oxford, 1923). There is no need to go over the ground again, and I have avoided so far as possible referring to the quarto in what follows. At the same time it is impossible fully to interpret the Plot without reference to the printed text, and I have perforce assumed many conclusions the evidence and arguments in favour of which will be found in my earlier work.

*Characteristics.*—When this Plot has been reconstructed so far as the evidence allows, it is found to correspond with the first four acts only of the quarto, and consequently it must have been continued on the back sheet. It will be noticed that the second column, which terminates at the end of a scene, is closed with a rule, while the first, which ends in the middle of a scene, is left open. The left and centre margins, but probably not the right, were used for notes of stage noises and properties required. One of these, demanding rather elaborate properties, is written in English script, but there is no reason to suppose that it is in a different hand, though it was probably added on a later occasion.

The play was regularly divided into acts by the appearance of 'a Portingall' who acted as 'Presenter' to the dumb-shows. These are regularly numbered in the Plot, but there is no formal act division. Comparison with the quarto shows that the scene division is perfectly regular. Final exits are marked in every case so far as the Plot is preserved, and there are also internal exits with correlative manets. While the scribe uses both 'exit' and 'exeunt' correctly, he makes 'manet' serve for both numbers.

It was clearly the scribe's intention, so far as the main characters were concerned, to mention the actor for each part on the first appearance but not subsequently. This avoided some sources of confusion, but increased the danger of omitting the actor altogether, since the scribe was liable to forget that a particular character had not appeared before. His execution is certainly not perfect. He forgot the actor for the Presenter in the first instance; the actor for Pisano he only recorded by accident; those for Calipolis and Sebastian he failed to record at all; and there may be a similar omission in III. ii. On the other hand he twice mentioned the actor for Young Mahamet (ll. 6, 21), and once probably entered the name of the actor instead of the character (l. 111). In the case of minor and what may be called group characters, the scribe naturally sought or tended to be more explicit, but he was perhaps even more erratic. The actor of Nemesis is mentioned twice (ll. 25, 56), of Sebastian's Page twice (ll. 46, 69); we get the list of Ghosts twice and of Furies three times. On the other hand when Mahamet's pages (ll. 7–8) reappear (l. 18) the actors' names are not repeated, nor are they when the Moor's pages, as we may suppose, are deputed to attend on his Ambassadors (l. 51). Once (l. 67) the scribe brings on an actor who cannot possibly be present.

The old inconvenient habit of massing characters and actors (a string of character-names being followed by a string of actors' names) is in theory at least abandoned, and the scribe sets out to mention the name of each actor immediately after the character (or character-group) to which he belongs. This avoids the danger of inversion that gives trouble in earlier Plots, but the scribe is not altogether successful in carrying through his innovation. The first dumb-show is impeccable, the first scene masses characters at the end, and so does II. ii. In I. ii the scribe got into a bad muddle: indeed the description here is a deplorable performance for so generally competent a plotter. For competent he is, and his work on the whole marks a high degree of technical evolution.

Like *Troilus and Cressida* the present Plot rather specializes in stage noises: partly no doubt because both are much concerned with battles. We find 'sound' eight times, 'sound sennett' four times, 'Alarũ' once. Many properties also are mentioned, some in the text, others in the margin, thus: a chariot (I. ii, III. iii), a whip, a bloody torch or brand, and a chopping knife (II. cho.), chairs (?) and boxes for presents (II. i), raw flesh (II. iii), scales, a sheep's gather (consisting of heart, liver, and lights), and three vials of blood (III. d.s.), a chair of state (?, III. i), drum and colours (III. iii, IV. i), a banquet, two tapers, dead men's heads and bones, and more blood (IV. cho.), and finally torches (IV. ii). Of course further properties were required for the fifth act. And yet we have reason to suppose that the record is incomplete; for instance, according to the quarto a bed and a chair were required in the first dumb-show.

The question of the influence of the Book on the Plot ought to receive important elucidation from the present case: unfortunately the quarto version has been so far altered, particularly

in the crucial passages describing the dumb-shows, that the results of comparison are rather disappointing. As usual the directions for the dumb-shows in the Plot tend to be descriptive, but the language of them is less so here than elsewhere. The action is described, but scarcely more than is necessary for clearness. Only in the third dumb-show do we get the expressions 'Fech in' and 'Carrie him out', which are clearly literary, since from the theatrical point of view the actions would be properly described as 'out' and 'in'. There are also a few descriptive touches elsewhere. The Moor's chariot in I. ii has a page 'on each side' (perhaps to move it forward); in II. iii he enters 'w^th^ raw flesh'; in the last scene preserved the characters enter 'by Torch light to coun saile' if the reconstruction is correct. A clear case is the duplication in II. ii, 'Enter Diego Lopis: Gouernor of Lisborne', a description of a single character which must come straight from the Book. But for the most part the language is strictly theatrical: Nemesis appears 'aboue' in the balcony, the furies lie 'behind the Curtaines' in the alcove, and these no doubt served to reveal the Moor's chariot. Most notable of all is the demand for '3· violls of blood & a sheeps gather', a purely theatrical direction that throws a flood of light on the crudely realistic methods of the Elizabethan stage.

One or two points that come out by comparison with the quarto deserve passing mention. At the end of III. i Stukeley and the Duke of Avero remain together on the stage for a private conversation after the other characters have gone off. The printed text has merely 'Manet Stukley and another'. This is very characteristic of the relation between Book and Plot. The author did not care which of the courtiers served as confidant: the stage-manager had to be specific, but he recorded his choice of Avero not in the Book but in the Plot. Further, in the same scene the quarto makes Luis de Silva appear along with the Spanish Ambassadors. This happened to raise a difficulty of casting, and since his presence was not in the least necessary, the Plot simply omitted him. Lastly it may be mentioned between III. i and III. ii the quarto has a whole additional scene. This scene, which is indeed of no importance, has been omitted in the Plot. It was not through inadvertance, for as the Plot stands its insertion would raise a difficulty of casting; but this could easily have been overcome, and the reason for the omission remains obscure.

*Casting.*—There is some doubling among the main characters though it is not heavy. Among the actors distinguished by the prefix 'Mr.', Richard Alleyn played the Governor of Lisbon in addition to the Presenter, Edward Juby took Calsepius earlier and Avero later, Shaa was the Irish Bishop and also the Governor of Tanger and perhaps Celebin, Jones took three small parts probably, Charles three, Sam at least six, Hunt was well occupied as an attendant but played a Moorish Ambassador as well. It is clear that though these may have been sharers they were not all leading actors. One of the principal boys, James, doubles the parts of Ruben and Sebastian's Page. All this of course in the first four acts.

Apart from uncertainty introduced at some points by the mutilation of the Plot there are few serious difficulties in following the casting. The scribe accidentally omitted to give the name of the actor of Sebastian. As a leading part it would certainly have been filled by a sharer. It could easily have been doubled with Abdelmelec, played by Downton, but it is very doubtful whether it was, since two sharers, Singer and Birde, do not appear at all. Most likely one of these played Sebastian while the other was held in reserve.

Another part for which the actor is not named is that of Calipolis. Of course he was a boy. I conjecture that he may have been Will Barnes, but the evidence respecting boy-actors in general is extremely intricate and has to be considered as a whole (see pp. 66–9).

A curious point is the doubling of the parts of Pisano and a Messenger by Sam in the course of a single scene (I. ii). The description of this in the Plot is anomalous and confused, but the quarto enables us to determine the action with certainty. The scribe is involved in two errors over Kendall, whose name occurs erroneously as an attendant in III. i and by mistake for a character in IV. ii. There is certainly some confusion over

the Governor of Tanger and his Captains in III. ii–iii, and the quarto fails to clear it up sufficiently to allow of the certain restoration of the Plot at this point.

## *Notes—Textual*

(the references are to Transcript VI^A^)

10. *Abdelmenen*] sic, the name is properly 'Abdelmunen'.

12. *attendatę*] sic.

14. Between *George* and *them* a word has almost entirely disappeared through the decay of the surface of the paper: there is no hole. We should expect *to* but such traces as remain rather suggest *wth*. If this was indeed the reading it must have been an error.

22. *exeunt*] the *un* is represented by three minims only.

26–7. The small detached fragment near the end of these lines has been misplaced a line too high: the portions of words preserved on it really belong to ll. 27–8. In the upper line, before the *i*, is preserved a small trace of the *a*, another portion of which is seen after the *t* in l. 27; above the *n* can be traced the tail of the *&* belonging to l. 26; above the *es* are two slight marks that might be the feet of an *H*, and above the *3* a trace of a possible tail of a *y*; while on the main portion, also above the *3*, are two slight marks that might belong to the head of a *y* written rather high at the end of l. 26. There is therefore little doubt that in l. 26 the name *Dab* · was followed, as we should expect, by *& Harry*

32. The reading in the left margin is very doubtful. The only letters that are tolerably certain are the *ai*, before which are substantial traces of at least two letters, one a tall looped one. On the whole I am inclined to think I was right, when editing the *Henslowe Papers*, in supposing that the word intended was 'chairs', and wrong, when preparing my study of *Alcazar and Orlando*, in reading '⟨ ⟩aie:'. The traces at the beginning appear to me to be consistent with *Ch*. The letter after the *i*, though not unlike the scribe's Greek ε in shape, is much too high. It is not either of the forms of 'r' ordinarily employed by the scribe, nor is it like the superior 'r' he uses in 'm^r^'. Nevertheless I think it possible that a superior *r* is meant. The remaining mark is on a level with this superior letter, and therefore too high for a colon; but it might quite well be a superior *s*. I therefore read ⟨*Ch*⟩*ai^rs^*, though with a good deal of hesitation.

33. In the margin before the *es* is a letter which looks at first sight like *r* but is more likely a fragmentary *x*, while earlier is a trace of a tall

looped letter. The word was most likely *boxes*. There is a slight objection in the fact that the *x* would be an Italian one, and that elsewhere in this plot the scribe always uses a minuscule of the English form (see *exeunt* passim). But his majuscule (see l. 14 *Xeque*) is Italian, while in the other plot in his hand the Italian minuscule repeatedly occurs (*Troilus and Cressida*, see l. 10 *exit*, ll. 15, 37, 49 *Aiax*, l. 21 *exeunt*, l. 22 *exit*, ll. 44, 48 *Polixina*).

41. *Cartwight*] sic. 43. *a gains*] sic.

53. *exeunt*] the *un* is represented by three minims only.

57. What looks in the facsimile like a trace of writing at the end of this line is really an accidental mark.

58. Evidently Parsons's christian name was given in this place. It was, in fact, Thomas, but the trace that remains is not consistent with the usual abbreviation 'Tho'. He was, however, a boy and may very likely have been known as 'Tom'. With this the traces can be reconciled, if we suppose them to represent the first two minims of the *m*, the third having been written lower and being now lost.

Since the actors of the Furies are already known from l. 28, the recurrence of the names of George, Parsons, and Tailor in ll. 58–9 proves that nothing is lost at the foot of the first column as one might otherwise be tempted to suppose at first sight. The conclusion is, moreover, confirmed by a closer examination, since had another line followed below l. 58 some trace must almost certainly have remained. There is indeed a trace of a letter, probably *t*, below the *a* of *Parsons*, but it is on a detached fragment which is certainly misplaced; an apparent trace below the *S* of *Somersett* is in fact an accidental mark. Similarly if a rule had been drawn closing this first column some trace would most likely have remained. It was not drawn because it would have been liable to confusion with a scene division.

59. The gap at the end of this line should be filled by the small fragment now placed at the end of l. 107.

60. There is a trace of a tall pointed letter below the *e* of *them* in l. 59, which would be consistent with a *t*.

60–6. A narrow fragment of sufficient depth for about seven lines, containing a portion of the inner right side-rule, and in l. 65 a solitary final letter, *r*, has been placed here in repairing. That it is misplaced is shown by the absence of any trace on it of the rule between ll. 65 and 66. It is also too long for the gap in ll. 78–83, while other apparent gaps in this column we shall find otherwise filled. It follows that it cannot belong to the front sheet at all, but must have formed part of the description of Act v on the back.

[illegible]ed letter. The word was most likely *hand*. There is a slight coincidence in the fact that the word is on its last page and that elsewhere
in this play the scribe always uses a minuscule of the English form (see
[illegible]). But his majuscule (see I, 25, [illegible]) is Italian. While
in the other plays of his hand the Italian majuscule [illegible] rapidly [illegible]
[illegible]

21 [illegible] *Rynnd sir*

[illegible] the [illegible] represented by three minims only.

[illegible] in the facsimile like a trace of [illegible] at the end of this
line [illegible] accidental mark.

8. [illegible] It seems that some [illegible] was given in this place. It was
[illegible] but the trace [illegible] not consistent with the
usual [illegible] over a [illegible] and may very
[illegible] have [illegible] (both) this [illegible] can be
[illegible]. If we suppose there to represent the first two minims of
the [illegible] having been written lower and being now lost [illegible]
[illegible] of the [illegible] already [illegible] 1. 28, the
[illegible] and [illegible] in II, [illegible]
[illegible] at the foot of the first column at one might
[illegible]. The [illegible]
[illegible] another line
[illegible] almost certainly have required
[illegible]
[illegible]
[illegible] the [illegible] in that [illegible]
[illegible] first column [illegible]
[illegible]
[illegible]

[illegible] the small [illegible]
[illegible]

[illegible] of them in [illegible]
[illegible]

61–4. The note in the left margin is in English script and consequently it is impossible to say with complete confidence that it is by the same hand. Nevertheless the resemblance of the word *blood* in l. 62 with the same in ll. 97 and 98 establishes a very strong probability.

62. After the deleted word is a trace of a further letter, possibly another *F*.

64. There is a trace, above the *oo* of *Moor* in the line below, of what may be the tail of an &.

66. Another small detached fragment, bearing a portion of a horizontal rule and the letters *y Torch* (the last two defective), has been mounted near the end of this line. It belongs of course to the first line of a scene (or column), and its present position is by no means impossible. At the same time the only reconstruction of the present line (including the fragment) that occurs to me would be 'bringing in many Torches' and the slight trace that remains before the *y* does not agree well with *n*. Moreover, comparison with the text of the play suggests sound literary reasons for transferring the fragment to l. 107.

69. The numeral *1* has been altered from *2* and we may therefore infer that the next word was originally *Pages* (or *Pagę*) altered to *Page* subsequently.

76. The identification of the second name depends on rather minute traces but is not seriously open to doubt. The letter following the *J* is certainly *e* rather than *o*, which points to the name being Jeffes and not Jones. This is borne out by distinct traces of the tops of the *ff* below the *e* of *Tanger* in the line above. Again, before the *J* is visible the top of a tall pointed letter that exactly fits the top of the second stroke of an *H*. If the name were Jones it would have to be preceded by 'm^r^', which is not compatible with the trace that remains.

*exeunt*] the *un* is represented by three minims only.

77. Near the end of this line considerable traces remain of two letters, apparently *wi*. The word 'with' seems to be required by the context, and the *th*, for which there is room, may have disappeared owing to decay of the surface. On the other hand the *w* does not seem to be of the usual form, and 'with' is nowhere else written out in full. The reading cannot therefore be considered certain. Before the *w* is a mark which may be the top of a tall pointed letter, but may equally be accidental.

84. The traces that remain make the reading *Calipolis* certain.

85. Before *moores* are considerable traces of two letters: the second is almost certainly a badly formed *h* (unless it were a *k* as in l. 15), the first probably either *t* or *c*.

86. The letter before *ding* is I think more likely *n* than *r*.

87. The lower portions of & and *w* and *C* are plainly visible above *exeunt* in the line below.

89. *him*] the *im* is represented by three minims only, with a dot somewhere above the last.

92. The first sign in the margin must I think be meant for *2* but it is badly formed.

93. *banqvett*] the *v* has been altered from some other letter.

96–9. The right-hand portion of the column is here very tattered, and in reparation the ends of the lines have dropped rather low, thus obscuring the alinement.

96. The tail of an & is visible before *lights* in the next line.

97. Before *ghts* are certain traces which suggest the letters *li*, the allusion apparently being to the *tapers* of l. 92. A very slight trace after the colon is consistent with *o*.

99–103. A detached fragment is placed at the end of these lines. As it stands its position is one line too low. The first line of the fragment consists of the letters *ther*, which complete the word *another*, of which the *an* appears at the end of l. 98, while the *o* has left a slight trace both there and on the fragment. When the fragment is so placed it will be found that slight traces before the *J* in the third line and below the *e* of *the* at the end of l. 99 join together to form the head of the *k* needed for the name Dick before Juby. In the word *exeunt* which occupies the fourth line of the fragment the *un* is represented by three minims only.

100. The traces at the beginning of the line put Kendall's name beyond doubt, but he evidently does not appear here in his usual character of a ghost. His part must be indicated by the *w* . . of the fragment, and the only word that suggests itself to me as consistent with the traces that remain is 'war'. Presumably therefore Dick Juby personated some other allegorical figure. Traces below the words *to the* may supply the letters *dic* for his name. The deleted *D* is explained by the scribe being used to follow Kendall's name by Dab, that of the second ghost. After the deletion there is a blank and then what may be the beginning of a *w*.

102. There was certainly space for a line here though it is not certain that anything was written in it. The fragment already mentioned, containing what are really the ends of ll. 98–101, shows no trace of a rule below the word *exeunt* though there is plenty of room. Similarly the fragment next to be discussed, which bears slight traces of l. 101, shows the middle of l. 102 blank, though a very slight trace

on the left-hand edge suggests that some word may have stood at the beginning of it. If so (unless it was an error) the word must presumably have been *omnes*, although it does not elsewhere occur in this Plot (cf., however, *Troilus and Cressida*, l. 24). On the main portion of the sheet, below the word *Furie* in l. 101, there is a good deal of space which would certainly have shown the tops of any tall letters in the line below, though perhaps not of small letters. There is as a matter of fact no trace whatever, the small mark in the facsimile being accidental.

103. The reconstruction here is complicated, but not, I think, open to any serious doubt. Between the remains of ll. 101 and 104 on the main portion of the sheet there is rather ample room for two lines though not enough for three. It will also be observed that the description of this dumb-show extends in any case to thirteen lines (ll. 89–101) and is already the longest in the plot: to carry it on to l. 106 would make it run to eighteen lines. The probability is therefore that there was a rule somewhere between ll. 101 and 104. Now there is in ll. 105–10 a detached fragment bearing a portion of a rule (made to conform to that between ll. 106 and 107). The second line of writing on this fragment begins apparently with the letters *ue* while l. 104 begins with the letters *Ma*, suggesting the name Mahamet Xeque, while the following letters on the fragment appear to be *Cele* which suggests the name Celybin, that of a minor character who appears along with Mahamet Xeque in the first scene of Act IV of the printed text. There is therefore not much doubt of the position, in spite of some slight uncertainty as to the reading of the words of the fragment. The *u* at the beginning of the second line is not wholly beyond question though it seems very probable. What follows certainly looks more like *Cele* than anything else, but certain difficulties must be admitted. The *C* is rather loosely formed: the *l* is clear though damaged: the following letter is also damaged but seems to be an ordinary English *e*. There remains the letter between *C* and *l*. It certainly suggests a loosely formed Italian *e*. Now the scribe commonly uses three forms of minuscule 'e': the ordinary English 'e', the Greek 'ε', and a letter formed like a 'c' with a diagonal stroke added, 'e' (this form, apparently developed from the 'e' of roman fount, appears not infrequently in hands of this period and is often open to confusion with 'o'). The letter in question is none of these. However, I think, that in the word *shew* in l. 4 there is an ordinary Italian '*e*' which will justify our recognizing that letter here also.

105. The letters at the beginning of this line are not very clear, but *att* seems pretty certain, and is apparently followed by an English *e*,

while the back-sweep of a *d* shows above the *tt* exactly as in the word *attendant* in l. 6. Before the *a* is a mark that is apparently accidental.

106. At the beginning of the line we may presume that *m^r Jones* is meant. The scribe apparently wrote *Joes* by accident and crossed it out. The central portion of the line is preserved on the fragment: there are no traces, but the surface may have decayed.

107. Both the fragments in this line we have already utilized elsewhere, the larger (ll. 107–9) for ll. 103–5, the smaller in l. 59. In place of these, as already explained, we bring down the small fragment from l. 66, which here fits very comfortably into the reconstruction, the slight trace of a letter before the *y* being consistent with *b*.

The larger fragment at present mounted as ll. 112–8 clearly belongs to the right-hand bottom corner of a column, and since we now know that the first column is not defective we are bound to bring it up into ll. 107–13 if it is to belong to the front sheet at all. Sufficient remains to identify it with certainty as belonging to IV. ii. The first word preserved on it, *ſaile*, is unquestionably preceded by a blank, but in view of its position there can be no serious doubt that *counſaile* is intended. At the beginning of the third line *ors* is fairly certain, the word perhaps being *soldiors*, though the preceding trace is not altogether suggestive of *i* In the fifth line the last word seems to be *to*: it is blotted and may have been deleted, but it appears to be required.

109. The trace at the beginning of this line looks like the beginning of a *w* (the dot being accidental) and there is a trace of a tall letter following, possibly *t*. The remains should be more extensive but the surface of the paper has decayed.

110. Near the beginning of the line sufficient trace remains to make the letter *t* fairly certain. The decay of the surface accounts for the absence of any further marks.

115–8. On the left of the larger fragment, which we have moved up into ll. 107–13, is a smaller which has been conjoined with it. The reason for this seems to have been the belief that the curl of the *D* at the beginning of the fourth line of the larger fragment was continued onto the smaller. This, however, makes a *D* quite unlike the scribe's, and moreover throws out the alinement. The correct position of the smaller fragment is not known: it is impossible to say for certain that it does not belong to the front sheet, but I have failed to fit it into any reconstruction. In the first line the letters *ge* are clear, followed by a comma and after a blank by a trace that makes it almost certain that the next letter was *J* (probably *page*, *Jeames*). The third line shows an *s* probably preceded by an *r* and followed by a colon, and then an *m* followed by but detached from the beginning of some other

letter. The last line bears the certain remains of *rg* probably preceded by *o* and followed by *e* (no doubt *George*).

All the detached fragments have thus been accounted for except three: the long narrow strip in ll. 60–6, which pretty certainly belongs to the back sheet; the fragment in 115–8, just discussed, which also probably belongs there; and the small fragment bearing a trace probably of a *t*, now mounted below l. 58, which may belong almost anywhere. The possibility that any of the fragments do not belong to the Plot at all may fortunately be dismissed. It is true that *Troilus and Cressida* is written in the same hand, and that the two documents were probably at one time in a bundle together. They are, however, written in inks of strikingly different colours, and no confusion would be possible.

## *Notes—Critical*

(the references are to Transcript VI^B)

3. The Presenter (as he is subsequently called) is here described as 'a Portingall', or Portuguese, and was therefore not dressed in the traditional garb of the Prologue.

This line already illustrates the danger in which the scribe stood throughout of omitting mention of the actors: Alleyn's name was here added as an afterthought.

5–8. Notice that two principal and five minor characters enter together but that the actors' names are not massed at the end but placed immediately after the individual characters or group of characters they impersonate.

10. Kendall reappears in another character at the beginning of the next scene. This is rendered possible by the fact that the dumb-show ended (and in this case the curtains of the alcove closed) before the Presenter had concluded his speech, thus affording time for a change of costume. This arrangement can still be traced in the quarto. The same must be assumed in the cases of the later dumb-shows also.

11–6. The actors are again distributed at the beginning of this scene (ll. 11–4), but are massed at the close (ll. 14–6). Perhaps it was the string of 'attenda[n]tę wth the Bassa' that upset the scribe's intention.

14. 'Muly mahamet Xeque' is the name of a single character distinct from the 'Muly Mahamett' of l. 5.

15. 'Abdula Rais & Ruben' (called Abdil Rayes and Rubin Arches in the quarto) are female characters.

17–22. The description of this scene is altogether anomalous, the scribe having got badly muddled over the actors. In the earlier part six characters enter but only two actors are assigned at the end of the string. Mahamet has appeared before as played by Edward Alleyn, so there was no need to mention the actor here. Hunt and Cartwright were his attendants in the dumb-show and therefore here too: they are named because the characters are minor ones. We are to suppose that his pages likewise remain the same, namely Alleyn's and Towne's boys, though these are not here specified. But neither Calipolis nor Pisano has been on before, and the actors who took the parts should have been named. Who played Calipolis we are never informed; but the actor of Pisano appears incidentally from the anomalous description of the end of the scene. After adding to the former entrants 'young Mahamet' and unnecessarily specifying his actor, the scribe proceeds 'exit m^r Sam manet the rest', thus substituting the name of an actor for the character he played. But we know from the quarto that the character who went off in the middle of the scene was Pisano: therefore Pisano was played by Sam. Further the character who enters near the end is a Messenger who tells of Pisano's capture: when therefore we read 'to them m^r Sam a gaine', another substitution of actor for character, we have to suppose that Sam after changing re-entered to double the part of Messenger with that of Pisano.

26. The '3·ghosts' are apparently those of Abdelmenen and Mahamet's two young brothers, who are murdered in the first dumb-show: the actors Kendall and Dab correspond, and the third, whose name is lost here and at l. 61, must therefore be Harry (which the traces here confirm).

27. 'lying behind the Curtaines', i.e. in the alcove, and no doubt to be discovered by drawing the curtains aside.

34. It is Ruben's 'young sonne' who is played by Dab.

45. The name of the actor who played Sebastian was inadvertently omitted, nor was the oversight repaired on any of his later appearances.

51. No actors are assigned for the pages who accompany the ambassadors from Mahamet, and we are left to infer that the scribe had in mind the same pair that attended Mahamet himself at ll. 7 and 18.

54. The substitution of 'him' for 'them' shows that scribes attached some weight to the distinction and that we have been justified in drawing inferences from it.

67. The name 'w· Kendall' must have been here inserted in error: he cannot possibly be an attendant because he plays Hercules who enters immediately after. The attendants were not Hunt and Sam, for they were black as moors, and moreover the scribe first entered Hunt's name only to delete it again. I conjecture that Dab and Harry were

made to serve, and that Kendall's name was accidentally added owing to his association with them in the previous scene.

75–6. There is reason to suppose an error here, but the details are conjectural, depending on the relation of Plot to quarto and possible restoration of the extensive mutilations in the next scene, and cannot conveniently be discussed here. It must suffice to say that I believe 'a Captains' to be a mere slip for '2 Captains', and that Sam's name, as acting the second of these, has been accidentally omitted.

87. I believe Hunt's name to have been omitted before the first '&' of this line, but the reconstruction is of course quite hypothetical.

97 ff. The action here is obscure and the end of the description of the scene even more conjectural than usual. I think the 'blood' was used to extinguish the 'lights', i.e. the '2. tapers' of l. 92. I have no confidence whatever in the restoration of 'Dyppe', but it is the best I can do. Dip did have the sense of drench, as in *Comus*, l. 802: 'a cold shuddring dew Dips me all o'er.' A little later 'war' and 'weapons' are roving shots suggested by slight hints in the quarto.

111. Although the reconstruction here depends a good deal on inference, there seems little doubt that Kendall's name was erroneously inserted instead of that of the character he played, namely Hercules. Had the character been given there would have been no need to mention the actor.

113. This line, followed by a rule, ends the second column and the fourth act. The few small fragments unplaced presumably come from the back sheet and the fifth act, but they are too small to throw any light on its construction.

## VII—1 *TAMAR CAM*

*Preservation.*—Of this Plot the original has disappeared, and it is now known only through a transcript by Steevens which was printed by Isaac Reed in the 1803 'Variorum' Shakespeare. This renders the task of interpretation rather difficult, since we cannot be certain either how far Steevens's transcript was reliable, or how accurately it was followed by the printer. Some opinion on the point we are, however, able to form, for two other Plots, *The Dead Man's Fortune* and *Frederick and Basilea*, were printed at the same time from the same source. Happily, although small differences of spelling are numerous, more serious lapses are comparatively rare: we find 'sir' for 'hir' in the one, and 'Myron-hamet' for 'Myron-hamec' and 'goliors' for 'soliors' throughout the other. At the same time it must be admitted that Steevens took certain quite unwarrantable liberties. He transferred marginal additions to the text, and printed deletions as though they stood; he also substituted 'enters' for 'Enter' and 'servants' for 'seruant' to suit what he erroneously supposed to be the sense required. It would appear, therefore, that while his transcript of 1 *Tamar Cam* may be generally trusted as regards the main features of the Plot, considerable caution is needed in making inferences from points of detail. This is the more unfortunate in that the Plot is evidently in itself a particularly difficult and particularly interesting one.

*Identification.*—*Tamar Cam*, as it is called in the heading of the Plot, or *Tamber Cam*, as Henslowe spells it, was originally in the repertory of Lord Strange's men. The Second Part was acted by them at the Rose as a new piece on 28 Apr. 1592, though it does not follow that it was new except at that theatre. The First Part must of course already have been in existence; it was most likely written some years earlier, since it appears to have been planned as a rival to Marlowe's *Tamburlaine* (? 1587) which belonged to the Admiral's company. It would seem, however, that *Tamar Cam* passed, as his personal property, to Edward Alleyn during his association with Strange's

men, and that he brought it with him to the Admiral's company when the reorganized troop began playing again in London in the spring of 1594. For a couple of years the piece lay idle, but early in 1596 it was revived and possibly revised, for Part I was acted as new on 6 or 7 May, and Part II also as new on 11 June, that year. The former proved much the more successful, and it was presumably this if not the whole play that the Admiral's men purchased from Alleyn on 2 Oct. 1602 for £2, the usual price for an old Book.

The Plot clearly belongs to the Admiral's company and is late. The absence of Jones and Shaa from the cast presumably indicates a performance after Jan. 1602, while Singer who is present probably left early in 1603. We may perhaps conclude that when the company bought the play from Alleyn they were contemplating a revival. Alleyn may have been preparing to retire about this time, and in 1601 and 1602 he parted with a number of the Books in his possession. But he himself took part in the performance: the exact date of his retirement is not known, but we have no evidence that he acted regularly after Elizabeth's death, though his name appears in the warrant when the company was taken under the patronage of Prince Henry in 1604. The date 1602 is therefore pretty safe for the Plot.

The subject of the play is somewhat obscure. One can hardly doubt that by the name 'Tamar Cam' is meant Timur Khan, especially as 'Tamor' and 'Cham' appear as variant spellings in the text. It seems, however, unlikely that the hero was the figure known to history by that name, the grandson and successor of Khublai Khan, whose uneventful reign as second Mongol emperor of China lasted from 1294 to 1307. It is true that the name Timur Khan was sometimes applied (as by Peter Heylin) to Timur i Leng (Timur the Halt) or Tamerlane, but such an identification seems to be excluded here by the mention of 'Mango Cham', who can hardly be other than Mangu Khan (1251–9), grandson of Jenghis Khan and elder brother of Khublai. And this possibly gives us a hint for the correct solution. If the play was written as a rival to *Tamburlaine*, what more effective counterblast could there be than one celebrating the exploits of the far greater conqueror Jenghis Khan? The suggestion tallies well with the prominence given to the Persian Shah, who would in that case be Mahommed of Khwarizm, and the procession of subject races at the end of Part I would be entirely appropriate; while the Second Part might be supposed to have celebrated the Mongol successes in Russia and China. It is possible that the unknown author boldly altered the name of his hero to one more familiar to his audience, but it is also conceivable that he knew that Jenghis Khan is properly an honorific and that his real name was Temuchin, and made this an excuse for giving his play a title closely similar to that of the piece he sought to rival.

We may suspect that for all but the barest outline of the action the author drew upon his imagination, seeing that he appears to have done so for all minor characters. Geography rather than history supplied him with Colmogra, Pontus, and Ascalon. Otanes is possibly a perversion of Orcanes, the name of the second Ottoman emperor, Artaxes of Artaxias, that of a king of Armenia mentioned by Petrus Bizarus. I am indebted to Miss U. Ellis-Fermor for keeping a look-out for the names in this Plot while working at the sources of *Tamburlaine*.

*Characteristics.*—The form of the name 'Denygten', which can hardly be anything but Steevens's misreading of 'Doughton', the spelling of 'Downton' that appears in *The Battle of Alcazar*, suggests that the two Plots were prepared by the same scribe, though in the present case this name at least must have been written in English and not in Italian script. It is, however, most unlikely that the scribe discarded his very legible and fairly elegant Italian for English throughout. The script of the name may have been an accident (such as we see in *The Dead Man's Fortune*); or possibly the scribe was experimenting with a new distinction, writing the names of characters in an Italian and those of actors in an English hand.

The suggestion that the present Plot was the work of the same scribe as *The Battle of Alcazar* is borne out by the generally similar nature of the plotting, though there are some signs of technical development. The play is regularly divided

into five acts by entrances of the 'Chorus', but these are not numbered nor is the division otherwise recognized by the scribe. So far as can be judged the division into scenes is perfectly regular. Final exits are generally recorded, though there are exceptions (II. ii, III. i, III. v, V. i, V. iii), and so in many cases are internal exits (in connexion with which some apparent errors or omissions are discussed in the notes). The term 'manet' (for both numbers) is used, but there is a tendency to dispense with it where no ambiguity results.

In the case of the named characters it was clearly the scribe's intention to specify the actor on the first appearance but not subsequently. But as usual there is some inconsistency. Dick Juby's name appears unnecessarily as Chorus in l. 24 and as Diaphines in l. 39, Sam's as Ascalon in l. 54, and Charles's as Artaxes in l. 102. On the other hand no actor is specified for Tarmia, even on her first appearance at l. 59, or for Palmeda on hers at l. 69. Further, Charles's name appears in place of Artaxes in l. 45, and there is the anomalous mention of 'Jack Jones' in a deletion (l. 74). The specification of 'supers' also appears to be rather lax, though there is some suspicion that this may be due in part to Steevens (l. 13). The attempt to avoid massing the characters, observable in *The Battle of Alcazar*, appears to have been abandoned; but there is still some endeavour to keep groups distinct, as at the beginning of I. i where the noblemen, though massed with Mango, are separated from the attendants (and cf. l. 48). Here too an interesting experiment is made of numbering the actors for the '3 noblemen': it was not very successful apparently (less so than the numbering of the procession) and was not repeated. Other irregularities are discussed under *Casting*.

Something is obviously wrong with the description of IV. i (see ll. 78, 86 notes), but whether the error is due to the scribe or to Steevens there seems no means of knowing, and like uncertainty attaches to l. 13. There is clearly an oversight in the last line of all, where an actor's name is missing, and probably in ll. 15, 36, 38, 48.

The Plot is very explicit in the matter of stage noises so far as the first column is concerned: 'Sound' eight times, 'Alarum' twice, also 'Sound Alarm', 'Sound Sennet', 'Sound flourish', 'Thunder', 'Wind horne', 'Drum a far of'. That the second column has no such notes is almost certainly an error: whether due to the scribe or Steevens it is impossible to say, though not perhaps to guess. No properties are mentioned in the margins, and the text too is reticent. The Drum and Trumpet (ll. 36, 42, 48) imply these properties, though probably characters as well; there are also the 'Drom and Cullers' (l. 103), and I suppose something might be required for the 'orracle' (l. 72); otherwise the only properties specifically recorded are three severed heads in III. iii.

The influence of the Book is not evident in any very specific manner. We may perhaps see it in 'Assinico Drunk' (l. 36), 'Colmogra like a post' (l. 52), 'Tarmia his daughter' (l. 59), 'To her the orracle speakes' (ll. 71–2). There can be little doubt, however, that the uncertainty respecting the rebels in III. iii originates in too close a following of the Book, and to the same may be due that which attends the spirits throughout, though there seems to be some additional carelessness in the wording of ll. 33–4. An undigested direction seems to underlie an error in l. 88, while a careless handling of the Book may account for the muddle at ll. 74–5. No doubt it is also ultimately responsible for some of the problems presented by the casting.

We cannot, I am afraid, altogether trust Steevens for the formal arrangement of the Plot. Analogy would lead us to expect another ruled margin on the right. The position of the first entry of the Chorus as given is certainly anomalous.

*Casting.*—The doubling is not very heavy: Bourne plays Colmogra in Acts I–IV and Artabisus in Act V; Towne who plays the Shah is also cast for the Oracle, but it is not certain whether this involved an appearance; the parts of Tarmia's two Sons are doubled with those of the nymphs Heron and Thia; Dick Juby was busy as Chorus, Trebassus, the spirit Diaphines, a Messenger, and a Trumpet. The minor parts taken by Cartwright, Marbeck, Parr, George, and Parsons—Nobles, Rebels, Attendants, Guards—are constantly doubled, but exactly how, the ambiguity of some of the descriptions leaves vague: Mar-

beck also played the spirit Pontus, Parsons another Spirit and a Nurse. All this, of course, is apart from the procession for which every available actor and attendant was pressed into service.

Some uncertainty arises from the fact that characters who are named in some scenes appear to be included in unnamed groups in others. This is no doubt the result of the scribe having followed somewhat vague directions of the Book. Thus Charles and Dick are cast for the parts of Artaxes and Trebassus who enter with the Shah in I. ii: and when we subsequently find the Shah appearing with unnamed Attendants played by the same actors, it is natural to conclude that the same characters are meant. A similar argument suggests that Artabisus, who is named as Artaxes' companion in v. iii, is the unnamed Noble who accompanies him in v. i. At the same time we may compare the case of the Clown Assinico. The details of the evidence are discussed in the notes (ll. 11, 93, 39).

## *Notes*

3. Dick Juby, who speaks the Chorus throughout, is on as a Trumpet at the end of II. v and as Trebassus (see l. 11) at the beginning of v. i. In neither instance have we any warrant to assume an interval to allow of his changing, and it follows that as Chorus he must have worn the traditional black cloak that could be put on over his other costume.

4. 'Cham', though not actually applied to Tamor, is evidently only a variant spelling of 'Cam'.

5. There is no doubt that by 'Denygten' (cf. ll. 90, 106) is meant Thomas Downton, but the name as it stands is an impossibility, and must somehow have been substituted for 'Doughton', the form in which it appears in *The Battle of Alcazar*. The scribe could hardly have made such an error as this: it must be a misreading by Steevens. The confusion of 'e' and 'o' and of 'n' and 'u' might easily occur either in Italian or English script, but only in the latter could 'gh' be misread as 'yg' (cf. e.g. *The Battle of Alcazar*, l. 64 'gather'). It follows that in the original this name at any rate was written in English script.

   'w. Cart.' is of course William Cartwright.

6. Steevens prints '& (3) W. Parr.' I suppose the parentheses mean that he supplied the '3', and I have therefore omitted it. At the same time some scribes had a trick of enclosing numerals in parentheses. This

is the only instance in the Plots of an attempt to number 'supers', and it does not appear to have been very successful.

7. 'Tamar'. This is the only occasion on which the spelling of the heading appears in the text: elsewhere it is 'Tamor'. The uncertainty is awkward: for the title I have felt bound to follow the heading (*Tamar Cam*), but for the character I have preferred the more frequent spelling (Tamor).

11. The 'Persian Shaugh' (Shah) is elsewhere called 'King of Persia' (l. 59), and the actor (Towne) shows that he is 'the Persian' of l. 49 (cf. 51) and therefore of l. 86: he is also probably the 'Persian' of l. 92. Of course in l. 17 'a Persian' played by Parsons is distinct.

Artaxes, or Attaxes as the name is printed in l. 101, is apparently a follower of the Shah, and is played by Charles. Now Charles plays an Attendant in III. ii and IV. i, and a Noble in III. iii and V. i, always in close association with the Shah. It is natural, therefore, to assume that his part is that of Artaxes throughout, and I have done so in the table. In that case, in III. i, where his name appears by mistake for that of a character, it is likewise Artaxes who is meant to be on, and we shall see that this agrees well with the requirements of the situation.

The Shah's other follower here is Trebassus, who is not named elsewhere. The part is played by Dick Juby, who also appears along with Charles in III. ii, III. iii, and V. i, and may therefore be assumed to personate Trebassus in all those scenes. He does not appear with Artaxes in IV. i because Dick was required to act a Spirit. No doubt these ambiguities of the Plot reflect vague directions in the Book.

13. No actors are provided for the Attendants. It would be just possible to interpret the description as meaning that Charles and Dick played the attendants Artaxes and Trebassus. But it seems much more likely that the names of Parsons and George have been accidentally omitted—perhaps by Steevens, else why is the line so short? These actors are on as Attendants in the previous scene, and they subsequently appear as the Shah's Guard in l. 61 and as his Attendants or Soldiers in l. 87. They may therefore be common 'supers' ready to attend on any character that needs them. Parsons, however, is earmarked as a Persian, since he has little opportunity to change between this and I. iv where he is described as such.

15. A direction for 'attendants' or something of the sort must have been omitted, since none of the actors named played either Tamor or Otanes.

21. 'Exit Colmogra'. Notice that here (and again at l. 62) the plotter has discarded the needless 'manet the rest' found in some earlier Plots.

22. Parsons appears in this scene first as a Persian and later as a Guard. From what has been said above (l. 13) it is doubtful whether he needed to change, but anyhow he had time.

25. The first Spirit, played by Parsons, is not allowed a name, and apparently neither he nor Pontus appears outside this scene.

26–8. 'To him'. If this refers to Otanes, the Spirits do not count, though they remain on. But more likely 'To him another' means 'After him another' (cf. ll. 33–4).

30. 'Spirritts', number unspecified, not even 'the Spirritts'. There cannot be more than three, for Marbeck who played Pontus is required for a Nobleman at the beginning of the next scene. I think probably only Diaphines and Ascalon reappear here and also later on.

33–4. The description 'to him Spirritts: Ascalon. To him Diaphines' is obscure, since it looks as though the named characters were distinguished from the 'Spirritts'. But again not all four Spirits can be present, since Marbeck is engaged in the neighbouring scene. It becomes clear if we recognize that in the case of the Spirits 'to him' means 'after him'; the sense here being 'to Otanes enter Spirritts, first Ascalon, then Diaphines'.

35–6. The '3 nobles' have been specified in ll. 31–2, but none of them can have carried 'a Drum'. This must indicate a character here and not a mere property, and an actor should have been assigned. None of the usual 'supers' are available: perhaps Anthony Jeffes lent a hand.

38. '& George Parsons' can hardly be right. It is perhaps merely a slip for 'George & Parsons' as playing the 'guard'.

39. No 'clowne' has been mentioned (but cf. l. 68): he must therefore be identical with one of the other characters already on the stage. Doubtless he is the drunken Assinico, whose actor, Singer, was a recognized clown. The name is therefore significant: it is a Spanish diminutive, *asnico*, little ass, and occurs as 'Asinico' in Shakespeare's *Troilus and Cressida*, II. i. 49, where modern editors print 'assinego'.

40–2. The 'attendants' Cartwright, Parr, and Marbeck are probably still the three 'noblemen' of l. 31, since they have had little opportunity of changing since l. 35. Parsons and George, the other 'attendants', were probably Guards as in l. 37. Most likely the Book had no more than the direction 'Enter Tamor Cam and Otanes attended'. At the same time one cannot feel quite certain as to the identity of the 'attendants' since Cartwright and Parr certainly, and Marbeck probably, reappear as 'attendants' in IV. i, after the '3 nobles' have been executed in III. iii.

42. 'a Trumpet' is again a character, not a property, and is played by Dick since Parr is not available here as he is in l. 48.

45–6. Not a very clear description. But evidently Cartwright and Marbeck are the two 'pledges', and 'Mr. Charles' therefore appears by mistake for the name of the character he plays. Further the 'pledges' are clearly hostages to be exchanged between Tamor and the Shah: Otanes is a close attendant on Tamor, and it follows that the missing character is the Shah's representative, no doubt Artaxes, the part taken by Charles elsewhere.

48. We can hardly doubt that the name of 'George' as one of the 'Attendaunts' has been accidentally omitted.

49. 'To him'. There are, of course, several persons on the stage, but they are merely followers of Tamor, and the point is that it is to him that the Shah enters.

51. 'Exeunt', sc. Attendants only.

52. 'Colmogra' disguised 'like a post'.

53. 'To Otanes enter Ascalon'. The wording is very unusual. Since no exit is given for Tamor and the Shah, I take the meaning to be that Ascalon enters apart to Otanes, that is, the Spirit appears to him alone and speaks aside.

59. This is Tarmia's first appearance, and the plotter was kind enough to copy from the Book the information that she is the 'King of Persia . . . his daughter', but nevertheless failed to specify an actor for the part.

61–2. 'Exeunt Otanes and nobles w^th the 3 Rebbells'. This is obscure for nothing has been said of any rebels. But the 'nobles' are the 'noblemen' who enter with Otanes in the line above and are played by Charles and Dick (that is, Artaxes and Trebassus I assume, l. 11), since Otanes, Charles, and Dick re-enter each with a severed head, a rebel's of course. It follows that 'the 3 Rebbells' can only be the '3 nobles' of l. 55 (and previously, probably including II. v).

66. The 'Captaine' is probably not a new character but merely the first Guard whom George has played before. Parr, having been executed as a Noble, is now available to eke out the Guards.

69. Palmeda or Palmida, who is attached to Otanes here and in l. 79, is a new character, but the plotter failed to specify the actor. That it was a female part appears from l. 83.

70. Marbeck certainly did not act Tarmia, since he was on as a Noble when she entered in III. iii. There were, therefore, four Guards.

74–5. Steevens only recorded these deleted lines in a footnote, but in-

dicated that they were marked off by rules. I have restored them to their place. It does not follow that a scene was cancelled. It is possible that after the Chorus the scribe turned over two leaves of the Book, and finding an entrance at the top of the page concluded that it was the beginning of an act (cf. *The Dead Man's Fortune*, l. 49). The lines are in effect merely an anticipation of ll. 79–80. A Jack Jones appears to be recorded here as playing Tarmia. But nothing is known of any actor of the name, and since the passage has been deleted it would be risky to rely on the assignment.

76. 'Cam' is, of course, Tamor.

78. There is evidently an omission here, possibly of a whole line or even more. Marbeck and George can hardly have played the 'children', even if Parsons played 'the nurss', and I assume that these were Tarmia's '2 sonns' as in l. 89. Marbeck and George were probably Attendants. Moreover we require an exit for Otanes, who re-enters in the next line.

80. '2. spirritts', we are not told which. But since Marbeck and Parsons, who played the first two in II. i, are apparently already on the stage, we must assume that Diaphines and Ascalon are meant as in II. iii and III. v: their actors Dick and Sam are at liberty.

86. Again there is something wrong, apparently an omission. The Guard has to be got off in l. 85 or l. 86, since Parsons re-enters; and so has Tarmia before her re-entry at l. 89. Moreover, Dick Juby, one of the '2. spirritts' of l. 86, has to change for Trebassus (?) in V. i, which he cannot do while speaking the Chorus. A single exit for Tarmia, Guard, and Spirits at l. 86 would suffice.

88. No actors are assigned for the 'soldiers', and there may be another omission. But usually it is George and Parsons who play the Shah's Guard. It would seem, therefore, that the direction ought to have been 'the Persian with attendants and soldiers'. What is really required and what the Book presumably contemplated was the entry, with the Shah, of Artaxes and Trebassus (played by Charles and Dick) and his Guard (played as before by Parsons and George). But it happened that Dick was otherwise engaged (see 86) and his name was therefore omitted, thus leaving only three actors for four characters ostensibly. Probably his presence was immaterial.

93. 'Mr. Bourne' has hitherto been playing Colmogra, who is attached to Tamor. Here he is evidently a Persian Noble. Another Noble is Charles, presumably as Artaxes. But in V. iii Charles, as 'Attaxes', is accompanied by 'Mr. Boorne' as Artabisus, whence it seems to follow that Artabisus is the character intended here likewise.

97. 'the other little boy' was no doubt 'Mr. Denygtens little boy' as in l. 90.

101. 'Artabisus' has not been named before, but see l. 93.

103. No actors are assigned for 'Drom and Cullers', and I take them to be here merely properties (cf. ll. 35–6, also *The Seven Deadly Sins*, l. 26, and *The Battle of Alcazar*, ll. 79, 103). George and Parsons, as 'attendants', seem usually to be Soldiers; and we may suppose that they bear the 'Drom and Cullers' here.

105. There should be an exit for the 'supers' here, since George, Parr, Parsons, and Marbeck all reappear in the procession. The main characters presumably remain on the stage.

106–17. For convenience I have called this a procession, but, as I imagine it, what really happens is that envoys from twelve conquered races enter in turn to do homage to Tamor, and having done so group themselves for a final tableau. The designations are rather uncertain. 'Amozins' can hardly be other than Amazons, and 'Nagars' may be Niggers, especially since the next pair is distinguished as 'ollive cullord moores', that is, not blackamoors. 'Cattaians' of course are the people of Cathay, and 'Crymms' the Tartars of the Crimea. As regards the 'people of Bohare', we may observe that Peter Heylin gives 'Bochor' as the modern name of the capital of Bactria, which would make them the same as the 'Bactrians'. The 'Geates' are presumably intended for the Getae, a Danubian tribe, whose name, however, at least one oriental historian (or his translator) brought into connexion with that of Tamburlaine (Sheref-al-Dīn, *c.* 1425, trans. F. Petis de la Croix, 1722).

Several points arise respecting the casting. To some extent the pairs in the procession can be traced as already associated in the play, whence we may legitimately conjecture that the 'little Will' who pairs with Jack Grigorie as an 'Amozin' is 'Mr. Denygtens little boy'. He is called his 'little boy' not merely on account of his size but because Parsons too was or had been Downton's 'boy'. He is evidently distinct from 'little will Barne', so called to distinguish him from big Will Borne, i.e. Mr. Bourne or Birde. In the last line the name 'W. Parr' has been deleted, the actor being already engaged, but no other has been substituted. Apparently the only actor available is Singer. Since Tarmia is not on in the final scene there is no doubt that her impersonator, nowhere specified in the Plot, appeared somewhere in the procession. For further speculation on the point see the note on boys in the Actor Lists (pp. 66–9).

## VIII—*ENGLAND'S JOY*

*Preservation.*—The only known copy of the broadside containing 'The Plot of the Play, called *Englands Joy*. To be Playd at the Swan this 6. of Nouember. 1602.' is preserved in the collection belonging to the Society of Antiquaries, to whose courtesy I am indebted for permission to reprint it in facsimile.

From the evidence of the blocks used the sheet may be assigned (on the authority of Dr. McKerrow and Mr. F. S. Ferguson) to the press of John Windet, a printer who had a large business from 1584 to 1611. In 1603 he became printer to the City, and in the seventeenth century at any rate was mainly a trade printer, working more for other stationers than on his own account. There is some reason to suppose that he printed a good deal more in this way than he publicly acknowledged. The right of printing players' 'bills' belonged at this date to James Roberts, but there were circumstances in the present case that might suggest recourse to a less authoritative press.

*Identification.*—It is doubtful whether the play of *England's Joy* ever existed: it seems to have been a mere hoax by one Richard Vennar of Lincoln's Inn, who succeeded in attracting an audience at the Swan at a good price and then attempted to abscond. The relevant evidence is given by Sir E. K. Chambers in *The Elizabethan Stage* (iii. 500).

*Characteristics.*—The 'Plot' consists of descriptions of nine scenes depicting the triumphs of Elizabeth's reign. It bears no definite relation to the technical theatrical Plots, but its form may have been in some measure suggested by them. Since no regular Bills of the time survive, it is impossible to say how far it resembled them, but the matter has been discussed in an essay on 'The Origin of the Theatre Programme' by Mr. W. J. Lawrence (*The Elizabethan Playhouse*, ii. 57).

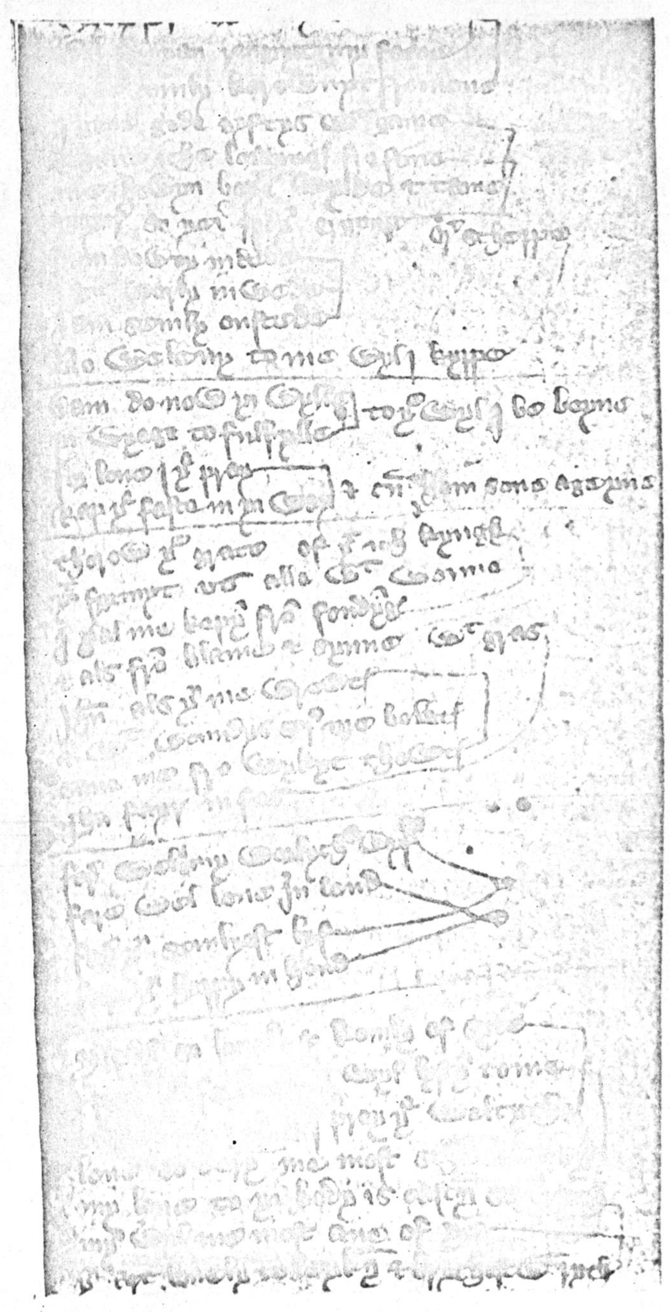

PORTION OF THE DUX MORAUD ROLL

*(slightly reduced)*

Pastores erant ī regione eadē vigilā
tes & custodientes gregē suū. Et ecce
angelus dnī astitit iuxta illos & timuerūt
timore magno.

PAGE FROM THE SHREWSBURY FRAGMENTS

*(slightly reduced)*

Sathan · suche pollicye in you

Bois

Whi not Sathan in all thinges that be · good:

Sathan yf prudent in mischefe

Bois

Yet the same may be the good mens releife

yt proves not that, for it is a mischefe done to [illegible]

Worth with pollicie & prudents fall downe in [illegible]

now wherfore here cannot be false in evell meaninge

That I, take prudently thy malicious workinge

But [illegible] falshod [illegible] such pollicy

are alwaies to covenant in thy nature [illegible]

Sathan · I am right sure

Bois

Why therfore playest here in the first

Aske them whom thou sholdest I saue not [illegible]

Thou callest them sinners [illegible] they are not

by that they be [illegible] from [illegible]

Now I do not [illegible] the [illegible] in this

Sathan · True that –

Bois

Then take the commissioners whom thou wilt [illegible]

I will abyde the iudgement of these

If it be [illegible] the commission [illegible]

That I have done thy wrong take them [illegible]

Againe wilt ye take or [illegible] lot [illegible]

Sathan · I cannot tell what

Bois

here is Abraham wilt thou have him ·

Sathan · not [illegible] you

PORTION OF THE PROCESSUS SATANAE PART

*(slightly reduced)*

FRAGMENT OF A MIRACLE PLAY ATTACHED TO A COURT-ROLL OF RICKINGHALL MANOR, SUFFOLK

# ACTORS' PARTS

## MEDIEVAL EXAMPLES

WE might well assume on general grounds that actors' Parts would be among the most ephemeral of dramatic documents, and the assumption is not contradicted by the available evidence. Perhaps we should hardly have expected that as many as three examples would have come down to us from pre-restoration days. As it is, the fourteenth, fifteenth, and sixteenth centuries contribute each an example (cf. p. 175). None appear to have survived from the seventeenth century previous to the closing of the theatres: whether any of the later seventeenth or eighteenth centuries exist I do not know: I have not heard of any.

The earliest is that of the chief male part in a miracle of the Virgin, the well-known tale of the incestuous daughter. It is headed 'Dux moraud' (Duke Vagabond), but whether this was the title of the play or the name of the character is uncertain. It is in stanzaic verse of various forms and is written in the usual manner of the time, with rules connecting the riming lines and the shorter lines placed in the right margin. There are no cues, and the speeches are separated by horizontal rules. As a result of this arrangement the document was supposed to be a collection of independent lyrics until its true character was recognized by Dr. W. Heuser, who published the text in 1907 (*Anglia*, xxx. 180–208). It is written on the two sides of a strip of vellum, 4 feet 2 inches long and $3\frac{3}{4}$–4 inches wide, cut off an assize roll for Norfolk and Suffolk, as appears from a few fragments of the original writing that remain. This suggests an East Anglian origin, which is borne out by scribal peculiarities. The writing is obviously of the fourteenth century, not I should imagine very early: this would make it about a century later than the original assize roll, which is assigned to the second half of the thirteenth century. The hand is very clear and legible, but the text is in parts faded or obliterated beyond recovery. The strip has been rolled for convenience of carrying or storing. The accompanying facsimile of one of the better preserved portions will give an idea of the general arrangement. The roll is in the Bodleian Library (no. 30519) now classed as MS. Eng. Poet. f. 2 (R).

The example from the fifteenth century is preserved in the library of Shrewsbury School, where it was discovered by W. W. Skeat and published in 1890 (*The Academy*, 4 and 11 Jan.). The volume is a *sequentiale* or collection of Latin sequences, tropes, or proses, with accompanying music, for use in the liturgy. The history of the manuscript is unknown, but it is just possible that it is of local provenance and was actually written at, or at least prepared for use at, Shrewsbury itself. At the end (fols. 38[a]–42[b]) are portions of some miracle plays in English. These are written in a different hand, or at any rate a different style, from the rest, but the Latin passages that accompany them, with musical setting, reveal the same writing as the earlier portion of the volume. This then evidently forms an organic whole, and must have been prepared for the use of an individual cantor to whom it fell to take the parts in question in certain liturgical plays. The plays and parts are three in number: *Officium Pastorum*, third Shepheard; *Officium Resurrectionis*, third Mary; *Officium Peregrinorum*, Cleophas. The first clearly has some relation to the corresponding play of the York cycle: indeed it appears to be a briefer version of that piece as it may be supposed to have existed before lines 37–85, which are in a different stanza, had replaced a passage metrically similar to the rest. The speeches are written consecutively with cues in the right margin. There are rime rules almost throughout, but they seem to have been added rather roughly at a later date. On the first page there is a paragraph mark at the beginning of each speech (see facsimile), but later the paragraphs appear to indicate the stanzaic structure while the speeches are divided by rules.

These examples afford unfortunately but a slender basis of comparison with that surviving from the sixteenth century. The point of contact afforded by the roll form of *Dux Moraud* may of course be accidental: at the same time the fact that the liturgical Parts survive in a volume is certainly no argument against the use of the conveniently carried roll in more popular

performances. We may fairly assume that when the former was written the use of cues was not yet general, but their presence in the Shrewsbury examples proves that they were at least as old as the fifteenth century, and once introduced they would hardly fall out of use again.[1]

*Postscript.*—While these pages were passing through the press another actor's part came to light. It was found in the library of the Duke of Portland at Welbeck Abbey, belongs apparently to the later sixteenth century (*c.* 1570–80), and contains the part of God in a miracle play. As repaired it forms a paper roll, six inches wide and nearly four feet long, consisting of three strips, and at the end the text runs over and is continued reversed on the back: it is, however, not certain that this was its original form. In arrangement it is the most explicit of the known Parts. It has a heading 'God the father speaketh', and contains one stage-direction referring to another character. Each speech is headed with the name 'God'. There are cues of three or four words generally, and the speaker of the cue is given: he is in almost every case 'Sathan'. The direction 'An houre space' marks the absence of God from the stage. At the end is 'finis' and a scribal (?) signature, apparently Jiggons. The text is printed in the Malone Society's Collections (ii. 237–50) under the title of *Processus Satanae*.

[1] It is possible, though not I think likely, that the beginning of another actor's part is preserved in a fragment of a miracle play in French and English, written possibly at Bury St. Edmunds, or at least in Suffolk, early in the fourteenth century, and acquired by the British Museum in 1921 (Add. Roll 63481. B). It was published by the late J. P. Gilson in *The Times Literary Supplement* of 26 May that year. In reply to a suggestion of mine that the leaf was scrivener's waste, having been cancelled owing to an error of the scribe, Mr. Gilson wrote: 'Your theory of the scribe's omission is very possible, but I can't satisfy myself as to the format [roll or leaf]. I think the holes on the right look like sewing, but if so it is a verso page with blank recto, which is odd. Was it written on the fly-leaf of some book whose main contents were different? If so, is it an actor's part? The *assit principio* [a superscription running: 'Assit principio sancta maria meo'] is not I think conclusive against this. The verse about the crow [following the superscription, and running: 'Coruum perfidie dapnant [*sc.* damnant] animalia queque'—'which may be mere scribbling'] is a little against its being a regular full-dress text of the play.'

## ORLANDO—DESCRIPTION AND CHARACTERISTICS

The only actor's part that has reached us from the Elizabethan theatres is that apparently used by Edward Alleyn for the title-role in Greene's play *Orlando Furioso*. This piece was apparently written in the autumn of 1591 soon after the appearance of Harington's translation of Ariosto, and contemporary gossip accused the author of selling it to the Queen's men for twenty nobles (£6 13*s*. 4*d*.), and when they were in the country selling it over again to the Admiral's men for a like sum. It was acted at Court before Elizabeth, probably by the Queen's men on 26 Dec. 1591. On 21 or 22 Feb. 1592 Strange's men (at this time in some sort of alliance with the Admiral's) gave a public performance of it at the Rose: it was not advertised as new and was not successful. It is highly probable that Alleyn, himself a servant of the Lord Admiral, was then acting with Strange's company, and it is possible that it was for this performance that the extant Part was prepared, or at least used. The fact that Alleyn's hand appears in it, proves that even if it was obtained legitimately from the Queen's men, gossip notwithstanding, it must have been carefully revised after it left their possession.

In 1594 appeared a quarto edition of the play printed by John Danter for Cuthbert Burby. The copy had been registered by Danter on 7 Dec. 1593 and transferred by him to Burby on 28 May following. The text of this edition is manifestly corrupt, and comparison with the Part shows it to be an altogether degenerate version or perversion which presupposes some quite exceptional circumstances of production. What these may have been is a problem which does not concern us here: I attempted a solution in my essay on *Two Elizabethan Stage Abridgements*. A reprint of the wretched changeling appeared in 1599, and these two quartos have perforce formed the basis of modern editions, though it would be unfair to charge Greene with the results. It is not surprising that Harington, compiling a catalogue of the plays in his library about 1610 (B.M., MS. Add. 27632, fol. 43[a]), should have entered his unwelcome god-child as 'Orlando Foolioso'!

Whatever may have been the origin of the extant Part it

remained in Alleyn's possession and is preserved among his papers at Dulwich, where it now forms MS. 1, item 138. Though both mutilated and defective it still contains some 530 lines representing the speeches and cues of Orlando for about two-thirds of the play. It has been several times printed: first and rather incorrectly by Collier as an appendix to his *Memoirs of Edward Alleyn* (1841, p. 198), again more incorrectly by Churton Collins in his edition of Greene's plays (1905, i. 266); next in my *Henslowe Papers* (1907, p. 156) still with some errors, and lastly in my *Alcazar and Orlando* (1923, p. 142). In this the Part is printed parallel with the corresponding portions of the quarto of 1594, and a renewed collation of the text for the present transcript has not revealed any material differences of reading, though I have occasionally altered my opinion on points of difficulty where the manuscript is obscure.

The Part is written on a number of strips of paper, which were pasted together to form a long roll. They were still at least in part joined together when first discovered and edited, but have now been separated and bound as leaves in a volume. The strips were formed by dividing a foolscap sheet lengthwise, thus giving a full measurement of approximately $16\frac{1}{4} \times 6$ inches. The width is more constant than the length and the edges were probably trimmed to ensure a tidy roll. The number of strips originally used for the Part cannot now be determined with complete certainty, but fourteen seems to be the most likely number and has been assumed in the following account. In that case the small fragment at the beginning of the extant portion is the end of the third strip.[1] Strips 4, 5, and 6 are continuous, with a small lacuna in 5 and the loss of the end of 6. After this a whole strip (7) is evidently absent. Strips 8 to 14 are continuous, but the end of the last, containing what corresponded to the last 21 lines of the quarto text, is again lost. Full-length strips vary by as much as a quarter or perhaps half an inch in length, but not all were entire when the Part was

[1] Were we to make the hazardous, but still possible, assumption that in the earlier scenes the quarto preserves Orlando's part in its entirety, the fragment would probably be the end of the second strip.

written. Strip 13 is only 13¾ inches long; strip 14 need not have been more than 10½ or 11. These last two strips have evidently been trimmed at the top, while some of the others may have been slightly trimmed at the bottom. Slips 6, 9, 10, 11, 12, 13 have the name 'Orlando' written at the head (it has been almost entirely cut away from 13, and may of course have been wholly removed from 14). Slip 6 begins a fresh scene and the name may be intended to mark an entry, like the direction 'Enter' at l. 219. But the other five instances occur in the middle of scenes, and the name must have been written to prevent the strips getting mixed with those of other Parts before they were made up into a roll. Perhaps it was proposed to cut the names off, as was done on strip 13, or possibly to cover them in the overlap when pasting the strips together, though the fact that the writing always stops well above the end of the strip suggests that the overlap was intended to be the other way, and indeed the traces of paste and the evidence of worm-holes shows that it actually was so in most cases. The overlap seems as a rule to have varied from ½ to 1 inch: if we take the average to be ¾ inch and the average length 16¼ inches, we get a probable effective length for the first twelve strips of 15½ inches each, and adding 12½ inches (with an unusually wide overlap) for strip 13, and 11 inches (without overlap) for 14, we arrive at a total length of 209½ inches, or almost 17½ feet, of which about 56 inches, or just over a quarter, is lost.

The Part was still in roll form when Collier saw it, but even without his testimony it would have been easy to reconstitute its form from the disposition of the holes eaten by the worms that attacked it from the outside. Their most extensive depredations are in strips 5 and 6: there is comparatively little damage to strip 4, and it is doubtful how far the loss of the earlier strips is due to them and how far to ordinary wear and tear: strips 13 and 14 are almost untouched. The different groups of worm-holes are found repeated with varying configuration over and over again, and enable us in some measure to trace the laps of the roll. On strip 4 the lap is of 5¾ inches, on strip 12 it is 4 inches. This means that near the centre the roll was just over 1¼ (1·28) inch in diameter, near the outside

over 1¾ (1·83) inch. In the nine strips (4–12) there must have been nearly thirty laps, and they must have been fairly tightly rolled, since the average difference between successive laps is only about $\frac{1}{20}$ inch, each increasing the diameter by less than $\frac{1}{50}$ inch. The last two strips were evidently less closely, i.e. more steeply, rolled, for in 13 the distance between the worm-holes decreases rapidly and in 14 appears quite irregular. The three strips lost at the beginning would have formed eight laps, so that the complete roll must have been almost exactly two (1·97) inches in diameter. The fact that the worms attacked mainly the outside of the roll might be supposed to be due to its having been wound on a stick, were not the suggestion negatived by the steeper pitch of the inner laps, while this sharper bending of the paper may account for the way in which it seems to have broken across.

The Part is written in a somewhat unusual, ornamental, and at times rather beautiful, secretary hand, varied by an elegant Italian script in the passages of Latin and Italian and some of the marginal directions. The two varieties may be seen at their best about the middle of strip 4 and in the lower half of strip 5. The scribe was presumably accustomed to the work, for on the whole he has made a competent and eminently tidy job of it. This in spite of occasional oversights: for example at ll. 264–5 he originally omitted portions of a speech, and just below (278–9) copied in, and deleted, a speech by another character; at l. 295 he omitted a cue (later supplied by the corrector), and at l. 459 entered the wrong cue in the first instance. It is also clear that he was sometimes unable to read his original, and had the grace to leave blanks in which the missing words could be inserted later. These blanks were, however, often inadequate even on the scale of his own writing. They were still more inadequate for the sprawling hand of the corrector, who filled most of them in and made sundry other emendations in the text. That this corrector was Alleyn admits of no doubt. All the major additions are in his hand, and while it would not be possible to identify the writing of many of the lesser alterations, and this writing does appear to vary a good deal, there is no sufficient reason to suspect that more than one revisional hand has been at work. Except in a few trifling alterations there is little possibility of doubt between the hands of the scribe and the corrector: the main exception is connected with the curious problem of ll. 450 and 455–6, discussed in the notes.

Besides the blunders already mentioned there are undoubtedly a certain number of errors in the text, occasionally involving the metrical alinement. This, however, is a matter that cannot be discussed apart from the question of the quarto text, and it has already been somewhat lengthily treated in my *Stage Abridgements*. I may be allowed, therefore, to refer those interested to the textual commentary that occupies pp. 202–48 of that volume, in which they will also find further discussion both of the extent of the defects in the Part (pp. 135–7, 200–1) and of the handwriting of the corrections (pp. 138–9), besides a fuller account of the composition, performance, and publication of the play (pp. 125–31). I may, however, repeat here that the errors remaining in the text of the Part after Alleyn's revision are generally trifling, and that it is evidently based on a thoroughly sound and authoritative copy, thus standing in marked contrast to the absurd pervertion of the quarto.

It only remains to give some account of the general characteristics of the Part. It is written as verse and the line division is mainly correct, such confusions as occur being quite possibly reproduced from the prompt book itself. The cues consist as a rule of two or three words, sometimes of no more than one. There is no indication of scene division, and it would be difficult to determine the distribution of the speeches in the play without recourse to the Book. In one place (l. 219) the word 'Enter' marks the entrance of the speaker at the beginning of a new scene; at another (l. 119) the heading 'Orlando' together with the marginal direction '*solus*' probably has the same significance. But there is no heading at l. 377 where the speaker enters in the course of a scene, nor in similar circumstances at l. 421.[1] Exits are usually marked: such an indication may have been lost in the mutilation of l. 118 (if it stood on the right) before 'Orlando. *solus*'; one remains in the left margin of l. 218 (before the 'Enter'), another at l. 375; that which should have

[1] At these points, however, cues are provided for Orlando's entrance.

stood at l. 420 was omitted by the scribe, but the corrector supplied 'Exeunt', rather incorrectly, for it is Orlando only who goes off.

There are some stage-directions in the left margin, though they are not very numerous. Among them (ll. 101–5) are '*dragges him in*' and '*enters w^th^ a mans legg*' indicating a momentary exit and re-entry in the course of a scene. Occasionally the directions refer to other characters, thus 'A[rgalio]. begins to weepe' (ll. 162–3), '*currũt*' (l. 301), '*Inchaũt*' (l. 308), besides, in form at least, 'N[amus]. victus', 'Oliuer victus', 'O[gier]. victus' (ll. 446, 453, 468). Some of these directions are written in English and others in Italian script, but beyond the fact that the latter is always used for Latin ones, no distinction can be observed. This use of Latin for stage-directions in an actor's Part is rather remarkable, and is perhaps a relic of Greene's university pretentions, but they must at least have been intelligible, or thought to be intelligible, to the actors. It is perhaps worth remark that the scribe's Latin is correct, while his attempt to write Italian called for heavy correction by Alleyn. All the more elaborate directions are in English.

How far this sole survivor is typical of the thousands of Elizabethan actors' parts that have presumably perished it is impossible to say. No doubt these differed somewhat in different companies and at different dates. But this much comparison with the earlier examples warrants our assuming: that the roll form was probably at least common, and that cues of two or three words at most were the general rule.

In the transcript whole words added or substituted by the corrector, presumably Alleyn throughout, are printed in heavy type, but alterations involving less than a whole word are only recorded in the notes. The present notes are mainly repeated from the transcript of the Part given in *Two Elizabethan Stage Abridgements* (*S.A.*), but a few depending on comparison with the quarto of 1594 (Q.) have been omitted. Differences of reading from this earlier transcript have been recorded, but it has not been thought necessary to mention errors in the *Henslowe Papers*. No notice is taken of a few cases in which letters previously marked as doubtful are now treated as certain and vice versa. The phrase 'altered from' means that the reading given in the transcript is the result of alteration from something else. Thus '*r* altered from *s*' (l. 31) means that the scribe originally wrote *s* ('his') and then altered the letter to *r* ('hir'). The phrase 'altered' by itself means that the reading given is the result of an alteration from something not now determinable.

4. After 'loue' there appears to be a very slight trace of a point on the edge of a worm-hole.

8. In 'lawdes' the stroke indicating the omission of 'n' (unusual above 'w') appears to have been added later, possibly by the corrector.

10. The name 'Clora' has been inserted by the corrector in a space left blank by the scribe.

13. The corrector crossed out the word 'for' and inserted before it a point that looks like a colon with a tick above it; the upper dot, however, is not quite certain.

31. In 'hir' the 'r' has been altered from 's'.

33. Before 'and' is a diagonal stroke which touches the 'a' but is apparently independent of it.

42. The word 'are' looks as though it had been inserted later: the hand is doubtful, but the ink apparently the same as in the rest of the line.

43. In 'for̃ming' the mark over the 'r' appears to be original. At l. 382 a similar mark seems to indicate a transposition, and it may be so here. The correct reading is probably 'framing' (Q.).

44. In 'making' the 'k' has been altered from 'ſ'.

45. The use of a long 'ſ' at the end of a word is anomalous, but occurs in some hands: cf. ll. 370, 469.

47. The deletion is rather untidy and might be due to the corrector; the ink, however, is apparently that of the scribe. The words are written in English script except for an Italian '*J*'.

50. The beginning of the line was left blank by the scribe, but nothing has been inserted.

53. In 'refuſd' there is an apparently unsignificant pen-flick after the 'd', which seems to have been altered from 'e'. In 'contemd' the 'm' has been altered from 'n'.

62. 'Ate' inserted by the corrector in a blank space.

67. In 'loue' the 'o' has been touched up or altered: probably a larger 'o' written over a smaller one.

69. The corrector has crossed out 'and for' and interlined 'offer' above.

71. The word 'cõpound' is rather crowded and may have been written in a space originally left blank. The deletion and interlineation are the corrector's.

83. In 'loues' the 'o' has been touched up.

87. In 'thẽ' the 'ẽ' has been altered from 'y', probably by the scribe. The deletion and interlineation are the corrector's.

92–9. The corrector has made numerous small alterations in these lines as follows:

95. In '*credi*' the '*e*' has been altered from '*a*'.

97. The cross of the '*đ*', standing for an apostrophe, has been added. In '*Conſiglio*' the '*C*' has been altered from '*l*', the '*ſ*' from '*g*', and the '*io*' from '*a*'; the scribe having written '*longigla*'.

99. In '*al*' the '*l*' has been altered from '*tt*'. In '*nate*' the '*e*' has been added to replace a deleted '*a*'.

100. The interlineation is the corrector's. The word transcribed as 'is' may have been altered and the reading is uncertain.

107. In 'Cerberus' the 'b' may have been altered from 'l'.

108. The alteration of 'you' to 'yea' seems to be the scribe's.

113. In *S.A.* an attempt to bring the text of the Part into relation with that of Q. led to the assumption that two lines were lost between 113 and 114. Further examination suggests that this is very unlikely, and the interpretation of certain traces formerly advanced in notes to ll. 113, 114 should be disregarded.

122. In '*non*' the first '*n*' appears to have been added.

137. The comma after the first 'rattle' is very faint.

137–40. The ends of these lines are mutilated and rather distorted in mending.

141. The word to be supplied after 'a' is presumably 'whore'. The letters transcribed 'ne' might equally be 'ue'.

142. The first word in the margin is hardly legible, being very faint and the paper discoloured.

167. The scribe began to write the 'a' of 'away' in the tail of the 'y' of 'Charlemayne', made a blot and started afresh.

183. The scribe wrote 'Ly e', leaving a blank for one letter; the corrector inserted 'r' and altered the 'e' to 'a'. At the end of the line the scribe wrote 'ſpears', the corrector first inserted an 'h' before the 'p', then crossed it out and inserted one after the 'p'.

185. The first word was no doubt 'run'. Of the 'u' only the first minim is visible, but had the word been 'ride', as Collier and Collins assumed, the head of the 'd' should be visible.

191. The alteration of 'are' to 'as' is the corrector's. In 'Jlythia' the 'l' seems to have been altered from 'b' either by the scribe or the corrector.

199. In 'lighte' the 'l' is blotted.

207. In 'heles' the first 'e' has been altered, apparently from 'o' and probably by the corrector.

208. The scribe left the whole of this line blank, and it was filled in by the corrector. It is carelessly written and the last letter is doubtful.

213. The first letter of 'clarkes' is almost entirely lost in a worm-hole: there can, however, be no reasonable doubt of the reading.

231. The word 'ryſing' is in the hand of the scribe, but the last three letters are very crowded. Probably the scribe originally left a blank (insufficient as usual) and subsequently discovered for himself what he thought was the correct reading (cf. 42).

232. For the defect 'euer' would be a possible reading: 'homer' hardly, for the 'h' and 'r' would probably have left traces.

239. The word 'crimſon' was inserted by the corrector in a blank space.

243. 'Galaxſia' was similarly inserted.

260. In 'talke' the 'a' is blotted.

265. The word 'poel' was inserted by the corrector in a blank left by the scribe, who interlined the following six words on finding that he had failed to complete the speech before entering the next cue.

269. Both 'child' and 'twins' were added by the corrector, one in a space left blank, the other at the end of the line.

The comma after the 'and' [illegible] is very [illegible]

The ends of these lines are mutilated and rather disturbed in meaning.

The word to be supplied [illegible] is presumably [illegible]. The letters transcribed [illegible] exactly [illegible]

The [illegible] very [illegible] and [illegible]

[illegible]

[illegible]

278–9. The scribe inadvertently copied in what is evidently a speech by another character. Probably, if we add the cue inserted after the mistake was discovered, the whole speech is preserved. On noticing his error the scribe crossed out what he had written, but not before he had corrected a minor mistake. This slip is interesting as telling us something of the hand of the original Book, for the scribe must have misread 'ye' as 'y^e^', which makes it probable that contractions were sometimes used and that the writing was perhaps rather uneven.

281. The word 'wandrng' was transcribed as 'wandring' in *S.A.* It is possible that an attempt may have been made to alter 'r' to 'ri'.

293. The point is uncertain, but the upper dot is apparently still visible, while the lower has probably been lost in a worm-hole.

295. The corrector's interlineation is presumably meant for a cue.

297. In 'Argalio' the 'r' has probably been altered from 'a'.

300. The reading of 'daring' is not quite clear; there appear to be three minims between 'r' and 'g' but the last actually touches the 'g'; there is no dot.

307. The word interlined by the corrector is either 'geſey' or 'goſey'; possibly *greasy* was meant.

315. The first word was inserted by the corrector in a blank space.

316. The first two words were similarly inserted: the first and last letters of the second are blotted.

318. 'Tyms' was, again, similarly inserted. The sense is doubtful, and the reading as it stands can hardly be correct.

319. The insertion is again similar. In 'thoſe' the 'o' has been altered from 'e' by the corrector.

322. In 'fruitleſſe' the 'r' has perhaps been altered.

327. In 'by' the 'b' is blotted.

334. In 'coach' the beginning of a 't' is visible above the second 'c' (cf. 387, 'ſcorth'.)

337. In 'woodes' the second 'o' has been altered from 'r', probably by the corrector.

351. The word 'wraſteld' was inserted by the corrector in a blank space.

353. The word 'brandȝ' was transcribed as 'brondę' in *S.A.* with a note that it could be read as 'brandę' with 'and' a minim short. The latter probably represents the intention of the scribe.

354. The interlined words were added by the corrector, who also crossed out the original reading. In this, if anything preceded 'ſtill' it is now quite illegible, but it seems more likely that the scribe left a blank.

360. In 'Clymene' the final 'e' is blotted.

382. Naturally 'frō' should stand for 'from' as in 391, 393, but it is possible that 'for' is intended (cf. Q.), the curl indicating a transposition (cf. 43).

387. In 'ſcorth' the 't' is presumably a slip for 'c'.

393. In 'frō' the 'r' is blotted and may have been altered.

394. The word 'proud' was prefixed in the margin by the corrector. The 'u' is apparently represented by a single minim. The corrector evidently should have altered 'what' to 'that' (Q.) but omitted to do so.

395. In 'Lampethuſas' the 'e' has been altered from 'a', probably by the corrector. In 'frō' the 'r' was probably altered from 'or', the 'ō' being then added.

396. The scribe left a blank, in which the corrector wrote a word, but so badly as to be indecipherable. The only letters tolerably certain are 'ſe', and these were probably preceded by two or three others and followed by one. It is difficult to see what word could have supplied the three syllables required.

413. In 'Nemeſis' the last stroke of the 'N' has been gone over and is blotted, but no alteration appears to have been made.

420. The direction was added by the corrector, who only allowed two minims for 'un'.

440. In 'Malgrado' the first 'a' is blotted.

450, 455. The last three words of each of these lines are written in a somewhat different manner from the rest, but the ink appears to be the same and there is no sufficient reason for supposing another hand (cf. 456, 520).

452. Between 'Jle' and 'taſke' is a stroke, probably the beginning of 'ſ' or 'f': 'yō' is intended to stand for 'you'.

453. The '*s*' has been altered, perhaps from a final 's' of the English form.

456. In this line the last four words are again different from the rest (cf. 450, 455). Here, however, the ink is fainter, and while the 'you' seems to be in the scribe's hand the writing of the last three words bears more resemblance to that of the corrector, though the likeness is not conclusive.

459. The words written by the scribe in the margin are presumably intended to replace the deleted cue.

480. 'Cliſias' and probably also '&' were inserted by the corrector in a blank space. The 'C' is a little indistinct but is hardly open to doubt.

485. The word 'cauſleſſe' was similarly inserted.

497. In 'trayto$^{r}$' the 'ay' is a minim short.

498. The 'on' might be read 'ou', as an error for 'out'.

510. In 'now' the 'no' has perhaps been altered from 'mo'. In 'frolick' the deleted letter is not quite certain.

514. In 'frend' the 'nd' is a minim short.

515. It seems probable that 'welcome' is an error of the scribe for 'welcomed', which may point to similarity between 'd' and 'e' in the original.

519. In 'com̃aund' the 'aund' is a minim short.

520. In 'Marſilius' the last six letters have been added in darker ink, but though less carefully written they are probably in the hand of the scribe (cf. 450).

521. The scribe left a blank for a word he could not read, and the corrector omitted to fill it in. The word may have been 'frankincense', in which case the space left was characteristically insufficient.

522. In 'fruitę' the 'r' has been altered.

526. In 'Thankes' two letters are blotted and illegible.

530. In 'while' a descending stroke through the 'w' is apparently due to the scribe having first begun to form the 'h' before he had completed the preceding letter.

531. In spite of the mutilation it is evident that the scribe left a blank between 'thoſe' and 'keles'. It was more than usually insufficient, since four syllables are required. (Q. supplies 'gallant Grecian'.) The loss of the remaining lines appears to be due not to casual mutilation but to a deliberate cut or tear, unless there was something to cause a fold in the paper here.

# PROMPT BOOKS

## THE MATERIAL

CONSIDERING their importance for textual criticism it is surprising that more attention has not been given to those prompt copies of early plays that have actually survived. Either in mere ignorance of their existence or in serene disregard of their testimony, critics have sometimes offered strangely erroneous opinions respecting the characteristic features of manuscripts of this type. In 1902 Sidney Lee announced that the typical features of an authoritative playhouse copy were 'complete divisions of a play into acts and scenes, stage directions, indications of "the scene", and lists of dramatis personae'. An examination of actual examples shows that three of these criteria are uniformly, or almost uniformly, absent, and that as regards stage-directions considerable divergency alike in type and fullness prevails. Indeed such attention as has been paid to the documents has been almost confined to the last ten years, and even so has been somewhat meagre apart from editions of individual plays, or articles dealing with particular points. I know of only two essays of wider scope. Dr. F. S. Boas has a chapter entitled 'A Seventeenth Century Theatrical Repertoire' in his volume *Shakespeare and the Universities and other Studies in Elizabethan Drama* (1923), but this is confined to the collection in MS. Egerton 1994 at the British Museum, and does not attempt to go very deeply into the character of the Books. The other is Mr. W. J. Lawrence's 'Early Prompt-Books and what they Reveal' in his *Pre-Restoration Stage Studies* (1927), which is an interesting and suggestive piece of work, but I cannot think that all his generalizations are warranted by the evidence to hand, and in detail he is often inaccurate.[1]

It is to be supposed that the general neglect of the subject has been due to lack of information as to the amount of material at the disposal of the critic. If we allow the term an extension

[1] An important chapter on 'The Book of the Play' in Sir E. K. Chambers's recent work on Shakespeare, which covers much the same ground as my sketch, was not available till the present volume was in type.

so loose as to cover the drama down to the closing of the theatres in 1642, there remain not less than fifteen manuscripts of Elizabethan plays showing reasonably clear signs of use or origin in the playhouse, and about the same number of manuscripts generally similar in type but less intimately connected with the stage. These thirty or so manuscripts afford a wealth of evidence that is of first-rate value, is indeed indispensable, to the textual critic and bibliographer, and there can be no question that its thorough investigation is among the most pressing tasks that await students of the Elizabethan drama. Not only do we need a study of the texts of these plays, the peculiarities of which will undoubtedly throw light on possible sources of corruption, but perhaps even more of the practice of act and scene division and indication, and of the stage-directions, both those of the original text and those added in the course of preparation for performance. Only when we are fully and certainly informed in these respects shall we be able to say with any confidence what features of a printed edition point towards, and what away from, the use of a playhouse manuscript as copy, and replace by sound knowledge the subjective and sometimes fantastic criteria which critics have applied in the past.

Such an investigation is obviously beyond the scope of a work like the present. Nevertheless something may be done to prepare the ground by supplying the student with a tentative survey of the extant material, together with specimen reproductions from a few typical manuscripts and notes on their peculiarities. The pages have been chosen with a view to illustrating different characteristics, and the choice amid such a wealth of interest has not been easy. For in this section of my work it has, of course, been a question of reproducing, not complete documents, but small samples only. However, I hope that such as they are they may not be without value both in accustoming students to the manner and appearance of the originals, and in directing their attention to the features that most require taking into account in relation to the textual problems of printed plays.

It may be of interest to add that two examples of what appear to be prompt books of single miracle plays survive from earlier times. Both are on vellum and of folio size, and have been

folded in such a way as to suggest that they were carried in the pocket and used either for the learning of parts—if special Parts were not provided—or for the superintendence of actual performances. One, containing the Antechrist play from the Chester cycle (in the National Library of Wales), dates from the late fifteenth century; the other, containing the Doubting of Thomas from the York cycle (belonging to the York Philological Society), from the earlier sixteenth. In neither, however, does the text show any peculiarities that can be associated with prompt use.

The classified list of extant manuscripts with which this volume closes is perhaps a rash venture which must plead for leniency on the ground of its being a first attempt. My concern is with plays written for production on the regular public stage before the outbreak of civil war closed the theatres. I have therefore generally excluded all the early drama—miracles, morals, interludes—all academic plays, masques, and Court entertainments, and lastly literary compositions of the closet drama type. My list of the remainder is doubtless incomplete, but such as it is I have divided it into three classes. Class A consists of prompt books proper. They are copies which either bear evidence of having been used in actual performance or at least prepared for such use, or else of being transcripts of such copies preserving their distinctive features or made for official purposes. Class B includes manuscripts of generally similar character but which show no definite evidence of having been used in the playhouse, and if written there were probably prepared for some private purpose. Class C is a rather miscellaneous collection, straying in some respects beyond the limits elsewhere imposed, of manuscript plays which for one reason or another seem to me to possess some particular interest deserving attention. It includes certain pieces that would have figured in earlier classes had I possessed fuller information regarding them, in particular an important collection the present whereabouts of which is unknown, and a couple of individual pieces that have only recently come to light. In each class, an attempt has been made to place the manuscripts in chronological order, and though this must necessarily be of a very rough kind, they have been given numbers for convenience of reference.

In the Elizabethan theatre the technical name for the prompt copy of a play was the Book. Two early manuscripts that have preserved their original wrappers are inscribed respectively 'The Book of Iohn A kent & Iohn a Cumber' and 'The Booke of Sir Thomas Moore', while in the case of a contemporary or even earlier piece, which was once kept within the fold of its own Plot, the later bore on the outside the inscription 'The Booke and Platt of the second part of The 7 deadly sinns'. This use gave rise to the term 'book-holder' or 'book-keeper' applied to the prompter in the early playhouses,[1] and there are many other evidences of its currency. Henslowe heads a list of plays in the repertory of the Admiral's men: 'A Note of all suche bookes as belong to the Stocke, and such as I have bought since the 3d of March 1598' (sc. 1597/8); moreover he uses the term regularly in recording the purchase of old plays, and such entries occur as late as 1603. Some interesting examples of its use occur in certain entries in the Stationers' Registers in which titles have evidently been copied direct from playhouse manuscripts submitted. They are:

[14 May 1594] Edward White. Entred for his Copie vnder thandꝭ of bothe the wardens a booke called the booke of David and Bethsaba.

[28 Oct. 1600] Tho. haies. Entred for his copie vnder the handꝭ of the Wardens & by Consent of m$^r$ Robertꝭ. A booke called the booke of the m$^r$chant of Venyce.

[20 May 1608] Edw. Blount. Entred for his copie vnder thandꝭ of S$^r$ Geo. Buck knight & m$^r$ warden Seton a booke called. The booke of Pericles Prynce of Tyre.

[29 June 1660] M$^r$ Hum: Moseley. Entred for his Copies (vnder y$^e$ hand of M$^r$ Thrale Warden) the severall Plays following. that is to say . . . The booke of y$^e$ 4. Hono$^{ble}$. Loves. a Comedy. by Wiłłm Rowley. . . .

Occurring as it does in a list of otherwise plain titles there can

[1] No doubt it is 'book-holder' that is strictly applicable to the prompter, while 'book-keeper' suggests one who had charge of the company's manuscripts. Indeed an attempt has been made to distinguish the terms according to the function implied, while admitting that the offices may often have been combined. On the whole, however, the two words seem to have been used indifferently.

be little doubt of the significance of the last instance in spite of the difference of form. Thus we get evidence of the use of the term in the King's company at any rate down to 1608, since *Pericles* was then probably a new play. The piece so belatedly entered at the Restoration is of unknown date: Rowley began writing about 1607 and continued twenty years or so. Exactly how late the use of Book as a technical term survived is not very clear. Evidently to Sir Henry Herbert when Master of the Revels it was familiar enough: on 21 Oct. 1633 he made a memorandum that 'The players ought not to study their parts till I have allowed of the booke', and the same day, in allowing the prompt copy of *The Tamer Tamed*, addressed to Mr. Knight, book-keeper of the King's company, the warning, 'Purge ther parts, as I have the booke'. At the same time it is noticeable that the word is absent from the wrappers of *Sir John Barnavelt* in 1619 and *Believe as you List* in 1631, nor does it appear on any of the title-pages prefixed to other late manuscripts.

One would suppose that the Book would usually be enclosed in some sort of wrapper or other limp binding to protect it both when in use and when lying with similar papers in the company's store. *John a Kent* and *Sir Thomas More* were sewn up in leaves of medieval manuscripts, *Believe as you List* in an indenture of 1595 the term of which had expired six years before. *Sir John Barnavelt* has the remains of a stout paper jacket.[1] *The Seven Deadly Sins* seems to have been kept in its own Plot as a folder, and this may have been a common practice, since all other Plots sufficiently preserved show similar signs of folding. It may well be that the practice varied in different companies according to their diverse needs. In three years, from the summer of 1594 to that of 1597, the Admiral's men put on fifty-five 'new' plays. The most successful, *The Wise Man of West Chester* (possibly a revision of *John a Kent*), ran to thirty-two performances, while five did not get beyond a first: the average was well under a dozen.[2] Such modest

[1] Only the front half, bearing the title, is preserved. It is of a sort of hand-made packing-paper, darkish grey in colour.

[2] Of the 55 plays there were 518 performances, giving an average of 9·4. But no doubt some of the pieces went on being acted later, and it may be fairer

prospects would hardly induce great care of the Book, and we may doubt whether wrappers were provided. On the other hand it is generally assumed, though I do not quite know on what grounds, that the Chamberlain's men contented themselves with a lesser number of new plays and were able to run them for a greater number of performances. If this was so, it would be worth bestowing more care on the Books.

The plays preserving any sort of wrapper have the title written on that alone, unless a censor's licence repeats it. Some others have it at the head of the text. Of these most likely the earliest is *Edmond Ironside*, which bears its original title *War hath made all Friends* above the initial stage-direction. This may be before 1600; no other instance seems to be recorded till about the end of the first quarter of the next century: of later examples *The Welsh Embassador* may be as early as any. Others again have the first leaf, or sometimes a fly-leaf, used for a sort of title-page. The one supplied for *Edmond Ironside* is difficult to date: the leaf is detached but seems to be of the same make as those that follow. The date of *The Poor Man's Comfort* is uncertain, for even if we take *c.* 1617 as that of composition the manuscript may be later, nor is it certain that the title is in the same hand as the text. Besides there is little or nothing to connect this manuscript with the playhouse. We can be rather more certain in the case of *The Two Noble Ladies*, for the title on the first leaf is pretty certainly in the hand of the text (in this case apparently the author's), and if the later inscription on the back of the leaf is correct the play cannot be after 1623. All other instances seem to be later. The additional inscription in *The Two Noble Ladies* is of unusual interest, running: 'The two noble Ladies: A Trage-comicall Historie often tymes acted w^t^h approbation At the Red Bull in S^t^: Iohns Streete By the Company of y^e^ Reuells', and followed by a list of personae. The wording of this hardly leaves a doubt that it was added with a view to publication. A rather elaborate title-page (giving, that is, the title, the authors' names, and a list of personae) is prefixed to *The Faithful Friends* (*c.* 1625?), but

to confine our attention to the 'new' plays of the first twelve months, which over three years reached an average of about 10·6.

this is part of the additions supplied probably in the eighteenth century. The only other that suggests publication is that of *The Queen of Corsica* in 1642: this play also has a list of personae. Of these three manuscripts only the first shows signs of playhouse use, and it is worth notice that only when it was prepared for printing was a list of personae added. Lists are also found in *Dick of Devonshire*, *Love's Changelings' Change*, and *Timon*, none of which can be connected with the playhouse. On the other hand, two prompt copies contain lists in the original hands, namely *The Welsh Embassador* and *The Seaman's Honest Wife*. The former may have been written about 1623: the list, though in the scribe's hand, was added subsequently. The latter, dated 1632, is autograph, but it is of course an altogether exceptional production.

In general then we may say that until a fairly late date the title of a Book was written on the wrapper and only appeared incidentally if at all in the manuscript itself, and that no list of dramatis personae was included. I have previously suggested (p. 73, n. 1) that the latter, including a cast of the parts, may have been kept as a separate document along with the plot: this, however, is mere conjecture since no example seems to have survived.

It is impossible to enter here upon any detailed examination of the textual and theatrical characteristics of the prompt copies and other related manuscripts that have come down to us: my task is only to collect and order the material for such a study. It may, however, be amusing and perhaps helpful to follow from a partly *a priori* standpoint the various operations that we may suppose to have been performed in the preparation of a completed Book, and to endeavour to relate them to different types of manuscript, or to various features in the individual manuscripts, we are fortunate enough to possess.

Most authors, when they set about composition, would probably produce a rough copy or mass of 'fowle papers' such as those upon which the scribe of *Bonduca* drew. That he was able to do so suggests that this rough draft had been handed over to the actors and preserved.[1] It had of course been from these

[1] Sir E. K. Chambers suggests as an alternative that the 'fowle papers' were

same papers that had been prepared the authoritative play-house copy—'the booke where by it was first Acted from'—which was mislaid when the scribe wrote, but which appears to have come to light again in time to supply copy for the Beaumont and Fletcher folio of 1647. But whether in that instance the Book was prepared by Fletcher with his own hand or whether the task was entrusted to a scribe connected with the King's company, such as Ralph Crane or the writer of the extant manuscript himself, is a question to which perhaps no conclusive answer is possible. It seems at first sight less likely that the author would hand over his foul papers along with his finished draft than that the former should be preserved if the fair copy was made in the playhouse. On the other hand, there may have been sound reasons from the company's point of view for obtaining possession of and preserving all the manuscript connected with any play they purchased. In the present instance the evidence which I have collected (from the differences between the foul papers as copied in the manuscript and the prompt copy as printed in the folio) incline me to the view that Fletcher prepared his own fair copy, but I should hesitate to say that the evidence amounts to proof.

It is probable that 'fowle papers' was often an apt enough description of the rough draft. There is, I think, good reason to suppose that the extant *Bonduca* manuscript was transcribed from an original that was sometimes far from legible and had undergone not a little alteration. This is interesting in view of what we are told by Humphrey Moseley in the 1647 folio: 'What ever I have seene of Mr. *Fletchers* owne hand, is free from interlining; and his friends affirme he never writ any one thing twice: it seemes he had that rare felicity to prepare and perfect all first in his owne braine; to shape and attire his *Notions*, to adde or loppe off, before he committed one word to writing, and never touched pen till all was to stand as firme and immutable as if ingraven in Brasse or Marble.' Here Moseley is of course expanding and adapting to his particular hero the famous words that Hemings and Condell had used in

obtained from the author's representatives. It is a possibility, but hardly, I should think, likely.

1623 of Shakespeare: 'His mind and hand went together: And what he thought, he vttered with that easinesse, that wee haue scarse receiued from him a blot in his papers.' It has been argued, cogently enough so far as logic is concerned, that these words, to have any significance, must be taken to apply not to a fair copy even autograph, but to the original drafts themselves. Certainly the textual and bibliographical critic of Shakespeare is bound to ask himself whether they do, and if so whether they are true. I do not pretend to know the answer, but I think the parallel case of Fletcher deserves consideration, and certainly a good deal of recent criticism of Shakespeare's text assumes a pretty sweeping negative.

The practice of an author making his own fair copy, which on general grounds one would assume to be normal, is well illustrated in the correspondence of Robert Daborne that the careful Henslowe preserved. It is quite clear that this minor playwright, who however thought he 'deservd as much mony as m^r^ messenger', made his own final draft and delivered it piecemeal against advances on the covenanted payment. Thus he promises to deliver '3 acts fayr written', has sent '2 sheets more fayr written', sits up 'till past 12 to write out this sheet', and again sends '2 sheets more so y^t^ y^u^ hav x sheets' in all. I have no doubt that when he speaks of sheets he means, not leaves or pages (as a modern author might), but four-page foolscap sheets, the unit of numbering in many playhouse Books (see below, p. 205). Sometimes the 'papers' Daborne sends are 'not so fayr written all as I could wish', and when he promises to bring his paymaster 'papers to the valew of three acts' we may suspect that only a rough draft is intended. The most significant of all, however, is the graphic note: 'Mr Hinchlow y^u^ accuse me with the breach of promise, trew it is I promysed to bring y^u^ the last scean which y^t^ y^u^ may see finished I send y^u^ the foule sheet & y^e^ fayr I was wrighting as y^r^ man can testify which if great busines had not prevented I had this night fynished'. Daborne's 'foule sheet', like Fletcher's 'fowle papers', affords a precious glimpse into the actualities of dramatic composition. There is by the way no hint that Daborne ever delivered his rough draft except as an earnest of his good intentions. But even the fair copy was subject to alteration at a late stage of the proceedings, for on one occasion he writes of his tragedy *Machiavel*, 'I have took extraordynary payns w^th^ the end & altered one other scean in the third act which they have now in parts'.[1] It must have been an annoying habit.

Daborne more than once hints in his correspondence, which belongs to the spring and summer of 1613, that the King's men would be glad to get his services. It is not certain whether he ever did write for them, but there is no doubt that his supposed rival, Massinger, who seems to have begun his dramatic career with Henslowe, was later one of the main supports of the King's company. For his practice with respect to fair copies we have to rely on inference. The prompt book of his *Believe as you List* is of course autograph, and this manuscript has been freely cited as the classic example of an author preparing his own fair copy to become in due course the authorized playhouse Book. At the same time the instance is not altogether typical, for it is safe to say that there never were any foul papers of *Believe as you List* properly speaking. The play was a revision of another piece on the subject of Sebastian of Portugal, which a few months before the censor had refused to license on political grounds. This earlier play, which for convenience we may call *Sebastian*, must, since it had been submitted for allowance, have reached the state of fair copy, but whether this was autograph or not we have no means of telling. Nor do we know in any detailed way how far divergent were the two versions, though certain relics that have survived in the extant copy suggest that in parts at any rate the alterations were merely verbal. Also, while the revision may in part have been carried out on the fair copy of *Sebastian*, there is some evidence, in surviving alterations of the text, that it was in part at least effected in the actual writing of *Believe as you List*. We arrive,

[1] The preparation of Parts, therefore, sometimes began before the Book was complete. This of course would be possible if the sheets were delivered piecemeal. The fact that Daborne seems to be taking credit for the fact that the actors already have the Parts for the third act, rather suggests that he prepared them, or was responsible for their preparation, himself. This is, however, unlikely and hardly a necessary inference from his words.

therefore, with some probability at the position that while the alterations required would practically necessitate a rewriting of the text by the author, they were not so extensive as to be difficult of incorporation direct into a fair copy. That in this case therefore the Book proves to be in the autograph of the author cannot safely be cited as evidence of the general practice, or even of Massinger's usual habits. And there is at least evidence that Massinger did not always prepare his fair copy himself. For another play of his that is extant in manuscript is certainly in the hand of a scribe. *The Parliament of Love* is imperfect, and it contains nothing (beyond one duplicated entrance direction) to indicate stage use, but if, as seems most probable,an excision from the last leaf has removed the censor's licence, there can be no doubt of its being an official playhouse copy. There may of course have been some reason for making a transcript of an autograph Book for the purpose of licence, but on the whole it seems easier to suppose that the manuscript was prepared from Massinger's rough draft by a scribe connected with the playhouse expressly for allowance to the Cockpit company (i.e. the Lady Elizabeth's men, for whom Daborne was writing a decade earlier). It would therefore be rash to assume that the prompt copies of Massinger's plays were always or even habitually autograph.

Other autograph Books of course there are. Of earlier date, Munday's *John a Kent* is in his own hand, and though the evidences of stage use are not very conspicuous, they are sufficient to connect it definitely with the playhouse. Later *The Two Noble Ladies* is pretty certainly in the hand of the unknown author, and there is some, though less clear, indication that *Charlemagne* is likewise autograph, though in that case the play cannot be by Chapman as literary critics have supposed. Mountfort's *Launching of the Mary* is of course in his own hand, but this piece cannot be taken as in any way typical.

In cases of collaboration the fair copy would naturally be prepared either by one of the authors or by a playhouse scribe. We probably possess examples of each. *Sir John Barnavelt* is by common consent the work of Fletcher and Massinger (some critics finding traces of a third hand) and the prompt book was written for the King's men by their scribe Ralph Crane. The original Book of *Sir Thomas More* was written throughout (we must presume) by Anthony Munday, but fairly good reason has been shown on literary grounds for supposing that he was only one of several authors engaged in its composition. The additions that have been made to this piece are in five different hands, four of which are clearly those of authors, while the other certainly belongs to some one connected with the theatre, who acted as general editor for the revision. The greater part of the autograph additions may safely be described as foul papers that have for purposes of convenience been inserted (and in some instances very clumsily inserted) into the existing fair copy. Whether the play was submitted to the censor in its original or revised form is a point that has been disputed: some attempt was apparently made to cast it, but it seems very unlikely that it was ever actually produced. Certainly the revised manuscript would have needed a good deal of tidying up before it could have served as a prompt copy, and it is at least possible that an entirely new transcript would have been made. In spite therefore of the inscription on the cover, I very much doubt whether the manuscript can be regarded as a 'live' Book at all: in any event it is a quite exceptional example, and I am inclined to regard with suspicion certain far-reaching inferences that have from time to time been based on its peculiar features.

No doubt those who see in the chaotic state of this particular 'Book' no obstacle either to its submission for licence or to its use as a prompt copy, can point to an apparently parallel case in *The Launching of the Mary*, which in spite of extreme untidiness actually bears the censor's allowance and the prompter's notes. But before the parallel be allowed as confirmation there are several considerations to be weighed. It is true that the unlucky censor read, marked, and actually with reservations licensed this appalling stuff, but having done so he proceeded to demand a revised 'fairer Copy' of the 'Bookeeper'. Unfortunately no entry relative to the play has been preserved from Herbert's office-book, so that we are rather in the dark as to his dealings with this particular piece, but I cannot help doubting whether he ever got his fairer copy. The prompter's

annotations suggest that it was actually this copy that was used on the stage, though to pilot through a performance from such a Book must have been something of a *tour de force*. But there is reason to suppose that the circumstances were exceptional. I find it impossible to believe that any company would have considered the production of the play on its merits, or that any public audience would have tolerated even a single performance of it. Perhaps the facts of its licence and production are best explained on the assumption that the East India Company paid the actors to stage this piece of blatant propaganda. The author's untidy manuscript, the product of his weary twelve-months' voyage round the Cape, may have been made to serve the censor and prompter for a single exceptional performance and the whole then allowed to lapse quietly into well-deserved oblivion.

But though I would suggest that neither *Sir Thomas More* nor *The Launching of the Mary* can be taken as at all typical prompt books, whether of the last decade of Elizabeth or the first of Charles, it would be a great mistake to suppose that no additions were ever made to the Book, nor a good deal of untidiness tolerated. The insertion of additional passages in the hand of the original scribe by means of slips of paper 'flown' on the page is a feature of the ill-named *Second Maiden's Tragedy*. This is a particularly neat prompt book, and the presence of additions should have hardly inconvenienced the prompter. The slips in this instance appear from the first to have been pasted by one edge onto the original leaf, but they were not always attached in this careful manner. The same device was used in *The Queen of Corsica*, a late piece surviving in a scribal copy and showing indeed no stigmas of playhouse use; but in this case the additional slips, two in number, were merely pinned onto the leaf, with the result that one of them is now missing. Pins, too, were used to attach a couple of slips which add to the untidiness of *The Launching of the Mary*; but here the slips perform a different function, containing not additions to the text but substitutions, and they might more conveniently have been pasted down over the cancelled passage, as was done in the case of *Sir Thomas More*. Thus *The Second Maiden's*

*Tragedy* is the only normal Book in which addition-slips appear, and it should be observed that they have been written and inserted with noticeable care.[1]

But slips were not, of course, the only means of making additions to an already written Book. The writing in the margin of passages intended for insertion in the text was an old practice. It was followed by Bale in revising his *King Johan*, and doubtless by many a medieval dramatist before him. It is hardly necessary to say that Mountfort makes marginal additions. So does Munday in *John a Kent*. They even occur in Crane's beautifully written Book of *Sir John Barnavelt*. But their most noticeable appearance is in *The Lady Mother*, and we are bound to admit that they and other alterations have given this manuscript a very untidy appearance. Originally a fairly neat piece of work, and bearing the censor's licence at the end, the Book has been scored and hacked about in the playhouse in a manner that must have made its use as a prompt book far from easy. We are of course at liberty to assume that the play thus roughly treated was one for which little future was anticipated on the boards, and upon which little care was in consequence bestowed; but this would be the merest speculation, hardly less idle than to suggest that, the manuscript having been rendered illegible by revision, a fresh Book may have been prepared while the old was still retained for the sake of the licence.

But though speculative, the question whether the playhouse manuscripts that have come down to us are all definitive prompt copies is one of some interest and importance. We have wandered rather far and I wish now to hark back to the relation between the rough draft and the fair copy. It can hardly be held impossible for a practised dramatist, particularly a rather facile one accustomed to swift and continual composition, to produce at once a rough copy substantially free from alteration and bearing no obvious or at least indubitable evidence to mark it as foul papers. It may be well to bear this in mind when considering such a play as *The Captives*. The manuscript shows

[1] Two carefully written additions were made by Crane to the Book of *Sir John Barnavelt* on leaves of smaller size. The method of insertion is not clear.

no more 'blotting', interlining, or alteration than many which we naturally accept as fair copies. At the same time there are three remarkable features about it. It is written in a hand so bad as to be almost illegible to any one who does not know the play almost by heart or has not leisure to puzzle it out word by word. The prompt notes are for the most part written in an almost equally careless script, and are so mixed up with the text that they would be a hindrance rather than a help to the prompter. We know that the play was licensed by Sir Henry Herbert on 3 Sept. 1624, but though the last page was blank no allowance was recorded there. These considerations make me doubtful whether we have here to do with a prompt book properly speaking, and not rather with something antecedent to it. I see no reason to believe that behind the extant manuscript there need be fouler papers: Heywood I suggest may have been quite capable of writing it straight away. I suspect that in this instance we see the book-keeper, instead of marking a fair copy for stage use as was his wont, annotating the author's rough draft with a view to the preparation in the playhouse of a Book ready alike for allowance and prompting. On no other assumption, so far as I am able to see, will the bibliographical facts make sense.

What a fair copy of the existing manuscript of *The Captives* might have been like we may to some extent gather from that of *The Welsh Embassador*. This is throughout in the hand of one scribe, including the playhouse stigmas such as 'bee redy Penda' and the rest. It is true that these have been added later in a different ink. They may have been inserted on the scribe's own responsibility. On the other hand, he certainly went over his copy again making corrections, and he may then have copied in the prompter's notes, which had possibly been added in the interval. It is perhaps just worth bearing in mind that *The Welsh Embassador*[1] is in the same hand as *The Parliament*

[1] It is possible, though by no means certain, that *The Welsh Embassador* should be identified with *The Welsh Traveller* licensed for 'the players of the Revels' by Herbert under the date 10 May 1622. This may be an error for 1623, since the Red Bull players only got their licence as 'the Children of the Revells' in July 1622, though the difficulty is perhaps not a serious one. Internal evidence fixes the date of *The Welsh Embassador* as 1622 or 1623, and the identification is therefore plausible. In that case of course it belonged to a dif-

*of Love*, and that the latter belonged to the same company as *The Captives*.

There can, I think, be little doubt that these two plays written in the hand of the same scribe were both intended for playhouse use. Of the extant manuscripts in Crane's hand only one, *Sir John Barnavelt*, was intended as a prompt copy; the rest, *The Witch*, *A Game at Chess*, and *Demetrius and Enanthe*, are all transcripts made for private persons. The third playhouse scribe who has been identified, the one whom it is convenient to call 'Jhon',[1] prepared Massinger's *Believe as you List* for performance with meticulous care, and his copy of *The Honest Man's Fortune* was made for the purpose of licence and no doubt for prompt use, though it was only to replace the original Book which had been lost. The Book of *Bonduca* had also gone astray when he made his transcript of that piece, but it would seem that he was then working for a private collector and not for the company.

Something has already been said on the subject of wrappers and title-pages. It is time to consider briefly certain other features of the physical constitution and formal arrangement of playhouse Books. All manuscripts that can be identified as such are in folio, and there is no reason to suppose that any other size was in use. This is what on general grounds one would expect, for it was essential that the prompter should be able to look ahead to see what action was coming, and the frequent turning of pages would have been inconvenient. This also perhaps accounts for the smallness and closeness of the writing in some examples: we occasionally find as many as eighty or even more lines on a page. The size of the paper used varies to some extent, but the deviation from a mean of say $12 \times 7\frac{3}{4}$ inches for

ferent company from the other two, which were licensed for the Lady Elizabeth's men at the Cockpit. On the other hand, the similarity of the damage which *The Parliament of Love* and *The Welsh Embassador* have suffered suggests that they must have long lain side by side. It would be strange if two plays written by the same scribe for different companies should have subsequently come together again. *The Welsh Embassador* bears no licence, though there was room for it on the last page.

[1] He may perhaps have been the Mr. Knight, book-keeper to the King's men, who is twice mentioned by Herbert in 1632–3. There were two Knights with the company in 1624, Anthony and Edward, but this is no obstacle to the identification since there is no real ground for supposing that 'Jhon's' name was John.

the leaf is not great in actual prompt books. The height varies from 11½ to 12½ or rather more, the width from 7¼ to over 8½. The tallest are *John a Kent* (12¾), *Charlemagne* (12½), and *Believe as you List* (12½); the widest *John a Kent* (8⅛), *Sir Thomas More* (8¾), and *The Launching of the Mary* (8⅛).[1] The smallest are *The Second Maiden's Tragedy* (11½×7½), *Sir John Barnavelt* (11⅝×7½), and *The Two Noble Ladies* (11⅝×7¼). None of the others seem to be more than 12¼ or less than 12 inches high, or more than 8 or less than 7¾ inches wide. Thus the size of the sheets used varied between about 15×11½ and 17×12½ inches. Comparing these with the sizes of the Plots (p. 70) we see that the makes are evidently the same, namely foolscap, but that the sizes run rather smaller. This may very likely be due to writing-paper being sold ready folded and trimmed of some of its deckle.

The usual practice seems to have been to write the plays on separately folded sheets, in units that is of four pages, and several manuscripts are so numbered. The most interesting of these is *The Telltale*, in which the scribe puts quite an elaborate inscription in the upper left-hand corner, e.g. '*6th sheete*' on the eleventh leaf. Even where no such numbering appears it may still be possible from the watermarks to demonstrate a regular succession of sheets, as in *The Welsh Embassador*, *The Parliament of Love*, and *Edmond Ironside*. But there are cases in which this is not so, for instance *The Two Noble Ladies*, of which it is the leaves that are numbered and these do not constitute successive sheets. Most likely the play was written on a single gathering. I may also mention that in *The Poor Man's Comfort* the numbering is ostensibly by sheets, though in fact the leaves are either separate or else form a number of small gatherings, which it would be easy to stab together and sew up as a Book. There is plenty of evidence that stabbing was the usual method of sewing. The same apply to *Dick of Devonshire*, while *Bonduca* is certainly written on four gatherings of three sheets each. Still *The Two Noble Ladies* appears to be the only prompt book that is not made up of successive sheets.

[1] The largest manuscripts, *Aglaura* (15⅝×10¼), *The Wizard* (14×9¼), and *Bonduca* (14×8¾), are very clearly not of the playhouse type.

A common practice, before starting to write, was to fold the leaf down the middle, and then fold the folded leaf yet again, so that when flattened out each page was divided into four equal columns some two inches wide.[1] In the left of these were written the speakers' names. The text was begun at the first fold, and if verse would fill approximately the two middle columns, leaving the right-hand column for stage-directions; if the text was prose it was written across all three columns. This practice of folding is not invariable, but the few manuscripts that show traces of ruled margins are mostly late. It was unusual to rule lines for the writing, except in the case of certain caligraphic manuscripts prepared for special occasions. Quite exceptional is *Edmond Ironside*, in which some leaves have been ruled on one side by an impressed style. This method, at one time universal, seems to have gone out of use in literary manuscripts about the twelfth century, but it survived in legal use till quite a late date, and its adoption in this play is one of the points that suggest that it was written by a scrivener.

In formal arrangement, as regards headings, directions, divisions, and the like, the manuscripts differ almost as much as they do in the frequency, content, and nature of the stage-directions. Some prompt copies are divided throughout into acts and scenes, some into acts only, others have no division at all. The second class is the most numerous, but the details are best reserved for consideration in connexion with the alterations made in the playhouse. As regards arrangement, out of the diversity of practice some sort of normal type seems to emerge. The directions for the principal entrances, including those constituting new scenes whether these are marked or not, are usually written across the page, beginning either a little outside or a little inside the first fold, and are often marked off from the text by rules. Sometimes, even when the scenes are not

[1] Mr. W. J. Lawrence, in his essay on 'Early Prompt-Books' (p. 384), remarks that this practice survived the Restoration. Of course, so obvious a device, though typical of prompt books, was in no way peculiar to them. I have found it employed in the pocket-books containing the lecture notes of William Harvey, and even on the fly-leaf of a printed book when the author wanted to write an epistle in a presentation copy (P. Heylyn, *Microcosmus*, 1627).

otherwise indicated, we can trace a tendency to reserve these central entrances, or else the rules, for new scenes, though how far this was deliberate is not easy to say. Less important entrances, or at least those requiring only short directions, are often relegated to the right margin without any break in the text: only occasionally do they appear on the left. Exits are almost exclusively marked on the right. Other stage-directions are also normally placed on the right: only when unusually elaborate do they take the central position: appearance on the left is exceptional unless in connexion with a speaker's name. It is, however, not uncommon to find 'within' added to a prefix, though 'aside' is generally placed on the right. Nor is it uncommon to find 'Enter' prefixed to a speaker's name to indicate his entrance, though generally only in the case of a minor character.

The usual practice is to write the text in English secretary script and distinguish the directions by the use of Italian script. In the case of the best hands, such as that of *The Second Maiden's Tragedy*, this is a quite adequate differentiation. Crane and 'Jhon' further distinguish their directions, or at least those most important from the prompter's point of view, by using a larger and heavier script. But in many hands the distinction is quite inadequate, and in order to make the directions in the right margin catch the eye resort is had to rules either under the direction, above and under, or all round.[1] This often has the desired effect, but when in *The Two Noble Ladies* every one of the lavishly scattered directions is enclosed in rules the practice tends to defeat its own end.

In all manuscripts intended for stage use every speech begins a fresh line of writing, irrespective of the metrical division The habit of writing speakers' names in the middle of a line would be distracting for prompt purposes, and may be taken to indicate a purely literary intention in the writer.[2] The speakers' names are in the margin, and the beginning of speeches are not indented as is usual in print, but a short horizontal rule is drawn separating the speeches. These speech-

[1] Such rules are even found occasionally in printed texts.

[2] The newly discovered *John of Bordeaux* may be an exception.

rules are a constant feature of all but the latest Books, but they vary very much in length. Evidently derived from the medieval habit of separating speeches by lines drawn right across the page (and having the name of the speaker added at the right-hand end), speech-rules are still of considerable length in *John a Kent*, become more modest in the original portion of *Sir Thomas More*,[1] and generally tend to shorten as time goes on. In some manuscripts they are reduced to mere ticks.

I have no intention of going in any detail into the form of stage-directions. It is a tempting study and one I believe of considerable bibliographical importance, but it offers a wide field of investigation, and I can do no more here than call attention to certain general features. Diversity is the characteristic that strikes the reader most and is most bewildering to the student. Prompt books are full of directions that at first sight suggest a purely literary origin. This is not really surprising, for plays are written by literary craftsmen, and even a playwright intimately connected with the stage may, when composing, think and write in dramatic as opposed to theatrical terms. What is noteworthy is that essentially literary directions are commonly left unaltered in prompt copies, and, as we have previously seen, sometimes find their way even into the purely theatrical Plots (cf. p. 88). On the other hand, even manuscripts showing no connexion with the playhouse at all contain at times distinctively theatrical terms and phrases. The use of 'within' for off the stage is sometimes cited as belonging to the theatre. Logically this is doubtless so, though in fact the use is common to nearly all writers. But there is no consistency even in the playhouse. A character leaving the stage goes 'within' from the point of view of the actors, and goes 'out' from that of the spectators. And, after all, the universal terms 'enter' and 'exit' assume the point of view of the audience, not the performers. Any writer, whether actually writing for the stage or not, will use 'within'—it is the only word available —even if the scene is a room and the noises come from the street: while on the other hand the phrase 'Carrie him out' (i.e.

[1] Mr. Lawrence is wrong in stating that the lines are lacking in this play (p. 388).

off the stage) has actually found its way into a Plot.[1] The fact is that 'in' and 'out', though seldom in practice ambiguous, had almost ceased to be correlative and had become synonymous terms. Actors and playwrights were well aware of this and made a joke of it. 'Within there', cries a character in *The Captives* (l. 68) to the Clown, who enters with the words: 'Within there is now without here!' Even the use of 'at one door' for 'on one side', though strictly belonging to the stage, may be used by a quite unprofessional writer, just as a playhouse scribe will sometimes use 'on the walls' instead of 'above'. Even imperative directions, though undoubtedly characteristic of the prompter, cannot be altogether relied on as indications of playhouse use. After all, 'enter' is itself an imperative,[2] and though 'exit' and 'manet' are grammatically indicatives, the frequency of their use where several characters are concerned suggests that they were rather felt as imperatives. Moreover many instances are ambiguous: 'kiss' may be an imperative, or it may be merely a shortened form of 'they kiss'.[3] It is quite true that there are some descriptive directions that suggest that the person who wrote them was recalling an actual performance of the play, that others of a literary character can hardly have been written by any one but the author in the act of composition,[4] and that certain types, particularly anticipatory and warning directions, are closely connected with the mechanism of production. But the whole question badly needs studying in relation, not to *a priori* expectation, but to the actual evidence of the Books themselves, and meanwhile the more we are able to suspend judgement perhaps the better.

[1] There are at least two such inversions of the normal usage in the Shakespeare folio: *The Comedy of Errors*, IV. iv. 149, 'Runne all out' (duplicating 'Exeunt omnes' a line below), and *The Tempest*, V. i. 255, 'Enter Ariell, driuing in Caliban, Stephano, and Trinculo'. I also note in *The Second Maiden's Tragedy*, fol. 56$^a$, 'The Spirit enters agen and stayes to goe out with the body'.

[2] The indicative singular 'Enters' occurs sporadically, but it is rare.

[3] In *Charlemagne* we find on fol. 129$^b$ 'giues y$^e$ ringe', but on the opposite page 'giue hym y$^e$ ringe', and later (fol. 133$^a$) 'giue y$^e$ letter', though in each case a singular is intended.

[4] To the author must likewise be credited permissive directions which leave the decision to the stage-manager. Such is the direction in *The Escapes of Jupiter* (fol. 77$^a$) 'A songe Iff you will', and that in *The Captives* (fol. 68$^a$) 'Eather strykes him w$^{th}$ a staffe or Casts a stone', a doubt which even the stage reviser failed to resolve.

And I think the point at which investigation might best begin would be the actual alterations and additions made by the prompter or stage-manager in preparing Books for use in performance. Upon this subject there are a few observations I wish to make in conclusion before leaving the further investigation to others. To begin with there is the vexed and vexing question of the division into acts and scenes. The evidence of the fifteen manuscripts here recognized as prompt books can be quite shortly stated. As originally written exactly one-third were fully divided into acts and scenes: *Sir John Barnavelt*, *The Two Noble Ladies*, *The Captives*, *Believe as you List*, and *The Launching of the Mary*. Three were undivided: *Sir Thomas More*, *Richard II*, and *Edmond Ironside*. The remaining seven were divided into acts but not into scenes.[1] The three undivided plays all belong, I believe, to the sixteenth century. Those fully divided range from 1619 to 1633. Those only divided into acts include *John a Kent*, probably the earliest of all (*c.* 1590), and *The Lady Mother*, perhaps the latest (1635); the rest range probably from 1605 to 1625. From this it would seem that lack of division is a sign of early date, that full division came in later, but that division into acts persisted throughout. This is borne out by the treatment these plays received in the playhouse. The crucial case is the well-known one of *Believe as you List*. Massinger divided his play most carefully into acts and scenes, duly marking them in his manuscript. But when 'Jhon' took the Book in hand he ruthlessly struck out Massinger's scene headings, while retaining and even emphasizing his division into acts.[2] It is consonant with this

[1] The only suggestion of any intention to divide a play into scenes but not into acts is the marking of '(i) Sceane' and '2 sceane' in *Richard II*. It is not uncommon for plays both manuscript and print to bear a heading 'Act 1: Scene 1' without further scene division, or act division either. And where there is a division into acts only we often find an indication of 'Scene 1' added to each act heading. Evidently some writers or scribes thought that it was the proper thing for a play to be fully divided.

[2] In two instances he wrote the word 'long' opposite the act division, apparently to indicate a longer interval than elsewhere. To this a close parallel occurs in Heywood's *Fair Maid of the West*, Part I (1631), where we find the direction: 'Exeunt. Act long. | Explicit Actus quartus'—a parallel to which Mr. Lawrence (p. 406) and Professor Sisson have both called attention. In *Believe as you List* the 'long' intervals occur before the second and fourth acts.

that playhouse revisers have at some time or other introduced act-divisions into *Richard II* and *Edmond Ironside*. Thus *Sir Thomas More* is the only play that remains without division of any sort, perhaps because it never reached performance. In *The Lady Mother* the division into acts was retained when the play was revised for production but the position of the breaks was altered.

To look at the question for a moment from the point of view of the scribes, it may be observed that the action of 'Jhon' in the case of *Believe as you List* agrees with his own practice in the case of *The Honest Man's Fortune*, which is divided into acts only, as is also his other manuscript of *Bonduca*. The scribe of *The Welsh Embassador* and *The Parliament of Love* likewise divides his plays into acts only. Crane alone, in his one prompt book, divides *Sir John Barnavelt* into scenes as well.[1]

It may seem curious that the division into scenes, those real dramatic units of the Elizabethan stage, should be entirely neglected in the Books in use thereon, while these Books emphasize the comparatively arbitrary division into acts, of which it is sometimes held the early stage took no account at all. I do not wish to enter upon a somewhat controversial field, and I would readily admit that acting practice may have varied in different companies and at different dates. But I do not think that the contradiction really goes very deep. The division of the scenes was not a matter of indifference, nor was it neglected. This is obvious from the notes made by the prompter in Heywood's *Captives*. One of his chief concerns is to mark the points at which the stage is empty—the points, that is, at which a fresh scene would begin according to the usual Elizabethan

The two plays were contemporary, but whereas Massinger's belonged of course to the King's men, Heywood's belonged to Queen Henrietta's, so that 'Jhon' is unlikely to have touched it, though the prompter's annotations must have been similar. I question whether this evidence would by itself warrant our assuming that the term 'act' was itself applied to the interval, but the famous Folio direction to *A Midsummer Night's Dream* (III–IV), 'They sleepe all the Act', seems conclusive.

[1] In so doing he may have been carrying over into a playhouse manuscript his practices in private transcripts. His four known quarto copies are all fully divided: two of these are of *A Game at Chess*, of which Middleton's autograph is divided into acts only.

practice. Again and again he writes 'clere'[1] for this purpose: elsewhere he marks an entry as 'to em' to indicate the contrary. He places a large star in the left margin at the points where new scenes should begin; and though it is true that he sometimes prefixes a similar star to other important entries, his object is, I take it, to ensure a clear indication of the changes on the stage when the Book was finally written. The solicitude for clear indication of the scene unit comes out of course in the Plots too. But the numbering of the scenes was a matter of complete indifference. And since the scenes succeeded each other without break, so long as the characters were got on and off the stage correctly, the scene division would be automatically achieved. The important point was to prevent an actor remaining on the stage when he ought to be off it, and this was ensured in the Book by the supply of precise and clearly visible directions, and in the Plots (in which originally exits were not recorded) by the rules that divide one scene from another.

With the acts it is different. If any act division was to be recognized in performance, the very arbitrariness of its nature necessitated clear indication in the Book. Intervals had to be marked, if necessary their duration indicated. It is possible that the insertion of act divisions in previously undivided manuscripts may point to a change in theatrical custom in this respect, but it would be rash to base any far-reaching deductions on this evidence until we have a clearer notion of the chronological relation of various hands than we can claim at present. But act divisions, arbitrary in nature, were not immutable, and as already mentioned were sometimes moved. It sufficed if due notice was entered in the Book, there was less need for the Plot to repeat it. This I believe to be the explanation of the treatment we observe of act and scene division, and of what is at first sight the curious anomaly that, whereas the

[1] Again Mr. W. J. Lawrence (p. 403) has adduced an interesting parallel. In *A King and no King*, at the end of v. i, the first quarto (1619) has the direction 'Exeunt' only, whereas the next (1625) has 'Exeunt clear'. It is difficult to see how the note got in, unless the quarto had been used in the theatre. The scene divisions are not marked. I do not think Mr. Lawrence is right in interpreting the word as a direction to 'clear the stage': it is merely a note that the stage is clear.

Plots preserve most carefully the scenic articulation but take little notice of the grouping into acts, the Books on the other hand lay all the stress on the acts and are comparatively indifferent to scenes.[1]

It is time we asked the question: What treatment did the book-keeper mete out to the author's stage-directions? The answer is that as a rule he left them alone. So long as they were intelligible it mattered little to him the form in which they were couched. Two things, however, did matter: that if important they should be neither inconspicuous nor too long to be taken in at a glance. If they failed to stand out clearly from the text so as to catch his eye, the prompter might yet make them serviceable by underlining or surrounding them with rules. If they were too frequent, or too elaborate and involved, the simplest thing was to note their essence in bold script in the left margin opposite. This it seems to me is the underlying principle of nearly all prompt annotation. Sometimes the original direction may be wholly cancelled: 'Jhon' even strikes out a direction of Massinger's for the entrance of minor characters, and substitutes one for the entrance of actors instead—but this is quite exceptional.

The author's directions being generally, though by no means always, confined to the right margin, the left was largely available for anything the prompter might wish to add. It is true that he did not always confine himself to it, but the fact that it was here that his annotations would most easily meet the eye gave it special advantages for his purpose. It was therefore here as a rule that he inserted his succincter duplications of the author's directions, and it was here too that he tended to make original annotations of his own. These are of course a miscellaneous lot, but they may perhaps be roughly classified as referring to action, noises, properties, and actors. All will be found illustrated in the notes added by a succession of playhouse hands to the Book of *Richard II*. Generally action seems the least frequent and important, since as a rule the author himself supplied the necessary directions. But notes some-

[1] I do not wish by any means to imply that the question of date may not be of importance.

times occur for 'Dance' or 'Song', and we should perhaps include here the special category of warning directions—'Antiochus ready: vnder the stage' and the like—of which more in a moment. The author also frequently provides for stage noises, but generally in a literary manner. The prompter is as a rule technically precise, and also supplies other directions called for by, or appropriate to, the text. If the author writes 'Trumpetts sounds' or merely 'sound' he may substitute 'Flourish', or perhaps some other technical phrase, such as 'Sennet'.[1] Elsewhere he will add 'Florish' or 'Music' of his own initiative. A demand for drums may be ambiguous. If the note is for 'Drum and Colours' it is clear that an entry of soldiers rather than a noise is intended, though doubtless the bearer of the former would not neglect the opportunity to use it. But in the note 'A Drome afare of'—a curiously literary note for a prompter—there is no question that what is asked for is a noise within. A drum and colours are of course properties as well as persons and a noise, and here we reach a category more closely associated with the prompter than the author. If an author mentions properties it is as a rule only incidentally: the prompter is precise and peremptory. We have 'A Bar brought in' for Barnavelt and 'A bed for woodstock' besides many lesser needs—tables, chairs, pens, ink, paper, books, and so on. We may assume, though we cannot prove, that in the categories of noises and properties there was a close correspondence between the notes in the prompt books and the requirements detailed in the more elaborate Plots. The stage-keeper, whose business it was to provide noises and properties at a particular juncture, would take the Plot as his guide and his performance would be checked by the prompter from the Book. A close correspondence would therefore be essential.

The most important, at least for the history of the stage, and

[1] In *The Two Noble Ladies* (fol. 239[a]) the author demanded 'Hoboys' for his dumb-show in IV. iv. The stage reviser struck this out and substituted 'Lesson Corn:'. A lesson was a set piece of music for performance, and the term was apparently a technical one, for in Act I of *The Virgin Martyr* (1622, sig. B 1) we again find 'A lessen of Cornets' accompanying a procession. These two plays were performed by the same company about the same time. 'Cornetts a Lesson' also forms part of the direction for a processional entry in *The Faithful Friends*, V. ii (p. 70), a play of which the history is unknown.

in many ways the most intriguing of the prompter's notes are those respecting individual actors. Of these quite a number are preserved, though they vary very much in frequency in different Books. *Sir Thomas More* preserves a single name only, *Richard II* three; while ten are mentioned in *Sir John Barnavelt* and nearly a dozen and a half in *Believe as you List*. But these high figures are quite exceptional, and the last-mentioned piece is further exceptional in preserving the names of some of the principal actors taking some of the leading parts. As a general rule it is only the actors filling minor parts and particularly doubled parts that are recorded. There is nothing distinctive about a servant or a messenger who has to come on for a moment and speak a few words; what the prompter requires to know, and what the writer of the Plot requires to know, is which particular hireling or boy is to fill the incidental role. That seems to be in general the rationale of the recording of actors' names.[1] And it really applies equally to the apparently anomalous case of *Believe as you List*, in which we are given the actors for several leading parts. For most of them are given not in the text but in a most exceptional list of minor properties required that is added at the end. And otherwise the actor of a principal part is only revealed quite incidentally. For instance, at one point we get the warning 'Gascoigne: & Hubert below: ready to open the Trap doore for M^r^ Taylor' (ll. 1825–31) and soon afterwards another 'Antiochus ready: vnder the stage' (ll. 1877–9), whence it follows that Joseph Taylor played the part of the hero Antiochus. But obviously this is no exception to the general practice.

At the same time I do not wish to suggest that we know everything we need about the occurrence of actors' names in texts whether manuscript or print. Far from it: the subject is one requiring particularly careful and cautious study. It has been lately argued,[2] and not without some show of reason, that

[1] The failure to realize this has led to some erroneous identifications. For example in *Sir John Barnavelt* it is certain that Gough was cast (on fol. 10^a^) not for the important part of Leidenberg, but for some attendant whose presence was afterwards cancelled.

[2] See especially Professor Allison Gaw's article on 'Actors' Names in Basic Shakespearean Texts' in *Publications of the Modern Language Association of*

in certain instances the actors' names that appear in stage-directions and as speech prefixes in printed texts were written not by the prompter but by the author himself. While I should not venture to deny that this is possible, I think it is at least pertinent to point out, what I believe to be the fact, that in every instance in which an actor's name appears in a manuscript play it is written in a different hand from the text, or at any rate in a different ink and style, showing it to be a later addition and not part of the original composition.[1]

And in view of the fact that it is in general only very minor actors who are mentioned in prompt copies, it is necessary to bear in mind a caution, which, obvious enough when once formulated, is easily overlooked. When we find an actor's name recorded in a play and again in the official records of a company, there is a very natural tendency to connect the play with the company and date of the record. But bearing in mind the fact that in the play the actor was probably an unimportant hireling and in the record a sharer in the company, it will be evident that so far from the play and the company being thereby brought into relation, we may be better employed searching for the play in the possession of some other company at an earlier date. Thus when in *The Two Noble Ladies*, a piece performed by the children of the Revels about 1622, we find George Stutfield appearing as a Spirit, the correct inference is not that the play was revived by the King's Revels or Queen Henrietta's men about 1635 or Beeston's boys about 1640, of all which companies Stutfield was a leading member, but that in his unrecorded youth he had acted with the Revels players at the Red Bull. It seems possible that disregard of this caution has already introduced an element of confusion into dramatic history.

The last topic that need engage us in this brief survey is the position of stage-directions with respect to the action in the text. Naturally an author will place a direction exactly at the

*America* (1925, xl. 530–50), and also his paper in *Anglia* (1925, xlix. 289–303), 'John Sincklo as one of Shakespeare's Actors'.

[1] When an addition was made to the text an actor's name was sometimes added at the same time, as in the solitary instance in *Sir Thomas More* and presumably one of those in *The Second Maiden's Tragedy*.

in certain instances the actors' names that appear in stage-directions and as speech prefixes in printed texts were written not by the prompter but by the author himself. While I should not venture to deny that this is possible, I think it is at least pertinent to point out, what [illegible] the fact that in every instance in which [illegible] a manu-script play it is written [illegible] hand from the text [illegible]

[illegible]

[illegible] Falstaff [illegible] When [illegible] a very natural tendency [illegible] the company and [illegible] the record [illegible] the play the scene was [illegible] the play and [illegible]

[illegible]

point where it belongs, subject only to the condition that unless he actually writes it at the same time as the corresponding text he may find there is no room to insert it just where he wishes. The prompter repeating an author's direction in the left margin usually places it opposite the original, approximately at least. We can watch his methods in detail in *Believe as you List*. As a rule the new directions are opposite the old, and the reviser draws a line to mark the exact spot where they belong. Occasionally, however, he marks an entry a few lines earlier than the author had done. It is not that he writes the direction in advance of the actual entry, for his line shows that it is the entrance itself that he has advanced. Clearly his intention is to bring the characters on at the back of the stage a few moments earlier in order that they may be able to enter into the dialogue at the correct point. It is sometimes assumed that, whether for this reason or because he needs warning of their coming, a prompter will tend to mark entries in advance of the actual point intended. There may be certain cases of this, but it is certainly contrary to the usual practice as revealed in the manuscripts. Provided the direction is clearly written the prompter can easily pick it up a few lines ahead, there would be no reason actually to write it out of place.

Such anticipatory directions must be clearly distinguished from warnings, which do not direct a character to do anything but be in readiness. Actually, however, there is one remarkable instance of a play whose directions are a cross between the two: they are anticipatory in form but presumably intended as warnings. The scribe who wrote the Book of *The Lady Mother* of course marked the entrance of his characters in their natural and proper places, but when he came to prepare the manuscript for the stage he re-marked all the entries in the left margin about a quarter of a page before his original directions, at the same time drawing a line down from his anticipation to the point in the text to which it referred. This example is, so far as my observation goes, unique.

Of true warnings the most complete and consistent set we possess is in *The Welsh Embassador*, where the scribe makes almost as much a practice of them as the scribe of *The Lady*

*Mother* of formal anticipations. Within a few lines of the opening we find 'bee redy Penda' followed some twenty lines later by 'Enter Penda like a Comon soldier', soon after 'bee redy Edmond & Eldred' followed after thirty lines by their entry, and so on throughout. Not all entries have warnings, but probably the majority have. Among the most interesting are 'bee redy Carintha at a Table' anticipating by about twenty-five lines 'Enter Carintha at a Table readinge', and 'sett out a Table' followed after a similar interval by 'Enter Clowne in his study writinge'. These constitute new scenes and the directions are evidently for the preparation of properties behind the curtains in readiness for a 'discovery'. The warning for the Clown is given some ten lines before that for his table.

Warnings though less persistent are still common in *Believe as you List*. I have already had occasion to mention one case in connexion with actors' names. The men who are to work the trap for Taylor-Antiochus are warned about l. 1830, the latter is warned about l. 1880, and he speaks 'belowe' at l. 1931. Thus for this ascent the actor has fifty and the stage hands a hundred lines' warning. Another interesting example occurs in the last act. About l. 2720 Massinger provided for the entry of two servants 'with many swords', the reviser specifying in the opposite margin the actors who were to bring them in. But about l. 2380 we find a warning 'All the swords ready', meaning possibly all that could be collected from the company's stock. But why should a warning of 340 lines be needed? The answer is that the direction is written in the first available space after the beginning of the act (l. 2367), and doubtless the collection of the weapons was to take place during the act interval. Act II supplies yet another instance. Where there was question of consulting the secret chronicles of Antiochus' reign, at about l. 1110, Massinger noted in the left margin 'the recordes brought in', a direction that the reviser amplified to 'Ent: Rowland w^th^ the booke of records'. As early as about l. 980, however, we find the warning 'the great booke: of Accompte ready'—apparently the company's ledger was brought in to do service for the chronicle. Some other, but

much less notable, examples are furnished by the Book of *Richard II*. Just before the end of Act IV we find the warning 'A bed for woodstock', but here the position is not very significant, for the bed is 'discovered' within fifty lines of the opening of Act V. The 'Blankes', i.e. blank charters, demanded at the beginning of Act III, are for immediate use. We find another warning, 'Peticions: Mace', just at the end of II. i (l. 790), but though Woodstock only 'giues the Mace vp' at l. 900, he presumably brings it in with him at the beginning of II. ii, while the petitions are mentioned within a few lines of the opening. Thus the directions for properties in *Richard II* are less distinctively warnings, while the note 'Shrevs Ready', which occurs significantly at the top of a page (fol. 179[b]), only anticipates the corresponding entry by a dozen lines. One instance occurs in *The Captives* (fol. 61[b]) where we find a note, 'Fellowes ready palestra: . . . .Sarly', anticipating the entry of the characters by about thirty lines, of which nineteen are marked for omission.

It will have been noticed that these warnings refer, with few exceptions, to the provision of properties and not to the entrance of characters, and are therefore of a different nature from those in *The Welsh Embassador*. They are, however, properly warnings and not anticipatory directions, and therefore still more different from the reviser's notes in *The Lady Mother*.

Now it is perfectly true that anticipations, as distinct from warnings, occur sporadically in printed texts, and it has been assumed that they imply a playhouse origin for the copy used. This is probably a quite valid inference, though it seems to have been based rather vaguely on the belief that such anticipations are normal in prompt books, which is not the fact. If we leave on one side the quite exceptional *Lady Mother*, anticipations are just as sporadic in manuscript as in printed plays. But they are not equally unmotived. Their rationale may best be seen in what we might almost call the *locus classicus*, first pointed out by Professor Sisson, on the page of *Believe as you List* chosen for reproduction in the accompanying facsimiles (fol. 20[a]). As Massinger wrote the manuscript there occurred near the top of the next page (fol. 20$^{b}$) a direction for music and a song (though the text of this was not given). This necessitated the bringing into position of a musician and a boy, and of this the prompter naturally required some warning overleaf. Massinger had written 'musicq & a songe' within three lines of the top of the verso: the stage reviser struck this out and wrote, with greater precision, 'the Lute · strikes & then the Songe', but placed his direction at the foot of the preceding recto. He might have left this as an anticipatory direction, but it would have been inconvenient seeing his habit to indicate the precise point where a direction belongs, besides it would not have quite served the purpose he had in view. He therefore proceeded to copy in as well, at the foot of the recto, the short speech which Massinger had written on the verso before the direction for the song, carefully deleting it in its original position. He thus had the whole of the text and business before him as he prompted the preceding passage, and having got the song under way could turn the leaf at his leisure during its progress. Finally, to complete the matter he placed in the margin at the top of the page some fifty lines earlier the warning 'Harry: Wilson: & Boy ready for the song at y$^{e}$ Arras'.

However, prompters were not always as careful and elaborate in their methods as this and were sometimes content in similar cases to duplicate a direction by way of anticipation. Two good examples are found in *Edmond Ironside*. The second line on fol. 105$^{b}$ is the direction 'Enter a messenger runinge', opposite which in the margin the reviser made a note of the actor, 'H. Gibs:'. But not content with this he made the further memorandum at the foot of the preceding recto 'Ent Messenger H Gibson', so as to have due warning of the coming entrance. And so again where the words 'Enter a Messenger' recurred at the head of fol. 107$^{b}$ he wrote 'Enter H: Gibs:' at the foot of fol. 107$^{a}$. It seems to me probable that we here have the explanation of the sporadic anticipations found in printed texts.[1]

[1] I have noted the following instances in other prompt books: *John a Kent*, fol. 8$^{a}$ near foot, 'Enter shrimpe' anticipating 'Enter Shrimpe skipping' at the head of the verso page; *The Second Maiden's Tragedy*, fol. 52$^{b}$ near foot, 'Enter soldiers w$^{th}$ the Ladye' anticipating by four lines the entrance at the top

This is as far as I am able to carry the analysis of prompt books for the moment. No doubt in the summary review I have attempted the problems have been made to appear simpler and the evidence less complex than is in fact the case, but I hope I have done nothing to confuse the issues or render more difficult than it must inevitably be the task of the detailed investigators who I trust will follow up the trail.

of the following recto; *The Two Noble Ladies*, fol. 238^a foot, 'Ent: Blood Caro' anticipating 'Enter Blood & Caro embracing', the third line overleaf; *The Captives*, fol. 56^a, 'Ent: scribonia' anticipating the direction on the verso by twenty-five lines, which however are marked for omission; fol. 61^a foot, 'noise w^th^in Clo: Ash: godf', attached to the scene heading and anticipating immediately the direction overleaf; fol. 62^a near foot, 'Raph: Tred: Clow' (twice) anticipating the formal direction overleaf, 'Enter m^r^ Raphael m^r^ Treadway and the clowne', by some sixteen lines which are marked for omission. There is probably another instance in *Charlemagne*, fol. 125^a foot, but the note is now illegible. Any of these would give rise to an arbitrary anticipation in a printed edition based on the manuscript. It will, however, be observed that, except where passages have been marked for omission, the anticipations are as a rule of a few lines only and would hardly be distinguishable from ordinary prompt duplications.

It has been no easy task to select for reproduction a limited number of representative pages from extant prompt books, in spite of the fact that I have confined my choice almost entirely to those accessible in the British Museum. The object I have kept in view has been to illustrate at once the great variety in the character of the Books themselves, and the individual methods of the various authors and stage revisers concerned. It is true that the small fragments from *John a Kent* (1) and *Sir Thomas More* (2 A, B) have been included on purely palaeographic grounds in order to illustrate the handwriting of one particularly important playhouse scribe. It was tempting to reproduce a series of passages from the second of these plays; but I was reluctant to claim it as a typical example, and moreover a complete facsimile is available. *Richard II* (3) appears to be an early and much worn prompt copy scored with the notes of a succession of stage revisers. *The Second Maiden's Tragedy* (4) is distinguished by its insertions. *Sir John Barnavelt* (5) illustrates Crane's work, and suggests his close association with the King's company. *The Two Noble Ladies* (6) is remarkable for the elaboration of its original stage-directions, which bear a significant relation to the prompter's notes. In Heywood's *Captives* (7) interest centres on the badness of the author's writing and the unusual nature of the annotations added in view of production. Massinger's *Believe as you List* (8), an author's fair copy prepared for the stage by another of the King's men's scribes ('Jhon'), again illustrates the book-keeper's attitude to literary directions. Lastly, *The Lady Mother* (9) is interesting both on account of the extensive revision carried out apparently by the author and of the prompter's systematic notes.

1. *John a Kent and John a Cumber*, by Anthony Munday. *c.* 1590?

The autograph manuscript preserves its contemporary vellum wrapper formed of portions of two medieval manuscripts, one of which also supplied that of *Sir Thomas More*. The title

inscribed on this wrapper is here reproduced for comparison with those of *Sir Thomas More* (2 A) and 2 *Seven Deadly Sins* (II). There can be no doubt, I think, that all three are the work of one hand. Clearly then the indications point to the two Books having once been in the possession of the same company at the same time, and serve to connect the Book of *John a Kent* with the playhouse, thus bearing out the few if distinct theatrical stigmas apparent in the text. This bears Munday's signature at the end, and below this another hand has added a date in Dec. 1596. This supplies a downward limit for the manuscript, which may, however, be considerably older. Various points in connexion with Munday's writing suggest that it was written some years before *Sir Thomas More*, and if 1593 be accepted as the most likely date for that play, the composition of *John a Kent* can hardly be placed later than 1590.

If 1593 is the correct date for *Sir Thomas More* there is little doubt that it belonged to Strange's men, or rather to the fusion of the earlier Strange's and Admiral's men that was then touring under that name, though led by the Admiral's servant Edward Alleyn. *John a Kent* may, therefore, have been in the same hands, though the inference is rendered somewhat uncertain by the fact that the scribe who wrote the titles on the two plays is known to have been later with the Admiral's men. But it is noteworthy that after Alleyn had re-established the Admiral's men as an independent company in the summer of 1594, we find among the new pieces in their repertory from Dec. 1594 till July 1597 a very popular play called *The Wise Man of West Chester*, the Book of which belonged to Alleyn personally (being sold by him to the company for 40*s*. on 19 Sept. 1601). This might well be an alternative title of *John a Kent*, and when we find among the company properties in 1598 an article described as 'Kentes woden leage', it is impossible to resist the inference that we have to do with a play somehow related to Munday's. But in the latter Kent has no wooden leg. We have then the choice of three alternatives. (i) The two may have been rival pieces on the same subject, in which case they must have been written for different companies. If *John a Kent* did not pass from Strange's to the Admiral's it must have passed to the Chamberlain's, or it may possibly have been originally written for one of the latter companies. Imitation by the Admiral's seems to imply an unlikely degree of success for the original play, though this is not perhaps an argument of great weight. On the other hand, *The Wise Man* was undoubtedly popular, and we might suppose that *John a Kent* was written as a counterblast for the Chamberlain's men some time in 1595 or 1596. This, however, would throw *Sir Thomas More* later than seems probable: moreover, while Munday is known to have written for the Admiral's men, there is no trace of his having ever been connected with the Chamberlain's. (ii) *John a Kent* may be a revised version of *The Wise Man* produced for the Admiral's men in 1595 or 1596. This would involve the same difficulty respecting *Sir Thomas More*, and moreover *The Wise Man* went on being played till 1597, while there is no trace of *John a Kent* in the repertory. (iii) Lastly, *The Wise Man* may be a revision for the Admiral's men of Munday's earlier *John a Kent*, written for Strange's. The revision may or may not have been the work of Munday himself. There appears no obvious objection to this supposition, which is the one which in consequence I provisionally accept. And this view carries with it certain important implications. For when in the spring of 1594 the Strange-Admiral's combination came to an end, the Book of *John a Kent* must have remained in Alleyn's hands, as did, we know, the Plot at least of *The Seven Deadly Sins*. And if this happened in the case of *John a Kent* it probably happened in that of *Sir Thomas More* likewise, seeing that the similar decay of the two manuscripts suggests that they may have long lain and mouldered side by side.

2. *Sir Thomas More*, by Anthony Munday and others. *c.* 1593?

The manuscript consists of an original fair copy written throughout in Munday's hand, though probably not all of his own composition, which has been largely altered and augmented by supplements in five other hands. A note by the censor insisting on drastic alterations, shows that production had been contemplated, and the addition at one point of an actor's name suggests that preparation had indeed begun,

though it is improbable that the piece was ever actually performed. The Book has a vellum wrapper like that of *John a Kent*, with a title inscribed by the same hand, which is here reproduced (2 A). The other reproduction (2 B) shows a portion of a scene in one of the additional hands (that known as C). Although in this Italian script is more sparingly used, there can be no question of the identity of the hand with that of the Plot of 2 *Seven Deadly Sins* (II), and therefore with that seen in the titles to *Sir Thomas More* and *John a Kent*. If the Plot and the Book are of approximately the same date the community of hand would point to their belonging to the same company, and a further link is afforded by the fact that the name of the actor, Thomas Goodale, preserved in the Book also appears in the Plot. I have previously argued at length the case for ascribing the Plot of *The Seven Deadly Sins* to Strange's men about 1590. The date of *Sir Thomas More* is much disputed, but there is a good deal to be said for 1593, a year to which I personally incline. If that is correct it almost necessarily follows that it belonged to Strange's men, or rather to the amalgamation of the Strange's and Admiral's companies that in 1593–4 was touring under that name. The scribe (C) was later with the Admiral's men and wrote for them the Plot of *Fortune's Tennis* in 1597–8. It is clear that he was some one closely connected with the playhouses, possibly in the capacity of book-keeper, a supposition that is borne out by the fact that in *Sir Thomas More* he seems to have acted as editor to the team of revisers, collating, combining, and in part transcribing their work. I see very little to indicate that he was himself part author of the scenes in his hand, though it is not impossible.

Only a few textual remarks on 2 B are needed:

l. 19. In 'Erafmus' there are six minims between 'f' and 's'.

l. 26. In 'beare' the 'b' has been altered from 'r'.

l. 27. In 'fhake' the 'k' has been altered.

---

The rules placed for greater distinction round the stage-direction of entry in the right margin (ll. 24–6) should be noticed.

3. *Richard II* or *Thomas of Woodstock*. *c.* 1592–5.

The play has been assigned to a date after 1592, since the author seems to have known *Edward II* and 2 *Henry VI*, and before 1595, since Shakespeare's *Richard II* appears to show knowledge of it; in any case the form 'Arden' (l. 15) would place it after Lodge's *Rosalynde* (1590). The manuscript, a much-thumbed prompt copy, probably dates from the original production, though it is not autograph; but the actors' names that occur, together with some of the prompt directions, may belong to one or more revivals in the next century. Neither the company to which it originally belonged nor that which revived it can at present be determined with any approach to certainty.

Textual notes are as follows:

l. 2. In 'tymeʒ' the 't' is blotted and has perhaps been altered. What in the facsimile looks like a stop after this word is really an accidental mark in the paper.

l. 5. The prefix '*ſer:*' was deleted by the reviser when he added the name 'Toby:'.

l. 10. In the reviser's direction 'Anticke' the letters 'ntic' have been written over and obliterate the initial '*W:*', sc. Woodstock, prefixed by the original scribe to the ensuing speech. In the reviser's 'fflorifh' the 'ff' appears to have been altered.

l. 18. The word 'fore·ſteʒ' is apparently so written, with a superscript 'r' above the 'e', but perhaps 'for$^{r}$eſteʒ' was what the scribe intended.

l. 36. In '*KingeRichard*' the '*e*' may have been inserted.

l. 37. In '*knights*' the first letter is not quite certain.

l. 41. What in the facsimile looks like a stop after 'yo$^{r}$' seems to be in fact an accidental mark.

l. 43. In the last word the missing letter may have been 'e' or 'i'.

l. 48. In 'loueʒ,' the 'ʒ' is doubtful, perhaps only a virgule ('/') was intended.

---

Not all the prompt directions on this page would seem to be in the same hand. The distribution is not quite certain, but most likely 'Toby:' and 'Muſick' are in one hand and the notes in ll. 10–11 in another.

Points to be observed are: the tendency to reduce prefixes to an initial; the long rules marking off the main entrance directions written across the page; the usual position of subsidiary entrances in the left margin, also between rules; the braces used in conjunction with marginal directions; the position of the reviser's direction in the right margin, together with its duplication 'Anticke' on the left; and lastly the catchword.

4. *The Second Maiden's Tragedy*, 1611.

The inappropriate title is the censor's, whose licence, dated 31 Oct. 1611, is at the end, and only means that it is another 'Maid's Tragedy' like that by Beaumont and Fletcher. Various worthless ascriptions have been made by later hands at the end. Massinger and Tourneur have been suggested as authors on no very substantial grounds. The Book is a very careful transcript by a professional scribe, with some alterations by the censor (see deletion at l. 40), certain literary revisions perhaps by the author (the hand has not been identified), and notes by a playhouse reviser. Of the last two appear on the page reproduced, one including an actor's name, Mr. Gough. Another actor mentioned is Richard Robinson. These suffice to identify the company as the King's. The most striking peculiarity of this Book is the addition of passages to the text by means of strips of paper 'flown' on the page, that is, pasted down by one edge. These additions, six in number, seem to have been written on one sheet of paper which was afterwards cut up rather carelessly into strips. The hand is that of the original scribe. Two of the additions are shown on the page reproduced, and the passages concealed by the slips run as follows:

of my proviſion, but a frend will beare,—wthin ther
*Enter* i *Soldier.* Sir
O 2 *Sold.* my lord
*Ty.* the men J wiſht for
for ſecrecy and imployemt;—Run *Atranius*
bring me the keyes of the *Cathedrall* ſtraight
i *Sould.* are you ſo holie now, do you curſe all daie
and goe to praie at midnighte?—*Exit.*

and:

J muſt not be ſo coozned; thoughe her life
was lyke a widdowes ſtate made ore in pollecy
to defeat me and my to confident heart
twas a moſt cruell wiſdome to her ſelf
as much to me that lou'd her,—what returnd?
*Enter* · i *Sould.* here be the keyes my lord
*Tyr.* J thank thy ſpeed
here comes the reſt full furniſht, follow me
and wealth ſhall followe you—*Exit*

i *Sould.* wealth, by this lighte
we goe to rob a church J hold my life
the mony will nere thriue, thats a ſure ſawe
what 's got from *Grace*, is euer ſpent in lawe — *Exunt*

The circles, one concealed, the other at the foot of the page, mark the position of the two insertions, the latter of which was to be spoken by Robert Gough, probably in the character of Memphonius.

Textual notes are as follows:

l. 5. What looks in the facsimile like a stop at the end of this line is really an accidental mark in the paper.

l. 11. In 'mee?' the upper part of the query seems to have been added above an original comma: the dot to the right is probably accidental.

l. 21. For 'vp,' the original has 'vp.,', but the dot looks modern.

l. 30. The addition of the reviser's direction, duplicating that covered by the slip at l. 32, shows that the revision was made after the additions had been pasted in their present position.

l. 32. The first two letters of the word '*Ent*[*er*]' do not appear in the facsimile owing to the bending of the paper at the inner margin.

l. 43 (on slip). In 'ſtraunge' the 'un' is dotted as though the scribe had first intended to write 'ſtrainge'.

l. 55 (under slip). In '*Exunt*' the '*e*' has been omitted.

In l. 48 (on slip) it is evident that the usually careful scribe has made a mistake. It would, of course, be easy to emend 'myndes' to 'mynde'. But in that case 'they' in the next line would refer to 'his moodes', whereas from what follows it seems clear that the lords of l. 52 are meant. Assuming this, the simplest emendation would be to read 'in his nobles mindes', but this clashes awkwardly with 'in ſpirrit or blood'. It is tempting to read and punctuate:

he waxes heavie, and in [*or* to] noble myndes

in imitation of *Hamlet*, III. i. 100. The query at the end of l. 50 stands for an exclamation mark, the two being used indifferently.

Notice the habit of marking subsidiary entrances by writing '*Enter*' before a speaker's prefix, as in ll. 32, 47.

5. *Sir John van Olden Barnavelt*, 1619.

The play, which was acted in Aug. 1619, is usually assigned to Fletcher and Massinger. The manuscript is known to be in the hand of a scribe named Ralph Crane. It was evidently

prepared with a view to use in the playhouse, the directions being written in large and heavy Italian script for the convenience of the prompter. They have occasionally been altered and others added in a much rougher style. These additional directions are indicated in the transcript by the use of heavy type, but it is not certain that the hand is different. Indeed the probability is that they are Crane's, and in that case his connexion with the playhouse was more intimate than one would gather from what he has himself told us.[1] A number of actors' names, incidentally added, show that the Book belonged to the King's company, for which Crane is known to have worked. There are also alterations and annotations in the hand of the censor, though there is no licence at the end. The page reproduced is fol. 23$^{b}$ of the official pencil numeration, corresponding to 21$^{b}$ of the original ink foliation.

Only one textual point arises:

In ll. 23–4 I cannot help suspecting that the scribe has blundered. The words 'that is being' show that the parenthesis is an expansion of the epithet 'weake' in the previous line. Then 'the bag . . . caſt behind' suggests a pedlar's pack thrown over the shoulder. If, then, we were to read 'him' instead of 'you', the idea would be that Barnavelt is discharged, useless, tramping off with his stock-in-trade (or perhaps his tools) packed up and slung on his back. But the phrase 'bag of his deferts' would remain awkward at best. It might be preferable to retain 'you' and alter 'bag' to 'lag', interpreting the line to mean, even the latest of his services cast to oblivion.

---

Observe the rules, unnecessary in connexion with the heavy directions originally written, but used to distinguish those added later in lighter script; also the subsidiary entrance marked in the right margin but with a short rule added on the left to indicate the exact point.

6. *The Two Noble Ladies and the Converted Conjurer*. 1622–3?

Nothing is known as to the authorship of this play, but it survives in what appears to be an autograph copy, containing alterations and corrections (cf. the direction at ll. 14–5) sometimes made *currente calamo* in the text, and further prepared for the stage in another hand by a playhouse reviser. At the

[1] See the article by Professor F. P. Wilson on 'Ralph Crane, Scrivener to the King's Players' (*The Library*, 1926, vii. 194–215).

beginning a third hand has added a title, apparently with a view to publication, stating that the piece was acted at the Red Bull by the company of the Revels. A short-lived company called the children or the players of the Revels did in fact act at the Red Bull in 1622–3, and there seems no reason to doubt that this play was in their repertory. But none of the five or six actors whose names are recorded by the stage reviser can be traced with this company, or indeed at quite so early a date, and it is possible that the revision may have been made for some other company a decade or so later (see, however, note on l. 16). At the same time the actors whose names appear would naturally be hired men taking only small parts, and they presumably began their careers some years before they are mentioned in the records (cf. p. 216). The manuscript is remarkable for the elaboration of the stage-directions supplied by the author in the right-hand margin.

Textual points are as follows:

l. 1. The writer began to run on the second line: this is not an uncommon error even in autograph manuscripts.

l. 4. In 'Archander' the first 'r' has probably been altered.

l. 5. In 'pow'r' the mark transcribed as an apostrophe is above the 'r' and looks like a deletion, but cf. l. 33.

l. 8. In 'madneſſe' the 'n' has been altered from 'e'.

l. 21. In 'yee' the 'ee' has been altered from 'ou'.

l. 27. In 'truce' the 'c' has been altered from 'e' and the 'e' added.

l. 35. In 'that' the 'at' has been altered from 'is', and in '*Tritons*' the '*T*' from '*t*'.

l. 38. In '*Souldier*' the '*l*' has been altered.

l. 39. In 'Alas' the 'A' has been altered, in 'ſtreame' the 'tr', and in '*Tritons*' the '*T*' from '*t*'.

l. 40. In '*Souldier*' the '*r*' has been altered; also—

l. 43. in '*Lyſander*' the '*yſa*', and

l. 45. in '*Cyprian*' the '*C*'.

l. 50. In 'Antiochs' the 's' has been added.

l. 51. In 'Egypts' the 'y' has been altered from 'i'.

---

In l. 16 it will be observed that the reviser has repeated on the left a direction written by the author on the right, and that in doing so

he followed the original form and not the substitute. A similar instance appears on fol. 242[a]. They may be accidental; if not, they show that the stage revision was contemporary with the author's final corrections, and that the actors named took part in the original performance.

In l. 41 the word rendered '*in*' must be regarded as doubtful. The Tritons go 'in' (i.e. off the stage) at this point: it is worth notice that the reviser has recorded the names of the actors on their exit instead of their entrance. A similar sign, also apparently connected with an exit, occurs in Specimen 9, l. 46 (though here again the reading is not certain) and in *Edmond Ironside* (fol. 104[b]) where, however, it is connected with an entry. It might possibly stand for '*m*[*r*]', but at any rate in the present instance the designation is unlikely to have been given to the actors of such insignificant parts.

---

Observe the rules surrounding the author's directions in the right margin: these are added by the author himself. The reviser repeats the more significant directions on the left, between rules, and assigns actors for small incidental parts.

## 7. *The Captives*, by Thomas Heywood. 1624.

The manuscript, which bears no title, is clearly autograph, and there is good reason to suppose that the hand is Heywood's. Herbert, the Master of the Revels, records on 3 Sept. 1624 the licence of 'The Captive, or The Lost recovered' by 'Hayward' for the Cockpit company, probably the Lady Elizabeth's men. This title, or rather *The Captives*, is so appropriate to the present play that the identification may be accepted.

The hand is an exceedingly bad one, whose chief characteristics are an utter indifference to the number of minims written and the habit of adding a meaningless stroke above a final 'm' or 'n', peculiarities that have been disregarded in the transcript. The manuscript has undergone elaborate revision in the playhouse. The revising hand varies a good deal (cf. ll. 9, 17, 78) but is probably the same throughout. It is at times so rough as to be liable to confusion with Heywood's, though there is little doubt that they are really distinct. Characteristic is the reviser's solicitude for what one might perhaps call the theatrical structure of the action. When the stage is left empty he puts the warning 'clere', and at one point adds 'to em' after a direction to indicate that the action is continuous: the large stars in the margin he seems to have prefixed to important entrances, whether on a clear stage or not. At the foot of the page he notes that the stage-hands are to be requisitioned to form a guard. All these notes are very roughly made, and there seems to be some careless duplication (l. 48 'w^th^in', ll. 76–7 'clere'). The final result both of the original writing and of the revision is so untidy and illegible that it is difficult to believe that the manuscript was designed for use as a prompt book. More likely the autograph was revised and annotated with a view to having a fair copy prepared for stage use by a scribe. In this connexion it is worth notice that though the play is known to have been allowed by the censor, and though there is a blank page at the end, there is no trace of any licence in the manuscript. Two or three actors are named in the reviser's notes. None are known to have been with the Lady Elizabeth's men, but as only small parts are involved they were no doubt hirelings who would find no mention in the records.

Textual notes are as follows:

l. 1. The sheet (not folio) number '10' was added by Heywood.

l. 9. Below this line the writer placed a short rule, indicating the end of a speech, erroneously, and wrote the next line over it.

l. 21. Before 'but' some letter has been begun and left: it may have been deleted. At the end of the line the paper is decayed.

l. 24. In 'him' the 'h' has been altered, perhaps from 'v'.

l. 43. The '&'' is very uncertain, but it is difficult to see what else can be intended.

l. 51. The upright bars between the names were added by the reviser, and so was the caret mark at the end. The latter perhaps means that Heywood's 'etc'' should be expanded.

l. 71. The word transcribed 'haunt' might equally well be read 'hunt'; there are three minims between the 'a' or 'u' and the 't'.

l. 74. There is apparently an apostrophe after 'alyve', as there is after the '&' in l. 43. In either case it might be a comma placed much too high.

l. 77. In 'Richrd' (a single minim does duty for 'ar') the 'Rich' is written over 'Jhon'. There seems to be a caret mark below the alteration, so that Heywood presumably imagined that he was inter-

lining his correction. It is not clear whether 'Jhon' is independently deleted or not.

---

Observe, beyond the peculiarities already noticed, the want of distinctness in the original stage-directions, and the fact that the reviser uses either margin indifferently for his additions.

8. *Believe as you List*, by Philip Massinger. 1631.

The manuscript is autograph and has been carefully revised in the playhouse. It has a vellum wrapper formed of an old indenture, on which the reviser's hand has written the title and an ascription to Massinger, while at the end is the censor's allowance dated 6 May 1631. Herbert's office book gave the date as 7 May (perhaps that on which he received his fee) and added that it was for the King's company. The play is a revision, with altered names and setting, of an earlier piece which on 11 Jan. the censor had refused to license on political grounds. The manuscript is therefore a transcript of another fair copy, but how far the revision was made in the course of transcription (which alterations in the present text suggest was sometimes the case), and how far, if at all, the rewriting was done in the rough on the earlier copy, is not exactly known. The stage revision was carried out by a scribe who may conveniently be called 'Jhon' (from a scribble in his *Honest Man's Fortune*), and who can be fairly classed as a playhouse scrivener. He worked for the King's company rather later than, perhaps in succession to, Crane, and may possibly have been their book-keeper 'Mr. Knight' mentioned by Herbert. His prompt notes are most careful and written, like Crane's, in a bold Italian script. His treatment of the author's own directions (which he often repeats in shorter form in the left margin, as at l. 23) form the most complete body of evidence provided by any single play for the customs of the stage. And the most interesting point in the whole manuscript is seen at the foot of the page reproduced; namely an elaborate piece of playhouse editing with an intimate bearing on the problem of anticipatory directions. The following page, as written by Massinger, began with a single speech followed by a song, for which the direction was duly inserted. This speech and direction the stage reviser transferred bodily to the foot of the previous (recto) page. The reason and significance of his action have been already fully discussed (pp. 219–20), but it is worth adding here that in copying the speech he disregarded the verse lining altogether and wrote it as prose, a fact of some bibliographical interest (cf. C. J. Sisson, 'Bibliographical Aspects of some Stuart Dramatic Manuscripts', *The Review of English Studies*, 1925, i. 421). The scribe also added near the top of the page a further direction warning the lutenist and singer to be ready at the back of the stage. At the end of the manuscript, after the censor's licence, the reviser copied in the prologue and epilogue, which may not be Massinger's, and added a list of special properties required in the play, a feature found in no other playhouse manuscript. They consist mainly of letters and papers which would be prepared for the occasion, and appear in fact to have been mostly dummies; but there is reason to suppose that on the Elizabethan stage such documents were sometimes actually made out in writing and read by the actors on the stage.[1] The reviser's notes further mention a number of actors by name, and several of these can be checked as belonging to the King's company.

Textual points are as follows:

l. 1. The sheet (not folio) number was added by Massinger in the inner margin. It has been altered from '8' to '9'.

l. 8. In 'to' the 't' has been altered.

l. 24. In 'Jaylor' the 'J' has been altered from 'i'.

l. 25. The deleted reading is not quite certain, but it was most likely

[1] Mr. W. J. Lawrence in his essay on 'Early Prompt-Books' (p. 406) appositely adduces the following passage from Marlowe's *Edward II* (1594, sc. xv, ll. 1798 ff.):

> *Edw.* Why man, they say there is great execution
> Done through the realme, my lord of *Arundell*
> You haue the note, haue you not?
> *Matr.* From the lieutenant of the tower my lord.
> *Edw.* I pray let vs see it, what haue we there?
> Read it *Spencer*. *Spencer reads their names.*
> Why so, they barkt a pace a month a goe,
> Now on my life, theile neither barke nor bite.

The list of names must have been given in the paper that Spencer read, for it is nowhere in the text—a fact that incidentally raises an interesting question as to the nature of the copy used.

a portmanteau miswriting of 'tem[ptinge fien]de', to which it has been corrected by the author.

l. 38. In 'this' the 't' has been altered, probably from 'l'.

l. 44. In 'ranſackde' the 'r' has been altered.

l. 58. The reviser's direction having interfered with the speaker's name, which happened to be written rather low, he deleted it with a heavy stroke and wrote it in again rather higher.

l. 59. The reviser placed a short thick dash to indicate the point where his direction belonged, and this partly obliterated Massinger's '&' at the beginning of the line. He therefore wrote another '&' over it.

---

It is worth observing that though this is an autograph fair copy there is little doubt that in l. 48 Massinger has written the opposite of what he intended. The 'not' was probably caught up from the line below.

9. *The Lady Mother*. 1635.

The manuscript of this piece, which Bullen ascribed to Glapthorne, would seem, to judge from certain errors in the text, to be probably in the hand of a scribe. It bears at the end the licence of the censor dated 15 Oct. 1635, and also contains a few corrections apparently in his hand. The play has undergone rather extensive literary revision and has also been carefully prepared for the stage. The page reproduced shows considerable marginal additions to the text. The hand in which these are written bears some resemblance to that of the text and might be a rougher variety of the same: it is, however, more likely to be distinct and may in that case perhaps be the author's. Some of the playhouse revision is certainly in the hand of the scribe, and it seems probable that he is responsible for the directions distinguished in the transcript by heavy italic type (ll. 15–6, 46–8) in spite of their difference of style. In the passage in question these refer to the author's marginal additions, and must of course have been inserted subsequent to the literary revision, but similar marginal directions occur throughout, anticipating as a rule by about a quarter of a page the directions in the text, and constitute the most distinctive feature of this Book. There are also certain short additions and a few prompt notes in yet other hands.

Textual points are as follows:

l. 35. The last letter of 'begin' is clearly visible under the mending paper.

l. 36. The mark at the end is only a flourish such as some scribes were wont to fill up short lines with.

l. 45. What looks like a comma after 'word' is an accidental mark in the paper.

l. 46. The reviser's '*in:*' is uncertain. There are certainly four minims, and though there seems to be a dot to the '*i*' it is not very clear. But there is apparently no doubt that he intends to mark the exit of the characters whose entrance he recorded above, and who have been making comments aside, for the remainder of the scene appears to be marked for omission. Cf. Specimen 6, note on l. 41.

l. 48. The last letter of 'freind' is clearly visible under the mending paper.

l. 51. Of the first word the top of the 't' is still visible, the 'o' has vanished. Of 'accõn' (i.e. action) mere traces of the first two letters remain. Of 'assault' the first four letters are represented by traces only, and there certainly does not seem to be any indication of tall letters; but it is hard to imagine what else the word can have been.

## DESCRIPTIVE LIST OF MANUSCRIPT PLAYS

The object and scope of the following list, as well as its general arrangement, have already been explained (p. 191), and it only remains to set forth some of the peculiarities and conventions of the descriptions. All the manuscripts in classes A and B are in folio: I have noted the size in inches, and whenever possible the make-up of the sheets (cf. p. 205). As a rule the leaves have been folded for margins in the manner detailed on p. 206, and the speeches divided by rules as mentioned on pp. 207-8. These points have been regularly recorded. The nature of the writing has been briefly indicated, and any details I have observed that might suggest its being the work of the author on the one hand or of a scribe on the other have been noted. Next I have dealt with indications of revision in the playhouse, and of censorship by the Master of the Revels. Particular attention has been paid to indications of division into acts and scenes, and to the style and position of the stage-directions, whether original or due to revision. I have also occasionally allowed myself a few remarks on their nature, but have preferred for the most part to let the reader form his own impression from the transcript of the more important directions and annotations with which my descriptions conclude, and which forms their most important feature.

The fullness of these lists of stage-directions varies considerably from play to play. In some instances it appeared necessary, or at least desirable, to quote the bulk of those that appeared in the manuscript. Others are far less interesting in this respect, and I have contented myself with collecting in full those occurring in the first act (or an approximately equivalent portion of the play)—at any rate all except bare entrances and exits—and from the rest of the play only those presenting some special feature of interest. This minimum is to be assumed where nothing is said to the contrary. Directions may be regarded as of three kinds: entrances, exits, and independent directions of all sorts unconnected with the entry or retirement of any character. But entrances and exits of course often include much beyond a record of the bare entry or retirement of the character or characters concerned. Again their position[1] may be defined as threefold; central, or in the left or right margin. By a central direction is to be understood one written across the page and interrupting the continuity of the text: it is of course the most important position, though not always the clearest. A direction that involves a break in the text is always classed as central, though it may begin in the left margin or extend into the right, or even be confined to one or other side of the page. The extremer cases require individual specification. Directions confined to the left margin, otherwise reserved for the speakers' names, are the best defined of all and need no further comment. The right margin is a far less certain location. Even when the paper has been folded it is effectually defined less by this than by writing of the text. In the case of verse the text usually occupies approximately the two middle columns of the folded page, and the blank space on the right is roughly equivalent to the folded margin. But in the case of prose the writing usually extends to or near the right edge of the page, and any right-hand directions have to be crowded in as best they may. Advantage is naturally taken of any short lines in the text, and consequently directions that have to be classed as right-hand ones, sometimes begin near or even before the middle fold, and also are apt to occur a few lines before or after their natural position.

There are a good many interesting points connected with the position of directions. Thus we sometimes find, in a play which is formally divided only into acts, that the writer has nevertheless shown his sense of scenic division by centring those, and only those, entrances that in fact constitute the beginning of a new scene. Then there is the question of how far the left margin was consciously left free for use by the prompter; the scribe confining his original directions to the right. Lastly there are the expedients adopted for emphasizing and calling attention to obscurely placed directions.

In the lists of manuscript directions (printed in smaller type)

[1] I am here speaking merely of the formal placing of the directions on the page. The more important question of the position the directions occupy in relation to the text has already been touched upon (pp. 216 ff.).

a few peculiar conventions have been adopted. A star (*) is prefixed to directions in another hand from the text[1]: it applies to the one quotation that immediately follows and no more. *Italics* indicate deletions in the original. Dots (. . .) indicate the omission of a mere string of names. Pointed brackets ⟨ ⟩ draw attention to mutilations in the original, and all letters within them are conjectural. Square brackets [ ] enclose editorial comments. A bar (|) indicates a line division in the original of a nature to merit record: in most cases it marks what might be called a fresh paragraph.

On the other hand, outside the small-type lists of directions, italics merely reproduce the italics or Italian script of an original quotation; original deletions are indicated by square brackets; and dots are used in a looser way for omissions.

The preceding explanations must be taken to apply particularly to classes A and B. The descriptions in class C are both briefer and more general and follow no definite scheme. This class includes quarto as well as folio manuscripts, and the format is therefore specified in each case.

## *CLASS A*

1. *John a Kent*, by A. Munday.
Huntington Library. *c.* 1590?

The play (see Plate 1) is written on thirteen leaves, forming a succession of six and a half sheets: of the odd leaf at the end only one corner now remains. The whole is enclosed in a vellum wrapper composed of fragments of two medieval manuscripts, one of which also supplied the wrapper for *Sir Thomas More*. The edges have suffered from damp and wear in a manner similar to those of *More*, and it would seem that at some time, apparently before it was provided with its wrapper, the manuscript was folded across, for there is a horizontal split in the paper half way down the inner margin of each leaf. The leaves must originally have measured about $12\frac{3}{4}\times 8\frac{1}{8}$ inches.

Wrapper, p. i: 'The Book of Iohn A kent & Iohn a Cumber'

[1] Occasionally to those added in a different style and at a different time, though perhaps by the same hand, as explained *in loco*.

(Plate 1) inscribed in gothic letters by the same hand as the title to *Sir Thomas More* (q.v.).

Begins, fol. 1$^{a}$: 'Act⟨us i⟩ Scena i | Enter Sir Griffin Meriddock of So⟨uth⟩wales, & Ieffrey⟨ P⟩ow⟨esse⟩'.

Ends, fol. 13$^{b}$: ⟨fin⟩is. | Anthony Mundy | ⟨ ⟩ Decembris 1596' the date being added in a different hand from the rest.

Written throughout, so far as the text is concerned, in the hand of Anthony Munday, whose autograph signature appears at the end. It is mainly an English script, with a rather sporadic mixture of roughly formed Italian. There is a normal use of exceptionally long speech-rules, extending almost the whole length of the lines, but varying with it. The leaves have been folded for margins. There are a few playhouse directions added in the margin by another hand, which is apparently identical with that of the stage reviser in *Sir Thomas More*, and if so with the hand that inscribed the ornamental title on the wrapper. The hand that added '⟨ ⟩ Decembris 1596' at the end is again different. There is no trace of censorship, but a licence may of course have been lost at the end, since the lower half of the last leaf has completely disappeared. Such passages as are marked for omission seem to have been condemned on purely literary or dramatic grounds. An addition of four lines has been written up the margin of fol. 2$^{a}$, in the hand of the text.

There is a regular division into acts only, the headings to which (with the addition 'Scena Prima') are centred except in the case of the third (fol. 6$^{b}$).

The stage-directions, which are not generally distinguished in script from the text, are decidedly full, both as regards entrances and independent directions. Entrances are centred with few exceptions: exits as usual are on the right: other directions appear indifferently in either margin, rarely in the centre. There is no definite use of rules in connexion with stage-directions; most of those that appear can be interpreted as speech-rules. The following list is exhaustive for all but bare exits.

1$^{a}$ [I. i, as above.] 'he shewes⟨ ⟩ letter⟨' (right). 'Enter S$^{r}$. Gosselin denvyle, S$^{r}$. Euan Griff⟨in⟩, and I⟨ohn⟩'.

2$^{a}$ [I. ii] 'Enter at one doore Ranulphe Earle of Chester, Oswen his sonn⟨e⟩ young Amery Lord Mortaigue, w$^{th}$ them the Countesse, her daught⟨er⟩ Marian, and fayre Sidanen. At another doore enter the Earles Pembrooke, Moorton and their trayne'. 'asyde' (right, thrice). 'exeunt. Countesse Sida & Ma⟨rian⟩' (sc. manent: right).

2$^{b}$ *'Enter' (left) one line before 'Enter Iohn a Kent like an aged Hermit' (centre). 'giue him somewhat' (right). 'he sees their handes' (right). 'he offers to depart' (right).

3$^{a}$ 'he pulles his beard' (right). 'Enter S$^{r}$. Griffin, and Lord Powesse'.

3$^{b}$ [I. iii] 'Enter Turnop w$^{th}$ his crewe of Clownes, & a Minstrell'. 'Enter Pembrook, Moorton, Oswen, Amery, to them this crew marching, one drest lik a Moore, w$^{th}$ a Tun painted with yellow oker, another with a Porrenger full of water an⟨d⟩ a pen in it, Turnop speaketh the Oration'.

4$^{a}$ 'exeunt Lordes'. 'exeunt. | Actus secundus. Scena Prima. | Enter at one doore Iohn a Kent, hermit lyke, as before, at anothe⟨r⟩ enter the Countesse, Sydanen and Marian'. 'Sydanen & h⟨e⟩ conferre' (right).

4$^{b}$ 'winde his horn' (right) one line before 'Enter denvyle, Griff. Powesse, *Euan*, and trayne' (left). 'he puts of his disguyse' (right).

5$^{a}$ 'exeunt—manet Iohn'. 'Enter Shrimp a boy' (right). 'round in his eare' (right). 'exeunt seuerally. | Enter Turnop, Hugh, Tom Tabrer, will the boy, and Spurling w$^{th}$ their Consort'. 'they play, the boy sings the welsh song' (left). 'Enter Shrimpe the boy' (centre). 'a Song of the Brydes losse' (left) opposite 'They play, and the boy singes, wheart [*sic*] the Bridegroomes come foorth in their nightgownes and kerchers on their heades, to them Oswen ⟨ ⟩ Amery making them selues ready' (centre) the last anticipating by 12 lines—

5$^{b}$ 'Heere enter Amery & Oswen vnbraste' (right). 'Enter the Earle of Chester in his night gowne, and Shrimpe following aloofe of, some seruants w$^{th}$ him'. 'exeunt clownes & seruaunts'. 'exit boy. | Enter Llwellen, his traine, and Iohn a Cumber a loofe of'. [speakes] 'to Iohn a Cumber' (right).

6$^{a}$ 'all embrace him' (right). 'Exeunt, man⟨et Cumber⟩'.

6$^{b}$ 'look in his glasse' (right). '⟨Actus⟩ tertius' (left) opposite 'Enter S$^{r}$. Griffin, Powesse, Gosselen and Euan'. *'musique' (left) one line before 'Musique whi⟨le⟩ he opens the doore' (right). 'ffrom one end of the Stage enter an antique queinlly disguysde and cōming dauncing before them, singes' (centre). 'a ducking curtesy—exit into the C⟨astell⟩' (right). 'ffrom the other end of the Stage, enter another antique, as the first' (centre).

7a 'exit into the Castell'. 'ffrom vnder the Stage the third Antique' (centre). 'exit into the Castell'. 'The fourth out of a tree, if possible it may be' (centre). 'exit into the Castell'. [Cumber] 'exit into the Castell, & makes fast the dore'. 'Enter Iohn a Kent talking with his boy'.

7b 'he tryes the doore' (right). 'Enter Iohn a Cumber on the walles lyke Iohn a Kent'. *'Musique' (left) two lines before 'whyle the musique playes, enters on the walles Llwellen Chester wth his Countesse, Moorton with Sydanen, Pemb. with Marian, Oswen and Amerye'.

8a 'they discend' (right). *'Enter shrimpe' (left) anticipating next page by three lines. 'manet Iohn' (left) presumably referring to an exit now lost on right.

8b 'Enter Shrimpe skipping'. [III. ii] 'Enter Iohn a Cumber in his owne habit, with him Turnop Hugh, and Thomas the tabrer'. *'Enter Iohn a Kent' (left) three lines before 'En⟨ter⟩Iohn a K⟨en⟩t listning' (right).

9a 'Actus Quartus Scena Prima. | Enter, Shrimp playing on some instrument, a prettie way befo⟨re⟩ the Countesse, Sydanen, Marian, Oswen and Amerye'. 'The boye playes roundabout them' (left). 'to her asyde' (right). 'they look about' (right). *'Musique Chime' (left) two lines before 'A daynt⟨y fit ?⟩ of musi⟨que⟩' (right). 'The boy trips round about Oswen and Amery, sing⟨ing a⟩ chyme, and they the one after the other, lay them ⟨down ?⟩ vsing very sluggish gestures, the Ladyes amazed S⟨tand⟩ about them' (centre).

9b 'Song, to the Musique wthin' (centre) and two lines later '⟨to⟩ be sung' (left). 'The chyme playes, & Gosselen wth the Countesse goes turning out' (centre). 'The chyme agayne, and they turne out in like manner' (centre) and 'exeunt'. 'The chyme agayne, and so they' (centre) and 'exeunt'. 'exit Euan'. 'they start vp'. [IV. ii] 'Enter Iohn a Kent lyke Iohn a Cumber, with him Llwellen, . . . foorth of the Castell'. [speakes] 'to Mooreton' (right).

10a 'Enter Iohn a Cumber lyke Iohn a Kent'. 'he poyntes to them' (right). 'he riseth and goeth to Iohn a Cumber' (right). 'suddenly starting to him, after the other hath do⟨n⟩e' (right). 'he suddenly too' (right, twice).

10b 'he sits downe' (right). 'Enter Sr Gosselen denvyle . . . and Marian'. [speakes] 'to Cumber' (right). 'Iohn a Cumber stamps about' (right). 'exeunt into the Castell'.

11a 'Enter Turnop & ⟨all⟩ his trayne w⟨ith musique ?⟩'. 'put it on him' (sc. a fool's coat: left). 'Enter Shrimpe leading Oswen

and Amery about the tree'. 'he lyes down' (right, twice). 'They e⟨spy?⟩ them' (right).

$11^{b}$ 'they help th⟨em⟩' (right). *'Enter' (left) one line before 'Enter Iohn a Cumber pulling of his foole coat, lyke Kent still' (centre). 'Iohn a Kent in his owne habit, denvyle, . . . and Shrimp on the walles' (centre). [speakes] 'to Shrimp' (right). 'the Ladyes' (right) gloss on text 'Ile deliuer them'.

$12^{a}$ 'Actus Quintus Scena Prima. | Enter the Abbot of Chester read⟨ing⟩ a letter, & one of ⟨his Seruaunts ?⟩'. [v. ii] 'Enter Iohn a Kent, denvyle, Griffin and Powesse'.

$12^{b}$ 'embracing' (right). [v. iii] 'Enter Llwellen, . . . Iohn a Cumber, and Abbot'. 'exeunt Coun. Syd. Ma. Ab.'. 'Enter Iohn a Kent a loof of, Griffin and Lord Powesse'. 'exeunt' [except Kent]. 'Enter Moorton and Pembrooke'.

$13^{a}$ 'Enter Chester. Llw⟨ellen ⟩'. 'E⟨nter ? ⟩'.

Printed: J. P. Collier (Shakespeare Society), 1851; M. St. C. Byrne (Malone Society), 1923. Facsimile: J. S. Farmer, 1912.

2. *Sir Thomas More* [by A. Munday and others].
B.M., MS. Harl. 7368. *c.* 1593?

The make-up of the play (see Plate 2) is complicated. The modern foliation runs from 1 to 22. Fols. 1 and 2 are the vellum wrapper, formed of two leaves of a medieval manuscript (cf. *John a Kent*): this allows twenty leaves for the text. Of the play as originally written thirteen leaves remain (fols. 3–5, 10–11, 14–15, 17–22), but the first speech on fol. $10^{a}$, most of the text on fols. $5^{b}$ and $11^{b}$, and all on fol. $14^{a}$ has been deleted, and the verso of the last leaf is blank. Moreover, one or more original leaves have been cancelled between fols. 5 and 10, and again between fols. 11 and 14. The other seven leaves (fols. 6–9, 12–13, 16) were inserted in the course of an extensive revision to which the piece was subjected, and so were two large slips found pasted over the lower portions of fols. $11^{b}$ and $14^{a}$ (now detached and numbered as fols. 11* and 13*). The original sequence of sheets can still be approximately determined. Assuming, as seems on the whole likely, that two leaves were cancelled between fols. 5 and 10, and one leaf between fols. 11 and 14, the sixteen leaves of the play as first written appear to have formed a regular sequence of eight sheets. Of the additional leaves, which include at least two distinct makes of paper, fols. 8–9 and 12–13 may possibly form sheets. The edges of many of the leaves have suffered rather severely from decay, mainly at the top and bottom, in much the same manner as those of *John a Kent*. In both manuscripts the injury is severest towards the end. This decay has affected the original leaves most, but is by no means confined to them; the difference being mainly if not entirely due to the fact that the additional leaves were rather smaller than the rest. So far as can be ascertained the original leaves must have measured not less than $12\frac{1}{4} \times 8\frac{3}{8}$ inches.

Fol. $2^{b}$ (reversed): 'The Booke of Sir Thomas Moore' (Plate $2^{a}$) inscribed in gothic letters by the same hand as the title to *John a Kent* (see below, hand C).

Begins, fol. $3^{a}$: 'Enter at ⟨one end Iohn Lincolne with ⟩ together, at the other end enters ffraunces ⟨de Bard with Doll,⟩ a lustie woman, he haling her by the ⟨arme⟩'. In the left margin is a note by the censor: '⟨Le⟩aue o⟨ut ⟩ y$^{e}$ ⟨i⟩nsur⟨rection⟩ wholy & y$^{e}$ Cause ther off & ⟨b⟩egin w$^{t}$ S$^{r}$ Tho: Moore att y$^{e}$ mayors sessions w$^{t}$ A reportt afterwardȩ off his good servic' don being' Shriue off Londō vppō a mutiny Agaynst y$^{e}$ Lūbardȩ only by A shortt reportt & not otherwise att your own perrilles E Tyllney'.

Ends on fol. $22^{a}$: 'ffinis' (verso blank).

The original portion is written throughout in the autograph of Anthony Munday, and is generally similar to *John a Kent* though probably a few years later. No less than five hands, distinguished as A, B, C, D, E, are concerned in the revision. A is the hand of Henry Chettle. B in some ways resembles Thomas Heywood's, but cannot be identified as his. C is the hand that wrote the Plots of *The Seven Deadly Sins* (*c.* 1590) and *Fortune's Tennis* (*c.* 1597–8), and comparison with these shows that the gothic titles on the wrappers of the present piece and of *John a Kent* are also in this hand. Hand D is thought by some to be Shakespeare's. E is Thomas Dekker's. The scribal technique is much the same throughout. The leaves seem to have been folded for margins by Munday, and possibly by A, C, and D, but not by B: E only completed a

page already partly written. All regularly use speech-rules. Munday's are rather long, though much shorter than in *John a Kent*. Those of A, B, and E are quite short: C's somewhat longer. D makes them as long as Munday's in *John a Kent*.

There are signs of revision even in the original version, for on the last page nine lines that seem to have constituted the original ending have been cancelled, and twenty-two others added in their place.

Fol. 6 contains the only contribution by A. The recto is full, and seven lines have even been written up the left margin, but the verso is blank. The leaf is misplaced, for the speeches it contains were evidently written in substitution of a passage on fol. 19ᵃ which is marked for omission and opposite which a reference mark appears in the margin.

Fols. 7–9 form a composite addition intended to replace original matter cancelled on fol. 5 and the two leaves probably that once followed it. Fol. 7ᵃ (on which the last two lines are written up the right margin) is connected by a double reference mark with fol. 5ᵇ and contains a revision by B of a scene (marked for omission) which occupies the central portion of that page. (The lower part of fol. 5ᵇ contains the opening of a scene that was rejected in revision.) Fol. 7ᵇ, written in hand C, contains a scene of which no trace remains in the original version. At the foot is the initial stage-direction for the following scene, which begins at the top of the next page. Fols. 8 and 9 (the verso of the latter blank) contain a revision by D (his only contribution) of the beginning of a scene, the concluding portion of which remains in the original version on fol. 10. The first speech on fol. 10ᵃ has been cancelled, having been included in D's revision.

Fols. 12 and 13 form another composite addition, a revision of the original cancelled scene which begins on fol. 11ᵇ and ends at the foot of fol. 14ᵃ (and included probably one intervening leaf). The bulk of the revision, down to about the middle of fol 13ᵇ, is in hand C; the last half page is a later addition, the sole contribution made by E.

Fol. 16 contains an addition by B to an original scene that

ends near the middle of fol. 17ᵃ, where a double reference mark indicates the intended position. The addition occupies the whole of fol. 16ᵃ and runs over for five lines on to the verso. Below this is a draft (also by B and uncancelled) of a short speech used elsewhere by C.

Lastly, there are the two slips, fols. 11* (verso) and 13* (recto), which contain afterthoughts of the revision. They are both in hand C. The former is an addition meant to be inserted at the beginning of the revisional scene on fol. 12ᵃ. The latter is more complicated. As first written it contained a speech for insertion at the beginning of the original scene on fol. 14ᵇ (this need not have been an afterthought). But after it had been pasted into its place at the foot of fol. 14ᵃ, yet another speech, intended to precede it, was written up the left margin, partly on the original leaf and partly on the slip itself. (This is the speech of which a draft by B appears on fol. 16ᵇ.) Opposite this latest addition C placed a reference mark and the direction 'Mess[enger] T Goodal'. This is the only actor's name that was entered in the manuscript (for the scribble, apparently 'Lanehã', in the margin of fol. 3ᵇ is probably modern): the little that is known about him will be found in the Actor Lists appended to the Plots (p. 45).

Besides the insertions that affect the structure of the manuscript, some of the same hands are found making marginal notes and additions, the details of which need not be specified here. It will be sufficient to observe that C, who acted as editor and stage reviser throughout, added many directions alike in the original and additional leaves and occasionally doctored the text as well; and that B made several marginal additions on fols. 10ᵃ, 10ᵇ, 11ᵃ. E appears at one point to have touched up the scene to which he appended his addition.

It is doubtful whether the revision was consequent upon the censor's criticisms: no attempt appears to have been made to comply with the demands of Tilney's note on fol. 3ᵃ (see above). Nor was any notice taken of two other directions in his hand: 'Mend yⁱˢ' (left) opposite eight lines on fol. 5ᵃ, and 'all altr'' (right) referring to some thirty on fol. 17ᵇ. On fol. 5ᵃ he also made three alterations in the text, substituting 'mã' for 'Eng-

lishe', and 'Lombard' for 'straunger' and 'ffrencheman', and there are probably other marks of his in the manuscript. The note on fol. 11[b], 'this must be newe written', directing the revision of sc. viii *a* (which was in fact carried out) is of doubtful authorship, but more likely by B than Tilney. At the same time the absence of any recognizable marks by Tilney in the additional pages leaves it doubtful whether these were ever before him.

There is no trace of any division into acts or scenes either in the original or the altered version.

Munday writes a current English hand of a literary type. He uses a rather rough Italian script sporadically, mainly for foreign words and certain proper names, but not in general for stage-directions. Normally the longer entrances are centred, but shorter ones are often noted on the right. Exits, as usual, appear on the right, and so as a rule do incidental directions. Occasionally, however, when owing to the use of prose the right margin is full, directions and even in one case an entrance are entered on the left. Right-hand directions are generally separated from the text by a diagonal line, and exits are usually preceded by a horizontal one; but otherwise no original rules appear in connexion with stage-directions.

A (Chettle's) is a small English hand of a literary type with some admixture of Italian capitals, but no distinctive use of Italian script. There are no stage-directions.

B (Heywood's?) is a very current and ill-formed hand of an English type and without any use of Italian. There are no stage-directions.

C (the editor's) is a hand of a more professional, but not distinctively legal, type. The English script is clearly differentiated from the rather ornamental Italian, which is reserved for foreign words and incidental purposes. In the longer passages written by himself C's usage respecting stage-directions is the same as Munday's, except that they are regularly in Italian script and sometimes within rules. But in his two slips and when adding directions in the margin of pages written by other hands he commonly uses English script. In the original leaves his additional directions are all in the left margin: in the revisional leaves he uses the top and bottom and the right margin.

D (Shakespeare's?) is a hand not unlike C in character, though rather more current and less professional in appearance. It is an almost pure English hand and makes no use of Italian script. The only stage-direction, an entrance, is centred.

E (Dekker's) is a rather rough, decidedly literary hand. English and Italian script are both used, but do not differ very clearly in appearance. The only direction is on the left, in Italian script, within rules.

In the following list the portions written in the different hands have been kept distinct. All starred directions are by C. The list is intended to be exhaustive for all but bare exits.

ORIGINAL TEXT.

$3^{a}$ 'Enter Caueler with a paire of dooues, Williamson the Carpenter and Sherwin following him'. [speaks] 'to Caueler' (left, prose filling the right margin).

$3^{b}$ [sc. ii] 'An Arras is drawne, and behinde it (as in Sessions) sit the L. Maior, Iustice Suresbie, and other Iustices, Sheriffe Moore and the other Sherife sitting by, Smart is the Plaintife, Lifter the prisoner at the barre'. 'Lord Maior and Moo<re> whisper'.

$4^{a}$ 'ex. L. Maior and Iust<ices> | ex. Smart'. 'Ent. Iust. Suresbie' (right). 'aside'.

$4^{b}$ 'aside'. 'action'. 'shrugging gladly'. 'Ent. Lord Maior &c.' (right). 'he sits downe'. 'aside' (with brace to 3 ll.).

$5^{a}$ [sc. iii] 'Enter the Earles of Shrewes<burie and Surrie Sir Thomas Palmer> and Sir Roger Cholmeley'. 'Enter a Messenger' (right).

$5^{b}$ *'Enter Lincolne betts williamson Doll' (left) opposite [sc. iv] 'Enter Lincolne, Betses, Williamson, Sherwin and other armed, doll in a shirt of Maile, a head piece, sword and Buckler, a crewe attending': the scene is cancelled and the marginal direction is meant to do duty for the revised version ($7^{a}$). 'ex. some and Sher.' 'En: Sher. & the rest' (right). [sc. v] 'Enter <t>hree or foure Prentises of trades, with a paire of Cudgelles': the scene is incomplete and cancelled.

$10^{a}$ [in sc. vi] 'they lay by their weapo<ns>'. 'they are led away'. 'Ent. Shrew.' (right) within rules probably added in revision.

$10^{b}$ *'Enter Crofts' (left) opposite 'Ent. Croftes' (right). 'exeunt seuerally' [sc. vii] 'Enter $M^{r}$. Sheriffe, and meete a Messenger'. 'Ent. Officers | ex. Mess.' (right). 'ex. some seuerally, others set

vp the Iibbit'. 'exit. enter another Officer' (right). 'The Prisoners are brought in well guarded' (right). 'he goes vp' (sc. the ladder).

$11^{a}$ 'he leapes off'. 'he kisses her on the ladder'. 'a great shout and noise. | Enter Surrey' (right). 'flinging ⟨vp cuppes⟩'.

$11^{b}$ [sc. viii *a*] 'A table beeing couered with a greene Carpet, a state Cushion on it, and the Pursse and Mace lying thereon Enter Sir Thomas Moore and his man Randall with him, attyred like him': the scene cancelled and incomplete. 'The waites playes within'. 'Musique, enter Surrey, Erasmus and attendants'.

$14^{a}$ [in sc. viii *b*, also cancelled] 'they lead him out'. 'Enter M$^{r}$. Morris. & ex. Sherif and the rest' (right). 'Faukener is brought' (right).

$14^{b}$ [sc. ix] 'Enter S$^{r}$. Thomas Moore, M$^{r}$. Roper, and Seruing men setting ⟨stooles⟩'. 'Enter his Lady' (right). 'ex. one'. 'ex. La. ent. Player' (right). 'En. Lady' (right). *'waites play here' (left) opposite 'The waites playes, Enters Lord Maior, so many Aldermen as may, the Lady Maioresse in Scarlet, with other Ladyes and Sir Thomas Moores daughters, Seruaunts carying lighted Torches by them': 'the waytes' are also mentioned in the text.

$15^{a}$ 'Enter Inclination the vise, readie' (right). 'The Trompet soundes, enter the Prologue' (centre) for the play within the play.

$15^{b}$ 'Enter Witt ruffling, and Inclination the vice' (centre). 'florishing his dagger'. 'Enter Lady Vanitie singing. and beckning with her hand' (centre). 'She offers to depart'. 'Enter an other player' (right).

$17^{a}$ 'Enter Luggins with the bearde'. 'exeunt. ma. players'. *'Enter To the players w$^{th}$ a reward' (left) opposite 'exeunt' (deleted): the entrance relates to the addition on 16. [sc. x] 'Enter the Earles of Shrewesburie, Surrey, Bishop of Rochester and other Lordes, seuerally, dooing curtesie to eache other, Clark of the Councell waiting bareheaded'. 'Enter S$^{r}$. Thomas Moore, with Pursse and Mace borne before him'. 'they sit'.

$17^{b}$ 'Enter Sir Thomas Palmer'. [delivers papers] 'with great reuerenc⟨e⟩'. 'he riseth'. 'they write'.

$18^{a}$ [sc. xi] 'Enter the Lady Moore, her two daughters, and M$^{r}$. Roper, as walking'. 'Enter S$^{r}$. Thomas Moore merily, Seruaunts attending'. 'daughters kneele'.

$18^{b}$ [sc. xii] 'Enter the Bishop of Rochester, Surrey, Shrewsburie, Lieutenant of the Tower, and warders with weapons'. [sc. xiii] 'Enter S$^{r}$. Thomas Moore, his Lady, daughters, M$^{r}$. Roper, Gentlemen and Seruaunts, as in his house at Chelsey'. 'lowe stooles'.

$19^{b}$ '⟨Enter a seruaunt⟩' (centre) at top of page. 'Enter the Earles,

Downes with his Mace, and attendants'. 'kinde salutations'. 'kneeling and weeping'. 'kneeling'. 'pondering to him selfe'.

20$^{a}$ [sc. xiv] 'Enter the warders of the Tower with Halbards'. 'Enter a poore woman' (right). 'Enter the Lords with Sir Thomas Moore, and attendants, and enter Lieutenant and Gentleman Porter'. 'he giues him his cap'.

20$^{b}$ [sc. xv] 'Enter Butler, ⟨Brewer⟩, Porter, and horssekeper ⟨seuerall wayes⟩'. 'Ent. Gough & Catesbie with a paper' (left, prose filling the right margin). [sc. xvi] 'Enter Sir Thomas Moore, the Lieutenant, and a seruaunt attending as in his chamber in the Tower'. 'hee giues it him'.

21$^{a}$ 'Enter Lady Moore mourning, daughters, M$^{r}$. Roper' (right). 'offring to depar⟨t⟩'.

21$^{b}$ [sc. xvii] 'Enter the Sheriffes of London and their Officers at one doore, the warders with their Halbards at an other'. 'Enter Lieutenant and his Guarde with Moore'. 'he weepes'.

22$^{a}$ 'As he is going vp the stayres, enters the Earles of Surrye & Shre⟨wsburie⟩'. 'walking' (left, prose right). 'giues him his gowne' (*ditto*). 'by the hangman' (*ditto*) deleted, a gloss on 'I am come hether only to be let blood, my doctor heere telles me it is good for the head ache'. [gives] 'his pursse' (*ditto*).

A-REVISION.

6$^{a}$ There are no stage-directions in this portion, nor in the passage it was intended to replace (on 19$^{a}$).

B-REVISION.

7$^{a}$ There are no stage-directions by B, though an internal exit and re-entry are needed and are given in the original version of the scene on 5$^{b}$. C wrote an initial direction opposite that of the cancelled original (see 5$^{b}$) and corrected a speaker's name. The erroneous direction at the end, *'Manett Clowne', may also be his.

16$^{a, b}$ Again there are no stage-directions by B in this addition to a scene ending on 17$^{a}$. C wrote the necessary entrance at the end of the original scene (see 17$^{a}$). At the head of the addition he also wrote *'Enter A Servingman' and lower *'Enter Moore w$^{th}$ attendaunts w$^{t}$ Purss & mace' (right).

C-REVISION.

7$^{b}$ '⟨En⟩ter At on dore S$^{r}$ Thomas moore and Lord maire: Att an other doore S$^{r}$ Iohn Munday Hurt' (centre). 'Enter A messenger' (right) within rules. 'Enter Shrowesberie Surrie Palmer · Cholmley'

centre). 'Enter Lincoln · Doll · Clown · Georg betts williamson others And A sergaunt at armes' (centre) at foot, the initial entry for the following scene supplied by D on 8ª.

11*ᵇ 'Enter moore' (left, at head) underlined.

12ª [see Plate 2ᵇ] 'Enter Sʳ Thomas moore and his man Atired like him' (centre) left unaltered when 11* was prefixed. 'Enter The Shreiue wᵗʰ Fawkner a ruffin and officers' (right) within rules.

12ᵇ 'Enter Surry Erasmus and Attendaunts' (centre).

13ª 'Enter sʳ Thomas moore' (left, prose right) within rules. 'et tu Erasmus an Diabolus' (right) apparently a gloss on the text. 'Enter mʳ Morris' (right).

13ᵇ 'Enter Faukner · and officers' (right). 'Enter a messenger heere' (left, English script, deleted): evidently a preliminary direction for the additional lines prefixed as an afterthought to 13*, which must therefore have been planned before, but probably written after, E had made his contribution at the foot of 13ᵇ.

13*ª 'Mess T Goodal' (left) opposite 'Enter A Messenger to moore' (centre) all written up the left margin.

D-REVISION.

8ª (The initial direction for the scene is written by C at the foot of 7ᵇ. C also altered or supplied a number of speakers' names.) *'Enter' prefixed to speaker's name 'seriant' 'Enter the L maier Surrey Shrewsbury' (centre). 8ᵇ, 9ª no directions.

E-REVISION.

13ᵇ 'weepes' (left, prose right) within rules.

Printed: A. Dyce (Shakespeare Society), 1844, and reprints; W. W. Greg (Malone Society), 1911. Facsimile: J. S. Farmer, 1910.

## 3. [*Richard II* or *Thomas of Woodstock*.]
B.M., MS. Egerton 1994[8]. *c.* 1592–5.

The play (see Plate 3), which has no title in the manuscript, occupies fols. 161–185 of the collection, and one leaf probably is missing at the end. The twenty-five leaves that survive constitute twelve and a half numbered sheets: the numbers 3 (fol. 165ª), 4, 6–13 in the top right corner remain. The extreme measurement of the leaves is about $12 \times 7\frac{3}{4}$ inches, but few are actually as large as this, owing to extensive decay of the edges. Catchwords are added irregularly.

Begins, fol. 161ᵃ: '(i) Sceane | Enter hastely at seucrall doores: Duke of Lancaster, Duke of yorke. the Earles of Arondell and Surrye, w$^{th}$ Napkins on ther armes & kniues in ther hands: & S$^{r}$. Thomas Chæney, w$^{th}$ others beareing torches, & some w$^{th}$ clookes & Rapiers'.

Ends at the foot of fol. 185$^{b}$, imperfectly, in the course of what appears to be the last scene.

Written fairly closely in a well-formed hand of a rather literary type, in which English script is mingled with elegant Italian for incidental purposes. The impression, however, is rather of a scribe than an author, and this is confirmed by the fact that at one point (fol. 163$^{b}$) the first half of a line was left blank and filled in by another hand. There is a regular use of speech-rules of moderate length, and the leaves have been folded for margins. The speaker's names, probably throughout, were added after the text had been written, in some passages in other hands, and in one or two instances even after other hands had supplied stage-directions. Several passages were cancelled before the speakers' names came to be added, and the scribe himself took part in this revision, as appears for example from a passage on fol. 170$^{a}$ where he inserted the words 'health to yo$^{r}$ matie' (*sic*) to serve as a link in place of the omitted lines. In four places (fols. 167$^{b}$, 180$^{a}$, 184$^{b}$, 185$^{a}$) directions appear which bear no relation to the present text and point either to confused alterations in the rough draft or to unfulfilled intentions of addition: they have all been deleted.

There is little doubt that certain alterations have been made in deference to the censor, if not by the censor himself. Twice on fol. 168$^{a}$ the term 'cuss', addressed by Woodstock to Richard, was struck out first in pencil and then in ink, and in the first case 'my leege' was substituted in another hand: on fol. 168$^{b}$ the words 'Superio$^{r}$ lord of Scottland' were struck out and crosses both in pencil and ink placed in the margin. Although the hand that wrote the words 'my leege' cannot be identified, the style of the marking so closely resembles that found in passages of *Charlemagne*, *The Second Maiden's Tragedy*, and

*Sir John Barnavelt*, on all of which Sir George Buc was unquestionably at work, as to suggest his presence here likewise. The piece may have been submitted to him on the occasion of a revival. The manuscript is now much stained and worn as if through long use in the playhouse.

As originally written the play was undivided except for '(i) Sceane' at the beginning and '2 sceane' on fol. 162$^{b}$. But another hand has introduced a full division into acts by adding the necessary notes in the margin.

The original scribe wrote central directions between rules for the main entrances, whether or not a new scene was intended. Entrances requiring only a short direction are normally marked in the left margin, very rarely on the right. Exits as usual are marked on the right, other directions left or right indifferently. All marginal directions are normally between rules and are often enclosed within braces. Apart from entrances, which are sometimes fairly elaborate, the original directions are usually brief and are not very numerous.

Additional notes and directions appear in probably at least five different hands. They are usually, but by no means always written in the left margin. The names apparently of three actors are introduced, namely 'Grad.' (?), 'George', and 'Toby', but there is no certainty as to their identification. The directions in this play, both original and supplementary, are of sufficient interest to justify making the following list substantially complete apart from bare exits, but into the complex question of the differentiation of the various revisional hands, and of their chronological relation, upon which the significance of the work in part depends, it is impossible to enter here.

161$^{b}$–162$^{a}$ 'Enter Thomas of Woodstocke In Freeze: The Mace ⟨ ⟩| The Lord Mayre & Exton, & others w$^{th}$ lightes afore them'.

162$^{a}$ *'G⟨⟩ad' apparently an actor's name prefixed to speaker's name 'Mayre'. 'Exitt L: May⟨re⟩'.

162$^{b}$ 'Exeunt omnes | 2 sceane / Enter Greene: Baggott and Tressillian in Rage'.

163$^{a}$ 'Exeunt Greene & Baggott Manett Tressill'.

163$^{b}$–164$^{a}$ [I. iii] 'sound A Senett / Enter In great state. King Richard Queen Añ, (Crownde) . . . | And Woodstock very braue . . .'.

166$^{a}$ 'wind Hornes w$^{th}$in' (left). 'Enter Cheney' (left). *'Act: 2$^{d}$.' and 'Trumpetts sound' and *'fflorish' (all left) opposite 'Exeunt omnes | Enter King Richard . . . and others'.

166$^{b}$ *'Booke' (left) required 18 lines later.

167$^{a}$ 'Enter. yorke' (left).

167$^{b}$ *'Peticions: Mace' (left) properties required for ensuing scene, mentioned about 10 and 110 lines later respectively. *'*Enter the queene dutches of gloster* ⟨&⟩ *Ireland*' (left) deleted and irrelevant to present text (possibly anticipating next scene on 169$^{b}$). *'fflorish' (left, twice) opposite 'Exeunt omnes' [II. ii] 'Enter Lancaster. (Arondell) Surrye. the queene, woodstock & his Dutches yorke meetes them. In hast'.

168$^{a}$ *'florish' (left) anticipating, and *'ff⟨louri⟩she' (right) duplicating, 'sound' (left) opposite 'Enter King. Richard . . . & others'. *'Paper' (right) required five lines later.

168$^{b}$ 'giues the Mace vp' (right). 'a florish' (left).

169$^{b}$ *'Flourish' (left) four lines before 'Trumpetts sounds Exeunt omnes' (right) [II. iii] 'Enter the Queene. the Dutches a Gloster the Dutches of Ireland and other mayds w$^{th}$ shirts & bands & other lyneing'

170$^{a}$ '*Enter, Cheney*' (left) deleted, with passage marked for omission, and repeated 'Enter Cheney' 14 ll. lower. 'A Florish' (left).

170$^{b}$ 'Exeunt both y$^{e}$ Dutchesse⟨ ⟩'. 'Exitt Queene'. *'Act: 3d:' (left) opposite 'sound a senett, Enter King Richard . . . & Scroope, Very Richly Attyrd In newe fashions & Trissilian whispering w$^{th}$ the King. a guard of Archers after them'. *'Blankes' (left), sc. blank charters required six lines later. 'Enter the queene' (left).

171$^{a}$ 'sound' (left) opposite 'Exeunt' (right) and 'Manett Trissillian' (centre, at foot of page).

171$^{b}$ 'Enter Crosbye & Fleming' (right). 'Enter Nimble' (left). [III. ii] 'Enter Woodstock: lancaster and yorke at Plashey'.

172$^{a}$ 'Enter Cheney w$^{th}$ blankes' (left).

172$^{b}$ 'Exeunt all but woodstock'. *'George' actor's name added above 'Enter. a seruant' (left).

173$^{a}$ 'Enter a spruce courtier a horsebacke' (left). 'Enter Cheney, Courtier & seruants' (left) opposite 'Enter C⟨ ⟩' (right). 'Exitt seruant w$^{th}$ the horse'.

173$^{b}$ 'Exeunt omnes' [III. iii] 'Enter M$^{r}$: Ignorance the Bayle of dunstable, Crossby Fleming & Nimble, w$^{th}$ blancks'.

174$^{a}$ 'Enter a Farmer. a Buther [*sic*] & a Graysher. very hastely' (centre).

174$^{b}$ *'3: B' (left) opposite 'seale them' sc. blanks (right). 'Exeunt officers w$^{th}$ them (3) men'. 'Enter a schoole master & a serueing man' (centre).

175$^{a}$ 'Exeunt The schoole⟨master⟩ & serui⟨ngman⟩'. 'Enter one A whisling' (left).

175$^{b}$ 'Enter Crossby & Fleming' (left). *'Actus quart$^{9}$' (left) opposite 'Exeunt omnes | Enter Trissillian w$^{th}$ wrightings & a man w$^{th}$ baggs of money' and after five lines 'Exit seruant'. 'Enter Busshey and Sroope [*sic*]' (centre).

176$^{a}$ 'Enter, Baggott' (left). '*sound*' (left) opposite 'Enter King Richard, Greene and others'.

177$^{b}$ 'sound' (left) opposite 'Exeunt omnes' [IV. ii] 'Enter Woodstocke and his Dutches w$^{th}$ a Gentleman, Cheney: & others'.

178$^{a}$ 'Exeunt Dutches & y$^{e}$ rest Manet woodstock'. 'Enter: Cheney' (left).

178$^{b}$ [Plate 3] 'Enter seruants' (left). *'Toby:' substituted for speaker's name '*ser:*' (i.e. servant). 'Enter Cheney' (left). *'Anticke' (left, obliterating speaker's initial 'W:') and *'fflorish Cornetts: Dance & musique: cornetts' (right) immediately above 'sound a florish, then a great shout & winding a hornes, Then Enters Cinthia' (centre). *'Musick' (left) immediately above 'Enter King Richard, Greene Busshey Baggott: like Dianas knights led In by (4.) other knights: (In Greene) w$^{th}$ hornes about ther neckʒ & borespeares in ther hands'.

179$^{a}$ '(Musicke) Then Enter Cheney' (left) opposite 'They Daunce' (right). *'A Drome afare of' (left).

179$^{b}$ *'Shrevs Ready' for entrance in next scene a dozen lines later. '(sound)' (left) opposite 'Exeunt omnes' [IV. iii] 'Enter Crossby, Fleming and Nimble'. 'Enter Trissilian w$^{th}$ the Shreeues of Kent & Northumberland: w$^{th}$ officers'. 'Exeunt w$^{th}$ the shreeues'.

180$^{a}$ 'Exitt nimble & there⟨st⟩ [*sic*] Manett Trissillian' (right) opposite '*Enter Dutches & a gentleman*' (left) deleted as irrelevant to the present text (also in text '*heere comeʒ the dutches*' deleted, after being copied in in error) followed immediately by 'Enter Baggott' (left, opposite text 'heere comes S$^{r}$ Edward Baggott'). 'Enter Busshye' (left).

180$^{b}$ 'Enter y$^{e}$ King *Greene* and Scroope' (left). *'A bed for woodstock' required for next scene and discovered about 50 lines later. *'Actus quint$^{9}$' (left) opposite 'Exeunt omnes | Enter Lapoole w$^{th}$ a light after hime the (2) Murderers'.

181$^{a}$ 'he drawes the curtaynes' (right) discovering the bed. *'musique' (left) before 'Thunder & lightning Enter the ghost of the Black Prince' (centre).

$181^b$ 'Thunder' opposite 'Exit Ghoste' and above 'Enter Edward the thirds ghost' (left). 'Enter Lapoole & the Murderers' (left).

$182^b$ 'Enter both the Murderers' (left) sc. come forward. 'strickes hime' (right). 'Exeunt $w^{th}$ the bodye'. [Direction for entrance of soldiers lost?]

$183^a$ 'Enter the $Murder^{rs}$' (left). 'They Kill the Murderers' (right). 'Exeunt sould: $w^{th}$ ther bodys'. [v. ii] '(Dromes March $w^{th}$ in) Enter Trissillian & Nimble $w^{th}$ Armour'.

$183^b$ [v. iii] 'Enter $w^{th}$ Drome, and Cullors, Yorke . . . $w^{th}$ the Dutches of gloster, & souldiers & Cheney'. *'Dromes' (left) repeated (right) eight lines below, the latter four lines above '⟨? Drome⟩s sounds ⟨$w^{th}$⟩ in' (left) before 'Enter Cheney' (left).

$184^a$ 'March a bout' (right) immediately before 'Enter $w^{th}$ Drome & Cullours: The King . . . and souldiers They march a bout (all'.

$184^b$ '*Enter Bragg: & Cheney* | *⟨E⟩nter Bushey: & Surry*' (left) deleted and irrelevant to the present text, opposite 'Exeunt omnes', and 'Alarume' (left) opposite [v. iv] 'Enter Greene & Cheyney: meets Armde'. 'Alarum' (left) opposite 'Th⟨e⟩y F⟨i⟩gh⟨t⟩' (right). 'Enter Arondęll' (left). '⟨? They fight⟩ & ⟨? Greene is slai⟩ne' (left). '⟨? Enter Kin⟩g . . . & souldiers' (centre). 'They Fight' (right).

$185^a$ 'To Them *Enter lancaster, yorke & Surry: & beats them all away* Manett the King'. 'Alarum' (left) immediately before 'Enter Baggott Busshy & Scroope to the King' (centre). 'Alarum' (left) opposite 'Exeunt omnes' [v. v] 'Enter Trissillian disguisd & Nimble' also 'Bush & lancaster Enter' (left) later addition written very faintly by the original scribe, irrelevant to the present text but not deleted. 'sound Retreat' (left).

$185^b$ 'sound a Retreat Then a Florish' and *'Drom Collours' (left) opposite [v. vi] 'Enter $w^{th}$ Victory Lancaster *Yorke* . . . & souldiers $w^{th}$ lapoole . . . Prisoners'. *'⟨w⟩ithin ⟨fflor⟩ishe' (left). 'Enter Nimble $w^{th}$ Trissillian. Bound & Guarded'.

Printed: J. O. Halliwell, 1870; W. Keller, *Shakespeare-Jahrbuch* (xxxv. 3–121), 1899; W. P. Frijlinck (Malone Society), 1929.

4. *Edmond Ironside* or *War hath Made all Friends*.

B.M., MS. Egerton 1994[5]. 1590–1600?

The play occupies fols. 96–118 of the collection. The twenty-three leaves (the first and last with verso blank) constitute eleven separate sheets with a single leaf prefixed. This pre-

liminary leaf is probably original, though the title on it may have been written somewhat later. The edges of the leaves are much worn, but the extreme measurements are about $12\frac{1}{8} \times 7\frac{7}{8}$ inches.

Fol. $96^{a}$: 'Edmond Ironside | The English King'. The first line is in large roman capitals, the second may be a later addition (verso blank).

Begins, fol. $97^{a}$: 'A trew Cronicle History called | Warr hath made all freindes: | Enter Canutvs Archbishope of Canterbury Earle of Southam⟨pton⟩ Edricus Duke of Mercia Leofricke Earle of Chester Turku⟨llus⟩ Duke of Norff' and Suff' Vskataulf and Swetho Da⟨nes⟩ They sitt about a table.' The first line is in elaborate gothic script; the second has been deleted, possibly in the ink in which the second line of the title-page was written.

Ends on fol. $118^{a}$: 'They goe hand in hand out off th⟨e stage?⟩ Edricus leadeinge the Drum̃e | Finis' (verso blank).

Written, rather loosely and untidily on the whole, in a hand of a distinctly legal type, using English script with incidental Italian erratically interspersed. The errors show it to be a copy by a not very intelligent scribe, who, there seems some reason to suppose, may have been a scrivener. His methods are not those usual in the playhouse. Such speech-rules as occur (and there are none after fol. $103^{a}$) have been added later, probably by another hand. Some of the leaves have been ruled, both for lines and margins, with a stilus; others have perhaps been folded for margins. But whatever its origin, the fact that the manuscript was used in the playhouse is shown by the presence of a number of directions added in one or more other hands and introducing the names of several actors. These, who most likely took part in a late revival, can be identified as H. Gibson, Henry Gradwell, Edward May, and George Stutfield. Gradwell alone has the prefix 'Mr.'. In the absence of any further indication of the occasion, it is not possible to determine the company concerned, but the date would most likely be somewhere in the twenties. The manuscript shows considerable signs of wear, but may have suffered from other causes as well.

There is no evidence of censorship, though it is possible that a desire to forestall criticism may account for one or two out of the numerous passages marked for omission. These are mostly short, ranging from one line to eight, with a single one of thirteen, but they aggregate just under 200 lines, which is nearly a tenth of the whole.

As originally written the play was wholly undivided, but a later hand has effected a division into acts by adding the required notes in the left margin. It is noticeable that the direction 'Act 4' is placed at the foot of the page after Act III, not at the head of Act IV.

In the original directions entrances are as a rule written across the page in the centre (beginning well away from the left margin, but extending towards the right) whether they mark the beginning of a scene or not, but a few of the shorter ones are entered on the right. Bare exits are as usual noted on the right, but the scribe occasionally combines them with an ensuing entry in a central direction, or even enters them centrally if of any elaboration. This is a most unusual habit. Other directions, if short, are generally written on the right, if longer, in the centre. There are no original directions in the left margin. English and Italian script are used quite indifferently. Central directions never have rules, but those in the right margin are occasionally written between them. The latter are also frequently divided from the text by a small brace, which serves the purpose of distinction where English script is used. The additions are mainly on the left, one duplicating an original direction on the right, but the right and bottom margins are also used. The following list of directions is practically exhaustive for the earlier half of the play.

$97^{a}$ 'hee ryse⟨th⟩' (right). $97^{b}$ 'he ryseth' (right).

$98^{a}$ 'Vskataulfe whispereth in Canutꝰ eare' (centre). 'Exit South: / Enter a Companye of cuntrymen makeinge a noyse' (whole centre).

$98^{b}$ 'Exeunt Swetho w$^{th}$ the poore Daines' (centre).

$99^{b}$ 'Exeunt omnes' (right) and 'Leofricke pulls Turkillus by the sleeve, as hee is goeinge and stayes him' (centre).

$100^{b}$ 'Exeunt' (right) and [I. ii] 'Enter Edricus solus' (centre).

$101^{a}$ 'Exit' (right) and [I. iii] 'Enter Edmond and Alfricke the generall

vnder the kinge' (centre). 'Enter Turkullus an⟨d⟩ Leofricke' (right). 'they kneell'.

101$^{b}$ *'Act 2$^{dus}$' opposite 'Exeunt e͞os [*sic*] | The Drum̃e and Trumpetts sound Enter [*'w$^{th}$' interlined] a banquet: Then Enter Canutus South: Arch: Bish: Vskataulf and Swetho Edricus'. 'Enter Egina' (right).

102$^{b}$ 'Exeunt omnes' [II. ii] 'Enter Edricke a poore man his wife and Stich'. 'Enter Edricus' (right).

103$^{a}$ 'he shewes his tongue'.

103$^{b}$ 'hee beates them about the stage Exeunt' [II. iii] 'Enter Canutus '*South:* ArchB: . . .'.

104$^{b}$ *'m: Grad: Stutf:' (left) actors' names added opposite 'Enter Swetho the Two Pledges and Stich w$^{th}$ an Axe'.

105$^{a}$ 'Hee cutts offe one hande' (centre). 'Hee Cutts offe the other hande' (centre). 'He Cutts off his Nose' (centre). 'Hee Cuttʒ his handę and Nose' (centre). 'Exit Pledes [*sic*]'. *'Ent Mess⟨e⟩nger H Gibson' (centre at foot) anticipating by a line—

105$^{b}$ *'H. Gibs:' (left) opposite 'Enter a messenger runinge' (centre). 'Canutus reades and then sayeth' (centre).

106$^{a}$ 'Exit Edricus' (1 line) 'Enter Edricus' (both right). *'Act 3' (left) opposite 'Enter at one doore: y$^{e}$ Arch B: of Caunter⟨bur⟩y ⟨and⟩ at th'other y$^{e}$ Arch B: of Yorke'.

106$^{b}$ 'yorke offers to Departe'. [III. ii] 'Enter Canutʒ . . . Harrold at armes and souldiers'.

107$^{a}$ *'m$^{r}$ gradell' (left) opposite 'The Herrold departeth from the kinge to the walls soundinge his trumpit The Balifes appeare aboue'. *'may' (left) apparently an actor's name added opposite the speech of '1 Balife'. 'Balifes departe Herrold retvrneth' (centre). *'assayle the walls' (right) and 'Enter H: Gibs:' (left at foot) anticipating—

107$^{b}$ 'Enter a Messenger' (centre at top). *'Alarum' (left) opposite 'Sound Drum̃ w$^{th}$in' (right). *'Ent: Edm' (left) opposite 'Enter Edmund w$^{th}$ souldiers' (right).

108$^{a}$ 'Alarum they fight Edmond drives Canutus offe the stage The drum̃e soundes a farr offe Enter attired in blacke sayinge' (Chorus 11 lines) 'Alarum Enter Canutus flyinge Edmond followinge they fight The Two kinges parley sounde a Retreate and parte' (Chorus 7 lines) 'Alarum Enter Canutus at one dore and Edmu⟨nd⟩ at the other they fight Canutus gives backe and flies Enter the souldiers of Edmond persuing Canutus and his lordʒ Edricus takes a dead m⟨ans⟩ head vppon his swordʒ poynt holdinge yt vppe ⟨to⟩ Edmonds souldiers they flie Enter Edmond a⟨gain⟩ Cheering them vp and makes Canutus flie' (Chorus 25 lines).

108$^{b}$ 'The souldiors shout et exeunt' (right).

109$^{a}$ 'Turns towards Vskataul⟨f⟩'. 'Edricus talkes to h⟨im⟩'.

109$^{b}$ 'Exeunt manet Edricus' and 'Enter Stich' (right). 'Enter Stich w$^{th}$ paper and an Inckehorne' (right). 'Edricus sittʒ downe writteth and blotteth' (centre).

110$^{a}$ 'Hee writteth and blotteth' (centre). 'Hee writteth and sayeth' (centre). 'hee fouldes yt vppe' (centre). 'Enter Stich' (right).

110$^{b}$ 'They shifte apparell'. [III. vi] 'Enter Stich in his lordę attire w$^{th}$ Blewcoates after him'. *'Act 4' (left) opposite 'Exeunt' anticipating—

111$^{a}$ 'Enter Edmond Ironside . . . w$^{th}$ Edricus disguised' (centre at top). 'The Letter' (centre) [text in English script] 'finis Letter' (right). 'he pulls of the velvet patch of his face' (right).

111$^{b}$ 'Enter a messenger runinge'.

112$^{a}$ 'Edricus talketh w$^{th}$ Edmund secretly Alfricke pulls him backe' (centre). 'they whisper Edm. saith :' 'they whisper againe' 'they whisper againe' (right in consecutive lines).

112$^{b}$ 'Enter Emma her Two sonnes Alphred and Edward in each hand Gunthranus goeinge before'.

113$^{a}$ 'they offer to depte'. 'they offer to depte'. 'Shee imbraceth them'. 'Shee sittę downe and settinge Edward on her knee a⟨nd⟩ Alphred in her arme' (right). 'Emma riset⟨h⟩'. 'they offer ⟨to depte⟩'. 'exeunt omnes' [IV. iii] 'Enter Canutus with a Letter in his hand and w$^{th}$ him : Vskataulfe . . . w$^{th}$ souldiers'.

113$^{b}$ 'The drum̃s sound afar off' (centre). 'The Drum̃e sound Enter Edmond w$^{th}$ Edricus other Lord and souldiers they fight Canutus gives et exeunt | Enter at one dore Canutus and at th' other Edricus'.

114$^{a}$ 'Alarum Enter Edmund chaseinge of Canutus Edricus backes Canutus Edmund flies: exeunt: and returne. Canutus w$^{th}$ Edricus'. *'Act 5' (left) opposite 'Enter Edmond Ironside . . . w$^{th}$ others'. 'Enter Edricus w$^{th}$ his hand in a skarfe, haultinge, with him Stich'.

115$^{a}$ 'exeunt omnes' [V. ii] 'Enter Canutus readinge of letter w$^{th}$ him Southampton . . . w$^{th}$ souldiers'.

115$^{b}$ [Letter in Italian script; no s.d.] 'The Drum̃e soundes a far off' (centre). 'Enter Edmund, Emma . . . and Turkillus'. 'They march a longe the stage one an other [*sic*] ' (centre).

116$^{a}$ 'he drawet⟨h⟩'. 'Hee Dr⟨aweth⟩'. 'They trayne theire souldio⟨urs on?⟩ the stage Edricus speake⟨th⟩' (centre).

116$^{b}$ 'The Armies make towardʒ one an other when Edricus standinge betwene sayeth' (centre).

117ª 'Edm: and Emma talkes togeither, Edm: turnes a⟨way⟩' (centre). 'Egina talkes w^th Canutꝰ, Canutꝰ turnes away' (centre).

117ᵇ 'The Trumpitte sound the Armies doe Compasse the Twoe kinge in the middest, they fight' (centre). 'Edm: drives : Canutꝰ about' (centre). 'they fight againe Edm: driues Canutꝰ | backe aboute the Stage' (centre, but beginning right).

118ª 'They imbra⟨ce⟩'. 'Edm: kisses Eg⟨ina⟩'. 'the Lorde imbrace'.

Printed: E. Boswell (Malone Society), 1927 (1928).

5. [*Charlemagne* or *The Distracted Emperor.*]
B.M., MS. Egerton 1994⁶. *c.* 1605?

The play, which has no title in the manuscript, occupies fols. 119–135 of the collection. The seventeen leaves form eight and a half numbered sheets: the numbers 2 (fol. 121ª), 3, 5, 6, 8 remain in the top inner corner. The leaves measure fully $12\frac{1}{2} \times 7\frac{7}{8}$ inches, but all are a good deal worn at the foot.

Begins, fol. 119ª: 'Actꝰ 1. Scena 1 | Enter La Busse, and Didier⟨'.

Ends on fol. 135ᵇ: 'Exe | finis [τελος added] | Terminat hora diem, terminat Author opus. | Nel la φ δ φ ν ρ la B' (i.e. Nella fideltà finirò la vita).

Written closely, in a small and rather ugly hand, of a literary type, which gets up to eighty and more lines onto a page. The script is English, with incidental Italian. Speech-rules of moderate length are used regularly, and the leaves have been folded for margins. It looks as though the manuscript might be autograph, and the impression is borne out by some of the alterations. Thus on fol. 129ᵇ a pencil cross (perhaps modern) draws attention to the following passage:

> why tys a bodye made by symetree
> & knytt together w^th more arte & care
> then [*Durers*] mathematycke cyrckles, *Durers* rules
> are ꝑfytted in hym . . .

One passage has certainly been censored. On fol. 127ª pencil and ink crosses draw attention to a line in which 'reverend p'latte' has been crossed out and 'preists' interlined, while in the left margin is written 'Read Priests'. The marginal note seems to be in the hand of Sir George Buc, so may that of the interlineation. There are a few other pencil marks (as above) but they do not suggest the censor. On the other hand, some of the deletions and omission marks may be his. On the same page as the note just mentioned there is cancelled a passage of five or six lines beginning:

> Oh nowe religion teach me to believe
> another god; or I must forfayte heauen . . .

which, in the mouth of Charles, may conceivably have been held offensive. Other deletions are clearly by the stage reviser (see below): a final speech of four lines by Orlando has been cancelled in order to give the last word to the Emperor.

The division is into acts only, though in each case the heading mentions the first scene as well. That to Act I is centred; the others are in the left margin.

Although scenes are not marked as such they are distinguished by having entrance directions centred and rules drawn across the page. The first two acts form each a single scene: there is one division in Act III, two in Act IV, and three in Act V. All other entrances, which are numerous, are marked in the right margin. Exits are, as usual, also marked on the right, and so almost without exception are the independent directions, which are rather numerous but seldom extensive. The play has been annotated for stage use by a reviser in a rather untidy hand—indeed there has pretty certainly been more than one reviser at work. The additional directions are almost always in the left margin. The original scribe usually distinguished his (right) marginal directions with a rule down on the left and another underneath: the reviser further emphasized entrances by adding a rule above. As will be seen from the following list, which is exhaustive for all but bare entrances and exits, the directions become more numerous towards the end of the play.

119ª *'ffiorish' opposite 'A crye w^th^in; god saue Theodora y^e^ Empresse'.

119^b^ 'Enter La Fue'. *'Hoboyes' opposite 'Ex: Fue' and 'Loude Musique Enter Charlimayne . . . & attendants', the reviser having also prefixed *'Ent^r^' to the speaker's name 'Char:' (to which he added an *'l').

120ª 'Enter Reinaldo'. 'Ex: Cha: The: Gab: & Attendants'. 'Exe: all but Gan & Rich'.

121ª 'Ex: Richard'. 'Enter Didier'. 'Ex: Ganelon'. 'Enter La Busse Gabriella and Bertha'. 'Ex: Didier'.

121$^{b}$ 'Ex Gabriella'. 'Exi: Bertha'. 'Enter Ganelon'. 'Ex: La Busse'.

122$^{a}$ 'Enter Didier'. 'Ente La Fue'. 'Ex: La Fue'. *'Actus 2' replacing '*Act$^{9}$ 2. Sce: 1*' (left) opposite 'Enter Orlando, Reinaldo, Oliuer, Souldiors attendants' (centre).

122$^{b}$ *'Ent$^{r}$ Busse' opposite 'Enter la Busse'.

124$^{a}$ 'Exe. all but Didier'.

124$^{b}$ 'Enter Charlimayn w$^{th}$ y$^{e}$ queene in hys armes Turpin, La Busse⟨'.

125$^{a}$ 'They place y$^{e}$ dead bodie in a chayre'. 'sitts by her'. *'Softe musique' opposite 'Musique | sleeps on her bosome'. 'He searches y$^{e}$ queenes poccetts, hands, necke Bossome & Hayre'. *'Exitt Tur' (right). [At the foot, right, is a direction, probably by the reviser, now illegible but perhaps anticipating the entry overleaf—]

125$^{b}$ 'Enter Richard La Busse and attendants' (top, right). 'Attendants la Busse & Gab: carie away y$^{e}$ dead'.

126$^{a}$ 'Kisses Turpin'. 'Ex: all but Didi'. 'Exi | ⟨Act⟩$^{9}$ 3· Sce: 1: Enter Eldegrad & Gabriella'.

128$^{a}$ 'capers' (twice).

128$^{b}$ [III. ii] 'Enter Eudon . . . & Gabriella'.

129$^{a}$ 'Exe: All but Gabr'. 'Exe. | Act$^{9}$ 4: Sce: i Enter Richard readinge a letter', and opposite the following passage *'Read'.

129$^{b}$ 'giues letters & money'. 'giues y$^{e}$ ringe' (left, the only instance: the right margin is crowded with prose).

130$^{a}$ 'giue hym y$^{e}$ ringe' (singular).

130$^{b}$ [IV. ii] 'Enter Ganelon; Eldegrad, & Gabriella'. 'giues letter'. 'giues hys coate'.

131$^{a}$ 'Eldegrad reads'. 'Ganelon reads'. 'Exe.' (with *'unt:' added) [IV. iii] 'Enter Orlando, Reinaldo, Oliuer'.

131$^{b}$ 'offer to drawe' (singular). *'Ent alofte Ganelon' (the letters 'Gan' being the original speaker's prefix) opposite 'Whisper, Enter Ganelon alofte'. 'Exe: all but Richard'. 'Act$^{9}$ 5: Sce 1 Enter Eldegrade & Didier'.

132$^{a}$ 'Hydes hym'. 'Richard knocks'. 'stabbs hym'. 'dies'. 'Didier stepps out'.

132$^{b}$ 'shoes y$^{e}$ key'. 'Exe. w$^{th}$ y$^{e}$ Dead' [V. ii] 'Enter Oliuer'.

133$^{a}$ [V. iii] 'Enter Didier w$^{th}$ a Letter'. [Didier] 'giue y$^{e}$ letter & Ganelon reads'.

134$^{a}$ 'He runns at Gab: & Elde: stepps betweene & he kills both'. 'dies'. 'dyes'.

134$^{b}$ *'Ent Dydier' opposite 'Oliuer taks y$^{e}$ letter & reads Enter Didier'. 'Enter a guarde and aprehends Gane: & Didier'. *'fflorish' opposite 'Exe: w$^{th}$ the dead Bodyes' [V. iv] 'Enter Charlimayne . . . &

Attendants . 'Ex: Eudon' (3 lines) 'Enter Eudon, & Busse leading in twoe lymes Byrtha & a Spaniell hym selfe cladd all in Nett'.

$135^a$ 'Enter la Fue in gallantrye'. 'Offers to kisse Charli:'. 'Ex: Fue & guard'. *'Dead marche' opposite 'Funerall sounde, Enter orlando, Renaldo leading ganelon, oliuer Didier; two herses one $w^{th}$ Eldegr. & Gab, $y^e$ other ⟨Ri⟩chard'.

$135^b$ 'Shoes the Deade'. 'giues $y^e$ letter'. 'Shoes $y^e$ ringe'. 'Ex: Gan. Did: & guard'.

Printed: A. H. Bullen, *Old Plays* (iii. 161–261), 1884; F. L. Schoell, 1920; U. M. Ellis-Fermor (Malone Society), in preparation.

### 6. *The Second Maiden's Tragedy.*

B.M., MS. Lansd. $807^2$. Licensed 31 Oct. 1611.

The play (see Plate 4), whose pointless title has been fastened on it through misunderstanding of the censor's note, occupies fols. 29–56 of the modern pencil numbering of this small collection, a numbering which includes (as fols. 31, 36, 46, 47, 53) five small additional slips 'flown' on other leaves. The twenty-three original leaves (of which the last page was at first left blank) form eleven and a half numbered sheets (the numbers '2' to 'ii' (i.e. 11) remaining in the inner top corner), the odd leaf being at the end. The leaves measure about $11\frac{1}{2} \times 7\frac{1}{2}$ inches.

Begins, fol. $29^a$: 'Actus $Prim^9$· | Enter the new Vsurping Tirant; The Nobles of his faction, Memphonius, Sophonirus, Heluetius with others, The right heire Gouianus depos'de'. A later hand has written the title 'The Second | Maydens Tragedy' in the outer margin near the top of the page.

Ends on fol. $56^a$: 'Recorders or other solempne Musique playes them owt. | ffinis', followed by the censor's licence: 'This second Maydens tragedy (for it hath no name inscribed) may $w^{th}$ the reformations bee acted publikely. 31.$octob^r$.1611. G. Buc'.

Fol. $56^b$: 'The Second Maydens Tragedy | October $31^{th}$ | 1611 | By [Thomas Goff] | A Tragedy indeed'. This title has been added in a later hand, and in place of the name has been substituted '[George Chapman]' in another hand, and in yet another 'By Will Shakspear'.

Written in an elegant professional hand, in which English script is clearly differentiated from the rather beautiful Italian

used for incidental purposes. The leaves have been folded for margins, and there is a normal use of short speech-rules. In the play so written a very rough hand has made some revisional alterations, which from their character might be the author's. In one instance (fol. 48ᵇ) this hand has supplied a word which the scribe had perhaps been unable to read in the copy. In others the reviser seems concerned with the niceties of language, substituting 'pathe' for 'waie' (fol. 38ᵃ), 'fearfull' for 'limber' (fol. 48ᵇ), 'lay to yoʳ handꝭ agen' for 'wher be thease lazie handes agen?' (fol. 49ᵃ), and 'but ffate is my hinderer' for 'but Fates my hindraunce' (fol. 54ᵃ).

Another revisional hand has added a number of stage-directions evidently in the playhouse. They include mention of two actors: Mr. [Robert] Goughe, who most likely took the part of Memphonius (Plate 4), and Richard Robinson, who played the Lady. Both are well known as members of the King's company at the date in question, though the boy is not heard of before that year.

Even apart from the licence the fact of censorship is evident. Buc with his own hand substituted 'I am poisoned' for 'yoʳ kinges poisond' on fol. 55ᵇ. In the margin opposite are crosses both in ink and pencil, apparently made by the censor. Similar crosses appear on fols. 43ᵇ and 49ᵇ and enable us with some confidence to assign to Buc the deletion of the lines:

> twas a straunge trick of her, few of yoʳ ladies
> in ordnary will beleiue it, they abhor it
> theile sooner kill them selues wᵗʰ lust, then for it;

as well as the alteration whereby a preference of life to honour is given as the opinion of 'many' rather than 'most' ladies—a somewhat subtle distinction which confirms the presence of Buc's hand on fol. 43ᵃ, where an alteration makes the fear of death a mark of 'some' great men only. Several other minor deletions, of oaths and the like, were no doubt made either by the censor or at his instigation.

There is a division into acts only, which are marked in the left margin.

Though the scenes are not numbered or recognized in any formal manner, they are indicated through most of the play by the position of the directions. All entrances constituting new scenes have directions written across the centre of the page, and in the first four acts these are the only entrances so centred. In the last act, on the other hand, several minor entrances are centred, in the sense that the directions break the continuity of the text, but these all begin in the left margin. Otherwise all minor entrances are indicated in the left margin, except for a couple on the right (fols. 43ª, 55ª, and these are hardly normal entries). Exits, as usual, are placed on the right, and so are the infrequent independent directions, with the exception of two longer ones that are centred (fols. 50ª, 52ª). The additional directions by the playhouse reviser are all added in the left margin. None of the original directions are distinguished by rules (though a few of the marginal entrances have braces), but some of the additional ones are provided with them. The following list is complete for all but bare entrances and exits.

29ª 'Actus Prim⁹·' (left) opposite 'Enter the new . . .' (centre). *'A senate' opposite the beginning of the first speech.

30ª 'Enter with the Lady clad in Black'.

30ᵇ 'Exiunt Lady and Govianus'.

32ª *'A florish' opposite 'Exiunt' [I. ii] 'Enter L Anselmus the deposde kinges brother, wᵗʰ his Frend Votarius'.

32ᵇ 'Enter Wyfe'. 33ᵇ 'Enter Wife'. 34ᵇ 'Enter Leonela'.

35ª 'Enter Bellarius Mufled · in his cloke'.

35ᵇ 'Actus: 2:ᵈᵘˢ·' opposite 'Enter the ladye of Gouianus, wᵗʰ a Servaunt'.

37ᵇ 'Enter Gouianus discharging a Pistoll'.

38ª [II. ii] 'Enter Votarius Sadly'.

39ª 'Exunt [*sic*] wife and Anselm⁹'. 'Exit Leonela manet Votarius'. 'Enter Bellarius passing ouer the Stage'.

39ᵇ 'Enter Anselmus: a dagger in his hand wᵗʰ Leonela'.

40ª *'A florish' opposite [II. iii] 'Enter the Tyrant with Sophonirus Memphonius and other Nobles'.

41ª 'Enter Guard', serving also as speaker's prefix. 'Exiunt Manet Sophonirus'. *'A florish' above 'Actus Tertius' opposite 'Enter Gouianus with his Ladye. and a servaunt'.

42ᵇ *'Knock' (twice) also 'With in' (twice) as speaker's prefix. 'Runs at her and falles by the way in a Sound'.

43ª *'Knock' (twice) opposite 'Kills her self | A great knocking agen'. *'Knock wᵗʰin'. 'Enter the Fellows well weopend' (right).

$43^{b}$ 'Exeunt Manet Gouianus'.

$44^{a}$ 'Actus Quartus' opposite 'Enter Votarius w$^{th}$ Anselmus Lady'.

$45^{b}$ [IV. ii] 'Enter Tirant wondrous discontentedly: Nobles a farr of'.

$48^{a}$ [Plate 4] *'Enter Soldiers' replacing 'Enter' twice prefixed to speaker's name '1 Soldier'. *'Enter m$^{r}$ Goughe' referring to additional slip (fol. 47).

$48^{b}$ [IV. iii]. 'Enter the Tirant agen at a farder dore, which opened, bringes hym to the Toombe wher the Lady lies buried; The Toombe here discouered ritchly set forthe'.

$49^{b}$ 'Exiunt Manet 1 Sol.'. [IV. iv] 'Enter Gouianus in black, a booke in his hand, his page carying a Torche before hym'.

$50^{a}$ 'Gouianus kneeles at the Toomb wrondrous [*sic*] passionatly. His Page singes' (right). 'On a sodayne in a kinde of Noyse like a Wynde, the dores clattering, the Toombstone flies open, and a great light appeares in the midst of the Toombe; His Lady as went owt, standing iust before hym all in white, Stuck with Iewells and a great crucifex on her brest' (centre) opposite which is added *'Enter Ladye Rich Robinson'.

$50^{b}$ 'Actus Quintus' opposite 'Enter Votarius with Anselmus the Husband'.

$51^{a}$ 'Leonella aboue in a Gallery with her loue Bellarius' (centre, but on left; the stage is not clear, for the exit marked for Anselmus is an error). 'Descendet Leonela' (right: i.e. exit from balcony). 'Locks him self in' (right). 'Enter Anselmus Lady with Leonella' (centre, but on left; only the lower stage is clear).

$51^{b}$ 'Enter Votarius to the doore w$^{th}$in' (left: i.e. outside the locked door).

$52^{a}$ 'kills Leonela' and opposite *'Ente: Bellarius' two lines before he speaks. 'They make a daungerous passe at one another the Lady purposely runs betwene, and is kild by them both' (centre). 'Ansel: dies'. 'Enter Gouianus with Servauntes' (centre, but on left).

$52^{b}$ 'Dyes' repeated on additional slip (fol. 53). [V. ii] 'Enter Tyrant with Attendauntes' (centre, but on left). *'Enter soldiers w$^{th}$ the Ladye' (left with rules) anticipating by four lines—

$54^{a}$ *'musick' opposite 'They bringe the Body in a Chaire drest vp in black veluet which setts out the pailenes of the handes and face, And a faire Chayne of pearle crosse her brest and the Crucyfex aboue it; He standes silent awhile letting the Musique play, becknyng the soldiers that bringe her in to make obeisaunce to her, and he hym self makes a lowe honour to the body and kisses the hande | A song with in in Voyces' (centre). 'Enter 3 Souldier with Gouianus' (centre, but on left).

$55^{a}$ 'Enter the Ghost in the shame [*sic*] form as the lady is drest in the Chayre' (right, with guide rule).

$55^{b}$ *'florish'.

$56^{a}$ '⟨T⟩he Spirit enters ⟨ag⟩en and stayes to ⟨go⟩e out with the ⟨bo⟩dy as it were ⟨atte⟩ndinge it' (left).

Printed: without editor's name (as No. 1 of *The Old English Drama*), 1824, and several times since; W. W. Greg (Malone Society), 1909 (1910).

7. *Sir John van Olden Barnavelt.*

B.M., MS. Add. 18653. Aug. 1619.

The play (see Plate 5), which is known to have been first performed between 19 and 27 Aug. 1619, occupies thirty-one leaves according to the modern pencil numbering. The first is the remains of a coarse paper wrapper. The play itself was originally written on twenty-eight numbered leaves (forming thirteen separate sheets together with two odd leaves, viz. the fifteenth and sixteenth, fols. 17, 18), but of these the eighth has been removed and replaced by a slip (fol. 9), while other slips (fols. 16, 30) have been inserted after the fourteenth and twenty-seventh. Two of these slips (fols. 9 and 30) are about three-quarters of a leaf, the other (fol. 16) a half leaf: all three are blank on the verso. The leaves measure about $11\frac{5}{8} \times 7\frac{1}{2}$ inches (except fols. 17, 18 which are a quarter of an inch narrower).

References are here given to the inclusive pencil foliation, but the original numbers are added in parentheses (being those followed in the latest edition).

Fol. $1^{a}$ (wrapper): 'The Tragedy of S$^{r}$ Iohn | Van Olden Barnauelt' in the hand of the scribe (verso blank).

Begins, fol. $2(1)^{a}$, with initial direction (see below).

Ends on fol. $31(28)^{b}$, without explicit of any sort beyond 'Exeunt'.

Written in the elegant professional hand of Ralph Crane (whose activities have been described by Professor F. P. Wilson in *The Library*, 1926, vii. 194–215). English and Italian scripts are used, directions are as a rule written in a larger and bolder style, and there is a normal use of very short speech-rules.

[illegible] the [illegible] (b), forms the [illegible] in the [illegible] with guide [illegible]

[illegible] enters [illegible] and [illegible] (Folt)

[illegible]

[illegible] MS. Add. 10,449 [illegible] 1619

[illegible] which is known to have been first per-formed between [illegible] occupies [illegible] one [illegible] according to the modern pencil numbering. The first [illegible] of a coarse paper wrapper. The play itself was [illegible] twenty-eight numbered leaves [illegible] thirteen [illegible] together with [illegible] leaves, viz. the fifteenth and sixteenth, [illegible] but of these the [illegible] had been removed and replaced [illegible] slips (fols. 16, 20) have been inserted [illegible] each and [illegible]. Two of these slips [illegible] and 20 [illegible] The other (fol. 17) [illegible] leaf [illegible] The [illegible] leaves measure about [illegible] which are a quarter [illegible] inch narrower.)

[illegible] the [illegible]

[illegible] Tragedy of Sir John Van Olden Barnavelt [illegible] the [illegible] (verso blank).

[illegible] with initial direction (Mc Bea[illegible])

[illegible] (fol. [illegible]), without [illegible] of [illegible] and [illegible]

[illegible] professional hand of [illegible] Professor [illegible] (fol. 10–21 [illegible]). English and Italian [illegible] written in a larger and bolder [illegible] and there is [illegible] of very short speech-rules.

The leaves have been folded for margins. The play has also been carefully revised by the scribe. Some passages he elaborately deleted (in certain cases clearly in obedience to the censor), at times substituting a few lines in the margin: he also wrote the additional slips. But there has also been an extensive playhouse revision; and many additional directions, including a number of actors' names, have been supplied in a much rougher hand. In the ensuing notes this hand has been treated, for the sake of distinction, as different from the scribe's: but in many instances the hand is in fact certainly the same, and probably it is so in all. Since the actors' names in this play have never been quite satisfactorily treated, I have added a special note on them at the end. The more important actors mentioned are all known to have been members of the King's company at the date in question.

There appear to be certain other alterations in the text made in a different and rather rough hand which is unidentified. Thus on fol. 3(2)[b] 'a kind wench' has been substituted for 'a fresh whore', on fol. 7(6)[a] 'Arminians' for 'Preachers' and 'meetings' for 'Pulpitts', and on fol. 14(13)[b] 'Roterdam' for 'Leiden'. The last looks like a correction, the others may owe their inspiration to the censor though they do not appear to be in his hand.

Sir George Buc's activity on the manuscript is, however, certain, though it bears no trace of licence. On fol. 5(4)[b] he wrote in the margin 'I like not this: neith[r] do I think y[t] the pr. was thus disgracefully vsed. besides he is to much presented. G. B.' Also, besides possibly making some minor alterations, he devoted his attention to a passage on fol. 26(24)[a], substituting 'cutt of his opposites' for 'took that course | that now is practisd on yo[u]', and 'another forme' for 'a Monarchie', and finally marking a dozen lines for omission. To this passage is appended a series of marginal crosses (similar to those found in *The Second Maiden's Tragedy*) which must clearly be credited to the censor. And similar crosses elsewhere enable us to trace his activity throughout the play. Both ink and pencil crosses condemn a long passage deleted by the scribe on fol. 25(23)[a] and a shorter one on fol. 8(7)[b], and call attention to phrases subsequently altered by him on fols. 2(1)$^{a}$, 4(3)$^{a}$, and 8(7)$^{a}$. The last of these is perhaps of special interest. One speech ran:

> I know yo$^{u}$ love the *Prince* of *Orange*, yet
> yo$^{u}$ must graunt him a Servant to the States,
> . . . . . . . . . . and . . . should he be
> disloyall . . .

An ink cross was placed opposite the first line and a pencil cross opposite the last: the scribe altered the '*Prince* of *Orange*' to the 'valiant Prince' but left the suggestion of disloyalty standing. Neither did he take any notice of the pencil crosses that call attention to such phrases as 'the Armenian faction' on fol. 14(13)$^{a}$, and 'we may be o$^{ur}$ owne Iustice' on fol. 18(16)$^{a}$: he even disregarded the ink and pencil crosses that reprove an ambassador's allusion to 'the King o$^{ur}$ Master' on fol. 27(25)$^{a}$. There are also some pencil marks, apparently for omission, on fol. 28(26)$^{a}$ of which no notice has been taken. It was apparently assumed that pencil jottings were for the censor's private amusement.

There is a full division into acts and scenes all duly numbered. The insertion of fol. 16(14*) containing the additional scene III. iii, has lead to the renumbering of the later scenes of that act.

Scene headings, and these alone, are written across the centre of the page. All other entrances, exits, and directions are in the right margin, the only exceptions being one or two of the additions in rougher script which appear on the left. There are no rules of any sort to the original directions, though they frequently adorn the additions. The directions on the right are generally preceded by a short dash, which marks the exact place where it belongs, and in many cases a mark has been made on the left likewise with a similar object. These left-hand marks would appear from the ink to belong to the additions: they tend to appear a line or so above the corresponding dash on the right, though there is sometimes a greater discrepancy. The following list is complete for all but bare and unaltered entrances and exits.

2(1)$^{a}$ 'Actus pri$^{9}$: Scæ$^{a}$. pri$^{a}$. | Enter Barnauelt, Modes-bargen, Leidenberch, *Vandermitten*' for which is substituted *'Grotius', while in

the text corresponding alterations have been made in the speakers' names.

3(2)[a] 'Enter 2. Captaines' to which is added *'Io: R: migh.'

4(3)[a] 'Scæ[a]. 2[a]. Enter Barnauelt: Modesbargen Leidenberch *Vandermitten:* Grotius: *Taurinus, Vtenbogart'*, for the last two is substituted *'Hogenbeets' with corresponding alterations in the text.

4(3)[b] 'Enter Bredero Vandort Officers'.

5(4)[a] 'Scæ[a]. 3[a]: Enter Pr. of Orange: *Gr. Henrie:* Gra: William. *Collonells* & Captaines' to which *'m[r] Rob:', the speeches of Grave Henry being transferred to William.

5(4)[b] 'Guard at dore'.

6(5)[a] 'Enter Barnauelt, Modesbargen. Leidenberch *Vandermitten.* [*'Grotius' interlined] Bredero, Vandort *&c'* for which *'Hogerbeets'.

7(6)[a] 'Actus Secundus: Scæ[a]. pri[a]. | Enter Barnauelt: Leidenberch, Modesbargen'. 'Enter Rock-Giles: 2. Burgers Captaines Leiutenn̄t *Soldiers'*.

8(7)[b] 'Scæ[a]. 2[a]. *Enter Holderus: & a dutch Widow'*: the scene is cancelled, involving the removal of the original eighth leaf, for which a slip, fol. 9, is substituted.

9(7*=8)[a] 'Enter Holderus: Duch-woemen: & an English-gent'w:' (centre).

10(9)[a] 'Enter *2*. 1 Burgers: *Vandermitten'* for which *'Grotius'. 'Enter Leidenberge' to which *'*& m[r] Gough'* (apparently deleted).

10(9)[b] 'Enter a Messenger' *'R: T'. II. iii 'Enter . 1 . Captaine: [*'Io: R1·' interlined] & Soldiers' to which *'migh'. II. iv 'Enter Pr. of Orange: ['Wiltm' interlined] Captaine: [*'m[r] Rob:' interlined] Leiutenn̄t &c.'. 'Enter Cap[n]. [*'Io: Ric' interlined] on y[e] walls'.

11(10)[a] II. v 'Enter Leidenberge: *Vandermitten*: [*'Grotius' interlined] Rock Giles'. 'Enter Messeng[r]' * R: T:'. (in II. vi) 'Enter Holderus' * 'T p:'. 'Exeunt. Enter Orange Leidenberge: Burgers. Captaines. Sold[rs].' to which *'and Arminiã[s]', the addition anticipating by half a dozen lines and replacing—

11(10)[b] '*Droms Enter y[e] Arminians*' and *'*pass ouer*' (right, with mark on left also deleted). III. i 'Enter Bredero, Vandort: *& 2. Lords*' the Lord's speeches in the text being transferred to Vandort.

12(11)[a] 'Ent' (right) probably the beginning of an abandoned direction. 'Enter Barnauelt & his Son'.

13(12)[b] III. ii 'Enter: P · of Orange, *Henrie*, William . . . Lords: Collonells: Captaines' *'Table: Bell', the addition anticipating by some thirty lines and replacing—

14(13)$^{a}$ *'*Table : Bell*'. 14(13)$^{b}$ 'Enter officer' *'R. T:'.

15(14)$^{a}$ 'Enter Captaine' *'m$^{r}$ Rice'.

15(14)$^{b}$ ☞ reference to additional slip, fol. 16, containing III. iii. 'Scæ$^{a}$. 4$^{a}$ [altered from '3$^{a}$']. Enter Barnauelt, & Prouost'.

16(14*)$^{a}$ 'Scæ$^{a}$. 3$^{a}$. Enter 2. Captaines' to which *'m$^{r}$ Rob: mighell'.

18(16)$^{b}$ III. vi 'Enter Leidenberch & Boy' to which *'Taper : pen & inke Table' (left) between rules.

19(17)$^{a}$ *'Son abed' (right) between rules. 'Boy w$^{th}$in' (speaker's prefix).

19(17)$^{b}$ 'Enter Prouost & Seru$^{ts}$.' *'R: T.'. (IV. i) 'Enter Captaine, & Soldiers' *'cap: Io: R'.

20(18)$^{a}$ *'Hornes' (left and right) between rules, before 'Exeunt. Enter Modes-bargen & Huntesmen' *'migh'. 'Enter 2: Huntesmã.' *'R: T.'. 'Ex$^{t}$. Enter Capt$^{n}$ & Soldiers'. 'Ex$^{t}$. Enter Modes-b⟨argen⟩ & Huntesmen'.

20(18)$^{b}$ 'Enter Captaine & Soldiers'. IV. ii 'Enter Orange, Bredero, Vandort: *Lords*' *'Tho: po:' (cf. 21$^{a}$).

21(19)$^{a}$ 'Enter Captaine' *'m$^{r}$ Rob:'. *'T: p:' added to speaker's prefix 'Ser.' (cf. 20$^{b}$). IV. iii 'Enter Barnauelt (in his studdy)' the words in parentheses are not in heavy script. 'Enter S$^{r}$uant' *'R: T'.

21(19)$^{b}$ 'Enter Daughter' *'G: lowen'. 'Enter Wife' *'nick. and daught.'.

22(20)$^{a}$ 'Enter Seru$^{t}$. *w$^{th}$ wine*' *'R: T' and three lines lower *'Ent: w$^{th}$ wyn'. 'Enter Seru$^{t}$' *'w$^{th}$' (left unfinished).

22(20)$^{b}$ 'Enter Wife & Daughter' (the corresponding mark on left is five lines above). 'Captaine w$^{th}$ in' *'m$^{r}$ Rob:'.

23(21)$^{a}$ IV. iv 'Enter Orange : & 1 Captaine' *'Io: Rice'. 'Song: Enter wife, aboue'.

23(21)$^{b}$ [Plate 5] '*Daunce*' and five lines lower *'Daunce' between rules. IV. v 'Enter Orange; . . . William *Henry*: Lords' to which *'Barre' (left) and *'Table' (right) both between rules, and one line lower *'A Bar brought in'.

25(23)$^{b}$ 'Enter *Captaine* w$^{th}$ Modesbargen' and interlined above the deletion *'*prouost*' and below *'Captaine'.

26(24)$^{a}$ v. i 'Enter Wife : Daughter : Seru$^{t}$ w$^{th}$ Peares' *'m$^{r}$ Rice'.

26(24)$^{b}$ 'Enter Prouosts Wife' *'T: Holc:'.

27(25)$^{a}$ 'Enter Orange, *Henry* [*'w$^{m}$.' substituted] Vandort Bredero *Lords*' with mark on left three lines before at foot of fol. 26$^{b}$. 'Enter *Boisise* [*'2 Embas' substituted] Morier wife, daught$^{r}$ attend$^{t}$s' and

*'m$^{r}$ Rob:' added after speaker's prefix 'Boi.'. '2. Chaires' *'S$^{tr}$: [?]$^{r}$ Bir.' (the reading here is doubtful and something appears to have been deleted; presumably the servant who brings in the chairs is meant).

28(26)$^{b}$ v. ii 'Enter. Harlem. Leyden, & Vtricht Executio$^{rs}$'.

29(27)$^{a}$ 'Song. Ex$^{t}$'. v. iii 'Enter 2. Captaines: & y$^{eir}$ Soldiers, seu'ally' *'m$^{r}$ Rob: m$^{r}$ Rice'. 'Enter Prouost Sold$^{s}$. & Execu$^{rs}$ w$^{th}$ a Coffin' *'& a Gibbett'.

29(27)$^{b}$ 'Enter Prouost Barnauelt: Lords: Guard. (a Scaffold put out) Execution$^{r}$' (right) and between this and the text *'Scaffold' between rules (which looks like a note for the stage-direction). Here the mark on the left is four lines below that on the right.

31(28)$^{a}$ ∘∘∘ reference to additional slip, fol. 30, containing two extra speeches.

The following is an attempt to identify the actors mentioned in the additional directions with the parts taken.

George Birch ?
'[ ]$^{r}$ Bir' a servant?, 27(25)$^{a}$.

Robert Gough.
'm$^{r}$ Gough' an attendant on Leidenberg (cancelled), 10(9)$^{a}$.

Thomas Holcombe.
'T: Holc' the Provost's wife, 26(24)$^{b}$.

G. Lowen.
'G: Lowen' Barnavelt's wife, 21(19)$^{b}$.

Nick, possibly Nicholas Underhill.
'nick' Barnavelt's wife, 21(19)$^{b}$.

Michael.
'migh' 'mighell' a captain, 3(2)$^{a}$, 16(14*)$^{a}$; a soldier, 10(9)$^{b}$; a huntsman, 20(18)$^{a}$.

Thomas Pollard.
'T.p.' 'Tho. po.' Holderus, 11(10)$^{a}$; a servant, 20(18)$^{b}$ and 21(19)$^{a}$.

John Rice (but can Mr. Rice be the same?).
'Io. R.' 'Io. Ri.' 'Io. Ric' 'Io. Rice' a captain, 3(2)$^{a}$, 10(9)$^{b}$ twice, 19(17)$^{b}$, 23(21)$^{a}$. 'm$^{r}$ Rice' a captain 15(14)$^{a}$, 29(27)$^{a}$; a servant, 26(24)$^{a}$.

Richard Robinson?
'm$^{r}$ Rob.' a captain, 5(3)$^{a}$, 10(9)$^{b}$, 16(14*)$^{a}$, 21(19)$^{a}$, 22(20)$^{b}$, 29(27)$^{a}$; an ambassador, 27(25)$^{a}$.

R. T.
'R. T.' a messenger, 10(9)$^{b}$, 11(10)$^{a}$; an officer, 14(13)$^{b}$; a servant, 19(17)$^{b}$, 21(19)$^{b}$, 22(20)$^{a}$; a huntsman, 20(18)$^{a}$.

Printed: A. H. Bullen, *Old Plays* (ii. 201–314), 1883; W. P. Frijlinck, 1922.

8. *The Two Noble Ladies.*

B.M., MS. Egerton 1994[11]. 1622–3?

The play (see Plate 6) occupies fols. 224–244 of the collection, but a leaf is missing between fols. 225 and 226. Of the original twenty-two leaves the first was treated as a fly-leaf and the rest numbered 1–21. (This foliation is added in parentheses below.) The whole appears to have formed a single gathering of twelve sheets, of which the last two leaves, presumably blank, are now lost (as well as leaf '2'). The extreme measurement of the leaves is $11\frac{5}{8} \times 7\frac{1}{4}$ inches. There are regular catchwords throughout.

Fol. 224[a]: 'The 2. Noble Ladys, | and | The Converted Coniurer'. This title is probably in the same hand and ink as the text.

Fol. 224[b]: 'The two noble Ladies: A Trage-comicall Historie often tymes acted w[t]h approbation At the Red Bull in S[t]: Iohns Streete By the Company of y[e] Reuells | The Actors Names | . . .'. This page is written in a different and perhaps later hand.

Begins, fol. 225(1)[a]: 'Act. i. Sce. i. | Alarum, . . . | Enter . . .' (see below).

Ends on fol. 244(21)[b]: 'Exeunt. | Finis'.

Written in a small neat hand, of a decidedly literary type, using English script with a not very distinctive Italian for incidental purposes. The manuscript is evidently an author's fair copy containing numerous alterations and corrections, often made *currente calamo*. There are no speech-rules, but the leaves have been folded for margins.

Use in the playhouse is shown by a few directions and several actors' names added in another hand. The actors can be probably identified as George Stutfield, [H.] Gibs[on], [Thomas?] Bond, Anthony Brew[er?], Tay[lor], and a Stage-keeper. Some of these were leading actors in the thirties, but there is nothing to show that they were more than hired men when they acted in this play. They may or may not have taken part

Printed: A. H. Bullen, *Old Plays* (ii. 201–[illegible]), 1883; W. P. Frijlinck, 1922.

8. *The Two Noble Ladies.*

B.M. MS. Egerton 1994. 1622–3 [illegible]

The play ([illegible]) occupies fols. 224–2[illegible] of the collection [illegible] Of the original [illegible] and the [illegible] in parentheses [illegible] a single cancelled [illegible] leaves, presumably [illegible] in [illegible] regular [illegible]

[illegible] Converted [illegible]

[illegible] Hall in St. [illegible] The Actors [illegible] and perhaps

[illegible]

[illegible] of a decidedly literary type [illegible] very distinctive [illegible] evidently [illegible]

in the Red Bull performance. A Revels company (late Queen's men) were acting there from Anne's death in 1619 till they broke early in 1623. (Actually they did not receive the title of Children of the Revels till their patent of July 1622, but it may have been applied retrospectively.) The licences do not include any of the actors named. There may well have been earlier performances, and again the play may have been revived later. The text certainly looks earlier than the title and personae on fol. 224[b], which appear to have been added with a view to publication. The hand of this addition has a certain resemblance to that of *The Welsh Embassador* (which may possibly also have been a Revels' play), but is in fact almost certainly distinct.

There are no traces of censorship, unless underlining and marginal crosses indicate that objection was taken to two passages: 'know that I being a courtier can finde a tricke to stop a souldiers pay, and keep him bare enough' (fol. 234(11)[a]), and 'Hide vs yee mountaines, couer vs yee rockes' (fol. 242(19)[a]).

There is an original division throughout into acts and scenes, duly numbered, which has not been interfered with. Scenes are regularly divided by a rule across the page, acts by a row of dots enclosed within rules.

Entrances, whether constituting a new scene or not, are mostly centred. Exits, as usual, are marked on the right. Other original directions, which are very numerous, are normally entered in the right margin. Most right-hand directions are completely enclosed within rules, though occasionally there are rules on two or three sides only: directions without rules are rare. In some cases central directions, associated with entrances, are similarly enclosed. The directions added in another hand are generally in the left margin, and often repeat original directions on the right. They are usually written between rules, but sometimes only underlined. In two instances it looks as though the reviser had duplicated an original direction which was subsequently altered in the hand of the text (fols. 235[b], 242[a]), which would make the revision contemporary with the writing, but it is possible that the duplication is accidental. The following list is far from exhaustive for the later acts.

225(1)[a] 'Alarm, then Flourish and Shout within' (left, no rules) opposite 'Act. i. Sce. 1. | Enter Iustina flying, Doron wounded meets her'.

225(1)[b] *'shoute' opposite 'Shout within'. 'Alarm still' (left, no rules) opposite 'Sce. 2. | Crie within, Kill Kill Kill. Enter Barebones (a poore Scholler) running' (centre, 'Crie . . . Kill.' within rules). 'within, Kill Kill Kill' (right, twice). 'Ciprian discovered at his booke' (right). *'shoute w[th]in' opposite 'Shout within'. 'Hides him vnder the table'. 'Enter Lysander and Miranda with they [*sic*] swords drawne' (centre).

226(3)[a] (in I. iii) 'asside'. 'Kisses her'.

226(3)[b] 'asside' twice to a single line with rules, thrice to two to four lines with brace.

227(4)[a] 'Sce. 4. | Enter *Eumenia* ['Iustina' interlined] supporting Doron deadly wounded'. 'He falls to the ground'. *'ffollow ffollow w[thin]' with guide line, opposite 'Crie within follow, follow this way'. *'Anth: Gibs:' apparently the names of two actors added opposite 'Enter 3. Souldiers' (centre, with rules). 'Dies'.

227(4)[b] 'Enter Miranda in Mans apparell'. 'They fight, while Iustina kneels by Doron and looks on him'. 'Enter Clitophon, hee parts them'.

228(5)[a] 'asside'. 'Exeunt. man⟨et⟩ Miranda'. *'Act 2: Flor Corn:' opposite 'Act. 2. Sce. 1. | Enter Souldan . . . 2. Eunuchs, and other attendants'.

228(5)[b] *'guard Tay: Stage k:' three lines before 'The Guard hurrys them away'. 'asside to Cyprian' and 'asside to Lysander' left standing though the speakers' names have been removed.

229(6)[a] 'asside to Lysander', 'asside to the Souldan', 'asside to Colactus', and 'asside' (each time with brace). 'The guard stands fixed, their eys rowling from the King to Cyprian, and so too & fro'. 'beats them'.

229(6)[b] 'He stands fixed in a posture of running at him with his sword'. 'Kneeles with a fearfull countenance and so is fixed'. 'Both Kneele'.

230(7)[a] *'Florish' opposite 'fflourish : Exeunt. | Sce. 2. | Enter Barebones with a satchell of meate, and a bottle of Wine'. 'Hee sits down' (left, with rules, prose right). 'Drincks. Enter Sinew, a Souldier' (right).

230(7)[b] 'gives him money'. 'Enter Lysander and Cyprian conferring' (right). 'They whisper'. *'Ent Canth:' opposite 'Enter Cantharides' (right).

231(8)[b] *'Act 3' opposite 'Exeunt. | Act. 3. Sce. 1. | Enter Iustina, Clitophon following her'.

232(9)[a] *'Ent. Anth Brew:' opposite 'Enter a Lord of Babilon with his sword drawn' (centre, within rules). *'Ent:' opposite 'Enter *Armidan* Miranda': Armidan is her male disguise. *'Shout wthin'' with guide line, opposite 'Shout within'. *'Ent Califfe' opposite 'Enter The Califfe with Attendants and Souldiers' (centre, within rules).

233(10)[a] *'Tay. Gib: Stage k:' actors' names added apparently for Soldiers called on three lines below. 'Drag her in'.

233(10)[b] *'fflor' opposite 'Sce. 2. | Enter Blood and Caro', but rather for preceding 'Exeunt'. 'Enter Sinew and Cantharides' (left with rules: prose right).

234(11)[a] *'Ent Bareb:' two lines before 'Enter Barebones stands beholding Caro' (centre within rules). 'They whisper'. 'Cantharides claws her'. 'fixes her eie on Barebones'.

234(11)[b] [speakes] 'to Blood'. 'to Sinew'. 'Exeunt severally'. *'Enter' opposite 'Sce. 3. | Enter *Cyprian and* Lysander and Cyprian'. *'Thunder' (left, third line from foot) and *'Ent Spirrit Geo Stut' (centre, at foot) anticipating third line of next page—

235(12)[a] *'Thunder' opposite 'Thunder. Enter a Spirit, Like a souldier in armour on his breast a sable sheild written on with Golden letters' (centre, within rules). *'Musique' opposite 'Recorders play. The Spirit vanishes' (centre, within rules). 'Recorders still. Enter an Angell shaped like a patriarch vpon his breast a blew table full of silver letters, in his right hand a red crossierstaffe, on his shoulders large wings'. 'Exit Angelus'.

235(12)[b] [Plate 6] *'Noise wthin'' opposite '*Noise within*' deleted in favour of 'Crye within. help help'. *'Anth: Gibs:' opposite 'Enter 2. Souldiers dragging Iustina bound'. *'Thunder' opposite 'Thunder. | Enter 2. Tritons with silver trumpets. | The tritons ceaz the souldiers' (right, within rules). *'Tritons in: Bond Stutf.' opposite 'The Tritons dragge them in sounding their trumpets'.

236(13)[a] 'Alarme' (left) opposite 'Act. 4. Sce. 1. | Enter *Miranda sol*< > ['Colactus wounded' interlined] with his sword drawn' (cf. sc. ii). 'Alarm still' (left) opposite 'Sce. 2. | Enter Miranda with her sword drawn' and three lines later *'Low Larum'. *'fflor Trump: Shoute' opposite 'flourish and Shout within'. *'Califfe Souldan Clittophon. Lords' (centre, at foot) anticipating entry third line over leaf—

236(13)[b] *'Flor Trump.' and *'*Sennit*' (left) two lines before '*Flourish. & Sennet*' (centre) preceding 'Enter in state the Califfe, Clitophon leading the Souldan bound; noblemen, and souldiers' also *'Tay: Gibs:' (right) actors' names added apparently for the Soldiers.

237(14)$^{b}$ 'his sword' (right, within rules) glossing text 'this shall be theyr passe to hell'. 'The Souldiers drop away' (centre, within rules).

238(15)$^{a}$ (in IV. iii) *'Ent: Blood Caro' (left, at foot) anticipating entry third line over leaf—

238(15)$^{b}$ *'Ent:' opposite 'Enter Bloud & Caro embracing' (right). 'stands close'. *'Ent Synew' two lines before 'Enter Sinew disguised with a letter' (right).

239(16)$^{a}$ 'Cantharides bites him'. 'He draws his sword and runs vp and downe crying sa sa sa tarararara; so Exit'. *'Lesson Corn:' replacing '*Hoboys*' (left) opposite 'Sce. 4. | A Dumb Shew. | Enter at one Dore the Souldan with souldiers, from the other a Herald meets him, delivers him a paper. The Souldã sends in a souldier, who brings Lysander. Hee kneels, the Souldan embraces him, and shews him the paper, hee kisses it, beckons to the Herald, houlds out the paper with his left hand and lays his right hand on his sword. With courtesy they part. The Souldan and Herald goe of severally. Lysander stays' (and speaks).

240(17)$^{a}$ *'Act 5' opposite 'Act. 5. Sce. 1.' and *'Dromme *Trump* Colo$^{rs}$' replacing '*Flourish*' preceding 'Enter Claudius a Roman Generall with Captains and Souldiers'.

240(17)$^{b}$ *'Low March. w$^{thin}$' with guide rule opposite 'A drũ far off'. *'Drom̃' opposite 'Enter Clitophon with Captains and Souldiers'.

241(18)$^{a}$ *'March' opposite 'Exeunt'. (in V. ii) *'Enter Cantharides' two lines before 'Enter Cantharides' (right). 'Iustina is discovered in a chaire asleep, in her hands a prayer book, divells about her' (right).

241(18)$^{b}$ *'Musiqꝫ' opposite 'Musick. A song' (centre, within rules).

242(19)$^{a}$ 'The feinds roare and fly back' (centre, but to right, within rules). 'Musiqꝫ Ent: Angell' opposite 'Recorders. [interlined above '*Soft musicke*'] Enter the patriarch-like Angell . . .' (right). 'The Devills sinck roaring; a flame of fier riseth after them'.

242(19)$^{b}$ 'Exit Angelus'. 'Throws his charmed rod, and his books vnder the stage. a flame riseth'. 'The Angells booke' (right, within rules) glossing text 'This sacred trueth alone shall be my studdy'. *'Ent: Souldan Colactus Califfe Herald' opposite 'Sce. 3$^{a}$. et Vltima. | Enter at one dore the Souldan, Colactus, & Souldiers at the other the Califfe, a Nobleman, Herald, & Souldier⟨s⟩' also *'Drums and Coloures' replacing '*Flourish*'.

243(20)$^{a}$ *'Tuckett' (left) with guide rule opposite *'Tuckett' (right) replacing *'*fflor:*'. *'*fflor Corn*' opposite 'flourish. Enter Herald with Lysander in armour' (right). *'Tuckett' (left) replacing '*fflorish*' (centre) opposite 'Flourish. Enter' (right, at foot) really a catchword, made into a direction by the addition of rules, for—

243(20)[b] 'Flourish. Enter Herald, Miranda following him in her Owne Amazonian attire . . .' (centre, with rules). *'Larum w$^{thin}$' six lines before, and *'Larums within' opposite, 'Alarme within'.

244(21)[a] *'Larum' opposite 'Enter Claudius with Souldiers at one dore . . .' (centre, within rules). 'This while Clitophon presents Iustina to the Califfe, & they whisper, kindly embracing' with brace to eight lines.

244(21)[b] 'All this is ⟨in ?⟩ private disc⟨ourse⟩ betwixt Lys⟨ander,⟩ Clitophon, I⟨ustina⟩ and Cyprian⟨ ⟩ The rest ⟨ ⟩ to minde⟨ ' with brace to ten or twelve lines.

Printed: R. G. Rhoads (Malone Society), 1930.

9. *The Welsh Embassador*. Cardiff Public Library. *c.* 1623.
The play occupies nineteen leaves (the first and last pages of which are blank) forming nine separate sheets preceded by one odd leaf. The foot of every leaf is more or less injured by damp, but the measurement can be determined as about $12\frac{1}{8} \times 8$ inches.

Fol. 1[b] (recto blank): 'The Welch Embassador' followed by list of characters.

Begins, fol. 2[a]: 'The Welsh Embassador. | Act 1$^{us}$ | Enter the Duke of Cornewall, the Earles of Chester and mercia; and Edwin; Elfred [*sic*] and Edmond y$^{e}$ Kings broth⟨ers⟩ disguizd like souldiers'.

Ends on fol. 19[a], the last lines mutilated (verso blank).

Written throughout, in a hand of a rather professional type, by a scribe who also wrote *The Parliament of Love*. It is a neat and regular hand in which the English is clearly distinguished from the rather elegant Italian script. There is a normal use of short speech-rules, and the leaves have been folded for margins. There is no trace of any second hand and no actual evidence of prompt use, though the nature of the directions show that the play had been certainly prepared for the stage. A few passages near the end have been marked for omission, but there is no indication of censorship unless such can be seen in the deletion of a mention of 'the raigne of this kinge heere' on fol. 18[a].

There is a regular division into acts only, a finis appearing at the end of each (except the last) and the number of the next being marked in the left margin. In one instance the finis and number appear at the foot of a verso, the entrance being at the head of the next recto.

Though there is no formal division into scenes, all entrances constituting them are written across the page (i.e. centred but beginning in the left margin), but so are a few others of importance (fols. 5ᵇ, 7ᵇ, 10ᵃ, 18ᵇ). All other entrances are marked in the left margin and so are independent directions with only one or two exceptions. As a rule only exits and like directions appear on the right. The principal feature is the insertion of warnings for actors to be in readiness. These are always in the left margin and usually anticipate the entrances by a quarter to half a page, the average being about a third, or say twenty lines. They are in the hand of the scribe, but the ink shows that they were added later. These warnings are regularly enclosed between rules, but similar rules also mark certain other directions likewise and are even occasionally added (near the end) to entrances as well.

2ᵃ 'Act 1ᵘˢ' opposite 'Enter the Duke of Cornewall, . . .' (centre) see above, 'Elfred' is an error for 'Eldred'. 'Enter yᵉ Kinge' (left). 'bee redy Penda' anticipating by 22 ll. 'Enter Penda like a Comon soldier'.

2ᵇ 'bee redy Edmond & Eldred' (30 ll.) 'Enter Edmond & Eldred' (there is no previous exit).

3ᵃ [I. ii] 'Enter Carintha; Cornewall and Chester'. 'Bee redy Penda' (30 ll.) 'Enter Penda'. 'Enter King'.

3ᵇ 'Bee redy Winchester' (28 ll.) 'enter Winchester'. 'bee redy Colchester' (20 ll.)—

4ᵃ 'Entᵓ Colchester'. 'bee redy Winchester & Armante' (43 ll.) [I. iii] 'Entᵓ Winchester and Armante'. 'bee redy Clowne' (8 ll.)—

4ᵇ 'Entᵓ Clowne'. 'bee redy Kinge' (20 ll.) 'Entᵓ Kinge'. 'bee redy Clowne' (30 ll.).

5ᵃ 'Entᵓ Clowne'. 'Enter Colchester'. 'Act 2ᵈᵘˢ' opposite 'finis Actus Primi | enter Eldred, Edmond, Penda, and Captaine Voltimar'.

5ᵇ 'bee redy Kinge Cornewall & Chester' (30 ll.) 'florish' before 'Enter Kinge; Cornewall and Chester the 3 step to the K' (centre).

6ᵇ 'Enter Colchester & Kent' (without warning) and 'exeunt: manet winchester'.

$7^{a}$ [in II. ii] 'bee redy K: Cornewall Chester: Edm: Eldred & Penda' (36 ll.)—

$7^{b}$ 'florish' before 'Enter Kinge: Cornewall, Chester, Edmond, Eldred, and Penda; followinge' (centre) and 'Exit Corn:'.

$8^{a}$ [II. iii] 'Enter Cornwall; and Carintha, Vaild in black'. 'bee redy Penda and Voltimar aboue' (no entrance marked, but 25 ll. lower) 'shews Penda w$^{th}$ a Leadinge staff voltimar at his back: his sword in him' (right, with index left).

$8^{b}$ 'exeunt ões manet K: & Vol:'. 'Act 3$^{us}$' opposite 'Finis Actus Secundi | Enter Armante and Clowne'.

$10^{a}$ [in III. ii] 'bee redy Penda Eldred; winchest' Chest' Colchest Kent' (12 ll.) 'Hoboyes' opposite 'Enter winchester; Colchester, Chester, Kent; then Penda the Welsh enbassador braue; Eldred as a Welsh seruingman: wincheste and his faction kiss the Kings hand; & then place them selues for Audience' (centre).

$10^{b}$ 'florish' opposite 'Exeunt Pen: Eld: & Voltimar'. 'Ent' voltimar and Edmond like an Irish man'. 'bee redy Carintha at a Table (26 ll.)—

$11^{a}$ [III. iii] 'Enter Corintha at a Table readinge'.

$11^{b}$ 'finis Actus Tertij' (centre) and '⟨Act⟩ 4$^{us.}$' (left) at foot.

$12^{a}$ 'florish' opposite [IV. i] 'Enter Kinge; Cornewall; Chester, and Penda'. 'bee redy Armante & *Edmond* Eldred' (30 ll.) 'Ent' Armante & *Edmond* Eldred'.

$13^{b}$ [in IV. ii] 'florish'. 'Daunce'. [speaks] 'w$^{t}$h in'.

$14^{a}$ 'Act' 5$^{us}$ | florish' opposite 'finis Actus Quarti | Enter Kinge Cornewall and Chester'. 'bee redy Winchester & Prince' (8 ll.) 'Enter winchester like a fryer leadinge the prince vaild' (centre).

$14^{b}$ 'vnvailes him' (right).

$16^{b}$ 'sett out a Table' (27 ll.) [V. ii] 'Enter Clowne in his study writinge: one Knockes w$^{t}$hin'.

$17^{a}$ 'Knock w$^{t}$hin | Enter Edmond'.

$17^{b}$ '⟨bee⟩ redy K: Winchest' Cornewall; Colchester ⟨K⟩ent Carintha Armante & Voltimar' (18 ll.) [V. iii] 'florish' before 'Enter Kinge Winchester, Cornewall, Carintha, Armante & Voltimar followinge' (centre) (6 ll.) 'Ent' Colchester: & Kent' (left). 'bee redy Clowne' (22 ll.) 'Ent' Clowne w$^{t}$h a Booke'.

$18^{b}$ 'Hoboyes | Ent' Edmond'. 'bee redy Lords & Prince' (10 ll.) 'Enter Cornewall w$^{t}$h his sword drawne, after him Colchester and Kent drawne the Prince like Cupid Voltimar keepes in the midst, Penda Edmond & Eldred draw & guard the Kinge; Winchester & Ladies step betwene all' (centre).

$19^{a}$ '*Ent' Clowne like Vulcan*' and following 11 ll. deleted.

Printed: H. Littledale and W. W. Greg (Malone Society), 1920 (1921).

10. *The Parliament of Love* [by P. Massinger].
Dyce MS. 39. 1624.

The play, as preserved, occupies nineteen leaves (the last page having been originally left blank), but two most likely have been lost at the beginning. Those that remain constitute nine separate sheets, with an odd leaf at the end. The foot of each leaf has suffered decay through damp, but the measurement can be determined as about $12 \times 7\frac{7}{8}$ inches.

Begins, fol. 1[a], imperfectly, probably in the fourth scene of the first act.

Ends on fol. 19[a]: 'finis'. Below this a strip has been cut out of the leaf: it probably contained Herbert's licence of 3 Nov. 1624, which is given from his office book as: 'For the Cockpit Company; A new Play, called, The Parliament of Love: Written by Massinger'. The Cockpit seems to have been occupied by the Lady Elizabeth's men.

Fol. 19[b]: 'The Parliam[t] of Loue', added apparently in the hand of a reviser. The rest of the page is blank.

Written in the same hand and in the same manner as *The Welsh Embassador*, while the close similarity of the injury to the two manuscripts (though more extensive in the present case) suggests that they once lay together in a damp receptacle. The lower portion of fol. 8[b] (at the end of what was probably the fifth sheet, and near the beginning of III. iii) was accidentally left blank, and subsequently filled with cross hatching to show that there was no gap in the text. In the last two acts there are a number of cuts and alterations in another hand, evidently made from a literary or dramatic point of view. The reviser was careful to preserve the grammar but paid little regard to the verse, which perhaps suggests that he was not the author, as does one passage in which he possibly misunderstood the original (fol. 16[d]). It is certainly not Massinger's hand. There is no evidence of censorship, for the toning down of the heroine's phrase 'to whore mee' can hardly be regarded as such (fol. 17[b]). Except for the presumption of the licence

there is nothing to connect this manuscript with the playhouse.

There is a regular division into acts, a finis appearing at the end of each (except the last) and the number of the next being entered in the left margin.

Though there is no formal division into scenes, the entrances constituting them are written across the page (that is centred, but beginning on the left), while no other directions are so treated except one particularly elaborate one (presumably involving a discovery) on fol. $15^a$. Other entrances are regularly marked in the left margin (one only being repeated on the right). Exits, as usual, appear on the right. Independent directions, which are few, appear in either margin indifferently. In general all directions in the left margin are between rules, exceptions being apparently fortuitous. There are no warning directions such as are found in *The Welsh Embassador*. The following list is exhaustive for all beyond bare entrances and exits.

$1^b$ 'Ent' Beaupre' (left) opposite 'Ent' Beaupre like a More' (right). 'Exeunt' [I. v] 'Enter Charles, Orleans, Philamore, and Lafort' (centre).

$2^b$ 'Exeunts' and '⟨finis Actus⟩ Primi' (centre) at foot.

$3^a$ 'Act' $2^{dus}$: ' opposite 'Enter Clarindore, montross, Perigot, & Novall'.

$3^b$ [II. ii] 'Enter Leonora, & a Seruant'. 'Ent' Clerimond'.

$5^a$ [II. iii] 'Enter Clarindore and Beaupre'. 'Ent' Bellisant'. 'Exit Beaupre'.

$6^a$ 'Ent' Seruants'. 'Act' $3^{us}$' opposite 'finis Actus Secundi | Enter Chamont, Perigot, Nouall, Dinant, Lamira & Clarinda'.

$6^b$ 'Exeunt, manet Nouall & Perigot'.

$9^a$ [in III. iii] 'Knock' (left).

$9^b$ 'offers to kill him self' (right).

$10^a$ 'Act' $4^{tus.}$' opposite 'finis Actus Tertij | Enter Nouall and Dinant'.

$11^b$ [in IV. ii] 'they draw' (right, between rules).

$12^a$ 'fight Cleremond vnder montross' (right).

$13^a$ [in IV. v] 'w$^t$h in Nouall' (speaker's prefix) (3 ll.) 'Enter Nouall'.

$14^a$ 'w$^t$h in Perigott' (speaker's prefix) (2 ll.) 'Enter Seruants w$^t$h Perigot'.

$14^b$ 'Act' $5^{tus}$' opposite 'finis Actus Quarti | Enter Chamont, Philamor, & Lafort'.

15ª 'Enter Charles: the Lords ioyne w^t^h the troopes · A preist w^t^h the Image of Cupid A barr sett forth: then enter Cleremond, Clarindore, Bellisant Leonora, Beaupre Perigot, Nouall, & officer montross on a beere before the barr' (centre).

Printed: W. Gifford, *Massinger* (ii. 233–322), 1805, and reprints; K. M. Lea (Malone Society), 1928 (1929).

11. [*The Captives*, by T. Heywood.]
B.M., MS. Egerton 1994³. 1624.

The play (see Plate 7), which bears no title in the manuscript, occupies fols 52–73 of the collection. The twenty-two leaves (of which the last page is blank) form eleven numbered sheets (most of the numbers being still legible in the outer top corner). The leaves measure up to 12×8 inches.

Begins, fol. 52ª: 'Actus primus. Scen⟨a⟩ pr. | Enter M^r^ Raphael a younge Marchaunt M^r^ Treadway his companion and ffrend. Etc''.

Ends on fol. 73ª: 'Finis' (verso blank).

The manuscript, autograph by Thomas Heywood, is written rather closely in an exceedingly rough literary hand of a generally English type, with occasional directions in equally rough Italian script. There is a normal use of rather short speech-rules, and the leaves were probably folded for margins. It has been prepared throughout for playhouse use by another rough hand: possibly more than one appears. Among other notes occur the names of several actors, namely Taylor, Gibson, Jack (unless this is Gibson's first name, which is unlikely), and a Stage[-keeper]. None can be traced outside prompt-books. The badness of the original hand and the roughness of the reviser's notes suggest that the manuscript may not have been itself intended for a prompt copy, but that it was meant to be transcribed for that purpose. If so, it was presumably the transcript that was licensed by Herbert, according to an entry quoted from his office book, on 3 Sept. 1624: 'For the Cockpit Company; A new Play, called, The Captive, or The Lost recovered: Written by Hayward'. The present manuscript at least bears no licence and shows no sign

of censorship. The Cockpit was apparently occupied by the Lady Elizabeth's men.

There is an original division throughout into acts and scenes, duly numbered, which has not been interfered with. Each act except the last has an explicit.

Original entrance directions, as well as scene headings and the explicits of acts, are centred and usually underlined (the reviser sometimes adding a second rule above). Exits are, as usual, marked on the right, and so in general are the rather scanty independent directions. The reviser's directions, which appear indifferently in either margin and are usually either underlined or between rules, are of peculiar interest in relation to the scene divisions. At the end of a scene he often adds the word 'clere' to indicate that the stage is left empty; and equally in other scenes, in which the locality remains unchanged and the action is really continuous, but in the course of which the stage is repeatedly left empty for a moment, he adds the same warning. Elsewhere he several times adds 'to them' or an equivalent to a direction, to indicate that the entry is not upon an empty stage. Further he often draws attention to an entrance by placing a large star in the left margin (not always noted below after the first act), and in the direction marks off the several characters by upright bars (not noted here: cf. *Believe as you List*). The following list is fairly exhaustive.

$52^{a}$ 'Enter the clowne' to which a star and guide rule are added (left).

$52^{b}$ 'Enter the clowne wth Mildewe, and Sarleboys his guest and, ffrende' with star.

$54^{a}$ *'cleare' added after 'Exnt' before 'Actus 1 scena $2^{a}$. | Enter An abbot wth his Covent off ffryars, amongst them Fryar Ihon, and ffryar Ritchard' to which are added *'Chaire' (left) and *'Iack: Gibsen' (right) presumably the actor or actors to set the chair.

$54^{b}$ *'⟨m⟩anet' prefixed to speaker's name 'ff Ihon' and rule added above his speech.

$55^{a}$ *'cleare' (right) and star (left) before 'Actus $pr^{s}$: scen: $3^{a}$. | Enter After a greate Tempestuous storme $m^{r}$. Ashburne, an Englishe Marchant, and his man godffrey' to which added *'Thunder' (left) and *'Ashb: godfry' above. *'Thund:' (left). 'Enter Raphael Treadwaye and the clowne' with star.

56[a] *'Act: 2 Storme continewed' opposite 'Explicit Actus pr[s]:' 'Actus 2[s]. scena pr[a] | Enter palestra, all well [for 'wett'] as newly shipwracke and escapt the fury off the Seas'. *'Ent: scribonia' (left, with star) anticipating entrance over leaf, the intervening 25 lines marked for omission.

57[a] 'They go in'. 'Enter *ffryar Ihon*' and *'Fryer Iohn' substituted, with star. *'Ent: Fryer Richard' (right) with star (left). 'Enter the Abbot wth other fryars' with star (left) and *'Fryers' (right).

57[b] *'Bell Rung' (right) two lines before, and 'Lo: Lad: Dennis' with star (left) opposite, 'The bell ringes to mattens. enter the Lord de Averne and his Lady Etc' Dennis and others' (last three words added). '*Musicke and* vayles' (left) opposite 'The quire and Musick: the ffryars make a Lane wth ducks and obeysance' (right). *'Manet Iohn' added to 'Exnt'.

58[a] *'Tempest' (left) and *'Thunder' (right) opposite 'Actus 2[s]: scena 2[a] | Enter, 2 ffishermen'. *'Ex: fish.' (right).

58[b] 'Enter scribonia wth an empty pale' to which added *'to y[e] Clow'. 'Knocke'. *'Ent: Godfr:' above 'Enter Godfr' (left in place of speaker's name, 'fr' and rules added by reviser).

59[a] *'Exit' (right) sc. Godfrey? and *'Ent: Myldew & Sarlaboys to her' (left with guide rule) anticipating next scene (27 of the intervening 35 lines being marked for omission) and making the two continuous (but this is apparently an error). '*Enter godfrey wth water*'. 'Actus 2s scena 3[a]. | Enter the Bawde Mildewe and sarlaboyse'.

59[b] two stars opposite 'Enter godffrey' the direction being rather obscure.

60[a] *'clere' added to 'Exeunt' before *'Act: 3' opposite 'Explicit Actus 2s. | Actus 3[s]. scena pr[a.] | Enter The Lady de Averne wth a letter in her hand readinge, and wth her, mayde *weepinge* [?]'.

60[b] *'Ent L D'Auerne Dennis. to h' (left) opposite 'Enter the Lord de Averne, wth som ffollowers: his mã Denis' and *'Lo: Den: followerę' (right). 'Ink: paper ready' for next page some 20 lines later.

61[a] 'Enter Dennis' to which added *'w[th] pen Inke & paper'. 'Wrytes' (right). *'Exeunt clere' before 'Actus 3[s] scena 2[a]' to which added *'noise w[th]in Clo: Ash: godf' anticipating direction over leaf.

61[b] 'Enter after a great noyse wth in: The Clowne meetinge wth Ashburne and God-ffrey'. *'Fellowes ready palestra: Scribonia. w[th] Godfry. mildew. Sarly:' (left) anticipating entrance by some 30 lines, of which 19 are for omission. 'Musick' (left). *'Gib: Stage: Taylo[r]' (left) actors for Country Fellows some three lines (for omission) before 'A tumult wth in and suddein noyse enter att one doore godffrey wth

Coontry Fellowes ffor theire reskewe at the other Mildew sarlaboys. palestra scribonia' to which added *'⟨Gi⟩bs: Cont: fellowes' (left).

$62^{a}$ *'Raph: Tred: Clow' (right) five lines from foot, and *'Raph: Tred: Clow: to them' (left) at foot, anticipating entrance over leaf, the intervening lines marked for omission.

$62^{b}$ 'Enter M$^{r}$ Raphael M$^{r}$ Treadway and the clowne'.

$63^{a}$ *'Exeunt / clere' before 'Actus 3$^{s}$ scena 3$^{a}$. | Enter The Lord de averne, his lady [*'Dennis' interlined] and the waytinge mayde'.

$63^{b}$ 'Enter the ffryar wth a letter' to which added *'Iohn to them' (right). *'Fry: strangled' (left).

$64^{a}$ *'clere' (right) before *'Act 4' opposite 'Explicit Actus 3s.' 'Actus 4$^{s}$ scena pr$^{a}$. | Enter The Clowne'.

$65^{a}$ *'Noise' (left) opposite 'Noyse w$^{t}$hin' three lines before *'Noise within' immediately above 'Enter after a noyse or tumult: Ashburne, his wyffe. palestra scribonia and godffrey'.

$65^{b}$ *'Ex$^{t}$ ma: Ashb:' (right) but the Clown also remains.

$67^{b}$ *'clere' (left), the rest of the scene, over 30 lines, being meant for omission. 'Actus 4$^{s}$. scena 3$^{a}$. | Enter Dennis wth the ffryar [*'from aboue' interlined] vpon his backe'.

$68^{a}$ *'Fry: Io: post' (left, 'post' replacing *'Arras'). 'Eather strykes him wth a staffe or Casts a stone' (left). *'carry him vp' (left) opposite 'Exit' with *'clere' (right). 'Enter the knight. halff vnredy, his Lady after him' to which added *'Dennis' who is called for here though he first speaks some 25 lines lower, where *'w$^{th}$in' is added before his name.

$68^{b}$ *'Fryer sett vp & left' (left) opposite 'Exit' with *'clere'. 'Enter L. D'averne' to which added *'to dennis'. *'Exeunt / clere w$^{th}$ y$^{e}$ Fryer'.

$69^{a}$ *'w$^{th}$in Baker' (left) and *'Bak: w$^{th}$in' (right) opposite his first speech. 'Explicit Actus 4$^{s}$: | Actus 5s: scena pr$^{a}$: | Enter Thomas Ashburne the yonger brother to Ihon A Merchant wth one off his factors' to which added *'fact: Gibson' (right).

$69^{b}$ *'Trample' anticipating direction on next page some 17 lines below. *'clere Exeunt' before 'Actus 5s. scena 2$^{a}$'.

$70^{a}$ [Plate 7] *'Ent: Rich: Baker' (right). *'Trampling noise' opposite 'A Noyse wthin Trampling off Horses'. *'clere' (right) before entrance. 'Noyse'. 'Enter the baker rooninge' to which added *'to em'. 'Noyse wthin'. *'w$^{th}$in' added to speaker's name 'ff Rich' and repeated right. *'clere' (left and right) before 'Enter The Abbott the baker ffryar Richard prisoner and guarded Etc'' to which added *'stagekeepers as a guard'.

70[b] *'clere (left and right) before 'Actus 5s. scena 3ª. et vltima'. *'*Barre ready*' (right). 'Enter gripus the ffisherman' to which added *'to him'. *'godfry' (left) above 'Enter godffrey' (centre) to which added *'to them'.

71[a] 'Enter . . . gripus' to which added *'to 'em'.

71[b] *'to them' (left) opposite 'Enter at one doore . . . at the other . . . & the clowne aloofe'.

72[a] 'Enter godffrye in hast'.

72[b] 'Enter the L de Averne and his man Dennis'.

73[a] 'Enter the Lady Averne and her Maid Millesant'.

Printed: A. H. Bullen, *Old Plays* (iv. 99–217), 1885; A. C. Judson, 1921; E. C. Dunn (Malone Society), in preparation.

12. *The Honest Man's Fortune.*

Dyce MS. 9. Licensed 8 Feb. 1624/5.

The play is written on thirty-four numbered leaves, forming seventeen separate sheets, and preceded by a fly-leaf: the numbers 4–32 remain. In the first nine sheets the leaves measure up to $12\frac{1}{8}\times7\frac{1}{2}$ inches, in the last eight $12\frac{1}{4}\times7\frac{3}{4}$. There is some decay at the bottom edge, but only near the end is the text damaged.

Fly-leaf: 'The Honest mans fortune | Plaide | In the yeare 1613' (verso blank).

Begins, fol. 1[a]: 'Actus : 1: Scæna : 1: | Enter orleans: And Amiens At Seuerall doores'.

Ends on fol. 34[b]: 'Exeunt | ffinis', below which is a smudged scribble in a large hand 'Ihon', and below again Herbert's autograph licence: 'This Play, being an olde One and thir Originall Lost was reallowd by mee, this: 8. febru. 1624 Att the Intreaty of Mr ⟨Taylor⟩'. The last word has been supplied in the margin by a modern hand, the original being mutilated. The corresponding entry in the office-book is quoted as: 'For the king's company. An olde play called The Honest Mans Fortune, the originall being lost, was re-allowed by mee at Mr. Taylor's intreaty, and on condition to give mee a booke [The Arcadia], this 8 Februa. 1624'. (The significance of the bracketed words, which are omitted by one authority, is not clear.)

[illegible] (left and right) before 'Actus 3a. scena 1a.' [illegible] Lady' (right). [illegible] 'Enter' [illegible] to which added 'to [illegible]' [illegible] above 'Enter' [illegible] (centre) to which added 'to them'.

[illegible] which added 'to them'.

7 [illegible] (left) opposite 'Enter at one doore, [illegible] at the other [illegible] the doores aloofe'.

[illegible] in haste'.

[illegible] Enter the [illegible] and [illegible]

[illegible] Enter [illegible] and [illegible]

Printed [illegible] *Plays* [illegible] in preparation.

## 12. *The Honest Man's Fortune*

Dyce MS. 9. [illegible] Licensed 8 Feb. 1624/5.

The play is written on thirty-four [illegible] leaves, forming [illegible] separate sheets, and preceded by a fly-leaf [illegible] [illegible] first [illegible] leaves [illegible] bottom [illegible]

[illegible] *The Honest mans fortune* [illegible] the [illegible]

[illegible]

Written throughout in the hand of a playhouse scribe, who also wrote the manuscript of *Bonduca* and revised that of *Believe as you List*. It has been thought that the name 'Ihon' scribbled at the end is intended for a signature. This seems to me very unlikely (it is by no means certain that the hand is the same) but since it provides a convenient label for a very important scribe I propose to refer to him as 'Jhon'. The hand is clear and well formed, though more current than in the other examples: the script is English with incidental Italian. Stage-directions are usually in a bolder form of the Italian. The writing grows somewhat closer as the play proceeds, the number of lines to the page rising from just over forty to a little under fifty. There is a normal use of speech-rules, which are of moderate length but begin farther to the left than usual; and the leaves have been folded for margins. The names of three actors appear, having been added to the directions by the scribe himself subsequent to the original writing. They are G. Ver[non], J. Rho[des], and a G. Rick[ . . .?]. The first two are known from a document of 1624 as being with the King's company, and no doubt acted in the revival rather than the original performance. Many passages are marked for omission, probably by the original scribe, since in some cases he has altered the directions to correspond. In one of these cases, however, another hand inserted a connecting link (fol. 20[b]). Again on fol. 25[b] this hand possibly added a one-line speech in the margin, but failed to adjust the text satisfactorily to the alteration. (This speech is found in the printed text: see below.) There are probably one or two other shorter alterations by the same hand.

Besides the passages marked for omission evidently on theatrical grounds there are several others that have been deleted or altered as offensive, presumably by the censor or at his direction. On fol. 9[b] a dozen lines relating to male-stews have been elaborately scored out, and on fol. 10[b] a fairly innocent jibe at courtiers; on fol. 23[a] 'gallantę' instead of 'ffrench lordę' are censured for familiarity with their pages. In each case the printed text preserves the original reading. On the other hand, there are several similar cuts in the printed text, and this also has many blanks left for oaths and the like which are retained in the manuscript though perhaps not always in their original strength. There seem to be only one of two expressions of this sort actually cancelled in the manuscript. However, on fol. 19[b] a line or so has been elaborately deleted: it does not correspond to anything in the print, and though not decipherable, does not seem to be a scribal error.

The play was printed in the Beaumont and Fletcher folio of 1647. The two texts frequently correct one another, neither being markedly superior, though the print is much more carefully (but by no means always correctly) punctuated. Both are marked by accidental omissions besides the castrations already mentioned. Their relation is, however, very close, and there are frequent common errors, particularly of line-division. The stage-directions differ as a rule more than the text. The printed version contains an unimportant scene between lackeys just before the banquet (in v. iii, fol. 31[b]) that is not in the manuscript. Also the manuscript gives a different ending (from near the foot of fol. 34[a] down to the last speech but one) in place of the rather unseemly jesting of the folio. Although it appears from Herbert's licence that the 'Originall', that is the copy previously authorized by Buc, was then lost, the present manuscript does not give the impression of having been prepared from 'foul papers' like that of *Bonduca*. More probably some sort of stage version came into the hands of the King's men from Lady Elizabeth's company, who seem to have originally produced the play. Such a manuscript may have been too worn or untidy to submit to Herbert, but it would seem to have underlain both the extant manuscript and the folio text.

The division is into acts only, though in each case there is mention of the first scene. In this the folio agrees. The headings are centred.

The stage-directions, in addition to entrances and exits, though fairly frequent are not very elaborate except in a few cases. The principal entrances, including nearly all those for fresh scenes, are centred between rules. Other entrances are usually in the left margin (only twice on the right) also between rules. These are all, so far as space allows, written in larger

and heavier script. One long descriptive direction is centred between rules, and one is in the left margin: these are not in heavy script. Exits and minor directions are on the right in ordinary script and without rules, but sometimes preceded by a dash or a brace. The following list is exhaustive for directions other than bare entrances and exits. In some instances directions from the folio have been added in brackets for comparison.

1[b] 'Ent: Montaigue: Dubois: Longauile. Viramor·' (centre) [F° 'Enter Montague having a Purse, Duboys, Longueville, and Voramer [*sic*] the Page with two Caskets'].

2[a] 'Ent: 2: lawiers: &: 2: Creditors' (left).

5[a] 'Ent: y[e] Creditors' with later addition 'G: Ver: I: Rho:'.

6[b] [II. ii] 'Ent: Orleans: A Seruant: his ladye following' with 'G: Rick:' interlined before 'A Seruant'.

7[b] 'drawes' (right, twice). 'Exit Amiens' (right) [F° 'Enter [*sic*] Amiens in amazement, the servants following him' (centre)]. 'Ent: 2: seruante | G: Rick:' (left) the name was probably written at the same time [F° 'Enter servant' (right)].

8[a] [I. iii] 'Ent: Amiens: At one doore: Montaigue: and Veramour. At Another' [F° 'Enter Amiens drawne, Montague, Vercamor [*sic*] meeting'] and immediately afterwards 'they drawe' (right) [not in F°]. 'Ent: the ladye orleans' (right) [F° 'Enter Lady'].

9[a] 'Exeunt | Actus: Secundj: Scæna: pri: | Ent: Longauile: And Dubois'.

10[a] 'Exe' [II. ii] Ent: Lauerduer: And Captaine Lapoop'.

12[a] 'W[th]in: Clashing of weapons: Some crying downe w[th] theire weapons: then Enter Longauile: Dubois: their swords drawne: 3: or: 4 Drawers betwene em:' (centre: 'Drawers' interlined above 'Seruants' deleted) [F° 'Whithin [*sic*] a clamor, down with their weapons. Enter Longavile and Dubois, their swords drawn, servants and others between them'].

12[b] 'Ent: Amiens: w[th] Sword drawne' [F° 'Enter Amience in hast, his sword drawne'].

13[b] [II. iii] 'Ent: Longauile: Amience following him' [F° 'Enter Longaville, Amiens following him'].

14[a] 'Exeunt' [II. iv] 'Ent: Dubois' (left, at foot, text beginning over leaf).

14[b] 'Ent: Lauerdure: & Lapoope: w[th] disguises' [F° 'Enter Laverdine and Lapoope, with disguises']. 'Exeunt' (i.e. withdraw) and 'Ent: Montague: 3: officers: 3: Creditors' (centre) [F° 'Enter Montague in the hands of three Officers, and three Creditors'].

15ª 'Ent: Malycorne' deleted and repeated two lines lower [where it appears in F°].

15ᵇ 'Ent: Dubois Lapoop: Lauerdure' (i.e. come forward).

16ª 'Dubois Runs vpon Montague. and struglinge yeilds him his sword: the officers drawe: Lauerdure. and Lapoope: retires: Montague chaseth em About the Stage: himself wounded:' (centre, not heavy script) [F° '. . . Laverdine and La-poope in the scuffling retire, Montague chaseth them off the Stage, . . .'] and immediately afterwards 'they fight' (right, 'they' inserted) duplicating former action [not in F°]. '*Exit* Exeunt | Actus: 3: Scæna: 1: | Ent: Maddam Lamira: Ladye Orleance: And Viramour the page'.

17ᵇ 'Ent: Charlot: Wᵗʰ A letter'.

18ª 'Exe: Lamyra · et Charlote'. 'Ent: Montaigue' anticipating by six lines (marked for omission) '*A Songe* At the Ende of it: Ent: Montague : fainting : his sword drawne' [F° 'Musick a Song, . . .].

19ª [III. ii] 'Ent: Amience: Longauile: hauing A paper in's hand' [F° 'Enter Amiens and Longeville with a Paper'].

19ᵇ 'Ent: Orlean:' [not in F°, which also omits the prefix to his speech].

20ª 'drawe both' (right).

20ᵇ 'Ent: Montaigue: Lamira: Lady orleance Charlot: Page' anticipating by nearly a page (marked for omission)—

21ª 'Ent: Montague: bare: Lamyra: Lady orleance: Charlot: Viram:' [F° 'Enter Mountague bare-headed, Lamira, Lady Orleance, Charlo, [*sic*] Veramour, salute'].

21ᵇ 'Lamyra showes hir selfe at the Arras' (left) [not in F°].

22ª 'Ent: Lamyra: from the Aras' (left) [F° 'Exit [*sic*] Lamira from the Arras' (right)].

22ᵇ 'Ent: Viramoor' deleted and repeated a line higher [not in F°].

23ª 'Actus Quartij [*sic*]: Scæna: prj | Enter Montaigue: in meane habit' [F° '. . . alone, in . . .'].

23ᵇ 'Ent: Viramour' [F° 'Enter Veramour with Counters' required for gold coines].

25ᵇ 'Enter: Lamira: . . . Charlot: Viramour' (centre).

26ᵇ [IV. ii] 'Ent: Dubois: orleance: Longauile: Amience: · 2 · Lacqueyes: A Page wᵗʰ · 2 · Pistolls'.

27ª 'Wᵗʰin: cry: oh Stay their swords: Stay their swords' (left, without rules and not in heavy script) [F° 'A noise within, crying down with their Swords']. 'Ent: Ladye orleance: . . . 2· lacqueys: pag⟨e⟩' (centre).

29ª 'Actus Quintj: Scæna prj | Enter: Montaigue: and Charlote'.

30ª [V. ii] 'Ent: lauerdure: lapoope: and Maly-corne'.

31[a] Direction (left) damaged and illegible opposite 'Exeunt' followed by rule, apparently anticipating—

31[b] [v. iii] 'A Banquet: Set out: then Enter: orleance: & his Ladye: Arme in Arme: Amience: Lamira: Charlott drest as A Bride: Montaigue: veie [*sic*] braue, Longauile: Dubois: Lauerdure: Malycorne: Lapoop: & Attendantę' [F° 'Enter foure serving in a Banquet' followed by a scene not in the manuscript, then 'Enter Orleance, ... Charlote, like a Bride, Montague brave, ... La-Poope'].

34[a] 'Ent: Lauerdure: & Viram: as A woeman' (right).

The manuscript was used by Dyce in his edition of the play (*Beaumont and Fletcher*, 1843, iii. 329–452) and his notes supply a fairly complete record of its readings so far at least as important differences are concerned. But his text is of course modernized. In A. R. Waller's edition (*Beaumont and Fletcher*, 1912, x. 375 ff.) the manuscript is wholly ignored.

13. *Believe as you List*, by P. Massinger.

B.M., MS. Egerton 2828. Licensed 6 May 1631.

The play (see Plate 8) is written on twenty-four leaves (fols. 4–27), forming twelve numbered sheets (most of the numbers remain in the top inner corner), and followed by a single unnumbered sheet (fols. 28–9) containing the prologue, epilogue, &c. The whole was enclosed in a vellum wrapper formed of a sixteenth-century indenture, now bound in at the beginning (fols. 2–3), into which the sheets were stabbed and sewn. Of the second leaf (fol. 5) only a narrow strip now remains, and a few lines elsewhere are damaged through the decay of the edges. The leaves measure $12\frac{1}{2} \times 7\frac{3}{4}$ inches.

Fol. 2[a]: 'A new playe Call'd: Beleeue as you List: Written By m[r] Mæssenger May 6[th] 1631 A Tragedy' (the last two words, which are very faint, are probably a modern addition).

Begins, fol. 4[a]: 'Actus primi, Scæna p⟨ri⟩ma | Antiochus stoicꝫ in philosophers habits. . . .'.

Ends on fol. 27[b]: 'The Ende' followed by the censor's autograph licence: 'This Play, called Beleiue as you liste, may bee acted. this 6. of May. 1631. Henry Herbert.'

Fol. 28[b]: '⟨Prolo⟩gue' 22 lines (recto blank).

Fol. 29[a]: 'Epilogue' 14 lines.

Fol. 29[b]: certain notes of properties required (see below).

Written throughout, so far as the text is concerned, in the autograph of Philip Massinger. This is a hand of mixed character which makes no attempt at differentiating scripts. There is a normal use of rather short speech-rules, and the leaves have been folded for margins. The manuscript is a careful fair copy, considerably revised from an earlier draft or version, of which, however, some traces were inadvertently allowed to remain. The play was revised for production by the playhouse scribe 'Jhon' (see *The Honest Man's Fortune*), who removed the relics of the original version, made a few editorial emendations, and very thoroughly worked over the stage-directions with a view to adapting them to the requirements of the prompter. His most extensive interference with the author's manuscript was at the foot of fol. 20$^{a}$, where he inserted a direction for music and transferred a whole speech from the top of the next page, so that the prompter should be able to turn the leaf at his leisure during the progress of the song that followed. He also made certain adjustments in the minor parts, clearing up a confusion of the author's, and further adapting them to the exigencies of the cast. In the course of his revision he introduced the names of seventeen actors, several of whom are otherwise known to have been members of the King's company at the time. Lastly he appended the Prologue and Epilogue. These are written on the two inner pages of a sheet of different paper, which was evidently added to the manuscript after it had been submitted for licence. On the fourth page of this sheet he also inscribed the following memoranda of properties needed in the course of the play:

⟨Act: 1: A⟩ writing out of the booke w$^{th}$ a small peece of Siluer for M$^{r}$ Swantton:
·3· notes for m$^{r}$ pollard:
Act: 2: A writing for M$^{r}$ Taylor:
Act: 3: A letter. for M$^{r}$ Robinson
·2· letters for M$^{r}$ Lowin:
Act: 5: A letter for M$^{r}$ Benfeild/

The 'writing out of the booke' suggests that the words to be read (fol. 6$^{a}$) were actually copied out of the prompt book on to

the property letter, though they do not amount to five lines all told (cf. p. 234). The other letters were apparently dummies, and were not read at all.

The original version of the play had been submitted to the censor, who refused licence on political grounds on 11 Jan. 1631. After being rewritten by Massinger and revised by 'Jhon', the play was again submitted, and this time received licence on 6 May (or 7 May, according to Herbert's office book) for the King's company. So thorough had been the revision that the censor apparently found only one passage to which exception could be taken, and as this was on the now mutilated fol. 5, the nature of his alteration eludes us. Otherwise the only possible trace of censorship is the deletion of some lines on fol. 15ª touching the purposes of the deity (under the name of Jove), and these appear to have been struck out by Massinger himself with a view of forestalling criticism, though after the stage reviser had done his work.

The play was carefully divided by Massinger into both acts and scenes, according to the normal Elizabethan method. The headings are all centred except that to III. i, which was apparently omitted at the time of writing and subsequently added in the left margin. Those in Act I the reviser disregarded completely, all the rest he deleted (though the deletion was only partial in the case of III. i and IV. i). Having thus got rid of Massinger's headings, 'Jhon' showed no further interest in the scenes, but proceeded to reinstate the act division by emphatic notes in the margin. Moreover to his headings 'Act: 2:' and 'Act: 4:' he appended the word 'Long', which may be interpreted with some confidence as meaning a long interval. It appears, therefore, that the reviser's interest, so far as division went, was concentrated on the question of interval: scenes which were in fact continuous on the stage were for him continuous in action, while on the other hand he provided for the splitting up of the whole play by the introduction of two shorter and two longer pauses.

Massinger's methods with respect to stage-directions are of the simplest. Scene headings, and none but scene headings, are centred. All other entrances and exits, together with the rare independent directions, are entered in the right margin with few and possibly accidental exceptions. Whether this was done deliberately in order to leave the left margin free for the use of the prompter, or whether the reviser made such free and emphatic use of it just because the author's directions had been obscurely placed, there seems no means of determining. Massinger's directions are often surrounded, or partially surrounded, by rules: those of the reviser usually appear between heavy dashes.

The general principle upon which 'Jhon' worked is equally clear. Massinger's right-hand literary directions he replaced by left-hand directions of a more theatrical type and written in a bold, heavy Italian script that could not fail to catch the prompter's eye. Frequently in the case of minor characters he added the name of the actor who took the part. At times he deleted the original direction, at others he left it standing. And whereas Massinger usually marked the entrance of a character at the very point at which he first spoke or was addressed, the reviser habitually marked it a few lines earlier (indicating the exact point by a heavy dash) at the point at which the actor would have to enter at the back of the stage in order to come into the conversation at the desired moment. He further entered a number of warnings for actors or properties to be in readiness, though these are of an exceptional nature and not general. Lastly he supplied certain necessary directions for properties and stage noises with which the author had not concerned himself. It should be added that 'Jhon' occasionally made use of the right margin, though always in conjunction with the left, and that in some instances he made elaborate additions to the author's central directions, at times introducing upright bars between the names of the characters (after the manner of the reviser of *The Captives*).

The thorough revision to which the author's directions in this play have been submitted by the stage reviser makes the manuscript the most important document we possess for the study of the methods of contemporary prompting, and therefore for the critical analysis of the printed texts of the period. It is consequently desirable to give a fairly comprehensive

record both of original and additional directions, and the list appended below is substantially exhaustive for all but bare exits. At the same time it should be remarked that the work of the reviser is so elaborate as to make it difficult at times to appreciate its full significance apart from the text.

4$^a$ 'Actus primi, Scæna p⟨ri⟩ma | Antiochus · stoicqȝ · in philosophers habits. Chrysalus · [*'w$^{th}$ a writing ⟨&⟩ pen⟨y⟩' interlined] Syrus · Geta · bondeme⟨n⟩' but Chrysalus, &c., do not enter till at least 130 lines later (fol. 5$^a$). The points between the names were replaced by bars by the reviser.

5$^b$ 'exit stoicqȝ' (right).

6$^a$ 'reads' (left, twice). *'Ent: Berecinthius: w$^{th}$ ·3· papers: & ·3· Marchantȩ' (left) opposite 'Actus primi, scæna secunda. Berecinthvs a flamen. 3 Asian marchants'.

6$^b$ *'Ent: fflaminius: Calistus: Dimetr:' (left) seven lines above '*Enter Titus flaminivs · Calistus · Demetrius · 2 freedmen*' (right).

7$^b$ 'ex flaminivs cum suis'.

8$^a$ *'Ent: Antiochus' (left) three lines above '*enter Antiochus*' (right).

8$^b$ *'Act: 2: Long | Ent:—' opposite '*Actus secundi, scæna prima*. flaminius. & Calistus' to which is added *'R: Bax'. *'Ent: Demetrius W$^m$ Pattrick' one line above '*enter Demetrivs*'.

9$^a$ *'Ent: chrisalus Geta: Syrus: Demetrius:' opposite '*Enter* [*'*Demetrius*' interlined replacing '*Calistus*'] *Chrisalus. Geta Syrus*'. *'Table ready: & ·6· chaires to sett out' for II. ii, about 75 lines later. *'M$^r$ Hobs: calld vp' for entry in II. ii, about 170 lines later.

10$^a$ *'Ent:' prefixed to '*Actus secundi, scæna secunda* Amilcar · Hanno · Asdrubal · Carthalo [*'Rowland: w$^m$ Mago: Nick' replacing '*officers*']'.

10$^b$ *'Ent: fflaminius m$^r$ Hobs: & Rowland' (left) opposite *'Ent: fflaminius: m$^r$ Hobs: Rowland: ffan [*sic*] Balls' (right) replacing '*Enter flaminivs*'.

11$^a$ *'w$^{th}$in:' prefixed to speaker's name 'officer'. *'Ent: ['Antiochus:' speaker's name] Berecinthius: ·3· Marchantȩ: Garde' opposite *'Ent—' prefixed to 'Enter *officers* · Antiochus (Habited like a kinge) Berecinthius · the three marchants' and *'Garde' added.

12$^a$ *'the great booke: of Accomptȩ ready' for production about 135 lines later.

12$^b$ 'Exevnt officers with Berecinthivs'.

13$^a$ *'Ent: Rowland: w$^{th}$ the booke of records' three lines above 'the recordes brought in' (left) and repeated in larger script *'Ent: Rowland w$^{th}$ the Records' (right).

$13^{b}$ 'exevnt Carthaginians'. 'exevnt the ende of $y^{e}$ seconde Act' (right) 'Act $3^{d}$. | Scæne first' (left) 'Ent: flaminivs. Calistus. Demetrivs' (centre) the act heading an afterthought: the reviser added *'Act: 3:—' and 'Ent:—' (the latter written over 'Act $3^{d}$.' with the dash deleting the original 'Ent:') on the left, interlined *'$w^{th}$ ·2· letters' after 'flaminivs', and wrote *'$M^{r}$ Hobs: & Rowland' over the other two names.

$14^{a}$ *'Ent: Lentulus: $m^{r}$ Rob: $w^{th}$ a letter' two lines before 'Enter Lentulus'. *'Ent: Titus: R. Baxt:' opposite '*Enter Titus*'.

$14^{b}$ *'Ent: Antiochus & ·3· Marchant$^{e}$' before '*Actus tertij, scæna secunda. Antiochus. the ·3· marchants*'.

$15^{a}$ *'fflorish' three lines above '*flourishe*' (left). *'Ent: Berecinthi' two lines before '*Enter Berecinthivs*'. *'fflorish' deleted and repeated a line higher, opposite *'Ent: Prusius: Queen Philoxenes [*sic*]: Rowl: $w^{m}$ Mago $m^{r}$ Balls: Nick: & Lady' (right) two lines above '*Enter Prusias. Queene. Philoxenus. attendants*'.

$15^{b}$ *'fflorish' written over 'flourishe' opposite 'exevnt. Prusias. Antiochus Queene. Philoxenus attendants'. *'Ent: fflaminius & R: Baxter' three lines before '*Enter flaminivs & Demetrivs*' followed at once by 'exit Demetrivs' where the reviser has substituted *'Titus' for 'Demetrius' in the entrance but not in the exit.

$16^{a}$ *'Ent: fflaminius & Philoxenus' opposite '*Actus tertij scæna tertia. flaminivs. Philoxenus*'.

$16^{b}$ *'Ent: Prusius & Philoxenus:' two lines before '*Enter Prusias, & Philoxenus*'.

$17^{b}$ *'Ent: Antiochus: Queene: Philoxenes [*sic*]: Berecinth: 3: $March^{te}$: R: Baxt: & $Atten^{te}$' two lines before 'Enter Antiochus. Queene. Philoxenus. Berecinthivs the 3 marchants. Demetrius. attendants'.

$18^{a}$ *'Ent: Garde' (no original direction). 'they beare of the Queene'.

$18^{b}$ 'exevnt Prusias & Philoxenus'. 'exit Antiochus garded'. *'Ent: Garde'. 'the end of the thirde Acte' (right) 'Actus quarti, scæna prima. Æ metellus a procunsul of *Lusitania* Sempronivs a Centurion' also *'long Act: 4: | Ent: Metelus: & Sempronius: | 2 chaires set out' (left). *'Gascoine: & Hubert below: ready to open the Trap doore for $M^{r}$ Taylor' about 100 lines later.

$19^{a}$ *'Ent: fflaminius' two lines before '*Enter flaminivs*': the reviser first rewrote the name larger, then deleted and repeated the direction. *'Antiochus ready: vnder the stage' for his entry in IV. ii, about 55 lines later.

$19^{b}$ *'Ent: Iaylor: $w^{m}$ penn $w^{th}$ poniard & halter' opposite '*Actus quarti, scæna secunda. enter Iaylor. with a poniard & halter*' the last five words

295 'servant Cardoghianus' ... 'Exeunt' the ende of ye seconde Act ... Sceane past (?) ... at Samnyra, Calistus, Demetrius, ... [illegible] written like an exit though. The revisers deleted it 'Act ...' and ... letter written over 'Act 3' with the ... the original ... on the left, ... [illegible] ... and ... 'Mr Hobs & Rowland' over the other two names.

370 ... [illegible] ... before ... [illegible] ... opposite ... [illegible]

[illegible]

added. *'Antiochus below' written over same original direction, both serving at once as entrance and speaker's name. *'Ent: Metellus ffIaminius: & Sempronius (Aboue)' two lines after '*Enter Metellus. flaminivs. Sempronivs. aboue*' which was originally placed 25 lines later.

20$^{a}$ [Plate 8] *'Harry: Willson: & Boy ready for the song at y$^{e}$ Arras' about 55 lines later. *'Ent: Iaylor (w$^{th}$ bread & water)' two lines before 'Enter Iaylor. with browne bread, & a woodden dishe of water'. *'the Lute. strikes & then the Songe' (with speech transferred, see above) anticipating by three lines—

20$^{b}$ '*musicq; & a* songe'. *'Ent: Courtezan' written over 'Enter Courtezan' (left).

21$^{a}$ 'offers to kisse hym'. 'aside' (right).

21$^{b}$ *'Ent: Iaylor: & others Rowl:' seven lines before '*enter Iaylor with others*'. *'Ent: Berecinthius: & I: Hony: R: Baxt: & Gard' opposite '*Actus quarti Scæna tertia.* officers leadinge in Berecinthivs & the first marchant with halter'.

22$^{a}$ *'Ent: Metellus: & ffIaminius' (left, duplicated right) opposite '*Actus quarti, scæna quarta. Metellus. flaminius*'.

22$^{b}$ *'Enter: Sempronius' written over same original direction (left). *'w$^{th}$in: officer' over original speaker's prefix 'officer', and 'Ent: Antiochus: & Gard' opposite 'Enter officers leadinge in Antiochus. his head shaude in the habit of a slaue' (right).

23$^{a}$ '*Actus quinti, Scæna prima.* Marcellus (proconsul of Sicilie) 2. & 3 marchant' whereto the reviser prefixed on the left *'Act: 5:' and 'Ent:—' (before the deletion), interlined *'w$^{th}$ a letter' after 'Marcellus', added *'w$^{m}$ Pen: Curt:' after '2. & 3 marchant', and appended *'& Attend$^{te}$: Rowland: m$^{r}$ Bulls: Nick' below. *'All the swords ready' warning, near beginning of act, for their production in v. ii, about 340 lines later. '⟨th⟩e letter' gloss on text 'doe you knowe what this containes?'.

23$^{b}$ *'Ent: Cornelia: & a Moore Woman' two lines above '*Enter Cornelia. & a more waiting woman*' (left).

24$^{b}$ *'Ent: ffIaminius &: R: Baxt:' five lines before '*Enter flaminivs & Demetrivs*'.

25$^{a}$ *'Ent: Antiochus: Cap$^{t}$: (w$^{m}$ patt:) & Soldiers' opposite '*Actus quinti scæna vltima. Antiochus. Captaine. souldiers*'.

25$^{b}$ *'⟨E⟩nt: Marcellus: ffIaminius: Cornelia: Moore woman: R: Baxt: Rowl: & others' four lines before '*Enter Marcellus. flaminivs. Cornelia Moore woman & servants*'.

26$^{a}$ *'Ent: R: Baxt: w$^{th}$ Swords' two lines before 'enter servant with many swords'. *'Ent: Rowland w^th swords' opposite 'Enter another servant with more swordes'.

27^a *'Be ready: y^e · 2 · Marchant℮: w^m Pen: Curtis: & Garde' for entry nearly 40 lines later.

27^b 'enter the 2 marchants & a garde' (right, the left margin is torn away here). 'exevnt with flaminivs'. *'Ent: Garde (agen)' [the distinguishing of a re-entry is very rare]. *'fflorish' for final exit not marked.

Printed: T. C. Croker (Percy Society), 1849, and reprints; C. J. Sisson (Malone Society), 1927 (1928). Facsimile: J. S. Farmer, 1907.

14. *The Launching of the Mary*, by W. M[ountfort].
B.M., MS. Egerton 1994[15]. Licensed 27 June 1633.

The play occupies fols. 317–349 of the collection. There is also a slip, fol. 320*, which was originally pinned on to fol. 320^a, while fol. 333 is another slip originally pinned on to fol. 334^a. The thirty-two full leaves form sixteen separate sheets, of which two, fols. 342–345, are of a different paper and were inserted later in place of cancelled matter (perhaps occupying one sheet). The leaves measure up to fully $12\frac{1}{8} \times 8\frac{1}{8}$, but vary by as much as half an inch in different sheets. The last leaf has been bound in the wrong way round; it has been stabbed on both edges.

Fol. 317^a: 'Anno · 1632 ·' otherwise blank (verso blank).

Fol. 318^a: 'The lanchinge of the Mary · written by · W: M · gent. in his returne from East India. ão. 1632. | Or the seamans honest wyfe. | The actors. . . .'. This seems to have been written after the play was completed.

Fol. 318^b: 'Prologue' (14 ll.) 'exit'. Presumably also an addition.

Begins, fol. 319^a: 'Enter the Lo: Admirall surnamed Hobab · Capt: fitzIohn: naupegus wth an attendant or two' ('Iohn' has been substituted for 'Ioseph').

Ends on fol. 349^b (recto blank): 'exit. | ['finis' deleted] | ['Epilogue' deleted] · E · [12 ll.] exit. | Iamq; opus exegi &c'/' followed by the censor's autograph licence: 'This Play, called y^e Seamans Honest wife, all y^e Oaths left out In y^e action as they are crost In y^e booke & all other Reformations strictly

obserud, may bee acted not otherwyse. this. 27. Iune. 1633. Henry Herbert. | I commande your Bookeeper to present mee wth a fairer Copy hereafte⟨r⟩ and to leaue out all Oathes, prophaness & publick Ribaldry, as he will answer it at his perill. HHerbert'.

Written throughout in the autograph of Walter Mountfort, a servant of the East India Company. This is a current hand generally of an English type: there seems to be some attempt to use Italian script occasionally for proper names but it is neither consistent nor very distinctive. There are in general no speech-rules, but a few have been added later (e.g. on fols. 334–6). The paper has not been folded for margins, and these are rather narrow. There are extensive corrections and alterations by the author. Some of the additions are written on slips pinned on over the cancelled text, others in the margins. The most considerable change, however, is the insertion of fols. 342–345 (eight pages) after the play had been submitted to the censor and evidently to replace matter which he had condemned. A scene ends at the foot of fol. $341^{b}$, and the final speeches of Act IV are deleted at the head of fol. $346^{a}$, having been incorporated in the revision: also the last two lines of fol. $345^{b}$ are written in the margin, so as to conclude the scene on that page. There is some reason to suppose that only two original leaves were cancelled in this place.

There are a number of annotations by a playhouse reviser, mostly directions for music (one in a different hand from the rest). This reviser also made numerous cuts, and may have twice (fols. $322^{b}$, $337^{a}$) inserted a consequential alteration in the text: he also corrected or supplied a few speakers' names.

The censor made no annotations in the text, but numerous deletions may from their nature be ascribed to him. Many oaths are struck out, including 'faith', though 'by gisse' escaped his notice. (This was six months before Charles's famous ruling that 'faith, death, slight' were 'asseverations, and no oaths'.) Objection is taken to various minor matters, and more particularly to the theme of the Amboyna massacre, references to which are deleted, and to criticism of the Royal Mint, which seems to have been the subject of the cancelled scene.

There is a regular division into acts, and a very imperfect one into scenes, by the author. There is no division in the first two acts, though the second certainly consists of two scenes. In Act III three scenes are marked, but there should be a fourth. No attempt has been made to rectify these errors. The stage reviser duplicated the heading to Act IV in a marginal note. He also provided for music in each of the four intervals. Between Acts III and IV, however, the music is directed to play during the sort of dumb show that concludes the former, in which certain characters sleep on the stage and are later roused and go off (action which somewhat recalls the direction 'They sleepe all the Act' in *A Midsummer-Night's Dream*: F1, Act III end).

There is very little system in the author's directions. The main entrances and a few independent directions are centred. Shorter directions of all sorts are entered indifferently on right or left. Even one exit was marked in revision on the left. There is a tendency to write directions at the end of a line only partially full, so that in some cases directions that have to be regarded as technically on the right are in fact near the middle. A good many short ones occur (bracketed) within the line. There is no attempt to distinguish directions by the use of Italian script, but some, especially towards the right, are enclosed in parentheses. The long descriptive directions towards the end of the play are a notable feature. The stage reviser's directions are all on the left, except here and there where they have been added to central entrances. The following list is substantially complete for all but bare entrances and exits.

319[b] 'Bell ringes' (centre, at head). 'Enter · Truñell, okum, tallow, Tarre, & sheathinge nayle'. 'bringes in fire: & · 2 · full pottꝭ: 5 · 3 footed stooles. Sitt' (centre).

320[a] '(*drinke*) drinke' (right, near centre). 'Enter boye: | Exeunt' (left) added after the slip (320*) had been affixed.

320[b] 'exit Cap. &. Naup.' (right) added. 'Enter · gouer: deputie, & ['1 · 2' interlined above '· 2 · or 3 ·'] Comittees'.

321[b] *'Musick' (left) opposite 'Enter a small banquett, & wine. musique aloft. after a small respitt of tyme all taken awaye' (centre).

325[a] 'Enter · fitzI: Naupegus' added above 'Actus · 2 · scena · 1[a].' to which is added *'Musick'.

328[a] '*his purse* / giues his purse' (both left). 'Enter Mary Sparke. & Isabell Nutt. two seamens wyues. wth handbaskettę'.

329[a] [II. ii, not marked] 'Enter Truñell, . . . & Sheethinge nayle'. '(bringes. fire. stooles. & drinke—)' (right).

329[b] '(drinke round)' (right, near centre).

330[a] 'Bell ringes. enter Naupegus & Clarke of the Checke'. 'Here bringe a little table, & a paper booke: for Clerke of the Checke' after which 'Clerke · Calles' (left) a list of names, against which 'answeare wthin all but: Mend: & · Ele ·'(left) and 'where' (to 'Miles Mendpricke') and 'where yt must be the least man wth a long beard' (to 'Edmond Elephant') (right).

331[a] *'Musick' (left) opposite 'Actus tertius. scena 1ª. | Enter Lo. Ad: w^th^ ·2· or ·3· attendantę'. '(exeunt attend) (takes vp a paper)' (centre, towards right) and 'reades' (left). 'stands amazed' (left). 'scena ·2· Enter Locuples, wth a purse in his hand, wth dorotea hastinge frõ him & he violently holdinge her'.

331[b] 'aside' (left, below speaker's name).

332[a] 'Scena 3ª. enter Gou: deputie, 1 · 2 · Comittee'.

337[a] 'offers a paper. The Ad: refuseth the paper' (left).

337[b] [III. iv, not marked] 'Enter Mary Sparke at one doore & Isabell Nutt. at another wth handbaskettę. in one baskett a bricke batt wrapt in a Cleane napkin: & in the other ·3· or 4· peecę of painted Cloth in another Cleane napkin. Enter Truñell aside'. 'Tru: aside' (speaker's name).

338[a] 'Enter Truñell singinge'. 'aside' (in the middle of a line).

338[b] 'Trũ. aside' (speaker's name). 'aside' (in the middle of a line). '(bringes in a table & a towell & stooles)' (right, near centre). 'drawer w^th^ wine & bread' (left) '(Nutt holds vp her finger)' (centre).

339[a] 'drawer wth wine' (left) '—drinkes—' (in text, *passim*). '(Here they fall both drunke)' (in text). '(pluckes a new bricke batt out)' (in text). '(pluckes out · 4 or 5 · peeces painted Cloth)' (in text). 'enter boye' (left).

339[b] *'musicke' and *'Musick' (left) in different hands, opposite 'Enter the drawer, hastily wakinge the women. who startinge vp, & layinge hold on the bottome of the baskettꝭ, out falls the bricke batt, & the peecꝭ of painted Clothes. wch they (as yf no body sawe them) put vp agayne. exeunt. then enter boye agayne takes bush & all awaye. perfumes the roome. exit' then *'Act 4^th^:' (left) opposite 'Actus · quartus · scena 1ª. | *Enter dorotea Constance at one doore, at another doore a servingman who dđ her a letter*' replaced by *'Enter L^d^ Adm

Gouernor Deputye', the heading for the revised IV. iii (fol. 342[a]), scenes i and ii being intended and partly marked for omission. 'dorotea reades the letter' (left). 'teares the îre &c'.' (left).

340[a] 'knocke wthin. | enter Capt.' (left).

340[b] '⟨k⟩no. wthin' (left) opposite 'Enter boye wth a letter' (centre). 'Rreades [*sic*] to her selfe. startȝ as yf afrighted, shakes wth feare. & speakes' (centre). 'knocke wthin' (left) before 'Enter Capt. Goodman a sea Com̃aunder'.

341[b] 'scena 2[d]. | Enter Captayne fitzIohn. Naupegus, & Clarke of the Checke'.

342[a] 'scena 3[a]. | Enter at one doore · Lo · Ad: at another Go: dep: 1 · 2 · Com̃ittee'.

343[a] 'Exeunt at · 2 · seuerall doores. | scena 4[a]: | Enter doro: Constance ['alone' interlined] in a petticote & wastcoate. with her worke in her hand'. 'shewes her worke' (left). 'Sitts · to worke' (left) before 'Enter Truñell, . . . & Sheathinge nayle'.

343[b] '(offers to runne out) & Tarre stopps him' (centre).

344[a] 'Here they all see her' (left). 345[a] 'Sitts' (right) before 'Enter Capt fitzIohn'.

345[b] 'kicks them | offers to draw' (left) and '(they all runne out)' (right). 'giues his purse' (left). 'kneeles' (right).

346[a] 'Exe: om.' (part of cancelled text) then *'Musick' (left) opposite 'Actus quintus: the first sceane Consistinge more. in action then speech · as settinge of 2 · Crabbs. the heavinge at the Capsten the whistlinge of the Boteswaines wth the wordes, sometymes heaue sometymes lanche to lengthen the tyme, as shall be shewed before the daye of action. | after the settinge of the Crabbs, & bendinge of the Cables, there must appeare aloft, as many gallantȩ & ladies as the roome Canne well hold amongst wch must be Lo: Ad: Go: Dep: 1 · 2 · Com̃: then enter alowe in haste · at one doore · Truñell & tallow, & at another. Tarre, Okum, & Sheathinge nayle'.

346[b] 'Enter boteswayne whistlinge' (centre). 'wthin' (left, four times, once in text). 'whistles' (left, thrice). '(a great shout within)' twice, and '(a greate shout of all)' once (in text). '⟨En⟩ter · Capt: ⟨in⟩ hast' (left).

347[a] 'Scena · 2d̃a ·' then *'Trumpete' (left) opposite 'Enter Lo · Ad: Go: dep: 1 · 2 · Com̃. wth attendantȩ'. 'Enter Banquett: all sytt · | Musique aloft · | after a little while syttinge Lo: Ad: beginnes a health to the good successe of the Mary: wch must be Contynued wth shootinge of gunns to the last man: wch orderly discharged will be about · 11 · or 13 · gunns. wch ended (a loude shoute wthin) God

blesse the Mary. &c'. then all sytt agayne: & imediately enter: Tarre · Trunell · Tallow · Okum & Sheathinge-nayle. wth some daintie dance, euery one wearinge the embleme of his name, vpon his head. The dance ended, & all taken awaye the Lo: Ad: speakes'.

347[b] 'Exeunt · omnes. | Sce: 3[a]. | Enter Captayne fitz · alone'.

348[b] 'Scena · 4[a]. | Enter dorotea Constance alone'.

Printed: J. H. Walter (Malone Society), in preparation.

15. *The Lady Mother.*

B.M., MS. Egerton 1994[9]. Licensed 15 Oct. 1635.

The play (see Plate 9) occupies fols. 186–211 of the collection, the twenty-six leaves (of which the last contains an addition only, and the last two versos are blank) forming thirteen separate sheets. The fourth page of each sheet bore a catch-word, now sometimes lost. The edges are rather decayed especially at the outer margin, where the text has suffered some damage. The leaves measure up to $12\frac{1}{4} \times 7\frac{3}{4}$ inches, but many have been trimmed in the course of reparation.

Begins, fol. 186[a]: 'Act. 1. sc. 1. Enter Thorowgood Bonuill & Grimes'.

Ends on fol. 210[a]: 'Exeunt Oes [*sic*] | Finis' followed by the censor's autograph licence: 'This Play Call'd the Lady= moth⟨er⟩ (the Reformacōns obseru'd) may b⟨e⟩ Acted. October the xv[th]. 1635 Will: Blagraue dep[t] to the m⟨aster⟩ of the Reuell⟨s⟩' (verso blank).

Fol. 211[a]: an addition consisting of half a page of dialogue, intended for insertion in the text, apparently at the beginning of II. i on fol. 191[a], though there is no indication of the place where it belongs (verso blank).

Written in a clear though rather current hand, generally Italian in character. It suggests a scribe's, and this impression is borne out by some of the alterations: e.g. on the first page 'observe' has been corrected to 'obscure'. There is a normal use of short speech-rules; but the leaves have not been folded for margins, and these are rather narrow. Of the numerous corrections, alterations, and additions, some are certainly in the hand of the scribe, but that in which the most extensive additions (those on fols. 191[a] and 211[a]) are written, while bearing some resemblance to the scribe's, is probably to be distinguished from it. There are also other shorter additions on fol. $196^b$ (left margin) and fol. $205^a$ (foot), which seem to be in yet another hand, and it is therefore doubtful which if any of the hands should be regarded as that of the author. The scribe is also responsible for most of the prompt annotations appearing in the play, but a few of these (on fols. $187^b$, $192^{a,b}$) are in another hand, which may be traceable in other pieces in the collection.

There are clear indications that the play was censored before licence. Some oaths have been struck out: e.g. fol. $186^a$ 'ffaith', though this is left standing later. In the heading to the original v. i (fol. $206^a$) a hand that is probably Blagrave's has deleted 'Recorder' and substituted the less specific 'Iudg'; the same has altered 'recorder' to 'Iudge' in the first speech, 'M^r Recorder' to 'S^r' in the second, and so on throughout the scene. The scribe or reviser has conformed by substituting 'S^r Hu:' for 'Re:' as prefix to the speeches, and altering 'Recorder' to 'Iustice' on fol. $208^b$. The omission of a subsequent passage (fols. $208^b$–$209^a$) seems to have been decided on after the censorship, since, in the few words inserted to make a connexion, we find the title 'm^r Iustice' instead of 'm^r Recorder'.

A passage in II. i (fol. $192^a$): 'Now on my life this boy does sing as like the boy at the whitefryers as ever I heard', may imply that the piece was acted there. The only playhouse in Whitefriars about this date was Salisbury Court, and the only company known to have occupied it in 1635 was the King's Revels.

There is a regular division into acts only, though in each case the first scene is numbered ($191^a$ Act: 2. Sc: i.', $195^b$ 'Act. 3. Scen: i.', $201^a$ 'Actus. 4: Sce: i.', $206^a$ 'Actus. 5 Sce: i.'). But the original division was afterwards altered by the scribe himself who marked the beginning of Act III on fol. $193^b$ (likewise adding 'Finis Act. 2.' at this point) and 'Act: 5.' on fol. $204^b$, though he left the original headings standing.

Although the scenes are not numbered they are always distinguished by a line drawn across the page. The more im-

portant entrances, including all those constituting a fresh scene, are centred: minor entrances are marked in the left margin. Exits as usual appear on the right: the scribe is particularly fond of the formula 'Ex$^{t}$ õẽs'. The scanty independent directions are mostly on the right, and are often difficult to distinguish from the text, in spite of the occasional use of rules. The most striking feature of the manuscript is the almost regular duplication of entrances in the left margin about a quarter of a page before the original direction. With the latter they are often linked by a line drawn down the margin, and they seem to be mostly if not all in the hand of the scribe, though no doubt added later. They are even found in the additional passage on fol. 211$^{a}$. These anticipatory directions are of course in effect warnings for the actors to be in readiness. The only other book giving warnings on at all the same scale is *The Welsh Embassador*. A few only are noticed in the following list.

186$^{b}$ 'Lady ⟨ ⟩ Maudlin' apparently added by the scribe as a warning 20 lines before the direction 'Ent' Lady & Magdalin'.

187$^{a}$ 'Timothy' apparently added by the scribe as a warning for the entry, 12 lines later, overleaf.

187$^{b}$ 'S$^{r}$ Geff. Bunch' and 'Sucket Crackby' anticipating by some 20 and 10 lines respectively the direction 'Ex$^{t}$ õẽs | Enter *Suckett & Crackby*' replaced by *'S$^{r}$ Gefferie & Bunch'. The deleted names refer to the following passage, which is marked for omission. Those substituted duplicate a deleted direction near the top of 188$^{a}$, itself an anticipation of a later one (the intervening passage being also marked for omission). But the whole text here is very confused.

190$^{a}$ 'Kneele'. 'put vp'. 'sitt down'. 'Kiss him'.

191$^{a}$ [Plate 9.] II. i 'Enter Alexander Lovell with a Bottle of Sack and a Cup'. In revision the scribe has supplied the entrance required for the marginal additions to the ensuing scene written perhaps by the author.

191$^{b}$ 'Flings away y$^{e}$ Bottle & sleeps | Ent' ... with fflaggons of Wine'. 'Lovell grunts'. 'S$^{r}$ Geff Lady' scribe's warning (repeated later) for entrance on 192$^{b}$, the intervening passage being cancelled. 'Ent' *Musike*' (left, at foot).

192$^{a}$ *'Musike' three lines before 'A Song' (both left). 'Daunce' (right).

192$^{b}$ *'Musike softe', *'*Musick*', and *'sease Musick' (all left). 'Ent' *Musike* & Grimes disguisd'.

193$^{a}$ 'blowes his nose'.

193$^{b}$ 'Finis Act. 2.' added before 'Ex$^{t}$ õẽs' (right) and '⟨ ⟩Finis Act | ⟨ ⟩ 3' (left) added opposite 'Enter S$^{r}$. Geffry. & Lady' (centre).

200$^{b}$ (in III. i) 'beats them'.

201$^{a}$ (in IV. i) *'Enter Ale⟨ ⟩' (right) and a line later *'Enter' (left) added perhaps by the author.

204$^{a}$ 'Act: 5.' (left) added by scribe opposite [IV. iii] 'Enter Lady Marloue sola' (centre).

206$^{a}$ 'Actus. 5 Sce: i. | A Table | Enter Recorder, S$^{r}$ Geffery, Crackbie Suckett & Bunch'. 'A Table' is a later addition by the scribe: 'Recorder' has been struck out and 'Iudg' interlined probably by the censor, and there are consequential alterations in the text.

208$^{b}$ 'Offers itt y$^{e}$ Recor:'. *'florishe Horrid Musicke' (left) opposite 'Enter Death: Gri:' (centre) to which is added *'and furies'. The additions may be by the author: the passage was later marked for omission.

209$^{a}$ 'Recorders' (left) opposite 'Enter Hymen & y$^{e}$ lovers' (centre), the passage marked for omission and ending '*discover*'.

Printed: A. H. Bullen, *Old Plays* (ii. 101–200), 1883.

## *CLASS B*

### 1. [*Timon.*] Dyce MS. 52. *c.* 1600?

The play has no title in the manuscript, which consists of twenty-five leaves. The first of these is a fly-leaf, the rest are numbered 1–24 in a modern hand, but the numbers have in some cases been written over an earlier (identical) numeration. The twenty-four numbered leaves constitute a gathering of four sheets (fols. 1–8) followed by eight separate sheets (fols. 9–24). The latter must originally have been appreciably larger than the former, but they have been cut down to a uniform size of $12 \times 7\frac{3}{4}$ inches, with some damage to the text.

Fly-leaf (verso): 'The Actors Names' followed by list of characters and 'Scene. Athens' (recto blank).

Begins, fol. 1$^{a}$: 'The first Act: scen. j$^{ma}$. | Enter Timon and Laches'.

Ends on fol. 24ᵃ: 'Exeunt omnes · | Timon Epilogue' (11 ll.) (verso blank).

Written in two hands, one (A) mainly English, the other (B) Italian. A wrote the personae on the fly-leaf in Italian script, and fols. 1ᵃ–8ᵇ in English, leaving the lower part of the last page blank. B began II. iv on fol. 9ᵃ and went on till after the heading to IV. i near the top of fol. 19ᵇ. Here A resumed and continued as far as the foot of fol. 22ᵇ, in the last scene. B wrote fol. 23ᵃ to within eleven lines of the foot, A finished this page and wrote eighteen lines of the next, which B concluded. A might belong to the early seventeenth century: B looks rather later, but the two must of course be contemporary. The text is sometimes written continuously, but in fact lines are seldom divided between different speakers. There are no rules of any sort. Fols. 1–8 have been folded for margins, the rest have mostly ruled margins which are somewhat narrower. The manuscript has the appearance of a literary transcript, and there is nothing to suggest that either hand is an author's. There are few corrections of any sort. The play may perhaps be of academic origin, and certain resemblances to *Pedantius* have been thought to suggest a date about 1580–90. But it is tempting to see in the 'Leane macilente Grunnio' of III. iv (fol. 13ᵇ) an allusion to *Every Man out of his Humour*, since the word seems to scan as four syllables.

There is no indication of censorship, nor is there any actual evidence of playhouse use. At the same time the addition and alteration of certain stage-directions suggest that the play was prepared for production. Thus on fol. 20ᵃ a direction originally called for two spades, and this was altered to three on discovering that another was needed later in the scene.

The text is fully divided into acts and scenes, the latter being determined on the foreign method of beginning a fresh scene whenever there is a change in the principal characters on the stage.

The stage-directions, both for entrances and incidental, are rather elaborate. As a rule only scene headings with their accompanying entrances are centred, all other directions appearing in the right margin.

$1^{b}$ 'Exeunt | Scen: $2^{da}$. ['Knocking at Timons dore' added] Enter Eutrapelus and Abyssus the Vsurer. *$w^{th}$* [*'following' interlined] him, then Enter Timon & Laches'.

$2^{a}$ 'Aside to Abyssus' (twice). 'Aside'.

$2^{b}$ 'Exeunt. | Scen: $3^{a}$. Act. $j^{mi}$. | Enter Gelasimus and Pædio his Page · a table and a looking glass'. 'takes the glass'.

$3^{a}$ 'Enter Pseudocheus to them' (right) and 'Scen: $4^{ta}$. Act: $j^{mi}$.' (centre).

$3^{b}$ 'Aside to Pædio'.

$4^{b}$ 'Exeunt omnes. | Scen: $5^{ta}$ Act: $j^{mi}$ | Enter Tymon, . . .'.

$5^{b}$ 'Tymon houlds him'. 'Hee strikes him'. 'he shewes his gould giuen by Timon'. 'shews his gould againe'. 'Exeunt | Finis Act. $j^{mi}$. | Scen: $j^{ma}$. Act $2^{di}$. | Enter Gelasimus Pseudocheus and Pædio at one dore Philargurus and Blatte at th'other'.

$6^{a}$ [speakes] 'to Blatte'. 'to Galas: houlding his hand vnder his chynn'.

$7^{b}$ II. ii 'Enter Laches & Hermogenes $w^{th}$. a guilt Rapier'.

$8^{a}$ 'he lookes on his Rapier'. 'he beats him & hoodwincks him'. II. iii 'Enter to them Timon . . .'.

$10^{a}$ II. v 'Enter Lollio at one dore, and Timon . . . at another with feathers in their hatts Demeas . . .'. '(the signe of the 7 starr⟨es)⟩' gloss on text 'How many starres See?'.

$10^{b}$ '(Sounde Musicke ·)'. '(They daunce)'. '(Aside)'.

$11^{b}$ 'Exit Lollio the rest following | The thirde Acte the first Scene · | Enter Lollio . . . Etrapelus aduancing his flaggon Gelasimus . . .'.

$12^{a}$ 'Enter Philarg: at another dore'. 'Exeunt Callimela & Blatte'.

$12^{b}$ (in III. ii) '(two spratts or the like)' gloss on 'Grunnio make broathe of these two fishes'.

$13^{b}$ III. iv 'Enter Obba & the musitians · Obba bringing a baskette of flowers'.

$14^{a}$ (in III. v) 'The Musicians playe and Hermogenes page sings'.

$14^{b}$ 'Enter a shippwrackte Sayler' (centre) but no new scene is marked.

$15^{b}$ IV. i 'Enter Timon at one dore Demeas & Eutrapelus at another'. 'Exeunt Demeas & Eutrapelus' (right) and 'Timon solus' (centre) but the scene continues. 'Gelasimus giues him the gold'.

$16^{a}$ 'Timon lies downe. | Scena secunda. | Abyssus at one Gelasimus . . . at another dore'.

$17^{a}$ IV. iii 'Enter Hermogenes . . . in gownes'. 'Timon ariseth from the grounde'.

$17^{b}$ 'Timon beats him, Herm: runnes away, Tim: followes him in at one dore & enters at another' (right with brace).

$18^{a}$ 'Exit Timon at one dore Lach: at another · | Scena · $4^{a}$ · | Enter Obba with a basket about to spreade the table And Grunnio speakes to him out of his hole'. 'Hee offers to pull him out'. 'Hee pulls him out'. 'Scen $5^{a}$ · | Timon . . . Eutrapelus: Hermogines . . . Speusippus come awhile after'. 'Now enter Her: . . . Speu: and drawe backe'.

$19^{a}$ 'Stones painted like to them · [gloss on 'Artichokes'] & throwes thẽ at them'. 'Timon beates Herm: aboue all the reste'. 'Hee hitts Herm:'.

$20^{a}$ v. ii 'Enter Timon and Laches w$^{th}$ *either a* ['3' interlined] spade['s' added] in their hands'.

$20^{b}$ 'He discouers himselfe'. 'Timon diggs at one end of the stage and Laches at the other' (centre, at foot).

$21^{a}$ v. iii [heading cut away] 'Enter Gelasimus booted & spurd w$^{th}$. a watch in one hand and a Riding rodd in th'other'. 'he throwes dust on him'. 'Enter Pædio w$^{th}$. a Cappe made w$^{th}$. Asses eares'. 'deliuers him the Capp'. 'he puts the capp ⟨on⟩'. 'he offers to bur⟨ie⟩ him in the Earth he had digged'. 'He giues him a spade'. 'he puts of his ca⟨pp⟩'.

$21^{b}$ 'He diggs'. 'He fynds gould'. 'he offers to goe drowne it'.

$22^{b}$ (in v. iv) 'Timon . . . & Laches passing ouer the stage'.

$23^{a}$ (in v. v) 'he takes a pap⟨er⟩ out of his p⟨ocket?⟩'.

$23^{b}$ 'He beates them with his spade' (right, with brace).

$24^{a}$ 'Laches strikes h⟨im⟩'.

Printed: A. Dyce (Shakespeare Society), 1842; and a reprint by W. C. Hazlitt.

2. *The Poor Man's Comfort*, by R. Daborne.

B.M., MS. Egerton $1994^{13}$. *c.* 1617?

The play occupies fols. 268–292 of the collection. Of the twenty-five leaves (the second and last pages of which are blank) the first is a fly-leaf of different paper, and the rest are numbered as twelve separate sheets, though they do not really constitute sheets at all, the make-up being irregular. The numbers are in the inner top corner of alternate rectos, and the last two are erroneously given as 12 and 13. There are regular catchwords on each page. The leaves measure $12 \times 7\frac{1}{2}$ inches.

Fol. $268^{a}$: 'The poore mans Comfort' possibly in a different hand from the rest, but about contemporary (verso blank).

Begins, fol. 269ᵃ: 'The Poore Mans Comfort: | Enter lucius at one dore like a sheaphard & Vrania at the other as a shepherdess'.

Ends on fol. 292ᵃ: 'fins [*sic*] | By R. Dabourne | The poore Manns Comfort', this seems to be in the hand of the scribe: another hand, apparently, has added 'Finis' (twice in capitals) and also 'The Ende of the Pore manns Comfort | By P·Massam' (verso blank).

The text, of which a printed edition in quarto appeared in 1655, is written in a somewhat current hand of a literary rather than a professional type. It is not Daborne's, and the corrections are evidently scribal, while the text remains full of careless mistakes. No other hand appears, except in the scribble at the end and perhaps in the title on the fly-leaf. The leaves have not been folded for margins, and these are rather narrow: there are no speech-rules.

There is no trace of censorship, and no sign of use in the playhouse. A passage on fol. 275ᵃ has, however, been marked for omission, and most of this is absent from the quarto. The two texts differ at times elsewhere, though less than do the stage-directions.

There is a division into acts only, as in the quarto.

The stage-directions are fairly full and of a rather theatrical type. The main entrances, whether or no they mark the beginning of a scene, are centred: they are usually either between rules or with under-rules, but there is no consistency in the practice. Minor entrances, with exits and independent directions, are on the right. The stage-directions in general differ considerably from those in the printed text, which as a rule are less full, less theatrical, and also less descriptive. Some of the more interesting divergences are noted below, the quarto reading being added in brackets. It is clear from two actors' names in one of the directions (cf. fol. 271ᵃ below) that the quarto was printed from a playhouse copy.

270ᵃ 'enter at one dore Cosmo, and surdo at the other Licippus & Alexie' [Q 'Enter Cosmo, Lucippus, Surdo, Alexis'].

270ᵇ 'confir' [Q 'Whispers Lucius'].

271$^{a}$ 'Enter oswell——w$^{thin}$: ferdinand frdinad' (centre) [Q 'Enter Oswell Alarum. | (Within) A Ferdinand, a Ferdinand']. 'enter: 2 lords' (centre) [Q 'Enter 2. Lords, Sands, Ellis']. 'enter fernando. Vincentio bering a crowne other lords'.

272$^{b}$ 'Ext. | enter enter, [*sic*] Vrania as a bride Cosing [*sic*] Licippus, at the other dore qucius [*sic*] & gisbert' and 10 lines lower 'enter sheapherds. Dance' [Q 'Flourish. Ex. | Enter Vrania as a Bride, Gisbert, Lucius, Cosmo, Lucippus, Alexis, Surdo. | Dance'].

275$^{a}$ 'thonder & lighting / Actus secundus. | enter Adelizia' [Q 'Act. II. | Thunder. Enter Adelizia]. (There are four and a half lines marked for omission in the manuscript, only two of these are omitted in Q, and there are other differences in the text.)

276$^{b}$ 'knock him downe'. 'starts vp' [not in Q]. 'enter M$^{rs}$: gulman Vrania disguisd' [Q 'Enter Madam Gulman, Vrania disguised'].

278$^{a}$ 'Ent' Iaspero' (right) [two lines lower in Q].

278$^{b}$ 'Enter Iaspero Licurgo' (centre) [five lines higher (right) in Q].

279$^{b}$ 'messeng$^{rs}$: my honord lord the seanat doth attend yo$^{w}$:—— messengers' [Q '*Surd.* My honour'd Lord, the Senate doth attend you. *Enter one*'].

280$^{a}$ 'Actus Tertius | senate: Enter lucius betweene two senato$^{rs}$. one bearing his robes w$^{th}$ a Cap of Maintenance, officers & suters: off: manent' [Q 'Cornets for a dum shew. Act. III. | Enter Officers with robes fitting a Senator, Lucius betweene Leonardo and Silleus, the rest attendant, two Officers'].

281$^{a}$ 'all 3: yo$^{w}$ are too fforward vincentio——to answere first' apparently an explanatory gloss ['*Glisc.* You are too forward Vincentio'].

282$^{a}$ 'He ascends the state & acts the seaters [*sic*]' (centre) i.e. he imitates the senators ['He ascends the State'].

282$^{b}$ 'Enter King. licurgo Vincentio at alij' (*sic*) ['Enter Gisbert againe. Enter Ferdinand, Licurgo, Vincentio, &c.']. 'Enter Poast' (right) and 'Enter Gisbert' (right) [both centre in Q].

283$^{a}$ 'Takes the state' [not in Q]. 'Pluck him downe' ['Plucks him down'].

284$^{b}$ 'Actus Quartus' ('& Vrania' has been added to the direction in different ink, but she does not enter till the next page) [Q includes 'Vrania' in the heading].

285$^{b}$ 'Ext | Enter, Alexis Adalizią at a table' ['Enter Alexis, Adellezia, A Table', no exit].

287$^{b}$ 'Actus Quintus'.

$288^{b}$ 'offer to kill himselfe' and 'kills flav:' [not in Q].

$291^{a}$ 'Tucket' [not in Q]. 'Enter Oswell as a Combitant' [Q text differs somewhat here].

$291^{b}$ 'Tucket' twice, added to entrance [not in Q]. 'discover themselus' [also in Q].

The manuscript was used by A. E. H. Swaen in his edition of the play (*Anglia*, xxi. 373–440, 1899), but his collation does not profess to be complete. Indeed it is doubtful whether the manuscript deserves much attention, though it preserves a few lines not in the quarto.

3. *Nero*. B.M., MS. Egerton $1994^{12}$. *c.* 1624?

The play occupies fols. 245–267 of the collection. It was originally written on twenty-five leaves, of which twenty-three remain, two being lost between fols. 250 and 251 (*c.* 200 lines of the printed text). The six leaves between fols. 258 and 265 are also in reversed order: the first three should follow the second three. (The pencil numbering of these leaves has been altered to agree with the correct order, though the leaves themselves have not been moved. I adopt the corrected numbering in this description, and treat the leaves in their true order.) The make-up in sheets is irregular and is evidently connected, as will be seen, with the changes of scribe. Fols. 245–250 form three separate sheets, fols. 251–258 form one gathering of four sheets, fols. 259–264 form one gathering of three sheets (which was folded inside out, thus producing the wrong order of the leaves), while fols. 265–267 appear to be what remains of a gathering of two sheets after the loss of a final blank leaf. The leaves measure up to $12\frac{1}{8} \times 7\frac{3}{4}$ inches.

Begins, fol. $245^{a}$: 'The Tragedy of Nero | Actus primus. Scena prima. | Enter Petronius Arbiter. Antonius ⟨ ⟩'.

Ends on fol. $267^{b}$: 'F⟨inis Actus Qu⟩int''.

Written in six different hands, all apparently those of scribes, of which A wrote fols. 245–50, B fols. 251–5, C fols. 256–7, D fols. 258 and 265, E fols. 259–60, 263–4, and 266–7, and F fols. 261–2. The two leaves missing between the portions of A and B were probably written in hand A, since he normally gets about 50 lines on a page, whereas B gets more. These two

[illegible] Seale have [not in Q].

[illegible] Enter [illegible] is a [illegible] [Q text differs somewhat here].

[illegible] were [illegible] in Q [illegible] Become the [illegible] [illegible].

The manuscript was used by A. E. H. Swaen in his edition of the play [illegible] his collation [illegible] to be complete [illegible] manuscript [illegible] not in the [illegible].

[illegible]

The play [illegible] of which twenty-three [illegible] The [illegible] pencil numbering [illegible] correct [illegible] have not been removed. [illegible]

[illegible]

leaves therefore probably formed a separate sheet. It is only in the last two gatherings that the hands alternate. It will be observed that D completes the gathering begun by B and C, and writes the first leaf of the last gathering. E completes the last gathering (supplying the inner sheet) and writes the two outer sheets of the middle gathering; while F writes only the inner sheet of this gathering. This suggests that at least towards the end of the play the scribes were following a copy page for page and dividing it up. Hand E has a rather curious likeness to Massinger's but is clearly not his. There are hardly any alterations *currente calamo*, but in some places blanks have been left where the original was imperfect or obscure, and a number of corrections have been made by one other hand (see list below). There is a quotation from Juvenal in the margin of fol. $257^b$, and other quotations appear on fols. $250^a$, $251^a$, and $255^b$. At the end of the first act (on fol. $249^a$) the lower half of the page has been left blank. There are no speech-rules, and the leaves have not been folded for margins, which are irregular.

There is no trace of censorship, nor any indication of use in the playhouse. The presence of quotations and the multiplicity of hands suggest a purely literary origin.

The play was printed anonymously in a quarto dated 1624. The two texts agree in general very closely, though on the whole the quarto is distinctly the better. If we suppose the latter to have deliberately omitted the quotations, the two might well be copies of the same original. Each occasionally corrects the other.

There is a division into acts only, though some headings make mention of the first scene as well. The quarto has the same division without mention of scenes.

Directions for entrances, whether or not they constitute a fresh scene, are usually centred, though a few appear, together with exits and independent directions, in the right margin. There are no rules whatever, but occasionally a marginal direction is preceded by a brace. The directions are rather scanty throughout, and for the most part untheatrical. While in general they agree closely with those of the quarto, they occasionally show marked differences. Sometimes one text and sometimes the other is alone in supplying a necessary direction. A few of the more interesting differences are noted below, the quarto reading being added in brackets.

245$^{a}$ 'Enter Poppea royally attended and pass ou' the Stage in State'.

249$^{a}$ 'Exeunt. | Finis actus primi' (lower half of page blank).

249$^{b}$ 'Actus Secundus Scena prima | Enter Petronius solus'.

252$^{a}$ 'ffinis Act: 2. | Actus .3. | Enter Poppea sola'. 'Enter Nimphi:' (right with brace).

254$^{a}$ 'Enter 2 Romans' (correctly) [Q 'A Romane to them']. 'Enter a 3 Roman' [Q 'Enter Another Romane to them'].

254$^{b}$ 'Softe musiqȝ' (left) with a blank left for the direction in the centre [Q 'Soft Musique, Enter Nero aboue alone with a Timbrell']. Lower down another blank has been left [Q 'Enter a Woman with a burnt Child': after the Woman's speech Q has one line by Nero and the direction 'Enter a Man bearing another dead': these are not in MS. though there is no blank and the man speaks].

255$^{a}$ 'Cantat' (right with brace).

256$^{b}$ 'Finis act' .3. | Actus .4. Scæna prima. Enter Nero . . .'.

257$^{b}$ 'Exeunt omnes' [Q adds 'Pretor Nero' (*sic*) meaning correctly that Nero remains].

258$^{b}$ 'Exit' [Q 'He dies'].

261$^{a}$ 'he Spurrs [*sic*] her to death' [Q 'Spurns her and Poppæa falls'].

262$^{a}$ 'they bring wine' [not in Q]. 'Drinkes' [Q 'He drinks'].

263$^{a}$ 'Enter Physitio' (right) [not in Q]. 'Exeunt | Finis actus 4:'.

263$^{b}$ 'Actus quintus. Scæna prima. | Enter . . .'. 'a tickett' (right, at foot: ? for 'a tuckett') [Q 'Enter a Roman' correctly].

264$^{a}$ 'Enter a m⟨ess.⟩' (right) [Q 'Enter another Roman'].

264$^{b}$ 'Exeunt' [Q 'Ex. Ner. | Manet Neophilus, Epaphroditus']. 'Enter Nero · Nimph: & Tigell:' (right).

265$^{b}$ 'Enter Nero' (right, but near centre).

266$^{a}$ 'Exeunt Præter Ner' (right) [Q 'ex. preter Nero'].

267$^{b}$ 'Enter 2 of Galbaes frendes Antonius and othere w$^{t}$h Nymphydius bounde'.

The following is a list of some of the corrections made by the reviser in the manuscript, together with the corresponding readings of the quarto. As a rule the correction agrees with the quarto. Occasionally the reviser corrects an error com-

mon to the two texts. But other instances seem to show him botching the text by the light of nature and doing it wrongly. Once he wrongly alters a correct reading. Deletions are in italic, corrections in parentheses.

$247^{b}$ 'wanton *head* (bed)' [Q 'bed'].

$248^{a}$ 'a rowle [*sic*] (of) fidlers' [Q 'rout of'].

$249^{b}$ '*that* (thye) powrefull mace' [Q 'thy']. The scribe omitted a line [given in Q] and thereby made nonsense of the passage, which the reviser tried to botch up.

$250^{b}$ 'then *you* had *sate* (you sate)' [Q 'Then had you sate']. 'fill'd with shouts and *Cries* (triumphs)' (this correction is by the scribe) [Q 'noyse'].

$251^{a}$ 'most wilbe glad of *thrunge*' (marked as incorrect but not altered) [Q 'change'].

$251^{b}$ 'lettę not our cause with needles blood *distayne* (be stayn'd) '[Q 'distayne' correctly]. '*this* (his) sou'aignty' [Q 'his'].

$252^{a}$ 'was currant, noe nor (passant) at other sightę' (word supplied in blank left by scribe) [Q 'passant'].

$252^{b}$ 'was yt not as (you) look't for't' [Q 'you'].

$253^{a}$ 'how much the latine staynes the Thracian (Lyre)' (word supplied in blank to which the scribe drew attention by a cross in the margin) [Q 'lyar'].

$253^{b}$ 'yea *were* (whose) powers *that* not like (to) those aboue' [Q 'You severe powers, that not like those aboue'].

$254^{a}$ 'death weares this brauery (out) & the vgly feares' [Q 'mares this brauery, and']. 'Tother his house god *lawes*' (saves) [Q 'saues']. 'all banne the doer *with* & (with) wishes kill' [Q 'and with']. 'this wee *had* (haue done) before' ['This, we haue had before'].

$254^{b}$ 'Ô Rome the enuy late,
but nowe the pitty of the world the *gettę* (Getes)
the men of Cholcos at thy sufferingę greiue
the shaggy dweller on the Scythian rocke
the condemned to ppetuall snowe . . .'
[Q 'But now, the pitie of the world thee gets, . . .
the most condemned . . .'
(Bullen emended to 'the Getes', correctly, and conjectured 'The Mosch condemned')].

$258^{a}$ '$y^{e}$ proud rooffs and wanton *Cost* (Court) of Kings' [Q 'cost'].

The play was printed from the quarto by A. H. Bullen, *Old*

*Plays* (i. 3–98), 1882, and a partial collation of the manuscript was added on a leaf of Addenda.

4. *The Escapes of Jupiter* [by T. Heywood].
B.M., MS. Egerton 1994[4]. *c.* 1625?

The play occupies fols. 74–95 of the collection. The twenty-two leaves (of which several pages are partly or wholly blank) form eleven numbered sheets (all the numbers remaining in the outer top corner). The leaves measure up to $12\frac{1}{8} \times 7\frac{7}{8}$ inches. Catchwords are used rather irregularly, as a rule on the fourth page of each sheet.

Begins, fol. 74ᵃ: 'Calisto, | Actus primus scena prima. | Enter Kinnge Lycaon, wth his Lords, And Iupiter wth other Lords off Epyre · Ec'.' The title 'Calisto' is applicable to the first act only.

Ends on fol. 95ᵃ: 'Explicit Actus 5s. | Finis'.

Fol. 95ᵇ: 'The Escapes of Iupiter' in a different, probably somewhat later, hand. The page was originally blank.

Written throughout in the autograph of Thomas Heywood. The characteristics of the hand are generally the same as in *The Captives*, but the writing is rather looser. There is the same consistent use of rather short speech-rules, and the leaves have probably been folded for margins. The alterations clearly show the manuscript to be the work of the author. That it was written with a view to performance appears from such a direction as 'A songe Iff you will' (fol. 77ᵃ), but there is no trace of playhouse use. The piece is a revised version of certain scenes out of two of Heywood's own plays, *The Golden Age* and *The Silver Age*, printed in 1611 and 1613 respectively.

Though there are no indications of formal censorship, it is clear that a passage on fol. 87ᵇ has been cancelled through fear of offence. Here the writer has drawn his pen through the lines:

> and now is fought
> by Ioshua duke vnto the hebrewe nation
> the ffamous battayle gainst the Cananites
> And att his orison the soon stands still
> that his may have theire slaughter . . .

Dyce (? 1870), [illegible] and a partial collation of the manuscript [illegible] added on a leaf of Addenda.

4. *The Escapes of Jupiter* by T. Heywood.
B.M., MS. Egerton 1994. c. 1625?

[illegible] collection. The twenty-[illegible] leaves [illegible] wholly blank [illegible] remaining in [illegible]

[illegible]

[illegible] English [illegible]

[illegible] *The Escapes of Jupiter* [illegible]

[illegible] wholly blank.

[illegible] autograph of Thomas Heywood. The characteristics of [illegible] are generally [illegible] in *The Captives*, but the writing is rather looser. [illegible] use of rather short speech-rules, and [illegible] have [illegible] for margins. [illegible]

[illegible]

and [illegible]

Considering that he has just explained that the real cause of the phenomenon was Jupiter's desire to have his fill of dalliance with Alcmena, the fear of offence may not have been groundless.

There is an original division into acts only, each with an explicit. After Act I ($78^b$) the rest of the page is left blank, Act II beginning on the next leaf (the second of the sheet). At the end of Act II ($83^a$) the rest of the page and the whole of the next are left blank, Act III beginning on the next leaf (the first of a new sheet). After Act III ($87^a$) there is no blank, and after Act IV ($90^b$) a blank of two inches only, in each case the next act beginning on the same page.

Though there is no formal division into scenes, a certain distinction is observable. Entrances are marked in the centre, and whereas many have only a single rule below them, those constituting the beginning of a scene usually have a rule above as well as below: in other words a line is normally drawn across the page at the end of a scene, though the practice may not be quite consistent. Exits and the scanty independent directions are normally marked on the right, though there are exceptions, some directions appearing in the left margin and some, even including exits, being centred. The marginal directions are ill distinguished from the text. The stage-directions of the manuscript only agree in a very general way with those found in the printed plays.

$74^b$ 'A Confused ffray Lycaon: beaten off, Enter Iupiter'. 'An Alarme Enter Iupiter wth his Trayne and the Lords off Pelagia wth a Crowne'.

$75^a$ 'Exeunt. | In this Tumult, Enter Calisto as affrighted' with single rule only. 'Enter in a Hurry wth weopens Drawne Iupiter and the Lords on boath sydes'.

$76^a$ 'Exnt | Enter Diana wth her Nimphes wth Bowes arrowes Iavelines. Faunes satyres Etc'' between rules, and 'The sonnge' (centre).

$77^a$ 'A songe Iff you will' (left) before 'Loud Musicke, wch Doon Enter Iupiter in the habit off a nimphe or shepherdesse'.

$77^b$ 'aside'. 'Exent. | Bugles and a noyse off huntinge. Enter Nimphes wth diana'. 'Enter [error for 'Exeunt'?] | Bugles and showtes: Enter fawnes and satyres'. 'Exeunt. | The Noyse Continewd Enter Iupiter: Calisto' between rules.

$78^{b}$ 'Exit bearing her off'. | '*Explicit Actus primus*' between rules, and 'Enter Homer'. 'Explicit Actus primus' between rules.

$79^{a}$ 'Actus secundus scena prima. | Enter three or fower ould Beldams' with rule below each line. 'The bell ringes' (centre) with rule.

$80^{a}$ 'Enter Iupiter and his man lyke two pedlers wth Eather off them a pack att his back' between rules. 'Ringes the bell'.

$80^{b}$ 'Enter Danae wth the beldams Lookinge vpon their Iewells'.

$81^{b}$ 'They kisse'. 'lookes back'. 'Exeunt | Enter the Beldams Drawinge out Danaes bed shee In it they place ffower Tapers att the ffower Corners' between rules.

$82^{a}$ 'Enter Iupiter Crownd in a ritch habitt'.

$82^{b}$ 'Hee begins to putt out the lights and make vnready' (right) with brace. 'The bedd Drawne in and Enter the Clowne' with single rule only. 'Enter Iupiter and Danae in her night-gowne'.

$83^{a}$ 'Exent | Enter Homer' with single rule only. 'Explicit Actus 2s. | Actus $3^{s}$ scena prima' with rule above and below each line.

$84^{a}$ 'Actus 3s scena prima. | An Arbor discovered shephards and shephardesses discovered. Iupiter lyke a woodman wth semele | A songe'.

$84^{b}$ 'Exnt. | Lowd musicke, Enter in great state semele attended by gentlemen, and her Ladyes'. 'Enters Iuno in the shape off her Nurse Beroe'.

$86^{a}$ 'Exit | Enter Iuno and Iris in a Clowde aboue'. 'A bedd thrust out, and In it semele'.

$86^{b}$ 'Thonder and lightninnge Iupiter discends In his Maiesty his thonder-bolt burning in his hande'. 'Violent Thonder'. 'As hee approcheth the bedd Itt ffyeres and Iupiter ffrom thenc takes an abortiue Inffant' (centre with rule). 'Hee ascendinge in the throne and then Homer Enters: and speakes'.

$87^{a}$ IV. i 'The head off the kinge brought in' (left) with braces, opposite 'Enter on the one syde the Teleboans and on the other Amphitrio too Captaines Blapharo And socia After a battaile, and fflorishe'.

$87^{b}$ 'Exent. | Thonder and lightninnge, Enters Iupiter in the shape off Amphitrio' between rules. 'Enter Ganimed habited lyke socia'.

$88^{a}$ 'Hee knocks. | Enter three servingemen'. 'Enter Alcmena Thessala her maide the three servingmen: Iupiter and Ganimed stand vnseene'.

$88^{b}$ 'A Banquett brought In' (centre with rule). 'Musicke' (left) at foot.

$89^{a}$ 'Musicke and they lighted In wth Torches. Ganimed stayes beehind' (at head with rule). 'Enter socia wth a letter in his hand'.

90[b] 'Enter Homer' below rule, six lines then another rule, and 'End | Explicit Actus Quintus [*sic*]' and after a blank 'Actus 5[s] scena prima, | Enter Amphitrio socia wth his letter and too Captaines'.

92[b] 'Exit Amphitrio, beatinge out his men. the Capt: follow' (centre with rule).

93[a] 'Enter socia and Blepharo Mayster off the shipp'. 'Musick theire sever[al?] Antick conges' (right) and 'Enter Amphitrio in a rage beatinnge his servants beeffore him. wth him the Captaines stayinge his blowes To whom at another doore Enter Ganimed' (centre between rules).

94[a] 'Enter Iupiter Alcmena Ganimed: The servants alooffe'. 'Exeunt All but socia and Amphitrio' (centre with rule).

94[b] 'They lye to sleepe' (right) and 'Iuno and Iris descend' (centre).

95[a] 'Thonder and lightninge, Amphitrio and socia awake The Captaines servants and the rest as affright roon In: Iupiter appears in maiesty to whome they all kneele'.

Extracts in *Anglica: Brandl-Festschrift* (Palaestra 148, pp. 211–43), 1925.

5. *Bonduca.* B.M., MS. Add. 36758. *c.* 1625.

The play has the title written on a fly-leaf, and itself fills twenty-four numbered leaves, which constitute four gatherings of three sheets each (there is a modern foliation from 1 to 25 in pencil). The manuscript is a rather large folio, the leaves measuring $14 \times 8\frac{3}{4}$ inches, bound in a vellum wrapper with gilt tooling.

Fly-leaf (recto): 'Bonduca | Queene of Brittaine' (verso blank).

Begins, fol. 1[a]: 'Actus primus: Scæna prj[a] | Enter Bonduca: (hir Daughter) Hengo: (hir Sonne) Nennius: & Soldiers'.

Ends on fol. 24[b]: 'Exeunt | ffinis'.

Written throughout by the scribe 'Jhon' (see *The Honest Man's Fortune*). It is a beautiful piece of work in English script, with not very distinctive Italian for incidental use, and directions usually in a larger and bolder hand: evidently a transcript prepared in the playhouse for a private collector. The source of the text appears from a note on fol. 23[a]. Below the heading 'Actus: Quintj: Scæna: pri[a]:' the scribe, instead of continuing the text, gives a brief description of two scenes and explains that the play is incomplete because 'the booke where by it was first Acted from is lost' and that the present transcript is made 'from the fowle papers of the Authors' (see pp. 5–6, where the passage is given in full). The scribe naturally follows the normal habits of the playhouse in the preparation of his manuscript (except as regards gatherings). The leaves have been folded for margins, and there is a regular use of speech-rules, which (as in his other play) tend to begin rather far to the left.

The main interest of the manuscript lies in the opportunity it affords for comparison with the complete and authoritative copy printed in the Beaumont and Fletcher folio of 1647, and for thus observing the revision which the play underwent between the author's rough draft and the final stage version.

There is a division in the manuscript into acts only (whereas the folio marks scenes as well) but in each case the heading includes mention of the first scene.

The stage-directions of the two texts differ rather widely. While each has directions not found in the other, those of the manuscript are perhaps in general more numerous, and in particular tend to be fuller and more graphic. They suggest amplifications by the scribe writing for readers and with recollections of actual performance in mind. It seems unlikely that very full directions should have been found in the foul papers; though they were not entirely absent, as appears from the fact that at one point (fol. 8[a]) the scribe copied in, as part of the text, the words 'in mockage', which in fact belong to a stage-direction.

The main entrances are written in the centre between rules. These include all except one of those recognized by the folio as constituting new scenes, but many others as well. Other entrances are marked on the right, sometimes with a rule above or below. Independent directions are also on the right, and so of course are exits, which are sometimes between rules. There are no directions in the left margin. Corresponding directions usually stand a line or so earlier in the manuscript than in the printed text. In the following list a dagger marks those direc-

tions which do not appear in the folio, or appear there shorn of their peculiar features.

$1^a$ 'Enter Caratacke' (right).
$3^a$ [I. ii] 'Enter Iunius & petillius: (2 · Roman Captaines:)'.
$3^b$ 'Enter Corporal Iudas: & 4. Soldiers'.
$4^b$ 'Exeunt soldiers | Enter: Swetonius: Demetrius: Decius'.
$6^a$ 'Exeunt | Act: 2: Scæna: i:—Enter penius: Regulus: Macer: Drusus'. 'Enter Curius' (right).
$6^b$ 'Drums beate A March · w$^{th}$in'.
$7^b$ [II. ii] 'Enter: Iunius: (after him:) petillius: & a Herald'.
$8^a$ †'he sitte downe'. 'Songe'.
$9^a$ [II. iii] 'Enter: Bonduca: & hir Daughters: Iudas: (w$^{th}$ his Soldiers: (halters about their Necks:) Nenius: following'.
$9^b$ †'Enter: w$^{th}$ wine & Meate' (right).
$10^a$ 'Enter: the · 2 · Daughters (Aboue:)' (right).
$10^b$ †'Enter: younger Daughter: & an Attendant: she shewes her selfe but at y$^e$ Doore' (right).
$11^a$ [in II. iv] †'Exeunt all but Decius: | Enter Iudas: & his Company. 4 · Soldiers'.
$12^a$ 'Exeunt | Actus Tertius · Scæna: prima: | Enter A Messenger' and one line later 'Enter the Druides (Singing) The Daughters: (strowing flowers) Bonduca: Caratacke: Nenius: & the rest following'.
$14^a$ [III. iii] †'Enter: Caratacke: Nennius:—Drums Beate w$^{th}$in'.
$14^b$ [III. v] 'Enter Drusus: & penius (aboue)'. 'Enter the · 2 · Daughters: Soldiers (bringing in) Iunius: Curius: Drusus: & others' (right).
$16^a$ †'Enter: Swetonius: Iunius: & Soldiers: vpon the chase' (right).
$16^b$ 'Enter: Bonduca: ['&' interlined] Daughters: *& other Brittaines*' (right) [F$^o$ 'and Britaines']. †'Enter Caratacke: (at their backs:) & Hengo'. †'Bonduca flyes & hir Daughters'. 'fighte'. 'sitt downe'.
$17^a$ 'Actus Quartus · Scæna prima: | Enter: petillius: . . . (Singing)'.
$17^b$ 'Exe$^t$ Sweto et omnes' [before IV. ii].
$18^a$ 'Drum beate w$^{th}$in' and two lines later 'Enter Iudas: & his Company (peeping at the Doore:)' (right).
$18^b$ 'Enter Soldiors: (ronning)' (right).
$19^a$ 'Exeunt: [IV. iii]—Enter: penius: Drusus: Regulus' (right, with rule below).
$20^b$ †'*stabs himselfe* | strikes himselfe'. †'dyes'. 'A Noise w$^{th}$in'. †'Enter: Drusus: Regulus: (stopping the Soldiers · at the Doore ·)'. †'the Soldiers kneele about & weepe'.

21[a] 'Exeunt: Drums beating a Dead March' [before IV. iv]. †'Enter petillius: (talkes w[th] y[e] Generall' (right).

22[a] 'Enter one w[th] Swords: & A great Cup' (right). †'she dyes'.

22[b] †'dyes' (twice).

23[a] V. i (see above, p. 321).

24[a] [in v. iii] †'Iudas steales nere him and shootes him: & startes back'. †[Caratache] 'flings and tumbles him [sc. Judas] ouer: pulls him [sc. Hengo] vp againe'.

24[b] †'Enter: petillius: Iunius: (climing the rock: fight' (right). †'they come of the rocke'.

The manuscript has never been printed, or used by editors, nor has any collation been published. A text is in preparation.

6. *The Faithful Friends*, by Beaumont and Fletcher.
Dyce MS. 10. *c.* 1625?

The play occupies forty-two leaves, of which the first is a fly-leaf bearing the title and another an insertion in quarto. The versos of the third and last leaves are blank. A late pagination, 1–78, omits the fly-leaf, the insertion (between pages 69 and 70) and the two blank pages. But the first three leaves together with the last are not original, having been added, perhaps in the eighteenth century, to supply defects in the manuscript. The matter on the fly-leaf may have been then first added. The next two and a half pages (the lower half of the recto and the whole of the verso of the third leaf are blank) evidently supply the text contained on a single original leaf missing at the beginning; while the half page written on the last leaf of all contains the conclusion of the text that must have stood on an original leaf lost at the end. Whether these portions were supplied from some other source, or were copied from the original leaves themselves when these were found to be too decayed for preservation, it is impossible to say; but the latter is the more economical hypothesis. The fact that the quarto insertion is unpaged suggests that when the manuscript was restored it was lying loose among the leaves and was overlooked: it was probably margined to folio size and inserted in its present place when the whole manuscript was interleaved and put into its modern russia binding. There are, therefore,

thirty-seven original leaves remaining, and one has been lost from either end. The thirty-nine leaves of which the manuscript consisted evidently formed nineteen separate sheets with an odd leaf at the end. The original leaves measure $11\frac{7}{8} \times 7\frac{3}{8}$ inches, and have regular catchwords throughout.

Fly-leaf (recto): 'The Faithful Friends | By Francis Beaumont | & | John Fletcher. | Dramatis Personæ . . .'. On 29 June 1660 Humphrey Moseley entered in the Stationers' Register 'The Faithfull Friend. a Comedy. by ffrancis Beamont & Iohn ffletcher'. (The fly-leaf is mounted, and on the back of the mount a hand of the eighteenth or nineteenth century has begun a much altered transcript of the text. Perhaps it was intended to continue this upon the interleaving.)

Begins, p. 1: 'Actus Primus | Scena prima | Enter Marius a young Lord returned from Travel, w$^{th}$ him Rufinus & Leontius noblemen'.

Ends on p. 78: 'Finis' (the verso of the leaf is blank).

While there is only one original hand in the play, it is convenient to distinguish as A, B, and C the three main hands that have contributed to the manuscript in its present form. Thus A wrote pp. 4–77, B the two pages of the quarto leaf inserted between pages 69 and 70, C the title and personae on the fly-leaf and pp. 1–3 and 78. A, the hand of the original scribe, varies a good deal in appearance but seems to be clearly a single hand throughout. It is an Italian hand and makes no distinction for incidental purposes. At first sight it might be thought to belong to the later seventeenth century, but examination reveals a number of earlier characteristics, which suggest that it may even be as early as the middle of the first half. Moreover, it has undergone alteration (e.g. on p. 13) by another hand which can hardly be after the middle of the century. This correcting hand bears a certain resemblance to B, but is not to be identified with it. Hand B, of the inserted leaf, seems to be clearly that of the author who supplied this short scene, and may well belong to the middle of the first half of the century. It may be the hand of some one accustomed to theatrical writing since it makes use of normal speech-rules. There is no reason to suppose that it is the hand of Massinger, as has been suggested: the resemblance, such as it is, is quite superficial. Hand C, that of the restorer, is most likely of the eighteenth century. It would, of course, be tempting to suppose that the play was made perfect and received its title and ascription (together with a list of characters) at the time it was entered for publication in the Stationers' Register; but it is doubtful whether either the writing or the paper can be as early as 1660.[1] C also paid some attention to the text of the original leaves, adding apparently a few trifling directions, correcting 'Hyther boreans' to 'Hyperborean' on p. 56, and on the same page supplying the word 'wearyness' in a blank left by the scribe. These and similar failures on the part of A show that we have to do with a scribe and not an author. There may be yet other hands present in the correction of the text, and it is possible that among them may be that of the author, though there seems little to suggest this view. The leaves written by A have been folded for margins: he began by using speech-rules, but discarded them after a while.

The manuscript has been thought to be a prompt copy, but it bears no clear indications of playhouse use. It is true that the text has been much revised and that passages have been marked for omission in the manner usual with stage revisers. But revision and deletion may have a literary as well as a theatrical object. Some passages have been underscored in pale red ink which is probably old, though the intent is uncertain: others in pencil which is probably modern. That the manuscript had some connexion with the stage does, however, appear likely. The chief problem it presents is the nature of the inserted leaf. The scribe duly wrote the text of several scenes between a set of clownish characters, but when he came to the end of Act IV, where such a scene was apparently called for, instead of furnishing the text he merely entered what he described as 'The Plott of a Scene of mirth' describing the action required. The quarto leaf inserted contains the text of this scene. It is possible that the scene was originally left to be acted extempore, and that it was only later thought

[1] Mr. Edward Heawood informs me that he has been unable to trace any similar watermark before 1708 (cf. *The Library*, Mar. 1931, xi. 471, fig. 115).

desirable to have the text written out. In that case B is presumably the hand of the author who supplied the scene, or at least of the actor who reconstructed it. On the other hand, it is possible that the text of the scene had been lost from the Book from which our manuscript was transcribed, that the deficiency was made good by the inclusion of the 'Plott' based on recollection of the performance, and the words subsequently recovered and inserted from some 'foul papers' preserved. In that case B is presumably the hand of the original author of at least some parts of the play. It is also just possible that the insertion of the scene at this point was an afterthought, for a blank may have been originally left at the end of the act and the 'Plott' only later written in by the scribe. There are blanks of the sort elsewhere. Thus the lower half of p. 14 was left vacant for the end of a song of which the scribe apparently lacked the full text. At the end of Act II the lower half of p. 37 has again been left blank for a similar purpose. Above this blank is the direction 'Songe', while lower down the words 'Ah God a mercy Leftenant' have been deleted. Between, an 'Exeunt' has been added, apparently by C.

There is a division into acts throughout. Scenes are marked in Act I only.

The directions for the principal entrances are centred, including some that do not constitute new scenes. Other entrances, together with exits and independent directions, are marked on the right. Rules are freely, but quite irregularly, used both with central and marginal directions. Stage-directions are fairly full throughout, and there are some peculiar ones of noticeable length near the end.

4 'Enter Learchus a young Lord' (right).

5 'Enter Marcellus a Captaine leading Drum and Cullors, Titus Martius the Kinge Tellius Armanus freind to Tullius, and Souldiers' (centre).

6 *'To Armanus' (right) this may be modern.

7 'Exeunt omnes. manet Tutt & Mar.'.

9 'Scena secunda/ | Enter in an Alehouse [altered in another hand to 'a guesthouse']: Bellario a Totter'd Soldier Black Snout a Smith,

Snip snap, a Taylor, Colueskine [*sic*], a shomaker: euery one potts in there hand'.

12 'Enter Const' & officers'.

15 'Scena tertia | Enter Philadelpha Tullius Bride and Ianus her page' (centre).

16 'Florish Drum & Trum: & a shout'.

18 'Enter Rufinus' and 'Exit Ruf.' (both right).

19 'Actus Secundus. Scena prima'.

20 'Enter Learchus, . . . and an other Senator, then Titus. the Kinge talking to Armanus Cornetts short florish'. 'Exit omnes, manet King & Rufinus'.

24 'Enter Philadelpha, in a mourning habit and Flauia her wayting mayde'.

26 'Enter Sr Pergamus in an old Armor a Capons tayle in his Beauer, a long sword; and Dindimus a Dwarfe carying his Launce and Sheilde'.

30 'stands aside'. 'Enter Rufinus' (right).

34 'Parly Answered'.

38 'Actus tertius. Scena prima'.

53 'They martch together and at the Entrance of the Gate Marius is stabd'.

55 'finis Act ter'.'.

56 'Actus Quartus: Sce: ja:'.

59 'Enter Marius in disguise and Lelia like a post boy'.

61 'Exeunt' followed in large script by 'Enter in a Dumbe shewe: 2 · Flamines After them one bearing an Offering for the Kinge: then 4 · Senators, after them Titus Martius talking to Rufinus: Learchus and Leontius following, Then Philadelpha richly Attird, her Traine borne vpp by virgins all carrying in there hands seuerall kindes of Sacrifice So passe ouer the Stage. Exeunt' below which a rule, then 'Softe Musicke Strikes' (left) and 'A Banquett being sett forth, Enter Titus and Philadelpha Who sitt downe at each end of one Table, Then at an other side Table sitts downe certaine Senators ould Tullius, and Marcellanus, then Rufinus Learchus, and Leontius who waite on the Kinge'.

62 'All sitt downe'. 'He drinkes'. 'The health goes about'.

63 'Enter the Masque in wch is young Tull Marius & Armanꝰ & Lelia in ladies habit they followe ye three young lords like furies after daunce wth the Ladies' (right without rules).

64 'Exit King and Lords seuerally, all but y: Tull . . . & Ruf.' (right

with rules). 'Ex: y: Tull. Phy. & Ruff. then a rich Bed is thrust out and they enter againe' (right with rules) opposite the text:

Ruf Away before then
lead to the Chamber called Elizium

Y. Tut This is the Lodging called Elizium

'Tutt puts out y^e^ Torch< > and stepps behinde y^e^ Arras'.

69 'Exeunt |

*The Plott of a Scene of mirth*
*to conclude this fourth Acte.* [deleted]

Enter S^r^ Pergamus the foolish knight like a Bridegroome . . .
[for the full text of this direction see p. 2, note.]

. . . Then Bellario Sings a songe how they will fall to there old Trades, a clapp of Thunder and all run of/ | finis 4 Act' (this direction is again in larger script). There follows the inserted leaf giving the text of the scene.

70 'Actus Quintus. Scena prima / | Enter Learchus and Leontius, muffeld vpp in there cloakes, and walke ouer the Stage'.

72 'Cornetts a Lesson' two lines before 'Enter 4 · Senators Marcellanus, old Tullius and 2 · others, Then Titus Martius with attendance, young Tullius in disguise amongst other Peticõners'.

76 'Enter Sabinus in a Palmers habit' (right with rule).

Printed among Beaumont and Fletcher's works by H. Weber (i. 1–131), 1812, and A. Dyce (iv. 197–300), 1844, but not included in A. R. Waller's edition, 1910. A text is in preparation by R. G. Rhoads.

7. *Dick of Devonshire.* B.M., MS. Egerton 1994[2]. 1626?

The play occupies fols. 30–51 of the collection: of the twenty-two leaves the first is a little shorter than the rest, which are numbered 1–21. (This original foliation is added below in parentheses.) The make-up into sheets is uncertain: it is clear that there is an odd leaf at each end, and the remainder might form a series of separate sheets with the exception of fols. 43–46, but more probably they constitute five gatherings of two sheets each. At the foot of fol. 34(4)^b^ is a duplicate, reversed and deleted, of the heading on fol. 31(1)^a^, showing that fol. 34(4) is the end either of a sheet or a gathering. The leaves measure about $11\frac{3}{4} \times 7\frac{3}{8}$ inches.

Fol. 30^a^ (fly-leaf): 'The Play of Dicke of Devonshire. | A |

Tragi Comedy. | Hector adest secumqꝫ Deos in prælia ducit.

Fol. 30^b (fly-leaf): 'Dramatis Personæ. . . .'.

Begins, fol. 31(1)^a: 'Act: 1. Sce: 1. Enter don Pedro Gusman, Henrico, & Manuell, his sons, don fernando & Eleonora, his daughter: & Teniente'.

Ends on fol. 51(21)^b: 'Exeunt Omnes. | Finis'.

Carefully written in a small, very neat, and somewhat ornamental hand, of rather mixed character, with practically no attempt at distinction of script. The general effect is scribal; on the other hand, what little alteration and correction there is rather suggests the author, e.g. fols. 31(1)^a, 48(18)^a, and particularly 44(14)^b:

> pray heaven [you have not] *it prove soe*; haue not you defac'd
>
> . . . . . . . . . . . . . . . .
>
> In right of vertue & a womans hono^r
> [I dare] (this deare wrongd Ladies) I dare call thee William

(the words in square brackets are deleted, those in italic interlined). The text is written continuously, and speakers' names, when in the middle of a line, are surrounded by rules. There are normal speech-rules, which are placed below the line in which the speech ends. The leaves have not been folded for margins, and these are rather narrow. There is no indication of playhouse use, nor even of the manuscript having been prepared with a view to production, while the Latin motto on the fly-leaf and the continuous writing strongly suggest a purely literary intention. There is no trace of censorship.

There is a division throughout into acts and scenes.

The scene headings with their entrances are written across the page between rules, the scene number on the left and separated from the direction by a vertical line. Other entrances, with exits and independent directions, are usually placed on the right and surrounded by rules. The directions are fairly frequent and full, but not distinctively theatrical.

31(1)^a 'Peeces dischargd'. 'Ent: Bustamente'. 'Ex: Pedro & Manuell'.

31(1)^b 'Act: 1. Sce: 2. Ent: Two Devonshire Merchants, as being in Sherryes'.

33(3)$^{b}$ (in I. iii) 'Ent: Buzzano above'. 'Ent: fernando w$^{th}$ Eleonora'. 'Ent: Buzzano & Spaniards flying'.

34(4)$^{a}$ 'redit'.

35(5)$^{a}$ 'Act: 2. Sc: 1. Alarum. as y$^{e}$ soft musicke begins, a peale of Ordnance goes off; then Cornetts sound a Battaile, w$^{ch}$ ended; Ent: Captaine, Master of a ship, Dick Pike, w$^{th}$ musketts'.

37(7)$^{a}$ (in II. ii) 'He forces her in'.

37(7)$^{b}$ 'Ent: Henrico, & Eleonora, loose haired, & weeping'. II. iii 'Ent: Pike, w$^{th}$ his sword in his hand, a Cloake on his Arme'.

38(8)$^{a}$ (in II. iv) 'Ent:' prefixed to speaker's name 'Pike'. 'Three or 4 shott dischargd, .2. soldiers slaine, y$^{e}$ other falls on his belly'. 'Ent: Don Iohn arm'd. Pike drawes & wrapps his Cloake about his arme'. 'The fight'. 'He hath him downe & disarmes him'.

38(8)$^{b}$ 'Ent: 12. Muskettiers' (left, prose right). II. v. 'Ent: Don Ferdinando, y$^{e}$ Teniente, w$^{th}$ Attend$^{te}$.; Bustamente brought in w$^{th}$ a Guard'.

39(9)$^{a}$ 'Exit, w$^{th}$ a guard'. 'Ent: Don Iohn, Pike, (w$^{th}$ his face wounded,) a guard of musketts'.

39(9)$^{b}$ 'Exeunt omnes' before III. i: the entrance belonging to III. ii was first written and deleted.

40(10)$^{a}$ III. ii 'Ent: Pike in shackles, nightcap, playsters on his face, A Iaylo$^{r}$'.

41(11)$^{a}$ III. iii 'Ent: Don Pedro, reading a Letter; & Manuell'.

43(13)$^{b}$ IV. i 'Ent: Henrico, (as newly risen.)'. 'Ent: Buzzano w$^{th}$ Cloake & Rapier' (left, though there is room right). 'Buz: falls downe'. 'w$^{th}$in' prefixed to speaker's name 'Man:', the whole between rules and braces added.

44(14)$^{b}$ 'they fight. Enter ferdinand & Attendants'.

45(15)$^{a}$ (in IV. ii) 'knocking w$^{th}$in' (left) opposite 'Ent: 2. fryers' (right).

45(15)$^{b}$ 'Enter Pike' (left, though there is room right). 'Ent: Iaylo$^{r}$ & .3. Spanish Picaroes chaynd'. 'Ent: Bustamente shackled & Iaylor'.

46(16)$^{a}$ 'A Table out, sword & papers' (left, no room right) anticipating by five lines, IV. iii 'Ent: fernando bareheaded, talking w$^{th}$ y$^{e}$ Duke of Macador./Duke Gyron, Medyna, Marquesse d'Alquevezzes, 2 gent$^{s}$: one w$^{th}$ Pikes sword. w$^{ch}$ is laid on a Table, Iaylo$^{r}$, Teniente, Clarke w$^{th}$ papers'.

46(16)$^{b}$ 'Ent: Don Iohn below'. 'Ent: his lady & a gentlewoman above'. 'They all conferre'. 'Ent: 2. Drums; Teniente, divers musketts, fernando w$^{th}$ Pike (w$^{th}$out band, an Iron about his necke, 2 Chaines manacling his wrists; a great Chaine at his heeles) Iaylo$^{r}$, 3. or 4 Halberts, A Barre sett out' (centre between rules and braces).

47(17)[a] 'they consult'. 'The soldiers laugh'.

47(17)[b] 'One stepps forth'. 'They fight: Pike disarmes & tripps him downe'. 'Exit, biting his thumbs, y[e] soldiers stampe'. 'Another steps in'. 'Drums' (left) opposite 'They fight, one is killd, y[e] other .2. disarmd'. 'A noyse w[th]in of, Diablo Englese'.

48(18)[b] (in v. i) 'Ent: y[e] Nobles as before, fernando, Manuell, Clarke Iaylor'.

49(19)[a] 'fernando fetches in Eleonora'.

49(19)[b] 'Ent: Manuell to be rackt, Iaylo[r], & Officers'.

50(20)[a] 'Exit' (in the middle of a line).

50(20)[b] 'Ent: Pike, & a Gentleman w[th] Letters'.

51(21)[a] 'Ent: Teniente, Henrico, Manuell, Pedro (as a fryer) At another dore Eleonora' (centre between rules and braces).

Printed: A. H. Bullen, *Old Plays* (ii. 1–99), 1883.

8. *Aglaura*, by Sir J. Suckling.
B.M., MS. Royal 18 C. xxv. 1637–8.

The play occupies twenty-five leaves (fols. 2–26) and there is an original blank at the end; these twenty-six leaves constitute three gatherings of four, four, and five sheets respectively. The leaves, with edges cut and gilt, are large folio and measure $15\frac{5}{8} \times 10\frac{1}{4}$ inches. The manuscript has a contemporary binding of green morocco heavily decorated with gold tooling.

Fol. 1: fly-leaf, originally blank, on the recto of which have been entered some notes of the weather in 1639.

Fol. 2[a]: 'Prologue' (18 ll.) and 'Prologue for y[e] Court' (16 ll.) with (12) additional lines 'To y[e] king'.

Fol. 2[a]: 'Scena Persia' followed by list of characters.

Begins, fol. 3[a]: 'Aglaura | Actus 1: scena j[a]: | Enter Iolas, Iolina'.

Ends on fol. 25[b]: 'exeunt | Finis'.

Fol. 26[a]: 'Epilogue' (21 ll.) and 'Epilogue for y[e] Court' (8 ll.) (verso blank).

Written in a very beautiful English hand, with incidental Italian, by a professional scribe. The margins are ruled and the speakers' names placed on the left. There are no speech-rules. The manuscript is almost certainly a copy prepared for pre-

sentation to the King on the occasion of the original performance at Court shortly before 7 Feb. 1638.

The play was printed soon afterwards, being licensed on 18 Apr., with an alternative last act converting the tragedy into a tragi-comedy. The manuscript presents the original version. It has a good many alterations and some additions very carefully made mostly if not all in the same hand as the text. These almost all reappear in the printed version, which however has undergone further amplification. On fol. 13$^a$ appears the direction:

> Enter y$^e$ king [in his night gowne] and Lordes

where the print omits the words deleted in the manuscript. However, at one point at least the print only partly follows the correction of the manuscript. On fol. 15$^a$ is the line:

> from thence tis but [a short howers] *some few minutes* easie [buisnes] *journey*

and here the print accepts the first substitution (italicized) but not the second. (Indeed it looks as though alternative emendations, perhaps by different hands, had both found their way into the manuscript.) At another point the manuscript corrects and explains an error in the print. On fol. 18$^a$ there is a passage which stands exactly as follows (italic here indicates Italian script):

> *Aria:* Staie—the howre, and place. *Ar.* I will not faile yo$^u$ there
> *Zi:* eleaven, vnder the Tarras walke:—∧ *goes out turns back againe*
> *Zi:* I had forgott—

The interlineation in the second line and the speaker's name in the third are additions. The print duly inserted the additional speech, as a separate line, but by omitting the speakers' names assigned it to Ziriff. Apart, however, from definite revision the two texts are in very close agreement.

There is a division into acts only, as in the print.

The stage-directions of the manuscript and those of the print are almost identical in wording and arrangement.

No use has been made of the manuscript by editors.

9. *The Elder Brother*. B.M., MS. Egerton 1994[1]. *c.* 1630–40. The play occupies fols. 2–29 of the collection, and the twenty-eight leaves constitute fourteen separate sheets numbered in the outer top corner. The leaves, which vary a good deal in width and are much decayed near the beginning, measure up to $12\frac{1}{8} \times 7\frac{3}{4}$ inches. There are catchwords throughout.

Begins, fol. 2[a]: 'Actus Primus, | Scœna .1. | Enter: Lewis Angelina: Siluia'.

Ends on fol. 29[a]: 'Exeunt | ffinis: | Elder Brother' followed on the same line by a flourish that may possibly conceal a monogram.

Fol. 29[b]: 'Epilogue' (8 ll.) followed by three short poems in the same hand and 'ffinis'.

Written carefully, with hardly any correction, in a good but rather current hand, not markedly professional, but probably that of a scribe. There is a thorough but irregular mixture of English and Italian forms, but hardly any attempt to distinguish the two scripts. The text is in some places written continuously, the speakers' names within the line being distinguished by rules or brackets. Elsewhere there is a normal use of short speech-rules. The leaves have not been folded for margins, and these are rather narrow: they appear to have been ruled with a stylus on the recto. There is nothing to suggest that the manuscript was ever used in the playhouse, and the paucity of stage-directions makes it unlikely that it was even a copy of a prompt copy. The presence of the poems at the end suggests a purely literary origin.

The play was printed in quarto in 1637. The two texts do not differ widely either in the dialogue or the stage-directions (but see the detailed notes below).

There is a division into acts and scenes throughout. One scene, numbered in the quarto, is not distinguished as such in the manuscript.

Scene headings are written in the centre between rules. The number is on the left, followed by the direction: each sometimes runs to two lines, and they are then separated by a brace. Other entrance directions are either centred, usually in parentheses, or written in the left margin. Exits and the few independent directions are on the right.

2[a] 'Actus Primus Scœna i. { Enter: Lewis Angelina Siluia }

3[b] 'Act: i. Sce[a]: 2: Ent: Andrew, Cooke, and Butler'.

4[b] 'Trampling' (left) [not in Q]. 'Eent':' (*sic*) prefixed to speaker's name 'butler' [centre in Q]. '(Ent: Charles.)' (centre).

6[a] 'Ent' Eust: Egrem: Cons: & Andro.' (right) [so also in Q].

6[b] 'ffinis the first act' (at foot between rules) [Q 'Finis Actus primi'].

7[a] 'Act: 2: Sce: 1: Enter: Miramount: Brisac'.

10[b] (in II. iv) 'En':' prefixed to speaker's name 'And:' (again on 12[a]).

11[a] 'Act: 3. Scœ[a]: 1:' without finis to Act II.

12[a] 'Eeunt [*sic*] | andrew stayes' [Q 'Exeunt']. III. iii 'Noyse' (left) [not in Q].

13[a] '(Enter: Lewis, Aug: Ladies, Notary, Seruants)'. 'Exeunt: | Enter: Bris: . . .' (no new scene, in fact Lewis and Angelina remain) [so also in Q].

14[a] (in III. iv) 'Exeunt: | Ent: Lewis . . .' (no new scene) [III. v in Q].

17[a] 'ffinis the 3[th]: [*sic*] Act:' (at foot) [not in Q].

17[b] 'Act: 4 | Scæ[a]: 1:'.

19[a] IV. iii 'Enter: Angelina, & Siluia, w[th] a Tap:' (last three words perhaps added) [Q 'with a taper'].

20[a] [Q 'Enter Eustace, Egremont, Cowsy': not in MS.]

20[b] '(She strikes off Eust hat)' (right) [also in Q]. '(Snatches out his sword)' (right) [Q 'Snatches away his Sword'].

24[a] 'Act: 5: Scæ[a]: i:' (no finis to Act IV).

26[b] '(they fight)' (right, near centre) [not in Q]. 'Ent': Miramont' (as speaker's name) [Q 'Enter Miram.' (right) the speaker's name being in the middle of the line].

Another quarto of the play appeared in 1651. The text had evidently been revised, for besides misprints of its own it contained a number of minor alterations and a few additional lines. Where the two quartos differ the manuscript is found to agree sometimes with one and sometimes with the other. Some of the principal variants are given in the following list. It may be remarked that the manuscript follows the quarto of 1637 in the reading (II. iv, fol. 11[a]) 'nere have marryed a woman in thy bosome', where that of 1651 has the presumably correct reading 'nere have warmed'. On the other hand, the manuscript alone preserves the true reading in a later passage (III. iii, fol. 13[a]):

> She has a Cherubs [sc. face]
> couer'd & vayld with wings of modest blushes

where both quartos omit the words 'wings of'.

3[b] 1637 'sip thy Celler | Quite dry'. 1651 omits 'Quite'. MS. as 1651.

4[b] 1637 'serulating'. 1651 'service'. MS. as 1651.

6[b] 1637 'a dry-fat of new bookes'. 1651 'a shelfe of new books'. MS. as 1637.

10[b] 1637 'Have I swept your bookes so often'. 1651 'I have not swept your books so long'. MS. as 1637.

11[a] 1637 'The happy, that'. 1651 'the happy day that'. MS. as 1651.

14[a] 1637 'Doe I prithee'. 1651 'Doe I prithee, 'twill be tenne times better'. MS. as 1651.

20[a] 1637 'And on the perfum'd flowers wee'll feast our senses'.
1651 'And on the perfum'd flowers woe us to tumble'.
MS. '& one y[e] perfumed flowers woe vs to't'.
[The MS. evidently preserves the original reading: 1637 is bowdlerized: 1651 apparently a misunderstanding.]
1637 'But I am poore in all but in your love.
Once more, good night. *Cha.* A good night t'yee, and may
The deaw of sleepe fall gently on you, sweet one'.
1651 'But I am poore in all but your affections:
Once more, good night. *Cha.* The deaw of sleep fall on you'.
MS. 'but I am poore in all but in yo[r]: loue
once more good night
*Ch*: The dew of sleepe fall gently on ye sweet one'.
[The MS seems to show that the variant is due to the accidental loss of half a line: 1651 adapts what remains to the demands of metre.]

22[b] 1637 *omits*. 1651 '*And*. I warrant thee Wench'. MS. as 1637.

28[a] 1637 'but ruines it'. 1651 'but rather ruines'. MS. 'but ruines rather'.
1637 'up you destroy;'. 1651 'up: you destroy'. MS. 'vp, yo[u]: destroy'.

29[a] 1637 'we preserve you still'. 1651 'we continue still'. MS. 'we preserue yo[u]: still'.

There is a partial collation of the manuscript in A. H. Bullen's *Beaumont and Fletcher* (ii. 1–100), 1905.

10. *The Fatal Marriage.*

B.M., MS. Egerton 1994[7]. *c.* 1630–40?

The play occupies fols. 136–160 of the collection, and the twenty-five leaves constitute twelve separate sheets followed by a single leaf. The sheets are numbered in the top left-hand corner of the first recto: the odd leaf is apparently not numbered. The leaves measure about $12 \times 7\frac{7}{8}$ inches. There are catchwords on most of the pages: they become less regular towards the end, and some may have been lost in a slight decay of the bottom edge.

Begins, fol. 136ᵃ: 'The ffatall maryage or A | second Lucreatya: · | Enter Lodwick prince of Plazenza, & galeas'.

Ends on fol. 160ᵇ: 'ffinis'.

Written in a good hand, which, however, becomes somewhat less careful as it proceeds. The English script is diversified with Italian used rather irregularly for incidental purposes. There is a normal use of speech-rules, which incline to length, but they rather look as if they had been inserted after the text was written: at the beginning there is a tendency to space the speeches. The leaves do not appear to have been folded for margins, though these are of normal width, for the lines are rather uneven. The general appearance is suggestive of a scribe, but the evidence is not clear. A passage at the head of fol. 156ᵇ is repeated and deleted at the head of fol. 157ᵇ: but most likely the latter (on the fourth page of a sheet) was written first and cancelled on discovering that the inside of the sheet had been left blank. At one point on fol. 151ᵇ the writer began to copy in the wrong speech, and on fol. 157ᵇ he made a muddle over the speakers and speech division: these appear to be errors of transcription. On the other hand an alteration made *currente calamo* on fol. 151ᵃ suggests the author:

> martiall take you the manage
> of the state, [detaine] the ranger sumon hither
> and for knowne causes formerly decreed
> detaine him prissoner . . .

There is no trace of censorship, and no indication of playhouse use. It is true that in the top left-hand corner of the last page the word 'Enter' has been written in a different hand. But it has no apparent relation to the text, and its presence seems to be accidental. The writing resembles that found in certain marginalia in other plays of the collection, but may possibly be an imitation.

There is no trace of division into acts or scenes.

The principal entrances are centred and sometimes appear between rules or with under-rules (usually made up of a series of dashes), but the presence or absence of rules has no relation to scenic division. All other entrances, together with exits and independent directions, are on the right; entrances being occasionally distinguished by under-rules. Directions are usually in Italian script, but its use is not consistent nor is its appearance very distinctive, so that those written on the right are often difficult to distinguish from the text. There are very few beyond the bare entrances and exits.

136[b] 'Enter Duke, laura, martiall · Iaspero, attendante' (centre, without rules).

139[a] 'Laura & Iaspero sigh'. 'la: & Iaspero make signes' (centre, towards right).

139[b] 'Enter woodman, his daughter' (centre, without rules).

140[a] 'Enter galeas. & his mother' (centre, between rules).

140[b] 'Enter Iacomo' (centre, with under-rule).

141[a] 'Exeunt' and 'Enter Iaspero in's night gowne' (centre, between rules). 'Exit' and 'Enter Martiall' (centre, with under-rule).

141[b] 'Exit' and 'Enter Iaspero to laura aboue' (centre, without rules). 'Enter Martiall' (centre, with under-rule). 'Enter Martiall duke' (right, with under-rule) after a speech by M. and without previous exit.

143[a] 'Exeunt' and 'Enter galeas, & Iacomo' (centre, without rules). 'Enter Iouanny' (right, without rules).

143[b] 'Exeunt' and 'Enter Lucreatya' [also Curio] (centre, without rules).

144[a] 'Enter Iouanny & galeas & Iacomo' (centre but towards right, without rules).

145[a] 'Exeunt' and 'Enter Clowne w[th] a whim wham | Enter Iacomo, lucretia' (centre, with rule between).

146b 'Exeunt' and 'Enter prince & Clowne' (centre, between rules).
148a 'Trumpet' and 'Enter Iaspero like an Indian' (centre, without rules).
149a 'Exit Ia.' and 'Enter Mother' (centre, with under-rule).
150a 'Enter Martiall wth watchmen' (centre, at head, spaced but no rule: a new scene). 'Enter prince disguisd Clo: & galeas' (right, with under-rule).
151a 'Exeunt oes' (right) and 'Enter Leonara sola' (centre, same line).
153a 'Enter duke disguis'd' (centre, towards right, crowded in, without rules).
154a 'Enter Clowne' (right, with under-rule).
156a 'Enter duke, Martiall' (right, without rules).
156b 'Exeunt' and 'Enter galeas solus' (centre, without rules).
157a 'Enter leonara' (right, with under-rule).
158a 'Enter Iacomo' (right, without rules).
158b 'Enter martiall wth ye sword before ye prince, laura, Isabella, Iaspero, woodman & Clowne' (centre, below a rule).

Not printed.

11. *The Telltale.* Dulwich MS. xx. *c.* 1630–40?

There is a modern foliation (followed here) from 1 to 25, but the first leaf does not belong. The remaining twenty-four leaves form twelve sheets, numbered as far as the ninth. Of this sheet only a little more than a page is written, the lower part of fol. 18b and the whole of fol. 19 being left blank, owing to a gap in the copy. Of the twelfth sheet only the first page is written, the finis coming three-quarters of the way down. The numbering of the sheets is unusually elaborate: the numeration, placed in the inner top corner of the first page, running, e.g. 'i', '2 sheete', '4th sheet', '9th sheete'; after which only the word 'sheete' is written (usually with a flourish below) the scribe being uncertain of the extent of the lacuna. The leaves measure $12 \times 7\frac{7}{8}$ inches.

[Fol. 1a: 'The Booke and platt of the second part of the 7 deadly sinns' (verso blank). This leaf is probably part of the back sheet of the Plot of that play, which at one time served as a wrapper for *The Telltale* (see p. 106).]

Begins, fol. 2a: 'The telltale | A florish · enter Duke of florence solus'.

Ends on fol. 24a: 'A florish· | Exeunt | Finis'. The last word is immediately followed (on the same line) by a monogram of the letters NICHOLAS. (Verso and fol. 25 blank.)

Written throughout in a hand of literary type, which somewhat resembles, but is clearly distinguishable from, that of Robert Daborne. Both English and Italian scripts are used, but the latter is not very distinctive except when carefully written in some of the more important stage-directions. Speakers' names are in English script and underlined. There is a normal use of fairly short speech-rules. The paper has not been folded for margins, and these are rather narrow. The lacuna and the ignorance of its extent suggest a scribe rather than an author, but his methods are not distinctive of the playhouse. Some of the alterations might be due to the author changing his mind, but they can equally be explained as due to the uncertainty of a scribe working on a draft that had been heavily corrected. Again the incomplete state of the text forbids our supposing that, even if intended for the stage, the manuscript was ever in use. The word 'mine', written in a large and rather rough hand opposite the first speech and surrounded by rules, has been thought to indicate that the book was once in the hands of the actor who was cast for the Duke of Florence; but this is uncertain. There are no prompt notes and no trace of censorship.

There is a regular division into acts only.

The main directions for entrance are in the centre, whether constituting a new scene or not, but many more are on the right, and one even on the left, besides the curiously-placed initial direction. Exits of course are on the right, and so as a rule are independent directions, except one or two particularly elaborate ones in the centre and occasional noises noted on the left. The scribe was apparently conscious that his Italian script habitually lacked distinction, for he surrounded almost all his directions with rules. The following list is substantially complete for all but bare entrances and exits.

2ª 'A florish · enter Duke of florence solus' (left, with rule below). 'enter fidelio' (right). 'exit fid'. 'A florish' (left) opposite 'enter Aspero · Hortensio · Borgias victoria · elinor Isabell: Picentio · Lesbia · Coũt Gismond, Bentivolee'.

4ᵇ 'Enter Captaine Lieftenant Antient'.

is immediately followed (on the same line) by a monogram of the letters [illegible]. (Verso and fol. [illegible] blank.)

Written throughout in a hand of literary type, which some-[illegible] resembles, but is clearly distinguishable from, that of [illegible]. Roman, [illegible] and Italian scripts are used, but [illegible] is not very distinctive except when [illegible] written [illegible] of the more important stage directions. Speakers' [illegible] English [illegible] is a regular [illegible] short speech-[illegible] and there are marginal [illegible] names of characters [illegible]. Many of these are not certainly of the [illegible]. The [illegible] might [illegible] to the author [illegible] but they would [illegible] of [illegible] written [illegible] have been identified [illegible] supposing [illegible] manuscript was ever in [illegible] 'Licensed' [illegible] written in a large and rather rough hand [illegible] surrounded by rules, has been [illegible] was once in the hands of [illegible] who was cast for the Duke of Florence, but this is un-certain. There are no prompt marks and no trace of censorship.

There is a reference [illegible] only.

The stage directions [illegible] the [illegible]

$5^{a}$ 'exeunt | Enter victoria & picentio'. 'Ent Aspero Gismond Cosmo behind to obserue' (right).

$6^{a}$ 'enter Iulio as a slaue' (right). 'Enter Iulio (right). 'Exeunt' (right) and 'Actus Secundus' (centre) at foot.

$6^{b}$ 'Enter elinor. ferneste Garulo' at head. 'Ent benti. w$^{th}$ two wepens' (right).

$7^{a}$ 'ent Gismond whisp elinor' (left, prose right).

$8^{b}$ 'w$^{th}$in' (left, as prefix to speech) and 'A cry w$^{th}$in ent Count lik a foole' (right).

$9^{a}$ 'ent ij doctors' (right). $10^{a}$ 'Enter Duke like a hermit' (right).

$10^{b}$ 'enter Iulio like a slaue' (right).

$11^{a}$ 'ent a messinger w$^{th}$ a letter' (right). 'opens the letter'. 'exeunt | ent victoria in a poore habitt Iulio like A slaue'.

$11^{b}$ 'offers to cut her face' and 'vmbers her face'. 'exeunt | Actus tertius | enter Duke Cap: Leiftenaunt Antient'.

$13^{a}$ 'Enter a boy drest like elinor & doctor'.

$13^{b}$ 'Ent elinor & Count a foole' (right).

$14^{a}$ 'Ent a gent: whispers asp' (right). 'enter Doctor in hast' (right).

$14^{b}$ 'exeunt | Ent: Aspero Cosmo Gis: Fernesi Isabella sick Picentio as a doctor w$^{th}$ her water'.

$15^{b}$ 'enter picentio in his owne shape' (right). 'She offers to embrace him'.

$16^{a}$ 'Actus quartus'. $17^{a}$ 'enter Benti w$^{th}$ a letter' (right).

$18^{a}$ 'exeunt manet nobles'. 'Enter Captaine, . . . duke, barber as hauing trimed him'. 'ent victoria as before' (right).

$20^{a}$ 'enter picentio as a doctor' (right). 'discouer himselfe' (right) at foot.

$20^{b}$ 'embrace him' (right) at head. 'Actus quintus'.

$21^{a}$ 'wine'.

$21^{b}$ 'exeunt' (right) and 'A sennit' (left) opposite 'Enter Cosmo Gismond bare: 2 bearing the Crowne and scepter: then aspero · 2 Churchmen betwixt them Isabella · . . . Picentio as a doctor'.

$22^{a}$ 'Ent duk, dutches . . . antient lik ghosts' (right).

$22^{b}$ 'Daunce' (right) opposite 'The duke taks the Crowne the dutches the scepter, Captaine fetches of hortenzo · leiftenaunt elinor & the antient Borgias' (centre) and 'Another straine' (right) opposite 'in w$^{ch}$ they reioyse & embrace the duke dutches & the rest take a new state in order' (centre).

$23^{b}$ 'garullo brought in a Chaire w$^{th}$ a doctor' (right).

Not printed.

12. *Love's Changelings' Change.*

B.M., MS. Egerton 1994[14]. *c.* 1630–40?

The play occupies fols. 293–316 of the collection, and the twenty-four leaves appear to constitute eleven separate sheets with an odd leaf at the beginning and the end. The leaves measure about $11\frac{7}{8} \times 7\frac{3}{8}$ inches.

Fol. 293ª: 'Prologus' (12 ll.), followed by the title 'Loves Changelinges change' in gothic script, and the couplet: 'Th'old wits are gone: looke for noe new thinge by vs | ffor nullum est iam Dictum quod non sit dictũ prius'.

Fol. 293ᵇ: 'The Actoʳˢ. names. . . . The Scæne Arcadia'.

Begins, fol. 294ª: 'Loves changelings change | Enter 2 Shepharde' (in 'change' the 'e' has been altered from 'd').

Ends on fol. 315ᵇ: 'ffinis'.

Fol. 316ª: 'Epilogus' (6 ll.) (verso blank).

Written in a small, neat, current hand, of a literary rather than professional type, in pale grey ink on somewhat absorbent paper. There are no rules of any kind, and the leaves were probably not folded for margins. What correction there is seems mostly if not all in the same hand. The manuscript is of course a fair copy and there is little distinctive about the alterations, but on the whole they possibly point to the author rather than a scribe. There is no trace of censorship or indication of playhouse use.

The text is divided into acts only.

The principal entrances are distinguished by central directions, and these usually but not always indicate a fresh scene. The great majority of directions of all sorts, however, are written on the right, though some of the longer while beginning on the right continue as central directions across the page. There are none on the left. Both entrances and independent directions tend to be very elaborate, and the latter are pretty frequent. They were evidently written with a view to performance, though they are not distinctively theatrical.

294ª 'Musidorus drawne in wet and halfe dead wᵗʰ a chest' (right). 'They take him by the heeles while water runs out of his mouth'. 'offers to throw himselfe in againe: they stay him'.

11. *Love's Changelinge's Change.*

[illegible] MS. Egerton 1994 [illegible]

[illegible] the collection, and the [illegible] [illegible] covering the [illegible] [illegible] [illegible] the beginning and the end [illegible]

[illegible]

[illegible] The Arcadia [illegible]

[illegible]

[illegible] (verso blank)

[illegible] hand, [illegible] rather [illegible] [illegible] and [illegible] were pre- [illegible] [illegible] a course [illegible] [illegible] the whole [illegible] [illegible]

[illegible] divided into acts [illegible]

[illegible] by central direc- [illegible] a fresh scene. [illegible] of all sorts, however, are [illegible] while beginning [illegible] directions across the page [illegible]

[illegible]

[illegible]

[illegible] marked [illegible]

[illegible] in act and scene [illegible]

[illegible] out of the [illegible]

[illegible]

294[b] 'Exeunt Shepherdę'. 'a smoke frõ vnderneath'. 'Pyrocles aloft'. 'Throwes the rope to short'. 'Exeunt omnes' and 'Enter Musidorus fainting with two shepherdę' (centre).

295[a] 'Enter Kalander' (right). 'whispers him'.

295[b] 'Enter a boy w[th] a le[r]. to y[e]. Shepherdę they open it & read it' (right). 'offers them a Iewell'. 'hee faintę. Kalander holds him'. 'drawes the Curtaine' 'give him the picture'.

296[a] 'A Table spread'.

296[b] 'Enter Kalanders serv[t] w[th] a l[r]. hee reads it and deptę suddenly' (right). 'Exit serv[t]. Enter Kalander with his counsell hee reveals it in private w[ch] was to haue some poore souldiers dressed w[th] rusty armo[r]. w[th] boody [*sic*] shirtę hanging on staves in steade of banners and bagpipes in stead of drumes leading some gentlemen chaind as Prisners of w[ch] Musidorus was one · how dee like it my Lord' (centre but beginning right): the last words are apparently part of a speech. 'Enter the poore souldiers w[th] their prisoners chaind as aforesaid they get into the Towne where shifting of their chaines they put to flight the Helotę. A noyse from w[th]in of those that fled Musidorus psues them and by the way is encountred by their captaine. | Enter Pyrocles at one doore and Musidorus at an other' (whole centre). 'throwes of his helmet'.

297[a] 'Exeunt omnes' and 'Enter Kalander Clitophon attend[tę]. Pyrocles and Musidorus w[th] a box of Iewells' (centre). 'Exeunt Attendantę at one doore and Pyrocles & Musidorus at another. Enter Kalander & Clitophon' (centre, beginning right) but Musidorus seems to remain. 'Exeunt omnes' and 'Enter two Huntsmen winding their horne' (centre). 'windę againe, Enter Kalander . . . in hunting habit' (right).

297[b] 'Exeunt: a hoope from w[th]in'. 'hee misse Pyrocles'. 'Exeunt omnes. Enter Musidorus reading of a l[r].' (right). 'reads it againe'. 'gives him Iewells'.

298[a] 'Exeunt at seu'all doores' and 'Actus secundus Scæna prima. | Still musicke from aboue with shrill voice naming Philoclea. Enter Pyrocles in an Amazons habit' (centre). 'Steps behind the Curtaine and singes'. 'drawes the curtaine'.

299[a] 'aside' (right) added.

302[b] 'Actus tertius scæna i[a]: Enter Cecropia and Clineas' (centre). 'A Table brought in They sit and drinke'.

304[a] 'They march out. The Drũ sounding & weapons clashing they come forth bloody and running away Philinax meetes them'.

304[b] 'Exeunt. Enter Dametas and a Esq3' (right).

305[a] 'Exeunt. | Enter Dametas w[th] his Sq3 · bearing his sheild w[th] this devise vppon five at a blowe. Enter a Page at another doore w[th] a l[r]. to Dametas' (partly centre, partly right).

306[b] 'Exeunt Enter Amphialus dressed w[th] a messenger at one doore and Cecropia at an other | hee drawes the messengers sword Cecropia runs backward & falls dead, messenger carries her out and comes in againe' (right, though apparently a new scene). 'falls on his sword messenger seekes to saue him but could [*sic*] not carries him in'. 'Exeunt omnes | Actus quartus Scæna prima'.

307[a] 'They going out are stopt by loud musicke from aboue'.

309[b] [speaks] 'in th'aire aside'. 310[a] 'rages'.

310[b] 'shee steepes beehind the Curtaine'.

311[a] 'hugs her'. 'The kinge lyes Dead'. 'ffinis Actus quarti' (centre, at foot).

311[b] 'Actus quintus Scæna prima'.

312[a] 'o yes—o yes—o yes—from within' (as a line of text).

312[b] 'Evarchus stands vp to give Iudgm[t]'. 315[b] 'they take him out'.

Not printed.

13. *The Wizard* [by S. Baylie].

B.M., MS. Add. 10306. *c.* 1640?

The play occupies fifty-five leaves (with a modern foliation 1–55 here followed) paged (beginning on fol. 3[a]) 1–105, and forming twenty-seven separate sheets with an odd leaf at the end. On the first page is a pencil note: 'formerly in possession of Cartwright presented by him to Dulwich College then in Garricks' (this has been rubbed out and retraced), and on the second page: 'before 1640'. The leaves are large folio, measuring $14 \times 9\frac{1}{4}$ inches.

Fol. 1[b] (recto blank): 'Dramatis personæ . . .' a later addition.

Fol. 2[a]: 'The Wizard'.

Fol. 2[b]: 'Dramatis Personæ. . . . The Scene London' the original list, much altered and crossed off.

Begins, fol. 3[a]: 'The | Wizard | A Comedy. | Act. 1. Scene. 1. | Sebastian. Clerimont' (the second word in ornamental gothic script).

Ends on fol. 55[a]: 'Exeunt Omnes. | Finis' (verso blank).

Written in a calligraphic hand of an Italian type but retaining

some English forms, with a sort of formal roman for directions, &c. It is evidently a literary transcript prepared by a scribe. There are extensive corrections and alterations, in part by a reviser who might be the original author, but in part apparently of later date, some being in the same hand as the personae on fol. 1[b]. The margins are ruled in red forming a column on the left for the speakers' names. There are no speech-rules. Nor is there any trace of censorship or indication of playhouse use. The play may from internal evidence be assigned to *c.* 1620–40, but there is nothing to show that the manuscript may not be later.

There is a division throughout into acts and scenes.

Directions for entrances are mostly centred, without rules. Exits as usual are on the right. Independent directions, which are generally within square brackets, are also on the right though they sometimes form a separate line.

5[b] 'Scene: 2. | Enter S[r] Timothy Shallow eating his paper, and Pimponio'.

7[b] 'Scene: 3. | Enter Cælia sola'.

9[a] 'S[r] Oli. walks up and downe'.

9[b] 'Enter Clerimont disguisd like a Soldier with a patch on his eye, and a false beard'.

12[b] (in I. iv) 'As he is going off Antonio meets him & draws' (centre, towards right, and within brackets).

13[a] 'makes at him'. 'draws'. 'undisguises himself'.

14[b] 'Act. 2. Scene. 1'.

23[b] II. vi. 'Enter Antonio and the Cook at one end, and Clerimont at the other and listens'.

35[b] (in IV. i) 'Sebastian goes out at one end, and listens; *Antonio goes out at the other*' (centre).

39[b] 'Antonio presents Cælia & Violetta before Sebastian as Spirits' (centre).

46[b] V. iii. 'Enter Antonio in the habit of his ffather, Clerimont. A Parson. Pimp. disguisd, with a dark lanthorne in his hand, and some habbits in his arms'.

47[a] V. iv. 'Enter Cælia; sitting at a table perusing some papers, Lucee waiting'. 'speakes at the door'.

48[a] 'takes the taper and find's it not the same' (sc. person).

50 v. v. 'Enter S^r^ Oliver, with musick playing under Violettas window'. 'musitians play'. 'Sebastian speaks above' (centre, towards right).

51[b] 'v. vi. 'Enter S^r^ Tim: Shallow disguisd as a conjurer, Pimponio & Luce'.

53[a] v. vii. 'Enter Antonio in the habitt of the Conjurer Clerimont, Cælia, & Violetta'.

54[a] 'he & she kneels' (in the text).

55[a] 'The Dance' (centre, towards right).

A second manuscript of this play is preserved in the Cathedral Library at Durham, and has a title-page: 'The Wizard | by | Simon Baylie'. It is in a different hand, but is not autograph, though it may be nearer to the original. It too has been corrected and altered in later hands.

An edition is in preparation by H. de Vocht (Louvain, *Materials &c.*).

14. [*The Court Secret*, by J. Shirley.]
Worcester College, Oxford. *c.* 1642?

[The credit for the identification of this piece as a version of *The Court Secret* printed as Shirley's in 1653, is due to Mr. R. G. Howarth of St. Catherine's, Oxford, who has kindly communicated to me his notes on the subject. It seems probable that some of the writing in the manuscript is Shirley's own, but it would be unwise to pronounce with certainty until it has been further investigated. The material for comparison is a volume of poems in the Bodleian (MS. Rawl. poet. 88) written in a calligraphic hand with the signature 'I. Shirley' at the end, and Shirley's will at Somerset House signed 'Iames Shirley', which is a draft in a very current hand. There seems no reasonable doubt that the two signatures are in the same hand, but the extreme difference between the writing of the body of the two documents makes comparison very difficult. My own impression, which I believe Mr. Howarth shares, is that the will is holograph and the poems likewise, and that the same hand is to be seen in the revisions in the play but not in the original text.]

The play, which has no title in the manuscript, occupies twenty-seven numbered leaves, which are, however, followed by

50 or 51 *Enter* 2 *Clowns* with musick, playing under Tapstre [illegible] [illegible] ... cathedral, specially stage" (centre, towards right).

51 [illegible] *Enter* ... [illegible] disguised as a conjurer, Plymouth's [illegible]

55 [illegible] *Enter* ... in the habit of the Conjurer, [illegible] [illegible]

[illegible] ... on the stool.

57 *The Dance* (centre, towards right).

[illegible] ... is preserved in the Cathedral [illegible] ... and has a title-page: The Wizard [illegible] ... in a different hand, but is not autograph [illegible] ... may be earlier to the original. It, too, has been [illegible] and altered in later hands.

An edition of it [illegible] ... de Vocht (Louvain [illegible]).

[illegible] ... Smiles.]

[illegible] ... College, Oxford ... c. 1637

[illegible] ... for the ... version of this piece as ... [illegible]

[illegible]

[illegible] ... to ... the ... of the ... are ... [illegible]

[illegible] ... that ... in the scene [illegible] ... the ... of the [illegible] ... very carefully [illegible] ... that the [illegible] ... alterations.

The ... the manuscript ... [illegible] ... leaves ... and, however, [illegible]

three others unnumbered (fols. 28–30). Of the latter the first contains only an addition to the text, while the other two (which have been separately folded and must have long remained separate) contain an induction. Fol. 12 is a cancel pasted on to the stub of the original leaf. Originally fols. 1–20 seem to have formed ten separate sheets: the same may be true of fols. 21–28, but these leaves are without watermark. There is a watermark in fol. 29, apparently the same as in the earlier sheets. Catchwords occur very irregularly. The leaves measure about $12\frac{1}{8} \times 7\frac{5}{8}$ inches.

Begins, fol. $1^a$: 'Act $j^{st}$: | Enter Don Manuell at one Dore, . . .' (see below).

Ends on fol. $27^b$: 'Exeunt omnes. | Finis'.

Fol. $28^a$: a passage of 11 lines intended for insertion on the opposite page (verso blank).

Fol. $29^a$: 'Inductio. | Spectator & Prolocutor' (verso blank).

Fol. $30^a$: end of Induction, 'Exit | Finis'.

Fol. $30^b$: two endorsements to the folded packet, 'Induction to $y^e$ Court Secret' and 'Rose & Crown Court'.

Written originally throughout in a careful semi-calligraphic hand (apparently that of *The Country Captain*). The script is Italian, making no difference for incidental purposes, except that some of the more important directions are written rather larger than the rest. The leaves appear to have been folded for margins, but these are only one-sixth of the width of the page, whereas the usual measure is a quarter. There are no speech-rules. Each act except the last begins a fresh page.

The piece has been revised throughout in a different and more current hand, also Italian in style. Several passages have been deleted, the most extensive being on fols. $3^a$, $5^a$, $22^b$; while others on fols. $23^a$ and $26^a$, though not actually deleted, are apparently marked for omission. The most important substitution is on fol $15^a$, the longest addition that on the last page. The character name Clara has been altered to Clarissa throughout. Two minor alterations, on fols. $6^a$ and $21^a$, appear to be in a different hand from the rest, though of the same nature. Also two additional directions, on fols. $23^b$ and $27^a$, are written in a very different style, but probably by the reviser. There are also some pencil markings which may indicate further adaptation for stage purposes.

The induction is written in a calligraphic Italian hand. The text is continuous, with speakers' names within the line. It has been roughly corrected in another hand in one place in pencil. This hand is difficult to identify: it may be the same as that of the revision, or there may be more than one. There would be nothing to connect the induction with the play were it not for the endorsements. These seem to be in one hand, different from that of the Induction, but possibly the reviser's. The Induction was evidently written on the first and third pages of a sheet, that was then again folded in four for carrying. It is much discoloured.

The piece was printed in 1653 in Shirley's *Six New Plays*, in which it occupied the last place, and was said to have been 'Never Acted, But prepared for the Scene at Black-friers'. In an epistle dedicatory to the Earl of Strafford, Shirley explained that 'it happened to receive birth, when the Stage was interdicted'. The printed version has been extensively revised and indeed largely rewritten from that contained in the manuscript. Presumably this revision was made by Shirley himself, but the alterations do not in general agree with those made by the second hand in the manuscript. The name Clara is retained: on the other hand, both revisions remove a minor character called Claudia. Two examples of the revisions are given below.

The play is divided into acts only, and in this the printed version agrees.

Most of the directions for entrance are centred, irrespective of whether or not a new scene is implied. A few, however, appear on the right, and even one on the left. The reviser has also occasionally used the left margin. Exits, as usual, and independent directions are on the right. There are very rarely any rules, but one appears below the first direction. The following list aims at being exhaustive for all but bare entries and exits.

1ᵃ I. i 'Enter Don Manuell at one Dore, at the other Maria lead by a Nobleman, *Claudia* Ladies Attendant'. Claudia has only a single line in the text, and this the reviser has transferred rather illegibly to

another speaker, possibly '1 Nob.'. She has also been removed from the printed version, the corresponding speech being given to one of the Gentlemen. 'she letts fall a Iewell'.

1[b] *'Enter Pedro' (left) opposite '*Ent' pedro*' (right).

2[b] 'pedro offers to go of'. 3[a] *'shewes a letter'.

4[a] 'Enter Manuell and Clara [altered to *'Clarissa'] at the other Dore Maria'. 'Man: leaues Clara and goes to Maria', the reviser drew rules round the direction, and in 'Clara' altered the second 'a' to 'i'.

5[a] *'she veiles'.

5[b] 'Exeunt seuerally | Explicit Actus primus' (quarter of page blank).

6[a] 'Act..2[d]: | Enter King and Roderigo'.

6[b] 'Manuell carrying of | Enter piracquo' (right, at foot).

7[a] 'Enter Carlo' to which is added *'meeting Piraquo' (centre, towards right).

8[a] 'pedro comes forth'.

8[b] 'Enter Maria, and Clara [altered to *'Clarissa'], *Claudia*', but no speeches are assigned to the last.

10[a] 'Manuell in Prison' (centre). 'Enter Carlo and the Captaine of the Castle' (centre).

11[b] 'Exit' (two-thirds of the page blank).

12[a] (a cancel) 'Act the third: | Enter | Antonio . . .'.

12[b] 'Carlo rises' (left).

13[a] 'Carlo embraces Man:' 'Carlo whispers with Man | Ex: Men:'. 'Enter Isabella veild and ladies | Isabella vnveiles' (centre). 'all Rise' with rules added by reviser.

14[a] 'Men: offers to goe of'.

15[a] 'Enter Carlo, Clara [altered to *'Clarissa'] Manuell aloofe'.

16[b] 'Exit. | Explicit Actus tertius' (two-thirds of the page blank).

17[a] 'Act 4[th]: | Enter Pedro'. 'Enter *Iulio* [*'Lopez' interlined] and *Iaques* [*'Alphonso' interlined] they vncouer and cringe' (none of these characters are in the printed version). 'Enter Leonora she curt'sies and passes' (another character unknown in print).

18[a] 'drawes'.

19[a] 'Enter Carlo like a More' (centre). 'they fight'.

19[b] 'Enter Celio and Surgeon' (right). 'they carry him of'. [speakes] * 'to Clara' (right) a slip for Clarissa.

20[b] 'Enter Antonio and Isabella. after them Piracquo who whispers to Roderigo'.

22$^a$ 'Ex$^t$: | Explicit actus quartus. | Act 5$^{th}$: | Carlo and a Dominican discouered vpon a Couch | Enter Celio . . .'.

22$^b$ 'sit downe'.

23$^a$ 'Ex:' and 'Celio and the Surgeons follow Carlo | Enter Mendoza in the Castle with the Capt:' (centre).

23$^b$ 'Enter a seruant and whispers with Castellano' (centre). *'Enter Pedro' (right) with reference mark for a line above.

24$^a$ 'Enter Castellano and whispers to Mendoza' (centre). 'Ex: Enter Castell: againe with Clara [altered to *'Clarissa'] veild' (right) with under-rule. 'she vnveiles'.

24$^b$ *'Enter Pir: mendoz: Cast: they obscure' 7 lines above '*Enter pir: mendoza and the Castell: they obscure*' (both left).

25$^b$ 'exeunt seuerally'.

26$^a$ 'pedro a loofe' (right) opposite 'Enter king, piraquo, Mendoza' (centre).

27$^a$ *'Whispers 〈 〉 | Exit'.

Below are two examples of the alternative revisions drawn from the first act. In the later portions of the play the printed version is often too divergent for comparison.

Fol. 2$^b$: *original text:*

Ped. if your lordship slight me thus, I may find wayes
to vndoe my selfe. pedro offers to go of
Pir. Pedro? why in this passion Signior?
Come weele talke temperatly—
Men, therefore vpon my blessing if thou hast
such an ambitious thought, I charge thee leaue it.
Cla. Sir you may spare these jealousies, I haue not
giuen away my freedome, or by promise
of more then may become my duty, cherish'd
his Courtship; though some Ladies, that are offerd
so faire, would thinke it litle sinne to welcome
the title of a Princesse, but I am
not ignorant, he is designd a bridegroome
to the fair Isabella, and it were
saucy iniustice to distract a blessing
now houering o're two kingdomes!

*manuscript revision:*

Ped. if your lordship slight me thus, I may find wayes to my own
safety. pedro offers to go of

. . . . . . . . . .

Cla. Sir you may trust my obedience, I shall not
w^th more than may become my duty, answerd [*sic*]
his Courtship; though some Ladies, that are offerd

. . . . . . . . . . . . . .

*printed version* (p. 5):

*Pe.* Nay if you slight me, Sir, and pay my service
With this neglect, I can undoe my self
To make you find repentence—— [*offers to go in.*
*Pi.* Come nearer——
*Me.* Therefore upon my blessing, if thou hast
Such an ambitious thought, I charge thee leave it.
*Cla.* Sir, you may spare these preeepts, [*sic*] I have not
Given away my freedom, or by promise
Of more than may become my duty, offer'd
The Prince an expectation; I am
Not ignorant . . . . . . . . . .

Fol. 5^a: *original text:*

Cla: Sir I haue no art to decipher these Characters
vpon his brow, they carried some displeasure.
and if I not mistake he namd his sister,
with caution you be lesse ambitious
Man: tis so, some tongues haue misrepresented me
I should deserue his frowne, if I had thoughts [so high]
so high, to attempt my Courtship there. Maria
is sacred and aboue me, and you might
with something more of reason I confesse
resent this litle absence, if you had not
been witnes how I was comanded from thee
Cla. I did obserue it
Ma: Clara I will make
thee Iudg of my whole heart, and cheerefully
divest my soule of all these garments, that do
obscure it from thy Eye; and if thou find
within me, one ambitious thought reflect
on her, do thou accuse me to the Prince
and let his anger fall, or if that be
not punishment enough, be thou more cruell
and frowne vpon me too.

*manuscript revision:*

Cla: Sir I want art to decipher those Characters
vpon his brow, they carried some displeasure.

and if I mistake not he namd his sister,
with caution you be lesse ambitious
Man: tis so, I am misrepresented to him
Clarissa Ile make thee iudge of my whole heart
divest it quite of all these veiles, that do

. . . . . . . . . . .

*printed version* (pp. 12–3):

*Cla.* Sir, I have no art
To decypher mysteries, but if I erre not,
He nam'd his Sister.
*Ma.* Ha!
*Cla.* With caution you should be less ambitious.
*Ma.* 'Tis so, he's jealous of my courtship there,
It can be nothing else, can it, sweet Madam?
I dare make you the judge of all my thoughts,
Unbosom every counsell, and divest
My soul of this thin garment that it wears,
To let your eye examine it; if you find
Within that great diaphanal an atome
Look black, as guilty of the Prince's anger,
Let him doom me to death, or if that be
Not punishment enough, be you more cruel,
And frown upon me too.

An edition by R. G. Howarth is in preparation.

15. *The Queen of Corsica*, by F. Jaques.
B.M., MS. Lansd. 807[1]. 1642.

The play occupies fols. 2–28 of the modern pencil numbering of this small collection, a numbering which includes (as fol. 9) an additional slip. The twenty-six original leaves (of which two rectos and two versos are blank) constitute thirteen separate sheets. The leaves measure $12 \times 7\frac{1}{2}$ inches.

Fol. 2ᵃ: 'The Queene of Corsica A Tragædy Written by Fran: Iaques. Anno Dom̃: 1642' followed by a four-line quotation from Horace (fol. $2^b$ and fol. $3^a$ blank).

Fol $3^b$: 'Dramatis Personæ. . . . The Scene Corsica'.

Begins, fol. $4^a$: 'Actus Primi | Scen: $1^a$: | {A Wood} Florimond. Cleander Dorimant. Calidor {Wounded}'.

Ends on fol. $27^a$: 'Explicit. Act. Quint. | Finis' (fol. $27^b$ and fol. $28^a$ blank).

Fol. 28ᵇ: 'Epilogue' (heading only) and 'Francis Iaques'. Below several short lines of writing have been smudged out.

Written on inferior paper in a hand of professional type. The script is mainly Italian, though several English forms are retained. Proper names (including speakers' prefixes) are written in a purer style, but this barely distinguishes them from the surrounding text. In stage-directions the hand is slightly more formal, and in scene numbers and headings decidedly larger. There are no speech-rules, and speakers' names are indented instead of being placed in the margin. The leaves have not been folded for margins, which are rather irregular and tend to be narrow. The inserted slip (fol. 9) has on the recto an additional passage carefully written by the same scribe. This belongs to a point on fol. 8ᵇ, and the slip was originally pinned onto that leaf. Another slip was once pinned onto the verso of fol. 22, where there is a reference mark for another insertion, but is no longer preserved. There are a few alterations in a different ink and possibly a different hand, but they do not necessarily point to the author. On fol. 13ᵃ a royal scandal is reported 'Which is the generall Whisper', and for 'generall' is substituted 'priuate': one can hardly see the censor's hand in this. On fol. 8ᵃ a direction is added, and another on fol. 24ᵇ; on fol. 22ᵇ 'you' is corrected to 'mee', and on fol. 23ᵃ eight lines have been cancelled evidently on literary grounds. There is nothing to suggest that the manuscript, which is clearly of a literary type, is autograph, or that it has been used in the playhouse: neither is there any trace of censorship.

There is a division throughout into acts and scenes: the latter are divided according to the foreign method.

Scene headings are centred and consist of lists of names only, but they are often accompanied by marginal directions. Heavy rules separate the acts. Noteworthy are the occasional indications of locality. Exits are usually, but not always, on the right. The full descriptive directions, whether independent or attached to entrances, are almost always in the left margin, and appear only by rare exception on the right.

4ᵇ 'A Wood' (left) opposite the direction: 'Scen 2ᵃ. [centre] Wind Hornes—then as from Hunting Enter—[right] | Achæa. . . . Phocillus [centre]'. 'Shee Embraces & Kisses him. Natolion frowns' (left). 'Dorimond p$^{r}$sents Calidor to the Queene' (left).

$5^{a}$ 'Embraces him'.

$5^{b}$ 'Phocillus Courting Antiope Aside. Alceus ffretts'. 'Alceus comes up to Phocillus'. 'Achæa & Florim: fall from y$^{eir}$ whisper'.

$7^{a}$ (in I. vi) 'Exeunt Beotto. Capt. Diocles' (left). 'Explicit. Act. Prim. | Actus Secundi | Scena 1$^{a}$:' (centre).

$8^{a}$ (in II. ii) 'Achæa Beckens y$^{e}$ Ladyes to Depart. Exeunt' to which is added in different ink 'shee weepeth' (*sic*).

$8^{b}$ (in II. iii) 'shee Pauses a pretty while, & then goes on'.

$12^{a}$ (in II. vii) 'Exit' (left). 'Scena 8$^{a}$ | Ariste. Achæa. Lady Undressing to Bed'.

$16^{a}$ III. vii 'Soft Musique. Tapers lighted, as the Bridall Chamber'.

$16^{b}$ 'A shrike w$^{th}$in. Arist: and Lady runne ouer the Stage, in y$^{eir}$: Actions expressing feare. They enter againe, And say y$^{e}$ Court is up at the Noyse, & in y$^{t}$ perplexity runne in and out'. (in III. viii) 'A Shricke w$^{th}$in'. 'Beotto Breakes in, and enters agen'.

$17^{a}$ 'An Alarum' opposite 'Scen. II'.

$18^{a}$ (in IV. i) 'The Cittz. stare at one another in amazem$^{t}$.' 'seruant laughes, and strikes him'.

$18^{b}$ (in IV. ii) 'Crowns him'. 'Henceforward his name is Chang'd'.

$19^{b}$ 'The Cittizens Speake uery Low'.

$20^{b}$ (in IV. iii) 'Cleander reads the Letter' (centre) which follows.

$21^{b}$ 'Pho. calls her back; gazes on her a good while. then Exit' explanatory of the text: '*Pho.* Farewell—Madam.—My Heart haz limn'd your fface now'. 'A Wood, wherein a graue is discou$^{r}$d; and Achæa Burieing her Infant, and strewing fflowers upon it. Achæa in Disguised Country Weeds' (left) opposite 'Scena 5$^{a}$. | Achæa. Ariste' (centre).

$22^{a}$ 'The lute w$^{th}$in while this song Warbled'.

$23^{b}$ V. i 'Phocillus. Heads-man' (centre) and 'Phocillus in Mourning. a Coffin lyeing by Him' (left). 'Feeles y$^{e}$ Axe'.

$24^{b}$ V. iii 'Hymen's Priest . . . Beotto' (centre) and 'Soft Musique. Hymens Image Discouerd, upon an Altar. the Priest goes up. Then follow Florimond & Achæa, hand in hand; Garlands upon theyr Heads. The King & Lords by 2 & 2 following' (left). 'The Priest p$^{r}$sents 'em' in different ink. 'The Image Sweats Blood'. 'w$^{th}$ a knife shee Stabbs him and her Selfe. Flor. reeles against the Altar'.

$25^{b}$ (in V. iv). 'King kneeles and they all doe'. 'Enter a Messenger' (left) no new scene.

26ᵃ v. v 'Phocillus. Captaine' (centre) and 'Drums. A Cry with in (Downe w^th^ y^e^ Rascalls Downe w^th^ y^e^ Rebells) Enter Pho. Cap. Drawne'. 'Lycom. enters, & Phoc: runnes at him, Lyc. flees. Phocillus pursues him in and out. Antiope at the Hanging entring in hast to see what is the matter runnes upon Phoc: sword who is in pursuite of y^e^ King' (left); 'Lyc.' enters and speaks before the end of the scene, a new one beginning with the entrance of Antiope: 'Scena 6ᵃ: | Antiope. Phocillus' (centre).

Not printed.

## *CLASS C*

1. [*John of Bordeaux.*] Alnwick Castle. 1590–1600?

A folio manuscript of a play without title, but with Sir John of Bordeaux among the leading characters, which also include Friar Bacon and Vandermast. The play alludes as in the past to incidents narrated in *The Famous History of Friar Bacon*, and is therefore presumably later than Greene's *Friar Bacon and Friar Bungay*.

Written in a clear but rather rough English hand: a few directions in Italian script may have been added by another hand. Marginal directions by a playhouse reviser, which thrice include the name of John Holland, make it clear that the manuscript has served as a prompt book; but in most respects it differs widely from the normal type. The leaves have not been folded for margins, there are no speech-rules, no attempt is made to differentiate the script, and, most remarkable of all, verse is almost throughout written as prose, and the speeches are continuous, with speakers' names in the middle of the line. At one point a passage of twelve lines has been written (apparently in a blank left for the purpose) in the hand of Henry Chettle.

Holland was with Strange's men when they acted *The Seven Deadly Sins* (perhaps in conjunction with the Admiral's) about 1590, and is also mentioned in the stage-directions of 2 *Henry VI.* His appearance therefore tends to connect the present piece with Strange's men. This company also acted *Friar Bacon* in 1592–3, but that play seems to have belonged to

Alleyn personally, and had probably been originally written for the Queen's men about 1589. It is possible, therefore, that the present play may have been composed as a rival piece for Strange's men about 1590, before Greene's play came under their control, or as a continuation at a somewhat later date.

An edition is in preparation by W. L. Renwick.

2. [*Tancred and Ghismonda.*] B.M., MS. Add. 34312. *c.* 1600? The play, which bears no title, is written on forty-eight numbered quarto leaves, forming fols. 139–186 of the manuscript. The personae and a prologue occupy the first page and the text begins with 'Act i' on the verso. The last leaf has the epilogue on the recto and on the verso a note: 'Scriptum p Capellanum tuum deuinct- & deuot-issimum'. Written in a rough hand, using both English and Italian script, with practically no correction. The whole seems to be purely literary, though the epilogue contemplates performance. It is an entirely distinct piece from the *Gismund of Salerne* of MSS. Hargrave 205 and Lansdowne 786, of which the revised version by Robert Wilmot was printed in 1591–2 under the title of *Tancred and Gismund.*

3. *A Game at Chess,* by T. Middleton. Five MSS. 1624–5.
(*a*) Trinity College, Cambridge, MS. O. 2. 66.

The play occupies fifty-one quarto leaves.

Title: 'A Game | at | Chesse. | by T. M.', verso blank: next the prologue, also with verso blank: there follow the induction, text, and epilogue on 98 pages.

Written throughout in the autograph of the author, Thomas Middleton, a small current hand making no differentiation of script in the text. The play is divided into acts only.

(*b*) Huntington Library.

The play occupies fifty-three quarto leaves.

Title: 'A Game | at | Chesse. | by Tho. Middleton', verso blank: next the prologue, also with verso blank: there follow the induction, text, and epilogue on 102 pages.

Written for the most part in a clear scribal hand, but with the title-page, a hiatus in II. ii, and also V. ii–iii supplied by Middleton. The play is divided into acts only, except for the heading 'Scæna Vltima'.

(*c*) Dr. A. S. W. Rosenbach.

The play occupies thirty-nine quarto leaves.

Title: 'A Game | at | Chesse | As it was Acted Nine Dayes together. | Compos'de by Tho: Middleton', verso blank: the prologue is absent: there follow the induction (with a blank page at the end), text, and epilogue on 75 pages (the last verso being blank).

Written for the most part in one rather rough scribal hand, but a second has written a short passage in III. i and the first four and a half pages of the last act, and Middleton has supplied the title-page. The play is divided into acts only, except for the heading 'Scena vltima'.

(*d*) Bodl., MS. Malone 25.

The play occupies thirty-seven quarto leaves.

Title: '1624. || A | Game | at | Chesse.|| By | Tho. Middleton' (in three compartments) verso blank: next (on an inserted leaf) dedicatory verses (4 lines) 'To the Worthilie-Accomplish'd Mr: William Hammond' from 'A Seruant to youre Vertues T. M.', verso blank: the prologue is absent: there follow the induction, text, and epilogue on 69 numbered pages (the last verso being blank).

A careful calligraphic copy in the hand of the scribe Ralph Crane, with the exception of the page of dedication which is autograph, though in a more calligraphic style than Middleton's usual writing. There is a division into acts and scenes throughout. The text is surrounded by rules, there are no speech-rules, but regular catchwords.

(*e*) B.M., MS. Lansd. 690.

The play actually occupies fifty-two quarto leaves, but there is an extra blank leaf after the title, presumably intended for a dedication but not filled in.

Title: '1624.|| A | Game | att | Chesse || By Tho: Middleton' (in three compartments) verso blank: the prologue follows the induction, and these, together with the text and epilogue, fill 101 numbered pages (the last verso being blank).

A careful calligraphic copy entirely in the hand of the scribe Ralph Crane. There is a division into acts and scenes throughout, and the arrangement is the same as in (*d*).

The play was first printed in 1625, and the manuscripts, which were evidently prepared to satisfy the curiosity of readers, are all presumably earlier. It had been licensed by Herbert on 12 June 1624. The dedicatory quatrain in (*d*) runs:

> This which nor Stage nor Stationers Stall can showe
> (The Common Eye maye wish for, but ne're knowe)
> Comes in it's best loue wth the New-yeare forth
> As a fit Present to the Hand of Worth.

This must have been written between the suppression of the play and its surreptitious publication, and the New Year was therefore 1624/5.

With one exception the manuscripts are described and collated in the edition of the play by R. C. Bald (1929), and he has also dealt in an article in *The Modern Language Review* (1930, xxv. 474–8) with the Rosenbach manuscript (*c*), which only came to light in 1928. None of the manuscripts preserves a quite complete text. The one in the Malone collection (*d*) is much abbreviated, and has the further peculiarity of omitting most of the stage-directions and massing at the beginning of each scene the names of all the characters who appear in it. Apart from the absence of the prologue, (*c*) contains the most complete text, though it has a few omissions of its own. The relation of the manuscripts has been further considered in articles in *The Library* for June 1930 and Sept. 1931.

4. *The Witch*, by T. Middleton.
Bodl., MS. Malone 12. *c.* 1620–7.

The play occupies forty-nine quarto leaves, the pagination beginning on the second leaf.

Title: 'A Tragi-Coomodie Called the Witch, | long since Acted, by his Ma[ties]. Seruants at the Black-Friers. | Written

by Tho. Middleton', followed on the same page by 'The Sceane Rauenna' and a list of 'The Persons' in double columns.

Epistle dedicatory: 'To the truely-worthie and generously-affected Thomas Holmes, Esquier', subscribed 'Tho: Middleton' (not autograph), on the verso of the title-leaf.

The text begins on page 1 and ends on p. 95 (the last verso is blank), and there is a running title 'The witch' throughout.

A calligraphic copy, written throughout in the hand of Ralph Crane. There are rules round the text leaving margins at top and bottom and at the outer edge, which are only used for the running title and pagination: there are no speech-rules. The text is in English script with small Italian for incidental purposes and a larger and bolder variety for the headings. There are regular catchwords, and about twenty-five lines to the page. There are few directions apart from the headings, but the necessary entrances, &c., are marked on the right. The play is divided into acts and scenes throughout.

Printed: Isaac Reed (but without name), 1778; A. Dyce, *Middleton* (iii. 245–335), 1840; A. H. Bullen, *Middleton* (v. 351–453), 1885.

5. *Demetrius and Enanthe*, by J. Fletcher.
Lord Harlech's MS. 27 Nov. 1625.

A private transcript of the play printed in the Beaumont and Fletcher folio of 1647 under the title of *The Humorous Lieutenant*. The manuscript is in quarto and consists of 6 unnumbered and 126 numbered pages, written by the scribe Ralph Crane, who is known to have been working for the King's company about the date given in the manuscript.

On a fly-leaf (p. i) is the inscription 'K Digby Margrit'.

Title (p. iii): 'Demetrius and Enanthe. a pleasant Comedie written by Iohn Fletcher gent'.' followed by an epistle dedicatory (p. v) 'To the honorable Sir Kelham [*sic*] Digbie knight' subscribed 'Your Commaunded Beades-man Raph Crane: Nouemb. 27. 1625' and the text on pages 1–126.

Written in Crane's calligraphic English hand, with small Italian script for incidental purposes, and a bolder variety for the headings. There are only about twenty-four lines to a page, no speech-rules, but regular catchwords. There is very little margin either side; nevertheless all stage-directions other than scene headings (there is a full and formal division) are entered on the right in such space as is afforded by the irregularities of the verse. Apart from entrances and exits, which are not as a rule elaborate, directions are neither frequent nor full. The most significant, from the point of view of description, is 'she turnes ouer a Booke' in II. iii (p. 31), and the most elaborate 'He seemes to Coniure: sweete Musiq is heard, and an Antick of litle Fayeries enter, & dance about y[e] Bowle, and fling in things, & Ex[t].' in IV. iii (p. 88). Neither of these is in the printed version. The two texts may be compared in the modern editions. The folio gives a somewhat censored and occasionally a cut text, which omits some seventy lines in all. On the other hand, the manuscript has minor omissions of its own, and knows nothing of the two songs which the folio introduces at the point where the conjuring occurs in IV. iii. In general the relation is similar to that observable in *The Honest Man's Fortune* (A 12) and *Bonduca* (B 5) though each of the three cases presents features of its own.

Printed: A. Dyce, 1830. Collations in editions of *The Humorous Lieutenant* by A. Dyce (*B. & F.*, vi. 415–539), 1844; R. W. Bond (Bullen's *B. & F.*, ii. 455–581), 1905; A. Glover and A. R. Waller (*B. & F.*, ii. 508–18), 1906.

6. *The Wasp*. Alnwick Castle. *c.* 1630?

A folio manuscript, possibly autograph, written generally in a normal manner, with regular speech-rules, but with little attempt at differentiating the script. Prompt notes in another hand, introducing the names of actors, show that the manuscript has been used in the playhouse for performance. One actor is 'Ellis', who may be Ellis Worth (with Queen Anne's men 1615–9, Red Bull players 1619–23, and Prince Charles's 1631–5) or Ellis Bedowe (at Norwich with the King's Revels (?) in 1635); another 'Ambros', possibly Ambrose Byland (a hired man of the King's company in 1624)

An edition is in preparation.

7. *The Swisser* [by A. Wilson]. B.M., MS. Add. 36759. 1631?
The play occupies sixty-four quarto leaves.

Fol. 1ᵃ: 'Ex Dono Dominæ Reeve' in a different hand from the rest.

Fol. 1ᵇ: 'The Swisser Acted At the Blackfriers 1631'.

Fol. 2ᵃ: 'The Scæne. Lombardie: Persons. Actor⟨s⟩': the list shows that the piece was acted by the King's company.

Fol. 2ᵇ: 'The Prologue' 16 lines.

Begins, fol. 3ᵃ: 'Actus Primus Scæna Prima. | Enter two Souldiers ruñing, Andrucho meetes them'.

Ends on fol. 63ᵇ: 'Exeunt. | finis'. Fol. 64ᵃ: 'Epilogue' 14 lines (verso blank). There is an ornament of four *S*'s at the end of the text and again after the Epilogue.

A careful calligraphic copy in the autograph of the author, Arthur Wilson. The script is Italian. There are no corrections apart from a few erasures, and no other hand appears except in the inscription on the first page. There is a division into acts and scenes throughout. The leaves have been folded for margins, and there are normal speech-rules, but no trace of playhouse use appears in the manuscript, which may possibly have been prepared for the press. The piece was entered for publication on 4 Sept. 1646.

There is a sprinkling of marginal directions besides others in the centre:

5ᵃ 'Speakes fearfully'. 11ᵇ 'Knock'. 22ᵃ 'He kisses her'.
33ᵃ 'He rises out of yᵉ Coffin'.
38ᵃ 'Arioldus meets Eurinia, wᵗʰ her haire about her eares'.
41ᵇ 'hee hides himself'. 55ᵃ 'Offers to drink Poison'.
55ᵇ 'They drink'. 57ᵇ 'They close and fall downe together'.
58ᵇ 'Andrucho hides'.
59ᵇ 'Knocking wᵗʰin'. 'Presents him a Sword'.
61ᵇ 'He discouers'.

Printed: A. Feuillerat, 1904.

8. *The Inconstant Lady* [by A. Wilson].
Bodl., MS. Rawl. Poet. 9. *c.* 1632?
The play occupies forty-five folio leaves. The verso of the first leaf is blank, and on the verso of the last (pasted over) is the

title and personae of another play of Wilson's, *The Corporal*, written in the same hand.

Fol. $1^a$: 'The Inconstant Ladie Acted at Blackfriers. The Scæne Burgundie. The names of the Persons....'.

Begins, fol. $2^a$: 'The inconstant Ladie' (this is a running-title throughout). 'Actus Primus. Scena Prima. | Antonio Trebutio'.

Ends on fol. $45^a$: 'Finis' followed by an ornament of four *S*'s.

A careful calligraphic copy in the autograph of the author, Arthur Wilson. The script is English. No other hand appears: there are hardly any corrections, but a few words are written over erasures. There are ruled margins, that on the left containing the speakers' names, and speech-rules are normally used, but the manuscript is purely literary. There is a division into acts and scenes throughout. The piece was entered for publication on 9 Sept. 1653.

There are a few elaborated entrances and a fair sprinkling of marginal directions.

$7^a$ 'He talkes to La⟨via⟩'. $14^b$ 'Calls w$^{th}$in'.
$17^b$ 'He setts downe, she rubs his Temples. | Song'.
$20^b$ 'kisses Her'.
$21^a$ 'she kises Pant'. 'Drawes'. 'He hurts him'. 'Peepes vp'.
$21^b$ 'He lifts vp his head'. $22^b$ 'Whisper'.
$25^b$ 'Pantarbo in an old night gowne & Capp w$^{th}$ a foule napkin about his necke'. 'Shakes his leggs'.
$27^a$ 'Romilia two or three Wenches'. $27^b$ 'Pantarbo aboue'.
$28^a$ 'Knock w$^{th}$in'. $30^b$ 'Knock w$^{th}$out'. 'Millecert disguis'd'.
$38^b$ 'Mill: Discouers'. $43^a$ 'mille: Discouers'.
$39^a$ 'Emilia w$^{th}$ a vaile on her face lying on a Bed'.
$44^b$ 'Pantarbo in a thin Garbe, Romilia following'.

Printed: P. Bliss, 1814.

9. [*The Country Captain*, by W. Cavendish, Duke of Newcastle.] B.M., MS. Harl. 7650. *c.* 1635?

The play, which has no title, is written on seventy-eight quarto leaves, while a larger leaf at the end contains an addition.

Begins, fol. 1[a]: 'Act the first | Enter Captaine Vnderwit and his man Thomas'. Ends on fol. 78[b]: 'Exeunt. | Finis'.

A careful literary copy, divided into five acts only, made by a good scribe (cf. B 14), and containing a few corrections apparently by the author (e.g. fols. 24[b], 50[b], 60[a], 68[b]) and a larger number by other scribes. Many passages are marked for omission. The additional leaf is in yet another hand, but has some notes apparently by the main scribe.

The play was printed at The Hague in 1649. The two texts are in general agreement though there are considerable variations. The passages marked for omission in the manuscript are retained in the print. Of the alterations some are incorporated and others not, but the passages in which they occur are apt to be cut or recast in the print, which evidently represents a revised version. At the beginning of Act IV there is a song in the print where the manuscript only has the direction 'A song i'th tauerne' (fol. 43[b]). After this is a passage which has been a good deal altered in the printed text but which incorporates the addition found at the end of the manuscript.

The stage-directions in the manuscript are not very numerous apart from entrances which are sometimes elaborated.

55[a] 'they measure and Denice getts both weapons'.
55[b] 'Enter S[r]. Francis a taper prepar'd'.
56[b] 'S[r]. Richard and his Lady abed. Enter Dorothy with a Light'.
57[a] 'Dorothy towards the dore putts out the Candle and returnes'.
58[b] 'S[r]. Francis asleepe, a table inke and Paper. Enter Lady'.
69[a] 'Enter S[r]. Richard opening a Letter a footman waiting'.

The manuscript was printed by A. H. Bullen, *Old Plays* (ii. 315–416), 1883, under the title of *Captain Underwit* and ascribed to Shirley.

10. *The Royal Slave* [by W. Cartwright].
B.M., MS. Add. 41616[1]. 1636?

A small folio of twenty-four leaves, bound up with two or three other manuscripts of larger size in the seventeenth century.

Title: 'The Royall Slaue | A Tragicomedy | The Scene Sardes. | Acted before the King at Oxford' (fol. 1[b], recto blank).

'The Persons' are on fol. 2[a], 'The Prologue' to the King and Queen at Oxford on fol. 2[b]. The text begins on fol. 3[a] and ends on fol. 23[a] (verso blank). 'The Epilogue' to the King and Queen at Oxford follows on fol. 24[a] (verso blank).

A calligraphic copy, evidently literary, and perhaps prepared for presentation. The absence of the later prologue and epilogue for Hampton Court connects the manuscript with the original performance at Christ Church on 30 Aug. 1636, and the absence of those to the University perhaps points to its being a presentation copy for the Court.

Except for occasional variants, possibly accidental, the text seems to agree closely with that of the version printed in 1639, including the stage-directions: it lacks, however, the descriptions of the scenes. There are a certain number of alterations in another contemporary hand, but it is doubtful whether they possess any authority. They include both corrections of obvious scribal errors and some more ambitious emendations. The former agree with the printed text, the latter as a rule do not. In one place (III. i, song) 'beasing' has been altered to 'leauing' where the print has 'Ceasing'.

11. *The Cyprian Conqueror.*

B.M., MS. Sloane 3709. *c.* 1640?

The play occupies fifty-one quarto leaves.

Title, fol. 1[b] (recto blank): 'The Cyprian conquerer Or The faithless relict | The scene Ephesus | Persons names' (among whom 'Dido Petronias maide a grase widdow'): 'The Preface' begins on fol. 2[a]: fol. 8[a] (verso blank) is a half-title partly in red: fol. 9 has 'The Prolouge' on the recto and 'The other Prolouge' on the verso.

Begins, fol. 10[a]: 'The faithless Relict or The Cyprian Conqueror' (another hand adds 'Act: prim. sc: prim.') 'Enter Philander'.

On fol. 49[b] 'Enter Eneas & speakes y[e] Epilouge': then fol. 50[b] 'The song sung in y[e] first act of Philanthes & Calista': fol. 51[a] 'The song sung y [*sic*] next daie b [*sic*] Eneas': and fol. 51[b] 'The song with y[e] soft mmusicke [*sic*] as Cupid descends'.

The manuscript is difficult to date, being written in 'printed'

letters by an illiterate scribe (one would almost suppose a child), corrected throughout in another rough hand, presumably by the author, whom the epilogue describes as 'a country man'. The composition is almost as naïve as the writing. Both prologue and epilogue contemplate performance, but the manuscript is purely literary.

12. [*The Benefice*] by R. Wild.
B.M., MS. Lansd. 807[4]. *c.* 1641?

An imperfect copy of the play (an old pagination running from 25 to 45) on eleven rather large quarto leaves constituting fols. 78–88 of this small collection (fols. 87ᵃ, 88ᵇ blank).

Fol. 78ᵃ: 'Act 3. Scen. 4. Enter Sʳ Homily'.

Fol. 88ᵃ: 'The Epilogue' 20 lines. 'Ceres after the Epilogue speaks' 8 lines. 'ffinis actus Qᵘⁱ | Robert Wild'.

Written in a neat literary hand, the same as that of the signature. There is very little correction, but one or two alterations made *currente calamo* suggest the author, e.g. fol. 81ᵇ: 'I faith therin we differ, you [scholars] black coats are towards . . .'. There is an original division into acts, and another hand apparently has added a division into scenes on the foreign method. There is no suggestion of playhouse use.

The play was printed in 1689, as written by Wild 'in his Younger Days', by some one into whose hands it had come 'now several Years since'. The printed text incorporates the corrections of the manuscript, and has the act but not the scene division.

The stage-directions of the manuscript are rather scanty.

78ᵃ 'Whips Homily'. 78ᵇ 'ffinis actus 3ⁱʲ.' at foot.

79ᵃ IV. i 'Enter bookworm like a ballad man'.

79ᵇ IV. ii 'Enter ffantastes like a scholar with one boot russet & another black'.

80ᵇ IV. iv 'Enter a Tinker Singing'.

82ᵃ IV. viii 'Enter Hob. drest like a Parson & Homily like his man'.

83ᵃ 'Exit cũ Homily'.

84ᵃ 'ffinis actus Quarᵗⁱ.' and *'Act 5: Sc: i:' also *'Scena pria'. 'Enter Hob with a pipe of Tobacco in his mouth'. 'fals downe'.

84$^{b}$ v. iii 'Enter a gypsie woman with a child on her back'.

85$^{a}$ (in v. iv) '< > puts y$^{e}$ rope a bout his necke' (a third of the page blank).

13. *The Lambarde Collection.* various dates.

A collection of seven manuscript plays in folio. It was first reported by J. O. Halliwell in the 'Early Illustrations of Shakespeare and the Drama' (section II) appended to his edition of *The Marriage of Wit and Wisdom* printed for the Shakespeare Society in 1846 (p. 85). It was then, according to his account, 'in the library of an ancient family in the East of England'. He enumerated the contents and transcribed the prologue to the last piece. The manuscript was next heard of in the possession of Mr. W. L. Lambarde, of Bradbourne Hall, Sevenoaks, when it came up for sale at Messrs. Hodgson's auction rooms on 19 June 1924 (lot 528). It was knocked down to a private purchaser for £350, and has since proved impossible to trace. The contents are as follows:

(a) *The Inconstant Lady, or Better late than Never.*

Arthur Wilson's play, already noted above (C 8). The second title is not given in the Bodleian manuscript, but the text there ends with the lines:

You ladie
Haue bene inconstant, therefore now indeuer
A Reformation. Better late then Neuer.

The present copy has alterations and additions, and may be autograph. In the title 'Lady' is altered from 'Woman' and the text, it is said, 'differs materially from the version printed by Bliss in 1814, in particular, certain of the songs being omitted'. It occupies 62 pages.

(b) A comedy without title, the characters of which include Jerome, Roderigo, Leander, Lidia, &c., occupying 68 pages.

(c) *The Lovers' Hospital.*

A fragment of two leaves only, presumably from the piece by George Wild, acted at St. John's College, Oxford, 29 Aug.

1636, a manuscript of which, entitled *Love's Hospital*, is in the British Museum, MS. Add. 14047[1].

(d) *The Woman's Prize, or the Tamer tam'd.*

The piece included in the Beaumont and Fletcher folio of 1647: 101 pages.

(e) *The Lost Lady*, a Tragi-Comedy, by Sir William Berkeley.

Printed in 1638–9: 70 pages. This has a list of characters and a prologue not in the printed version, but Act IV is not complete. There is also a note: 'A booke of her Majestye's most unchristianly handled by those to whom it was lent by her Majestye's most illfavord . . . dutifullest servant Captaine Peeter'.

(f) *The Beggar's Bush.*

Printed, as *Beggars' Bush*, in the Beaumont and Fletcher folio of 1647: 91 pages.

(g) *Hengist, King of Kent.*

Printed in 1661 as *The Mayor of Quinborough*, with an ascription to Thomas Middleton. It was originally entered for publication at the same time as the Beaumont and Fletcher plays, 4 Sept. 1646. The manuscript is said to differ materially from the printed version: it occupies 91 pages.

Another manuscript of this play, bearing the same title, is in the library of the Duke of Portland at Welbeck Abbey.

14. *The Percy Collection.* Huntington Library. 1647.

'Comædyes and Pastoralls with their Songs, As Also one Booke of Epigrammes By W. P. Esquier. . . . Excriptum Anno Salutis 1647', a folio volume containing six plays by William Percy, a younger son of the eighth Earl of Northumberland. The plays, which are individually dated, are as follows:

(a) 'The Cuck-queanes | And Cuckolds Errants | or | The Bearing down the Inne | A Comedye', fol. $7^a$, 1601.

(b) 'Arabia sitiens | or A Dreame of a Drye yeare | A Traga comadye', fol. $32^a$, 1601.

(c) 'The Faery Pastorall | or | Forrest of Elues', fol. $62^a$, 1603.

(d) 'A | Country Tragaedye in vacunum | or | Cupids sacrifice', fol. 92ª, 1602.

(e) 'The | Aphrodysial | or | Sea-Feast', fol. 120ª, 1602.

(f) 'Necromantes | or | The Two Supposed Heds. | A Comicall Inuention', fol. 152ª, 1632.

At the beginning (fol. 4ª) is: 'For The Faerye Pastorall Act 4 Scen 3 Sir Philip Sydneis Song', and at the end (fols. 192ª–194ᵇ): 'Songs That be vacant in the foresayd Pastorals and Comadyes. All of them made Anno 1636.' The 'One Singular Booke Of Epigrammes' (fols. 195ª–216ª) is dated 1610.

The nature of the corrections leaves no doubt that the whole manuscript is autograph. Many passages are written on slips pasted on to the leaves, sometimes over other slips and sometimes themselves corrected. The directions contemplate performance by Paul's boys, and are sometimes in the past tense as if recording actual performance, though of this there is no external confirmation. They are unusually full and elaborate and have been often quoted as evidence of theatrical conditions at least in the private houses; but in absence of any information as to the circumstances in which the plays were produced and acted, if at all, it is well to be cautious in drawing conclusions.

*The Cuck-Queans* and *The Faery Pastoral* were printed for the Roxburghe Club in 1824 with a preface by Joseph Haslewood.

Another collection of Percy's plays, in two volumes, said to be also at least partly autograph, is in the library of the Duke of Northumberland at Alnwick Castle. One volume agrees in content with that described above, and is dated 1646. The other appears to contain earlier drafts of (a) to (d) only. (See Historical MSS. Commission, Third Report, appx. p. 119.)

15. *The Apthorpe Collection.* B.M., MS. Add. 34221. 1640–50. A folio volume containing six plays and masques performed, or written for performance, at Apthorpe, Northamptonshire,

the seat of the earls of Westmorland. The pieces included are as follows:

(a) 'Candia Restaurata. Presented in a shew at Apthorpe the 12th of ffebruary 1640 · to the Lord and Lady of that place, by some of their owne Children and famelie', p. 1 (=fol. 1b). A list of the performers is given: women's parts are assigned to boys.

(b) 'Tymes trick vpon the Cards, prepared to be presented at Apthorpe by the youth and servante there the 22th of ffebruary 1641', p. 39.

(c) 'The Change. A Showe written in December 1642', p. 106.

(d) 'Vertues Triumph. This Comedy was writt in Ann. 1644', p. 151.

(e) 'Raguaillo D'Oceano This Show was written and prepared to be acted in Añ. 1640', p. 233.

(f) 'Φyxomaxia [*sic*] id est de pugna animi 1650', p. 267.

A list of the 'Seuerall Dramatic Entertainments' follows on p. 323.

The manuscript is in a number of different hands. The first four plays (a–d) are very tidily written by scribes. The rest is much rougher, and in this latter part there is one hand in which appear alterations *currente calamo*, and which seems to occur correcting others. This hand, which may therefore be that of an author, writes the latter part of *Ragguaglio d'Oceano* (e) from the middle of p. 250 to the end. It is that of Mildmay Fane, second Earl of Westmorland, as appears from comparison with a letter of 27 Feb. 1632(?) in MS. Harl. 3783, fol. 28a.

Another Apthorpe manuscript is now in the Huntington Library. It contains, besides some correspondence, two dramatic items, namely *Don Phoebus Triumph*, 1645, and *Candy Restored*, 1640. The latter is evidently the same as *Candia Restaurata* above (a), and is apparently in a scribe's hand. The former, however, is evidently autograph, and the hand, though much rougher than in the Museum manuscript, is clearly again that of the Earl.

## *REFERENCE LISTS*

### *Class A*

1. *John a Kent*, by A. Munday, p. 239.
2. *Sir Thomas More*, by A. Munday and others, p. 243.
3. *Richard II* or *Thomas of Woodstock*, p. 251.
4. *Edmond Ironside* or *War hath Made all Friends*, p. 256.
5. *Charlemagne* or *The Distracted Emperor*, p. 261.
6. *The Second Maiden's Tragedy*, p. 264.
7. *Sir John van Olden Barnavelt*, p. 268.
8. *The Two Noble Ladies*, p. 274.
9. *The Welsh Embassador*, p. 279.
10. *The Parliament of Love*, by P. Massinger, p. 282.
11. *The Captives*, by T. Heywood, p. 284.
12. *The Honest Man's Fortune*, p. 288.
13. *Believe as you List*, by P. Massinger, p. 293.
14. *The Launching of the Mary*, by W. Mountfort, p. 300.
15. *The Lady Mother*, p. 305.

### *Class B*

1. *Timon*, p. 308.
2. *The Poor Man's Comfort*, by R. Daborne, p. 311.
3. *Nero*, p. 314.
4. *The Escapes of Jupiter*, by T. Heywood, p. 318.
5. *Bonduca*, p. 321.
6. *The Faithful Friends*, by Beaumont and Fletcher, p. 324.
7. *Dick of Devonshire*, p. 329.
8. *Aglaura*, by Sir J. Suckling, p. 332.
9. *The Elder Brother*, p. 334.
10. *The Fatal Marriage*, p. 337.
11. *The Telltale*, p. 339.
12. *Love's Changelings' Change*, p. 342.
13. *The Wizard*, by S. Baylie, p. 344.
14. *The Court Secret*, by J. Shirley, p. 346.
15. *The Queen of Corsica*, by F. Jaques, p. 352.

### *Class C*

1. *John of Bordeaux*, p. 355.
2. *Tancred and Ghismonda*, p. 356.
3. *A Game at Chess*, by T. Middleton, p. 356.
4. *The Witch*, by T. Middleton, p. 358.
5. *Demetrius and Enanthe*, by J. Fletcher, p. 359.
6. *The Wasp*, p. 360.
7. *The Swisser*, by A. Wilson, p. 361.
8. *The Inconstant Lady*, by A. Wilson, p. 361.
9. *The Country Captain*, by W. Cavendish, Duke of Newcastle, p. 362.
10. *The Royal Slave*, by W. Cartwright, p. 363.
11. *The Cyprian Conqueror*, p. 364.
12. *The Benefice*, by R. Wild, p. 365.
13. *The Lambarde Collection*, p. 366.
14. *The Percy Collection*, p. 367.
15. *The Apthorpe Collection*, p. 368.

*Titles*

*Authors*

Wild, George,
? *The Lovers' Hospital*, in C 13

Wild, Robert,
*The Benefice*, C 12

Wilson, Arthur,
*The Swisser*, C 7
*The Inconstant Lady*, C 8, and in C 13

## *Autograph Plays*

*Apthorpe Collection, The*, C 15, in part: M. Fane.
*Believe as you List*, A 13: Massinger.
? *Benefice, The*, C 12: R. Wild.
*Captives, The*, A 11: Heywood.
? *Charlemagne*, A 5
*Country Captain, The*, C 9, corrections: W. Cavendish.
? *Court Secret, The*, B 14, revision: Shirley.
? *Dick of Devonshire*, B 7
*Escapes of Jupiter, The*, B 4: Heywood.
? *Faithful Friends, The*, B 6, addition.
? *Fatal Marriage, The*, B 10
*Game at Chess, A*, C 3 (*a*, and *b*, *c*, *d* in part): Middleton.
*Inconstant Lady, The*, C 8 (and ? in C 13): Wilson.
*John a Kent*, A 1: Munday.
*John of Bordeaux*, C 1, in part: Chettle.
*Launching of the Mary, The*, A 14: Mountfort.
*Percy Collection, The*, C 14: W. Percy.
*Sir Thomas More*, A 2: Munday; Chettle, Dekker, ? Heywood, ? Shakespeare.
*Swisser, The*, C 7: Wilson.
*Two Noble Ladies, The*, A 8
? *Wasp, The*, C 6

## *Autographs of Authors*

Cavendish, William, Duke of Newcastle:
*The Country Captain* (corrections), C 9

Chettle, Henry:
*Sir Thomas More* (part), A 2
*John of Bordeaux* (part), C 1

Dekker, Thomas:
*Sir Thomas More* (part), A 2

Fane, Mildmay, Earl of Westmorland:
*The Apthorpe Collection* (part), C 15

Heywood, Thomas:
? *Sir Thomas More* (part), A 2
*The Captives*, A 11
*The Escapes of Jupiter*, B 4

Massinger, Philip:
*Believe as you List*, A 13

Middleton, Thomas:
*A Game at Chess*, C 3 (*a*, and *b*, *c*, *d* in part).

Mountfort, Walter:
*The Launching of the Mary*, A 14

Munday, Anthony:
*John a Kent*, A 1
*Sir Thomas More* (part), A 2

Percy, William:
*The Percy Collection*, C 14

MANUSCRIPT PLAYS

Shakespeare, William:
? *Sir Thomas More* (part), A 2

Shirley, James:
? *The Court Secret* (revision), B 14

Wild, Robert:
? *The Benefice*, C 12

Wilson, Arthur:
*The Swisser*, C 7
*The Inconstant Lady*, C 8 (and ? in C 13).

## *Scribes*

Ralph Crane:
*Sir John van Olden Barnavelt*, A 7
*A Game at Chess*, C 3 (*d*, *e*)
*The Witch*, C 4
*Demetrius and Enanthe*, C 5

'Jhon':
*The Honest Man's Fortune*, A 12
*Bonduca*, B 5
*Believe as you List* (revision), A 13

Unknown:
*The Welsh Embassador*, A 9
*The Parliament of Love*, A 10

P. Massam:
? *The Poor Man's Comfort*, B 2 (but more likely a scribble).

Nicholas:
? *The Telltale*, B 11 (monogram).

## *Plays Printed before 1700*

*Aglaura*, B 8, 1638.
*Beggars' Bush*, in C 13, 1647.
*Benefice, The*, C 12, 1689.
*Bonduca*, B 5, 1647.
*Country Captain, The*, C 9, 1649.
*Court Secret, The*, B 14, 1653.
*Demetrius and Enanthe* (*The Humorous Lieutenant*), C 5, 1647.
*Elder Brother, The*, B 9, 1637.
*Game at Chess, A*, C 3, 1625.
*Hengist, King of Kent* (*The Mayor of Quinborough*), in C 13, 1661.
*Honest Man's Fortune, The*, A 12, 1647.
*Lost Lady, The*, in C 13, 1638.
*Nero*, B 3, 1624.
*Poor Man's Comfort, The*, B 2, 1655.
*Royal Slave, The*, C 10, 1639.
*Woman's Prize, The*, in C 13, 1647.

## *Licences of Masters of the Revels*

*Sir Thomas More*, A 2: Tilney (note only).
*The Second Maiden's Tragedy*, A 6: Buç, 31 Oct. 1611.
*Sir John van Olden Barnavelt*, A 7: Buc (note only).
*The Parliament of Love*, A 10: Herbert, 3 Nov. 1624 (cut out).
*The Honest Man's Fortune*, A 12: Herbert, 8 Feb. 1625.
*Believe as you List*, A 13: Herbert, 6 May 1631.
*The Launching of the Mary*, A 14: Herbert, 27 June 1633.
*The Lady Mother*, A 15: Blagrave (deputy), 15 Oct. 1635.

*Plays showing signs of Censorship*

*Believe as you List*, A 13
*Charlemagne*, A 5
*Honest Man's Fortune, The*, A 12
*Lady Mother, The*, A 15
*Launching of the Mary, The*, A 14
*Richard II*, A 3
*Second Maiden's Tragedy, The*, A 6
*Sir John van Olden Barnavelt*, A 7
*Sir Thomas More*, A 2
? *Two Noble Ladies, The*, A 8
? *Welsh Embassador, The*, A 9

*Plays containing Actors' Names*

*Believe as you List*, A 13: seventeen actors of the King's company.
*Captives, The*, A 11: Gibson, Jack, Taylor, stage-keeper.
*Edmond Ironside*, A 4: H. Gibson, H. Gradwell, E. May, G. Stutfield.
*Honest Man's Fortune, The*, A 12: J. Rhodes, G. Rick., G. Vernon.
*John of Bordeaux*, C 1: J. Holland.
*Richard II*, A 3: George, Grad. (?), Toby.
*Second Maiden's Tragedy, The*, A 6: R. Gough, R. Robinson.
*Sir John van Olden Barnavelt*, A 7: Bir., R. Gough, T. Holcombe, G. Lowen, Nick, Michael, T. Pollard, J. Rice, Rob., R. T.
*Sir Thomas More*, A 2: T. Goodale.
*Swisser, The*, C 7: a cast of the King's company.
*Two Noble Ladies, The*, A 8, Bond, A. Brew., H. Gibson, G. Stutfield, Taylor, stage-keeper.
*Wasp, The*, C 6: Ellis, Ambros.

*Actors' Names in Plays*

Ambros, C 6
Balls, F., A 13
Baxter, R., A 13
Benfield, R., A 13, C 7
Bir. (? G. Birch), A 7
Bond, A 8
Brew. (? Brewer), A., A 8
Ellis, C 6
George, A 3
Gibson, H., A 4, A 8, A 11
Goodale, T., A 2
Gough, R., A 6, A 7 (cancelled), C 7 (Goffe)
Grad. (?), A 3
Gradwell, H., A 4
Greville, C., A 13, C 7
Hobbes, T., A 13
Holcombe, T., A 7
Holland, J., C 1
Honeyman, J., A 13
Jack, A 11
Lowen, G., A 7, A 13, C 7
Mago, W., A 13
May, E., A 4
Michael, A 7
Nick, A 7, A 13
Pattrick, W., A 13
Penn, W., A 13, C 7
Pollard, T., A 7, A 13, C 7
Rhodes, J., A 12
Rice, J., A 7
Rick., G., A 12

# MEMORABILIA

I HARDLY think that a formal index is needed to this book. There should be no difficulty in finding the principal matters discussed in their appropriate sections. The actors whose names appear in the Plots can readily be traced through the lists which occupy pages 43–69. Similarly the reference lists at pages 370–6 should provide the necessary clues to the three classes of manuscript plays. There remain, however, a number of points incidentally discussed which are perhaps of sufficient interest to merit noting here.

THE END

PRINTED IN GREAT BRITAIN AT THE UNIVERSITY PRESS, OXFORD
BY JOHN JOHNSON, PRINTER TO THE UNIVERSITY